THE CHALLENGE
OF EASTERN ASIAN EDUCATION

SUNY Series
FRONTIERS IN EDUCATION
Philip G. Altbach, Editor

The Frontiers in Education Series draws upon a range of disciplines and approaches in the analysis of contemporary educational issues and concerns. Books in the series help to reinterpret established fields of scholarship in education by encouraging the latest synthesis and research. A special focus highlights educational policy issues from a multidisciplinary perspective. The series is published in cooperation with the School of Education, Boston College. A complete listing of books in the series can be found at the end of this volume.

THE CHALLENGE

OF EASTERN ASIAN EDUCATION

Implications for America

EDITED BY

William K. Cummings

and

Philip G. Altbach

STATE UNIVERSITY OF NEW YORK PRESS

Published by
State University of New York Press, Albany

For information, address the State University of New York Press,
State University Plaza, Albany, N.Y., 12246

Production by Diane Ganeles
Marketing by Nancy Farrell

Library of Congress Cataloging-in-Publication Data

The challenge of Eastern Asian education : implications for America / edited by
    William K. Cummings and Philip G. Altback.
        p. cm.—(SUNY series, frontiers in education)
    Includes bibliographical references (p.   ) and index.
    ISBN 0-7914-3283-1 (hc : acid free).—ISBN 0-7914-3284-X (pb : acid free)
    1. Education—East Asia—Cross-cultural studies.   2. Education—United
States—Cross-cultural studies.   3. Education and state—East Asia—Cross-
cultural studies.   4. Education and state—United States—Cross-cultural
studies.   I. Cummings, William K.   II. Altback, Philip G.   III. Series.
370'.95—dc20   96-34722
                                                                    CIP

10 9 8 7 6 5 4 3 2 1

Contents

Tables

Figures

Acknowledgments

This volume stems from an issue of *Educational Policy* that we edited and which was published in June 1995. We would like to thank the following publishers for their generous permission to reprint these articles:

Thomas P. Rohlen, *Educational Policy* 9.2, pp. 103–28. Copyright 1995 by Corwin Press, Inc. Reprinted by permission of Corwin Press Inc., 2455 Teller Road, Thousand Oaks, CA 91320-2218.

Catherine C. Lewis, *Educational Policy* 9.2, pp. 129–51. Copyright 1995 by Corwin Press, Inc. Reprinted by permission of Corwin Press Inc., 2455 Teller Road, Thousand Oaks, CA 91320-2218.

Harold W. Stevenson and Shinying Lee, *Educational Policy* 9.2, pp. 152–68. Copyright 1995 by Corwin Press, Inc. Reprinted by permission of Corwin Press Inc., 2455 Teller Road, Thousand Oaks, CA 91320-2218.

Gerald K. LeTendre, *Educational Policy* 9.2, pp. 179–84. Copyright 1995 by Corwin Press, Inc. Reprinted by permission of Corwin Press Inc., 2455 Teller Road, Thousand Oaks, CA 91320-2218.

Nobuo K. Shimahara, *Educational Policy* 9.2, pp. 185–200. Copyright 1995 by Corwin Press, Inc. Reprinted by permission of Corwin Press Inc., 2455 Teller Road, Thousand Oaks, CA 91320-2218.

Sam Stern, *Educational Policy* 9.2, pp. 201–17. Copyright 1995 by Corwin Press, Inc. Reprinted by permission of Corwin Press Inc., 2455 Teller Road, Thousand Oaks, CA 91320-2218.

Gay Garland Reed, *Educational Policy* 9.3, pp. 244–59. Copyright 1995 by Corwin Press, Inc. Reprinted by permission of Corwin Press Inc., 2455 Teller Road, Thousand Oaks, CA 91320-2218.

William K. Cummings, *Oxford Review of Education* 21.1, pp. 67–82. Copyright 1995 by Carfax Publishing Company. Reprinted by permission of Carfax Publishing Company, PO Box 25, Abingdon, Oxfordshire OX14 3UE, United Kingdom.

David Baker and Donald P. Holsinger, *International Journal of Comparative Sociology*, forthcoming. Copyright by E. J. Brill Publishers. Reprinted by permission of E. J. Brill Publishers, PO Box 9000, 2300 PA Leiden, Netherlands.

We are indebted to many colleagues who helped make this book possible. Funding from the Pacific Basic Research Center at Harvard University provided support to William K. Cummings. Jason Tan helped with the editing of the book at the Center for Comparative and Global Studies in Education at the State University of New York at Buffalo. We especially appreciate the cooperation of our colleagues who have contributed to this volume.

WILLIAM K. CUMMINGS
PHILIP G. ALTBACH

Introduction

WILLIAM K. CUMMINGS and
PHILIP G. ALTBACH

A Nation at Risk (1983) officially acknowledged weakness in American education and argued that this was detracting from national competitiveness. The report made specific reference to the educational successes of two Asian nations:

> The risk is not only that the Japanese make automobiles more efficiently than America and have government subsidies for development and export. It is not just that the South Koreans recently built the world's most efficient steel mill, or that American machine tools, once the pride of the world, are being displaced by German products. It is also that these developments signify a redistribution of trained capability throughout the globe. Knowledge, learning, information, and skilled intelligence are the new raw materials of international commerce. (pp. 6, 7)

In related documents the report identified Japan as a consistent high performer in international studies of academic achievement.

Building on these insights, in 1984 the U.S. Department of Education began an extensive survey of what was then known about Japanese education. The final report published in 1986 included a list of twelve principles of good education, whether Japanese or American, derived by then Secretary of Education William J. Bennett: among these were the importance of parental involvement in their children's education; the necessity of clear purpose, strong motivation, and high standards; the importance of maximizing learning time and making effective use thereof; the centrality of holding high expectations for all children and a firm commitment to developing a strong work ethic and good study habits.

While full of praise for Japanese education, the above report noted several weaknesses of Japanese education including its inflexibility in responding to individual differences and growing signs of student alienation. Some

1

U.S. commentators were not very enthusiastic about this interest in Japanese education; for example, James Fallows of the *Atlantic Monthly* wrote a controversial piece subtitled "You would not want your children to go to a Japanese high school."

But others have persisted in their efforts to probe the nature of Japanese and more broadly Eastern Asian education, seeking policy implications for the United States. The contributions to this book are written by several of America's most authoritative specialists on Asian education. Each of the authors has conducted extensive field work in Asia, and has, in their essay for this book, made an impressive effort to distill their findings in a form that is readily communicable to the U.S. policy audience. Each essay provides us with a specific policy insight that can be included in the U.S. debate.

The essays are organized in five parts: (1) curricular and classroom processes for basic education, (2) new developments at the secondary level, (3) innovations in the private sector and in (4) the linkage of education to society, and finally (5) four essays focusing on more systemic issues.

The focus of the various essays is on policy, with due consideration to the context in which policies are conceived and implemented. The emphasis on policy has led to considerable reflection on the title of the book. Many recent studies of the dynamic development in the Asian area use geographic references such as Asia or East Asia, but Asia covers too much and East Asia is too small and, moreover, has a strong Confucian cultural connotation. What's more, some Confucian nations have not been as impressive in their educational progressiveness as others; indeed non-Confucian nations such as Malaysia and Indonesia seem to be out-pacing certain of the Confucian nations. Thus the geographic scope of this book is larger than East Asia. Other analysts (Mackerras, 1995), facing a similar dilemma, have settled on Eastern Asia in order to indicate their interest in the fuller array of regional dynamism. This book follows that convention. Chapter Sixteen by Cummings says more.

Basic Education

Catherine Lewis, leading off the section on basic education, observes that a critical element in the success of education is the development of a pedagogy that responds to the "human" needs of young children. While American educators certainly believe their system is responsive to the needs of children, *Lewis implicitly argues that American education is overly slanted toward the enhancement of cognitive abilities, whereas Japan has developed a more balanced approach that emphasizes the "whole-child."* She observes how the Japanese approach encourages values of friendship and cooperation, self-discipline and active involvement in classroom projects, aesthetic expression alongside cognitive competence. Children are not separated by a single criterion such as cognitive competence into different groups or tracks but rather are kept together so they can profit from their diversity. Her chapter introduces nine characteristics of "whole-child" education and points out that some U.S. school systems practice it with apparent success.

Harold Stevenson and Shinying Lee pick up on the wholistic theme, this time focusing on the Asian approach of teaching to the whole class rather than to individual students. They begin by acknowledging the negative images associated with teacher-centered teaching where teachers serve as drillmasters leading robots through a series of mindless choral recitation; if this image ever fitted Eastern Asian education, they insist it is long outdated. They then go into a detailed illustration of the actual practices they have observed in over fifteen years of research in Japan, China, Taiwan, and the United States. Concerning Japan, they note that the resistance there to academic grouping results in greater in-class diversity in academic ability than is characteristic of an American classroom. Moreover, class-size in Japan is generally much larger than in the United States. Despite these apparent handicaps, *the Japanese whole-class teaching approach is comparatively more effective in making use of pupil time and engagement, and thus in promoting learning.* This finding raises an implicit challenge to those U.S. educators who insist smaller class-size should be a high reform priority. Among the many subthemes of their discussion is the Japanese reliance on "cooperative learning," but whereas in the United States the teacher often turns group work over to pupil leaders, in Japan the teacher carefully structures and supervises the several groups.

Gay Garland Reed contrasts the systematic moral education provided in Chinese schools with the aversion to such education in the United States. Her discussion explores three areas of contrast between the two societies: the relationship of morality and religion, the relationship of fact and value, and the relationship of the individual to the society.

Lynn Paine discusses Chinese teachers and the training they receive. She notes that China, just as the United States, has from the early eighties, devoted much attention to educational reform, and especially to the reform of teaching. She finds that China's reformers have tended to think of this reform as largely a technical issue, and that they have been blind to the deeply rooted culture of teaching with its economic, social, and political supports. As in the United States, China's reformers propose "external control and accountability systems" to induce change in teacher practice. But they typically fail to gain teacher acceptance for these systems, and thus teachers find ways to blunt the impact. She argues that it is equally important in China as it is in the United States to engage in the steady work of educational reform.

Secondary Education

Nobuo Shimahara begins the section on secondary education with a review of recent Japanese human resource policy discussions which finds that, *contrary to recent U.S. thinking, Japanese policymakers believe they need to loosen standards in order to promote greater diversity in youth learning experiences.* He reviews several new high school concepts that have been launched or are under consideration that seek to promote this diversity. As a footnote, it is interesting to note that Japanese reformers were able during the eighties to develop a national consensus on desirable reform directions but they at that time failed to make much dent on the system (Schopa, 1989). But over the past several years, apparently due to the disarray of party politics and hence the inattention of party politicians to educational affairs, many national and local educational officials are pushing through a variety of promising reforms.

Gerald K. LeTendre, drawing on extensive qualitative research in Japanese middle schools, tackles another sacred cow of American education, *the role of school counselors.* He notes that Japanese middle schools face an alarming incidence of misbehavior, often involving some pupils "bullying" others. Rather than rely on professional counselors to work with the deviant children as in the United States, the Japanese schools rely on counseling by classroom teachers backed up by school-community committees. The goal of this counseling is to restore the deviant to the classroom group rather than to administer punishment. LeTendre reports considerable success with this approach, and thus the incidence of deviance declines as the children proceed to high school. He also observes that some U.S. high schools are experimenting with similar approaches, and initially report improvement.

In reaction to the extensive comparative literature which argues that the Asian approach to human resource development has been different than that observed in other parts of the world, David Baker and Donald Holsinger review recent evidence on educational expansion over the 1960–90 period. They find that some Asian countries had relatively high enrollment rates in 1960, but that the annual rate of expansion in Asia since then has not been exceptional. Two case studies compare recent educational trends in Thailand and Malaysia. Malaysia has taken significant steps to modernize and expand secondary education, while Thailand has been less innovative. The authors suggest that Malaysia's efforts will be rewarded as the superior preparation of the Malaysian labor force will contribute to greater competitiveness. The authors reject the notion that there is a special Asian approach, but rather that history shows a close link between educational improvement and economic development in all parts of the world. Implicit in their observations is a warning that the United States also needs to continually renew its secondary schools if it wishes to remain competitive.

Private Education

Recent international interest in *alternatives to public education* leads William K. Cummings to survey private education in Eastern Asia. He finds that private education is quite prevalent in Asia, particularly at the secondary and tertiary levels and, moreover, continues to rapidly expand. Indeed in several Asian countries, over 75 percent of the places in postsecondary education are provided by private schools. Cummings observes that the vigor of the private sector both enables the public sector to contain costs and also stimulates policymakers to consider new approaches, such as secondary schools that combine both lower and upper secondary levels in an integrated curriculum.

Nancy Ukai Russell focuses on a particular sector of Asian private education, the informal schools (*Juku* in Japan, *Hagwon* in Korea, and *Buxiban* in Taiwan) established to supplement formal education. In all of these countries, they are a booming industry; in Japan, they now are reported to add $14 billion to the GNP, and presumably a significant increment to the national IQ quantum. Ukai notes that some Japanese firms are achieving success in *exporting their informal school technology to the United States*, and she suggests this may contribute to improvements in the quality of education in the U.S.

Education and Society

Sam Stern, who has looked extensively at the relationship between education and work in Japan, writes about the education-industry interface there in direct comparison with U.S. practice. He notes that Japan has had a policy for nearly 100 years in this area, whereas the United States, as illustrated in the School-to-Work Opportunities Act of 1994, is only in the early stages of developing a policy. A fundamental difference between the two systems is the higher evaluation in the United States of occupation-specific skills as contrasted with Japan's respect for company-specific skills. This difference accounts for the greater interest of Japanese employers in providing training. Stern suggests several implications for the United States, including the need for better understanding of the value of training and for greater focus and specificity in government-supported training programs.

Kin Bing Wu surveys education policies in Taiwan (China) and Hong Kong, two of the four Newly Industrialized Economies of East Asia, in order to provide the *context for understanding the diversity of educational policies and learning outcomes in the region.* She concludes that Taiwan's policies provide the foundation for movement into a new era of high-tech competitiveness, whereas Hong Kong will be less successful in this regard. With a generous leap of imagination, it is possible to apply the same strategy of comparative analysis to pairs of American states such as Ohio and Michigan, Massachusetts and Connecticut, and North Carolina and South Carolina. Some will be winners in the new era of global competition, while others will falter.

While the focus of the above studies is on the education-employer nexus, Chris Wheeler and his colleagues consider the *link of schools to the local community.* They observe that Thai schools have traditionally occupied an influential position in community life, yet many of the educational policies of the past century have tended to build up artificial barriers between school and community. In an interesting ongoing experiment, a number of schools in Thailand have sought with considerable success to break down the barrier, releasing the talents of school teachers and pupils to grapple with the challenge of forest depletion. Wheeler and his colleagues see a parallel between the recent Thai experience and that of many U.S. communities, where schools have tended to withdraw from local involvement. Under the right conditions and with the right strategy, they argue that schools can become a positive force for local improvement.

Systemwide Implications

Thomas Rohlen, author of a well-known study of the Japanese high school, begins this section with a useful caution that *it is important in approaching a foreign educational system to understand it in its entirety before focusing on specific practices.* Rohlen suggests we are moving into a new global era where the education of nations will be judged in terms of their contribution to national competitiveness. This is a new preoccupation for American education with its traditional humanistic and self-realizing concerns, and thus may strain the tolerance of the U.S. educational establishment. In contrast, Rohlen points out, significant elements of the Japanese educational establishment have been concerned with competitiveness since the Meiji Restoration (1868). Japan's concern to rely on human resources for catching up has resulted in the shaping of an educational system that is, comparatively speaking, well tuned for providing critical human resources correspondent with the changing needs of the global economy, and at reasonable cost. Thus Rohlen urges a rethinking of the goals of education, as a preliminary to evaluating the implications of Japanese and Asian education. More specifically, he notes the educational benefits of a nationwide consensus on curriculum, a minimum of tracking, the stick and carrot of high stakes examinations, and the pay-off from greater time-on-task both in and outside the school.

S. Gopinathan discusses *Singapore's strategy for nation-building and modernization*. He points out that Singapore's economy is based on human resources and that the state has taken an active role in guiding Singapore's very impressive economic development during the past two decades, and that the state has also been a central force in educational policy and planning. Education is emphasized and public funds have been spent to ensure educational opportunity and excellence. The government controls the curriculum and supervises both public and private educational sectors. Singapore's government has successfully attempted to combine the traditional Confucian emphasis on education with the contemporary need for high-tech skills. Gopinathan especially stresses the role of Singapore's education in fostering common values and norms, and he suggests there is need in the United States to revive earlier chapters in U.S. educational history, when there was a similar unifying emphasis.

Nina Borevskaya, a leading Russian scholar, looks to China for lessons concerning the options available to educators as the surrounding economy shifts from a command to a market principle. She concludes the principle shift will be from central control to central steering combined with extensive decentralization of certain functions. Observing that the United States also is experimenting with central steering, she suggests that some of *China's experiments with middle-level coordination and with the promoting of new sanctions and incentives* may be of interest to American educators.

In the concluding essay for this part and the book, William K. Cummings, one of the co-editors, presents his own *summary of the outstanding features of Eastern Asian education* and their policy implications for the United States. Much of what Cummings notes is consistent with the earlier chapters of this book—the Asian emphasis on basic education including the teaching of social values, the reliance on cooperative and wholistic learning approaches which contribute to lower per-student costs, the public sector focus on manpower and elite education, and the concern to coordinate educational outputs with labor force demand. Cummings suggests the seeming success of Asian education tends to provoke a defensive reaction among some Western educators, leading to an often exaggerated highlighting of some of the weaknesses of Asian education. Yes, there is delinquency in Asia as well as bullying and so on; but the level is not as great as some critics suggest. Perhaps the biggest challenge of Asian education is its assertion that young people are minors and should comply with the discipline and rules imposed by the schools, reflecting a more general societal preference for order over freedom. This Eastern Asian emphasis on control contrasts with the Western love of freedom. Each emphasis has its price.

I

Basic Education

CHAPTER 1

The Roots of Japanese Educational Achievement:
Helping Children Develop Bonds to School

CATHERINE C. LEWIS

We hear a great deal about Japanese academic achievement. By the late elementary grades, Japanese students outperform their foreign counterparts in science and mathematics, achieve widespread literacy, and become attentive, well-disciplined students (Stevenson & Stigler, 1992). Yet we know little about the roots of Japanese achievement. Is it the longer school year? The national curriculum? Better compensation for teachers? This chapter makes a fundamentally different argument: that Japanese elementary schools succeed because, like families, they strive to meet the needs of the whole child—for belonging, contribution, *and* intellectual competence. Children, in turn, develop strong positive bonds to schools that meet their human needs. They develop these bonds because, as Sergiovanni (1992) notes, "The more the school cares about students, the more students care about matters of schooling" (p. 139).

First-Graders Learn Science

Two student monitors stood in front of their first-grade class and quieted their classmates. When they had their classmates' attention, they announced, "Science class will begin" and invited the teacher to start the lesson. On tall

Author's Note: This article draws on the material from my book *Educating Hearts and Minds: Reflections on Japanese Preschool and Elementary Education* (1995), by permission of Cambridge University Press. The research presented was conducted with the support of the Abe Fellowship Program of the Center for Global Partnership, the Nippon Life Insurance Foundation, the Social Science Research Council, the Spencer Foundation Small Grants Program, and the Association for Asian Studies. The socialization model (or bonding model) of schooling was brought to my attention by Marilyn Watson of the Child Development Project and I am indebted both to Dr. Watson and to the research and program legacy of the Child Development Project.

stools around each laboratory table sat the four children of a *han*—a family-like small group that would spend three months working, playing, and eating lunch together. Mr. Yanagi introduced the lesson:

> I have some worries about this lesson, First, I have a feeling that about three people will fall over during today's lesson. You will hit your heads and say, "Ouch." I think it would be lovely if no one fell over today. Second, I'm worried that water will spray everywhere and get everyone wet. Please try not to get everyone wet. Finally, if we do have water spills, let's help each other clean up without saying things like "It's not my fault" or "You did it."

For the first ten minutes, the first-graders "introduced" the empty plastic bottles they had brought from home, explaining that they were bottles from orange juice specially bought for a picnic, Dad's favorite vinegar, or whatever. Encouraged by questions from Mr. Yanagi or their classmates, some students eagerly added details about the favorite beverages or foods that had recently inhabited the bottles. Then Mr. Yanagi filled two glasses—one short and wide, one tall and narrow—with water. "Our first problem is to decide which has more," he said. "Can we figure out the correct answer by looking at them? Talk within your groups about ways to figure out which has more." As the small groups talked, Mr. Yanagi circulated, listening to each group and occasionally making comments such as "Two groups seem to be talking together well." After several minutes of discussion within the groups, Mr. Yanagi asked each to report, saying, "It's all right to mention more than one way of comparing them. It's also all right to say you couldn't figure out the problem." Several groups reported that they could figure out which glass had more just by looking. Several groups suggested pouring the water into identical cups to compare the amounts. One group suggested weighing the water. Mr. Yanagi said, "Well, we have a disagreement. Groups 1 and 2 disagree with the groups that said you can tell just by looking; tell each other your ideas." Proponents of the two viewpoints debated about whether you could judge the relative amounts "just by looking"; Mr. Yanagi listened intently to the debate for several minutes, without commenting. Finally, he said, "This is an interesting debate, and we'll be finding out more about it. Now, let's all give a round of applause to Group 4; they were the only group that thought of investigating by weight."

With great drama, Mr. Yanagi announced that the time had come to see which glass actually contained more. A class member came up to pour the contents of the glasses into identical containers. As the child poured the water, other children shouted their predictions. When the amounts appeared to be exactly equal, a roar of excitement came up from the class, and many students rushed up front to inspect more closely. Mr. Yanagi allowed the students to inspect the glasses for a few minutes and then proceeded to the next activity. He filled two identical pitchers with tap water, adjusting the amount several times until all students agreed that the pitchers held equal amounts. Then he poured the contents into two glasses of different widths and said matter-of-factly, "See, now this one has more because it's higher." Children shouted out, "You're wrong, you're wrong" and "the lower container is wider." In mock defeat, Mr. Yanagi moaned, "You're too smart for me. I thought I could trick you." Then he explained the final problem: to work within each group and decide whose bottle had the greatest volume and then to announce the results and explain how they were obtained. Each four-person group received two measuring cups. Some students searched cabinets to find pitchers of the kind used by Mr. Yanagi; one enterprising group delved into a closet to find a scale. Students worked for about ten minutes in their groups, pouring, measuring, and talking. When all groups but one seemed to have finished, Mr. Yanagi announced, "We'll hear from each group as soon as Group 1 is finished. Please make a decision in your group about who will announce your results."

When Group 1 finished, Mr. Yanagi began his wrap-up:

> As I was thinking about this lesson yesterday, I was thinking about who would make a mess with the water. I imagined Group 1 and Group 4 would. Group 4 was neat, but Group 1 caused a major flood. Now, I'd like a representative from each group to tell us which bottle you predicted was biggest, which you found was biggest, and how you investigated.

As each group reported, Mr. Yanagi asked the whole class to predict what the result would be. Students shouted their predictions and eagerly watched the results. Mr. Yanagi recalled children's introductions of the bottles: "Aha, Yamaguchi-kun's juice bottle looks very tall and would make the juice he loves so much look delicious, but it turns out it doesn't hold much."

Nine Central Qualities of Japanese Elementary Education

Mr. Yanagi took the time to have children introduce their bottles and explain what favorite foods had inhabited them. He also took time to emphasize the social qualities important to the task—to share water without spilling, to clean up without recrimination if water was spilled. Children worked in family-like small groups, and children themselves were in control of many aspects of the lesson—from quieting classmates to debating whether measurement was useful. How do these qualities relate to Japanese educational achievement? This article argues that Japanese elementary schools meet children's basic human needs—for belonging, contribution, development of competence—and thereby lead children to care about school. Based on my own observations and interviews in Japanese elementary classrooms (see Lewis, 1995), and on the work of other researchers (especially Cummings, 1980; Sato, 1991; Stevenson & Stigler, 1992; White, 1987), this article lays out nine central qualities of Japanese elementary education that enable children to develop a positive attachment to schooling.

Observational Method

The account that follows draws heavily on observations I have conducted over the past decade. In 1985, I spent a minimum of 1 full day in each of fifteen different first-grade classrooms in a convenience sample of thirteen Tokyo public schools. The diverse sample included schools in wealthy and poor neighborhoods of Tokyo; the oldest as well as one of the newest elementary schools in Tokyo; classes that ranged in size from 23 students (in central-city areas of declining enrollment) to 45 (in rapidly expanding industrial areas); and teachers ranging from one to forty years of teaching experience. I also observed first- through sixth-grade classrooms and interviewed teachers in Tokyo, Kyoto, and Nagoya during four additional stays in Japan (in 1987, 1989, 1990, and 1993). The longest of these was 1993, when I observed in two Nagoya elementary schools intensively for four months, and when my own son attended the local elementary school in our mixed factory and residential neighborhood in Nagoya.

In my visits to Japanese schools, I interviewed teachers after observing them teach. I asked them standard questions about classroom organization and discipline and specific questions about incidents I had observed. These questions were ethnopsychological in focus: I asked teachers why they used particular instructional techniques and tried to elicit the thinking about children's learning and development that underlay the techniques. The sample of teachers I observed and interviewed cannot be assumed to be a representative sample. Yet some practices were so pervasive that it seems almost certain they would be prominent in any sample. For example, in all of the more than thirty elementary schools that I studied, in three cities, in observations that spanned ten years:

1. Children assumed responsibility for many aspects of classroom management, such as quieting the class and calling it to order.
2. All used fixed, small groups of children (*han*) as the basic units for many daily classroom activities.

Compared to a long-term ethnography, in which the observer spends many months or years at a single site, my observations no doubt give a more "model" view of educational practices: I saw less behind-the-scenes action and presumably more of what teachers and principals wanted me to see. Yet what I found is remarkably consistent with the independent observations of long-term ethnographers like Nancy Sato (1991).

Many of the practices that I describe below—such as use of *han* and children's assumption of responsibility for much classroom management—are long-term practices that could not possibly have been marshaled for the visit of a foreign researcher. On the other hand, lesson content or disciplinary force could more easily have been modified with my presence in mind.

Although this article focuses only on Japanese classrooms, it is worthwhile to note that my implicit comparative framework is the U.S. elementary classrooms I have observed over the past five years, mainly as part of special research projects and school change efforts, but also as a volunteer in my own children's schools. Like their Japanese counterparts, the American teachers I observed were not randomly or representatively sampled; as volunteers willing to be observed, they were probably among the more capable and confident teachers.

Nine Qualities of Japanese Education for Young Children

This section briefly outlines nine qualities of Japanese education for young children that, I argue, should be central to our understanding of Japanese educational achievement. Through these qualities, Japanese elementary education meets children's social, intellectual, and emotional needs and helps children develop enduring, positive bonds to school.

1. Whole-Child Education

> Japanese teachers believe in whole-person education.
> They feel that their most important task is to develop
> well-rounded whole people, not just intellects.
> —William Cummings

As William Cummings noted more than a decade ago, Japanese education focuses on the whole child. Nonacademic subjects—art, music, physical education, homemaking, and special class activities—account for more than one-third of instructional hours at first grade, and more than 40 percent of instructional hours by sixth grade (Monbusho, 1989). First-graders spend as much time in art and music (combined) as they do in mathematics.

The Ministry of Education's official Course of Study for Elementary Schools is striking in its focus not just on academic development but on social, emotional, and ethical development as well. Its goals for the elementary years include, for example, children's interest in language, affection for their country and its history, love of nature, love of music, richness of sentiment, fondness for exercise, and reverence for life. To be sure, Japanese teachers lead their students in learning mathematics, Japanese language, and other academic subjects. But they also lead them in brushing their teeth, thinking about ways to ease their mothers' workloads at home, discussing what it means to "do your utmost" at the upcoming athletics festival, and talking about whether all class members are building friendships.

At a time when U.S. educators are being pushed to be accountable on measurable achievement outcomes, the Japanese elementary focus on children's character, emotional engagement, and enjoyment of learning is striking.

2. Values-Rich Education

To enter a Japanese elementary classroom is to confront clear, explicit values. Students study beneath banners proclaiming their school, class, or group goals—a total of 94 goals in the nineteen first-grade classrooms I studied, written in *hiragana* (phonetic script) so that all children could read them. Of the 94 goals, about half focused on friendship, cooperation, and other aspects of social and emotional development:

Let's become friends.

Let's get along well and put our strength together.

Let's be kind children who easily say I'm sorry and thank you.

Let's think about others' feelings before we speak.

The remaining half of the goals fell approximately equally into five categories: perseverance, responsibility, enthusiasm, healthy habits, and academic striving. *Gambaru, doryoku, konki* (perseverance) included goals such as: "Let's become children who persist until the end" and "Let's become a class that does its best" (see also Duke, 1986). When children discussed persistence, they often chose specific personal goals, posted and illustrated these, and revisited them in later lessons. These goals chosen by children spanned many areas of development:

I want to run around the whole track without stopping.

I want to do my homework every day.

I'm going to eat my whole lunch, even the vegetables.

I'm going to stop punching my little brother.

The emphasis on *genki* (energy or enthusiasm) was reflected in goals such as "Be energetic" and "Let's play energetically." When children answered roll call, sang, responded in unison, or danced, a teacher's comment "there's not much *genki* today" would stimulate loud voices and exuberant gestures. That Japanese teachers value exuberant, enthusiastic behavior—perhaps because it shows wholehearted connection to the group—has been noted by other researchers (Peak, 1991).

The emphasis on responsibility included general goals such as *jibun no koto o jibun de suru* (self-reliance) and specific behavior such as being on time, keeping one's desk contents neat, and keeping the area around oneself neat. All nineteen first-grade classrooms where I systematically recorded wall contents had charts designed to help children self-manage. For example, lesson schedules posted in all classrooms allowed students to prepare for the upcoming lesson during the break that preceded it by laying out the right notebooks and textbooks, or by changing into gym clothes. These schedules also showed the length of the breaks between lessons (usually 10 or 20 minutes) and reminded children of options for that time: use the bathroom, play outside, and so forth. Charts showed the agenda for the daily class meetings, so that students could lead these meetings. Student-made charts proudly displayed each chore group's members and tasks—often with self-portraits and elaborate illustrations. In most classes, students reflected on some responsibility daily: Had they completed their chores? remembered to bring from home all required items? kept their desks neat? been ready for lessons on time?

Finally, 8 percent of the first-grade goals focused on academics. These goals emphasized effort, not outcomes, for example:

Let's become children who take initiative in learning.

Let's think carefully.

Let's try hard at Japanese.

At the upper elementary grades, classes often selected one goal related to their studies, *gakushu*, and one related to their daily life, *seikatsu*. In keeping with this, academic goals were more frequent in upper-grade elementary classrooms, but the focus remained on effort, not grades or honors.

Classroom goals generally follow the Ministry of Education's guidelines for moral education, which emphasize friendship, cooperation, responsibility, and perseverance; yet children often "chose" these goals after discussion of what kind of class they wanted to become (see below). Often the wording of the goals reflected the children's own language and experiences: "Let's play dodgeball without the boys hogging the ball" or "Let's stop goofing off during clean-up."

Values did not simply inhabit banners. Just as Mr. Yanagi encouraged his budding scientists to treat one another respectfully even if water was spilled, teachers brought values into the content or process of many—perhaps most—academic lessons. Social studies lessons asked first-graders to investigate the rules in nearby parks, to identify ways to help their mothers at home, and to study how adults help one another in the daily life of the school. Cooperative small-group lessons had goals such as "to enjoy each other's company while planning the itinerary for the field trip" and "to design a public park, making sure that you listen kindly to the ideas of all the children in your small group."

3. A Caring, Supportive Community

What's the difference between a collection of thirty-five individuals and a classroom "community"? This is a question that Japanese teachers provoked me to think about on a daily basis. At the beginning of the school year, Japanese teachers' magazines are filled with articles on *gakkyuzukuri*—promoting a classroom community. These articles urge teachers to provide chances for students to get to know one another as individuals, to have fun together, and to work together to shape classroom values and practices. For example, they recommend cooperative art projects and games, activities that help children find out about one another's families and hobbies, humorous songs and dances, and classwide discussions of "what kind of class we want to be." I was surprised that none of the nineteen first-grade teachers I interviewed mentioned purely academic skills (such as holding a pencil, writing, or recognizing letters) among the skills and attitudes that children need to learn during the first month of first grade. Two-thirds of the teachers mentioned children's friendships or sense of connection to one another. For example, here are three different teachers' goals for the beginning of the year, typical of many I heard:

> First, children need friends. Friends help make children at ease. What children like most about school is playing with friends, so I give them opportunities to play with everyone in the class.

> At the beginning of the year, I use music to help build our sense of classhood. I use music because I happened to be a music major in college, but you could use any subject—whatever happens to be your favorite. Using music, I give children the opportunity to create something bigger than any one child could create alone. The children share pleasure. They share the satisfaction of creating something together.

At the beginning of the year, I have children, at the end of each day, think of something nice other children did that day. Children naturally notice each other's bad points, but I have them notice each other's good points. And gradually their whole way of looking at others changes.

Japanese elementary students and teachers typically stay together for two years, providing a long time to create and experience a sense of community. Except for the 10- or 20-minute breaks between each academic lesson (when students are often completely *un*supervised), teachers spend the whole day with their students: students and teacher eat lunch together in the classroom, and the classroom teacher is responsible for all or nearly all subjects, including science, art, music, and physical education. If student work is posted, it is usually the work of every single student in the class. Likewise, activities that fragment the class—such as pull-out programs and ability-grouping—are avoided (Kajita, Shiota, Ishida, & Sugie, 1980).

Teachers help build connections among children through lessons that draw out children's personal experiences and ideas. In many classes, two children give one-minute speeches every day, to tell classmates about their favorite activities outside of school. As part of Japanese language lessons, social studies, and other subject areas, children compose and deliver oral reports on "my most precious possession," share memorable experiences involving their grandparents, draw each class member's house on a class map, discuss what each class member likes most and least about school, and find out a great deal about each other's experiences and preferences. Combined with the daily diaries that children in many schools write, these lessons give teachers an amazing array of information about students, which they often use to personalize lessons. Teachers draw individual children into lessons with comments such as "Your grandmother lives with you, so has she told you about what our neighborhood was like when she was young?" or "Writing is your least favorite subject, so what did you think about today's lesson?" In a society known for groupism and conformity, teachers' interest in personalizing lessons presents an odd paradox. Yet, as one teacher pointed out, "to nurture the group, you must nurture each individual."

4. Learning to Live in Groups

The groups of four children who worked together during Mr. Yanagi's science lesson would work together many times a day for several months. Their four desks were in two pairs immediately behind one another in the classroom, and they could meet together just by having two children turn in their seats. At lunch, they pushed their desks together to make a mini-dining table. At the end of each day (and sometimes each lesson, as well) the four children in each group talked about the strengths and weaknesses of their cooperation that day and thought about whether they had been kind to one another.

These *han* or fixed small groups of about four children are a prominent feature of life in nearly all Japanese elementary classrooms. *Han* differ sharply from the single-purpose, ability-based groups found in many American elementary schools: They include children with diverse abilities who together pursue a wide range of daily activities from art projects to science experiments. Japanese teachers often liken these groups to families and maintain the same groups for a relatively long time: an average of two months in first grade (Kajita et al., 1980).

Teachers frequently mention three kinds of goals for *han*. First, the groups are designed to promote participation and to provide a family-like home base for children. As teachers said, "It's hard for children to feel connected to a big class, much easier to feel connected to a group" and "It's easier to express your ideas to a small group than to talk in front of the whole class." Teachers conducted many group-building activities designed to give children shared, pleasurable experiences within their groups: Children built art and social studies projects together, played games, and interviewed one another about their interests.

Second, *han* were the basic units for classroom management. In the words of one teacher "Everything's easier if you have groups, because each group provides order." Teachers told me that a good group is "one that works well together" and has *matomari* (cohesiveness, or a sense of unity). They explained that, once groups had *matomari*, the class could easily take field trips, eat lunch outside the classroom, or undertake a complicated science experiment. Getting to know fellow *han* members and having fun together was the first step toward *matomari*; reflecting on the strengths and weaknesses of the group's effort and working to improve the group came next.

Third, teachers designed groups in ways intended to foster individual children's development: "I try to place a distractible child with a child who likes to take care of others, a generous child with a shy child." During the early elementary grades, groups were most often designed to help children build friendships and a family-like feeling. A common end-of-day question was "Did our group members do something kind for one another today?" As children progressed through the elementary grades, teachers thought carefully about the particular needs of their current students—social, emotional, intellectual—and formed groups that would help students with these needs. For example, groups might bring together shy children to help them develop leadership skills or might place each child who was falling behind in math in a group with someone "nurturant and skillful at math," and build each *han* around such a pair.

5. *Reflection or* Hansei

At the end of the day in Mr. Yanagi's class, each group reflected on its cooperation during the day, recalling whether they'd been ready to begin each lesson and whether they had shared materials without mishaps and in a friendly way. *Hansei*—reflection—pervaded daily activities (both non-academic and academic) in the Japanese classrooms I studied. In many class-rooms, students reflected daily or twice daily; some teachers ended each lesson with a time for reflection. Children might reflect, as a small group, on whether they had worked together well in doing chores; they might identify, individually, some goal for self-improvement (to study for one hour every night, to raise my hand at least once every day); they might reflect, as a class, on the past hour's, day's, or week's activities (did you do anything kind for others? anything naughty? what did you like best? least?). *Hansei* was sometimes formal and public. For example, students at one central To-kyo elementary school formally evaluated themselves each Friday on goals chosen by the class, discussing, for example whether they had made progress toward "becoming a friendly class." In other cases, *hansei* might be private or informal. Students might reflect quietly on their progress in meeting self-identified goals, or they might discuss the day's or week's activities, recall-ing favorite moments or problems.

Japanese children and parents consistently rate children's educational achievement less favorably than do American parents and children, an inter-esting anomaly in view of the higher actual achievement of Japanese stu-dents (Stevenson & Stigler, 1992). American and Japanese parents are equally accurate in assessing their own child's ranking relative to classmates; yet Americans as a whole rate children's performance more positively. Sim-ilarly, Japanese children report lower satisfaction with themselves than do U.S. or European children (Kashiwagi,1986). These findings could have many interpretations, but I wonder if they relate in some measure to chil-dren's experience with *hansei*. *Hansei* is designed to focus children's atten-tion on their shortcomings—on the fact that there's always room for self-improvement. Much research suggests benefits of a self-critical attitude: It can motivate striving for improvement, lead one to notice and care about problems that might escape a less critical eye, and catalyze creativity (Guilford, 1968; Lewis, 1992; Uchihashi,1983).

On the other hand, some Japanese commentators link a self-critical atti-tude to reticence and to a sense of inferiority or incompleteness, raising the interesting question of what's an "appropriate" level of self-criticism (Kurita, 1991; Nagano, 1983). Although we currently know little about *hansei*, I think it is an important puzzle piece in our understanding of Japanese education. In the months that I spent in elementary schools, I found myself powerfully affected by the reflection going on around me. As students and teachers earnestly asked themselves "What have I done to help others this week?" and "What are my goals for self-improvement?" I couldn't help asking myself the same questions.

6. Methods of Discipline that Promote a Personal Commitment to Values

Japanese elementary teachers choose methods of discipline that promote children's self-discipline and avoid strategies that build children's reliance on adult authority, surveillance, rewards, or punishment (Lewis, 1984, 1989). Four strategies are particularly striking. First, all Japanese elementary students—whatever their abilities or personal qualities—have regular opportunities for leadership. Every day, the *toban* (daily class monitors, sometimes called *nicchoku*) change; these monitors have a very visible role as classroom leaders. The *toban*—usually one boy and one girl—assemble and quiet the class before the teacher arrives for each lesson. In addition, they often lead meetings, evaluate other students' behavior, and lead the class in solving disputes or problems that arise.

The *toban* system capitalizes on children's natural interests—for attention, prestige, and a chance to lead others—and gives children a chance to experience the pleasure, and headaches, of responsibility. The child standing at the front of the class struggling to quiet classmates could be you—and would be in a matter of days or weeks. As one teacher said, the *toban* system "teaches how hard people can make it for you and how much better it is to have help." As another teacher pointed out, the *toban* system extended the experience of leadership to all children:

> The *toban* system allows even a child who can't normally be a leader a chance to be a leader. The children who are least able to lead others in daily encounters are often the ones who work the most carefully when they are *toban*.

Second, students helped shape the rules and norms of the classroom. At the beginning of the year, students and teacher discussed "what kind of class we want to become." This discussion provided the grist for individual, group, and class goals. Usually, the class's major goal was written on a banner over the front blackboard, for example: "Let's be a friendly class that persists until the end" or "Let's all get along well, cooperate, and do our best." Daily, students talked about whether they were making progress toward their goals and what they might do to improve. Children (not teachers) usually suggested the committees and chore groups needed to help the class run smoothly, volunteered for these, carried them out during designated times set aside in the day, and discussed the strengths and weaknesses of their efforts. These jobs were often quite simple during the early elementary years—turning the television on and off (for moral education programs once or twice a week), arranging flowers, caring for class animals, opening and shutting windows—but became increasingly demanding with age—monitoring sports equipment for recess, taking responsibility for delicate science equipment, writing a class newspaper, or creating a "student news" bulletin board. At brief meetings twice a day and longer weekly meetings, students often discussed their successes and problems in working toward the kind of class they wanted to be. Students raised incidents of kindness and exclusion, problems and successes in chores, and ideas for class projects. Often these meetings were student-run.

Third, teachers kept a low profile as authority figures. One first-grade teacher waited, without saying a word, for seventeen minutes while the student monitors tried unsuccessfully to quiet the class. "I could have quieted them by saying one word, but I don't want to create children who obey just because I'm here," explained their teacher. Later, the class devoted a long class meeting to discussing why they had had trouble quieting down and what they could do to improve. Although teachers' de-emphasis of control flies in the face of American conventional wisdom that firm control promotes good behavior, it is quite consistent with attribution theory and research, which suggest that children are most likely to internalize adult values when they see themselves as obeying those values willingly—rather than when they attribute their behavior to external rewards or punishments (Lepper, 1981).

Fourth, as several researchers have noted, Japanese teachers tend to attribute benign motives to children (Peak, 1991; Tobin, Wu, & Davidson, 1989). Children do not purposefully break rules; they "forget their promises" or "don't understand." Misbehavior is called *okashii* (strange) behavior. Belief in children's inherent goodness is a dominant theme in Japanese child-rearing, historical and contemporary (Boocock, 1987; Hara & Wagatsuma, 1974; Kojima, 1986). And research suggests that, when adults believe children to be good, it may be a self-fulfilling prophecy: adults' interpretations of children's motives affect children's self-attributions, which in turn affect their behavior (Lepper, 1981).

7. Children's Thinking Helps Drive Instruction and Classroom Life

Just as Japanese students' ideas shaped the kind of class they wanted to be, students' ideas often drove academic lessons, too. As students discussed the reasons for the rules they found in public parks, reflected on why the boats they built from plastic bottles sank or floated, or devised ways to measure their classrooms, their teachers acted more as gadflies than as authorities. Teachers might summarize the points made by children and point out the similarities or contradictions among them, but teachers rarely supplied correct answers. Tsuchida's (1993) study of fourth-grade American and Japanese science lessons found that Japanese teachers, compared to their American colleagues, more often exhorted students to express agreement or disagreement with classmates.

The death of two of the five crabs in a first-grade classroom provided the catalyst for a science lesson in a downtown Tokyo elementary school. The teacher began the class by asking, "Why do you think they died?" Students offered many suggestions, which he wrote on the board. Among them was the suggestion that the crabs' cages were too dirty. "What makes you think they're dirty?" asked the teacher. "They stink" yelled out several students. Another student said "It's not the dirty cages that stink. It's the crabs that stink. I've smelled them at the ocean and they stink there." This disagreement—about whether the crabs stank naturally or because of dirty cages—was seized upon by the teacher, who polled students' views, found the class was evenly split, and challenged students to devise an experiment that would resolve the question. The students, after brainstorming in small groups and as a class, eventually came up with the idea of washing one of the remaining live crabs and its cage, and then seeing how it smelled. The teacher questioned and challenged the students, encouraging them to state and to clarify their thinking, but gave no answers as students devised, conducted, and drew inferences from their experimental crab washing.

Like the first-grade crab lesson, Japanese science and social studies lessons often revolved around a single problem: What effects does moving water have in a stream? What happens to the starch in a seed potato when it sprouts? When you put a plastic bag over a plant, where do the drops of water come from? How does our neighborhood get water and dispose of sewage? What do our mothers do to help our families? A standard pattern for these lessons is for the teacher repeatedly to move back and forth between whole-class discussion and small-group work, with the teacher acting as gadfly, catalyst, and often synthesizer (Lewis, 1995; Tsuchida, 1993). This pattern allows students' ideas to help drive instruction and provides small-group activities likely to involve all children, while at the same time ensuring that the teacher's expertise is brought to bear. Japanese elementary mathematics lessons often follow a similar pattern, although individual hands-on activity or problem solving often replaces small-group activity in the case of mathematics (Easley & Easley, 1983; Stigler & Stevenson, 1991).

In summary, Japanese academic lessons tend to begin with a concrete problem, close to children's everyday lives—what happens to your heartbeat when you run up the stairs, or how can you figure out whether your bottle is bigger than the differently shaped bottle of your neighbor. Students volunteer their ideas and then discuss and evaluate these ideas, at some length. Typically, the teacher withholds his or her opinion during these discussions, urging students themselves to explain their responses and question their classmates. Although this pattern declines somewhat across the elementary years—with the discovery learning of the early years giving way to a curriculum more densely packed with facts and procedures—the ideal that students' ideas and curiosity should help drive learning continues to be in evidence, especially in mathematics and science.

8. "Wet Learning"

Why did Mr. Yanagi take the time to have students introduce their bottles, telling about the favorite beverages that had recently inhabited them? Japanese sometimes use the English words *wet* and *dry*—*wetto* and *dorai*—to describe emotional styles. A dry approach is rational, logical, unemotional (and often, by implication, Western); a wet approach is personal, emotional, interpersonally complex (and in contrast, Japanese). When I observed Japanese first-grade lessons, I was struck by how wet the learning was. Lessons were designed to spark children's personal interest, grip them emotionally, and involve them intimately with classmates, I noted above the fusion of academic and social content in many classroom lessons, as children investigated their mothers' work or discussed the rationale for playground rules. But even when the content was science or mathematics, learning was often an emotional enterprise. Children might spend two hours decorating the plastic bottle "boats" they would use to study sinking and floating in science class, or science class might start with each child telling a brief personal story about the fruits, flowers, or containers brought from home to use in the day's experiment.

Learning was active. It took children:

To the floor: Children thought up as many ways as they could to measure it—including human body lengths.

To every room in the school: They investigated who was in the room and what kind of work they did to help the school.

To the school yard: They drew the flowers and vegetables in the class garden.

To the neighborhood: They made maps and recorded play equipment in local parks.

I quickly learned not to rely on electric outlets, particularly for science and social studies lessons.

Finally, wet lessons emphasized process. The point wasn't just to obtain a correct answer: it was to be engaged in a wholehearted way and to reflect on one's work, whether or not these led to correct answers. Persistence and elaboration were often singled out for praise, quick-and-dirty work for criticism. Pictures that filled the paper or were elaborate were held up by teachers as examples of children who "really had autumn in their hearts as they drew pictures of autumn." Pictures dashed off quickly were returned to their owners for elaboration: "Weren't there more classmates on your field trip? Why is just one child playing here?" or "Look how lonely that chestnut looks on the paper. Can't you draw something to keep the chestnut company?" The emphasis on wholehearted engagement as an important criterion for judging children's work explained a paradox to me: that academic lessons often seemed more "soft" than I expected, as children shared their feelings about the lesson, but that enrichment subjects were taken more seriously (even art and music called for wholehearted involvement, not dashed-off creations).

9. A Standard Curriculum, Supportive of Child Inquiry

Japanese teachers have at their disposal carefully crafted lessons that support a view of children as active, thoughtful learners. These lessons are generally dominated by a single, important goal for children's learning—for example, to discover that heat rises or that measurement is useful—and a single problem to explore in depth. Supported by such lessons and examples, Japanese teachers are free to focus on how they will interest and motivate students— not on culling important concepts and information from textbooks and teachers' manuals jam-packed with lists of new concepts, information, vocabulary, and application problems, as is often the case for American teachers. A critique of American science textbooks has noted that the average science lesson contains more new vocabulary than a foreign-language lesson. Stevenson and Stigler (1992) argue that the pressure on American teachers to create original curriculum materials, rather than to provide skilled interpretations of standard curricula, is broadly detrimental to American education:

> In America, teachers are judged to be successful when they are innovative, inventive, and original. Skilled presentation of a standard lesson is not suffi-

cient and may even be disparaged as indicating a lack of innovative talent. It is as if American teachers were expected to write their own play or create their own concerto day after day and then perform it with expertise and finesse. These two models, the skilled performer and the innovator, have very different value in the East and West. It is hard for us in the West to appreciate that innovation does not require that the presentation be totally new, but can come from thoughtful additions, new interpretations, and skillful modifications. (pp. 167–68)

A Model of Education's Underpinnings

Why should the nine qualities just described provide the underpinnings for educational achievement? Work on Japanese education presents various—generally implicit—models of how Japanese children become highly motivated, knowledgeable, thoughtful learners. (There's remarkably little disagreement that they do become all these things during the elementary years.) These include behaviorist models that view learning as a function of time on task and rewards, models that emphasize the family's role in teaching and motivating children, and models that attend to the social structural, policy, and bureaucratic supports for education (e.g., Barrett, 1990; Hess & Azuma, 1991; Lynn, 1988; U.S. Study of Education in Japan, 1987; White, 1987).

Yet Japanese teachers themselves regard strong, positive human relationships as fundamental to children's educational success. Shimahara and Sakai (1992), who studied on-the-job training for new Japanese elementary teachers, noted that *kizuna*—the bond between students and teacher—is seen as the central principle of good education. In training new teachers, establishment of this bond takes precedence over technical competence. New teachers are urged to "mingle with students without disguise and pretense." They are coached on how to build enduring relationships with children and how to see things from a child's point of view. Here's the kind of advice experienced teachers gave their new colleagues:

> Teaching is a kind of art. Emphasis should be placed on the relationship of hearts, the nurturing of bonding between the teacher's and children's hearts.

> When I get a new class I do not teach subject matter immediately. Instead I play with children intensely for a week to gain a good understanding of them. Then I will begin to know what kinds of children they are and gradually direct them toward the goals of learning on the basis of happy and trustful *kakawari* [personal relations] with them.

How does one develop the "bonding between the teacher's and children's hearts" that is fundamental to children's success in school? The nine qualities of Japanese education just described make Japanese elementary schools extraordinarily responsive to children's needs—for friendship and belonging, for a sense of control over the environment, for opportunities to shape lessons with one's own ideas. Research and theory suggest that adults will succeed in establishing bonds of trust with children to the extent that they meet three basic needs of children: for autonomy, belonging, and competence (Connell & Wellborn, 1991; Deci & Ryan, 1985; Solomon, Watson, Battistich, Schaps, & Delucchi, 1992).

Autonomy is the child's need to shape the environment—to be self-directed and free of arbitrary restraint. Japanese schools provide for children's autonomy in many ways:

By giving all children a chance to lead their classmates, on a rotating basis;

By allowing children to help shape classroom rules and goals and to solve problems that arise;

By emphasizing *self*-evaluation rather than evaluation by the teacher, and self-management, rather than adult control.

Japanese teachers often use the terms *murinaku* (without force) and *shizen ni* (naturally) to describe children's willing acceptance of discipline that comes from within children themselves, rather than from the outside.

Belonging is the need for stable, mutually satisfying relationships. As noted above, Japanese schools emphasize belonging in many ways:

By avoiding ability grouping and pull-out programs;

By keeping teacher and students together for an extended period;

By using special events to build a schoolwide sense of community;

By emphasizing the importance of friendship and kindness;

By helping students develop connections to family-like small groups.

Schools emphasize goals—friendliness, persistence, cooperation, energy—that all children can achieve, whatever their level of academic skills.

Competence (or agency) is the child's need to act upon the world successfully, and to pursue activities regarded as worthwhile. Even without rewards or encouragement from others, children naturally explore the human and physical world and try to make sense of it, constantly forming and revising hypotheses. Children are likely to find school gripping and important to the extent that it connects with this quest to make sense of the world. As noted above, Japanese lessons are often driven by children's own thinking and may revolve around tasks that are inherently interesting to children—crafting boats that float, designing the ideal playground, finding out who works in each room of the school, using measurement to compare objects around them. Such meaningful, child-driven activities are much more likely to meet children's need for competence than would a focus on isolated, "basic" skills whose purpose and meaning are not clear to children. The breadth of the Japanese curriculum, with its emphases on art, music, physical education, and social development, further increases the likelihood that all children—not just an academically able few—will find areas of competence. The weight given to goals such as friendliness, persistence, and responsibility also provides opportunities for all children to succeed at valued goals. When a first-grade class monitor asked classmates to raise their hands if they succeeded on the week's goal of "playing energetically," all hands shot up eagerly.

Conclusion

In school, children's needs for autonomy, belonging, and competence must be reconciled with the needs of adult society: to create an orderly environment where children can efficiently acquire the knowledge, skills, and attitudes needed to become productive members of society. Yet whether students will be amenable to such learning may depend, in large part, on whether schools meet children's own needs for friendship, self-direction, and meaningful accomplishment. Japanese elementary schools—with their strong, nationally mandated emphasis on friendship, contribution to group life, and development of the whole child—have many qualities that help them effectively meet children's basic needs for autonomy, belonging, and competence. In return, children are likely to see school as a place responsive to their needs and to take on willingly its values of hard work, group participation, self-discipline, and self-critical reflection.

As noted at the outset, comparative research on Japanese and American education is in its infancy, and hence this article is speculative. We know little about how Japanese students view their educational experiences: Do students themselves see their schools as responsive to their needs for belonging, competence, and autonomy? Also, we know little about the changes in Japanese schooling over the elementary grades, a troubling gap in view of some evidence suggesting that, by junior high, Japanese schools may become quite *un*responsive to students' needs for autonomy and for meaningful learning. And we don't know whether there might be drawbacks associated with the strong bonds Japanese students establish to schools. If Japanese elementary schools are successful in promoting students' attachment to school, and their consequent internalization of the values of the school, they might also dull students' capacity for principled dissent—unless it is explicitly valued by the school.

Research in U.S. schools demonstrates that schools meeting children's needs for autonomy, belonging, and competence are likely to promote students' academic achievement as well (Solomon et al., 1992). Hence these "new ABC's" (autonomy, belonging, competence) are at least a plausible puzzle piece in understanding Japanese academic achievement. The fact that Japanese students are "off-task" a tiny fraction of the time that their American counterparts are—with less direction from adults and more student responsibility—suggests that students' acceptance of school values and their capacity to handle autonomy must be components of any adequate explanation of Japanese academic achievement. And it's important to note that the habits of mind that underlie academic achievement—asking critical questions, reflecting, justifying one's own point of view, understanding the thoughts and experiences of others—develop not only during academic lessons but throughout the school day, as students discuss why it took their class seventeen minutes to quiet down, or whether they are becoming a "friendlier" class.

As we reflect on Japanese practices and their relevance to American education, we should paint as rich and complicated a picture of Japanese education as we can: one that recognizes the interwoven threads of intellectual, social, and ethical development. Part of this complicated picture, I have argued, is the effectiveness of Japanese schools in meeting children's psychological needs—for autonomy, belonging, and competence—and thereby helping children develop strong, positive bonds to schooling.

What are the implications of Japanese elementary education for U.S. practice? At least one well-researched American program—the Child Development Project (CDP)—employs practices that are remarkably similar to Japanese practices, with the goal of creating a "caring community to learners" in order to promote children's social and ethical as well as intellectual development (Watson, Solomon, Battistich, Schaps, and Solomon, 1989). More than a decade of longitudinal research on Child Development Project schools and matched comparison schools indicates that the CDP program does promote children's bonds to school, increasing their friendships, helpfulness toward one another, commitment to democratic values, and higher-order intellectual skills. So there is reason to believe that the strategies widely employed by Japanese elementary teachers—the emphasis on warm, caring personal relationships, opportunities for children to shape the environment, and values such as helpfulness, kindness, and responsibility— may be important keys to good schooling in the United States as well. In our haste to explain Japanese academic achievement, we should not overlook what Japanese elementary teachers themselves regard as their central goal: warm, trusting relationships among all members of the school community.

CHAPTER 2

The East Asian Version of Whole-Class Teaching

HAROLD W. STEVENSON and
SHINYING LEE

As Americans strive to improve the quality of the nation's education, many parents and educators argue that the solution lies in the adoption of a more child-centered, individualistic approach. This often means reducing class size and rejecting whole-class instruction as much as possible in favor of organizing the class into small groups. Having children work in small groups, the argument goes, allows dull lectures to be replaced by stimulating experiences of self-discovery. We argue that reducing the time spent on whole-class instruction can have harmful effects on children's learning because it reduces their opportunities to learn from experienced and knowledgeable adults—their teachers.

Faced with the relentless findings of cross-national studies showing American students falling below the average of other industrialized nations, we Americans are seeking models that will enable us to improve our status. In this quest, some of us have looked at East Asian education, a system that relies nearly solely on whole-class instruction and is producing students who are consistently among the world's top performers in comparative studies of academic achievement (e.g., Garden, 1987; Stevenson, Chen, & Lee, 1993; Stevenson et al., 1990). Some observers reject the East Asian teaching methods as being unacceptable; others—and we are among them—find many interesting ideas in East Asian teaching practices.

The Stereotype

If one asks the typical American about East Asian education, the answer usually conforms to a stereotyped image: tense, robotlike children and a stern, demanding teacher who stresses mechanical learning and rote memory.

Author's note: A longer version of portions of this chapter will appear in a book edited by T. Rohlen and G. LeTendre, *Teaching and Learning in Japan*.

Lectures, choral recitation, and daily drill characterize the classes, they say, and resigned submission describes the students. The students are believed to lack creativity and problem-solving skills. It is suggested that they are able to attain their high levels of academic competence only by spending long hours in classes and grueling hours after school doing homework.

This high-pressure stereotype of whole-class instruction in East Asian schools may have been appropriate fifty years ago, but it is no longer a valid description of the typical East Asian classroom. Indeed, Westerners whom we have accompanied to classrooms in East Asia are shocked when they first visit the schools.

The Image

The first thing Western visitors to an East Asian elementary school comment about is how noisy the children are before school and during their frequent breaks between classes. Visitors inevitably say that they were unprepared for the wild activity that occurs on the playground, as scores or even hundreds of children engage in vigorous games of badminton, basketball, rope skipping, or tag. And they are surprised to know that the day is punctuated by 10- or 15-minute breaks that occur after every 40- to 45-minute class, so that nearly an hour a day is spent in recesses.

Noise continues as the children enter their classrooms. Then, with remarkable speed, the children assume a calm, attentive attitude when the teacher announces, "Let's begin." Expecting to find the teacher as the sole source of information and lone arbiter of what is correct, visitors are surprised by the frequency with which the teacher calls upon students for their opinions or explanations of a problem and then seeks the reaction of other students to what has just been suggested. Visitors who understand the language are impressed by the skill with which teachers guide students through the lessons. They often describe the teachers as skilled professionals who approach their classes with a confident intensity and who present interesting lessons to their large classes with enthusiasm and vigor. They are surprised by the teachers' clear organization of the lesson and their polished mastery of teaching techniques.

All teachers are not equally successful, of course, but the pattern described above is evident in the vast majority of classrooms. The teacher does not assume the role of lecturer but acts as an informed guide who knows that teaching is most effective if students participate in the lesson and if students realize that they may be called on during the course of the hour for their opinions and reactions.

We found that Japanese children spent most of their time at school working, watching, and listening together as a class; they were rarely divided into smaller groups. American children, on the other hand, spent as much time working alone as they did working together as a class. American children worked on individual activities 47% of the time. This percentage was much greater than that for Japanese children (28%).

The Data

We have written descriptions of the teaching practices we have observed in Japanese and Chinese elementary schools (Lee, Graham, & Stevenson, 1996; Stevenson & Stigler, 1992; Stigler & Stevenson, 1991) and of formal observational studies we have conducted in Japanese, Chinese, and American kindergartens (Stevenson, Lee, & Graham, 1993) and elementary schools (Stevenson et al., 1987). These reports provide the background for the descriptions we present in this article. (For additional descriptions of teaching in Japanese and Chinese classrooms, see Lewis, 1984, 1989; Peak, 1991; Rohlen, 1983; Sato & McGlaughlin, 1992; Stigler & Perry, 1988; White, 1988.)

We rely in the present report on data from a large observational study we conducted more recently in elementary school classrooms in East Asia and the United States. We will describe the East Asian approach to whole-class instruction by concentrating our attention first on Japanese schools; however, the conclusions we draw from the descriptions of Japanese schools also apply to the Chinese schools we visited. In a later section we compare the Japanese and Chinese schools.

We conducted our research in the metropolitan areas of Chicago and of Sendai, a large city several hundred kilometers northeast of Tokyo. In each metropolitan area, observations were made in representative samples of schools, including some of the least successful and some of the most outstanding. Ten Sendai schools were chosen to represent the range of elementary schools found in a large, traditional Japanese city. Twenty schools were selected in the city of Chicago and its suburbs. The large racial, ethnic, and economic diversity found throughout the Chicago metropolitan area required the larger sample of schools. We will also refer to data from the metropolitan area of Beijing, China, a third site for this research.

The results we quote are based on 480 class periods of narrative descriptions of mathematics lessons made by observers who observed one class period on four separate occasions in each of two first-grade and two fifth-grade classrooms in each of the Japanese and American schools. Observations were made only during mathematics classes, but on the basis of our own experience and of the data we obtained in an earlier study (Stevenson et al., 1987), we believe that lessons in other subjects do not depart greatly in form or approach from what we describe.

The essential features of the observational methods used involved having two observers visit each classroom at the same time. One observer followed a time-sampling procedure and noted the presence of certain predefined categories of behavior during brief, successive observational periods. The second observer, focusing on the teacher and his or her interactions with the students, wrote a narrative description of what occurred during each lesson. Other people then coded the narrative observations according to a scheme developed on the basis of our earlier experience in East Asian and American classrooms.

Whole-Class Instruction

We focus our attention on whole-class instruction, a type of classroom organization in which teachers teach to the whole class. This occurred in over 95% of the Japanese lessons. American teachers also relied on whole-class instruction: first- and fifth-grade teachers worked with the whole class between 75% and 85% of the time.

The whole-class approach gives the largest number of children the greatest amount of their teachers' time. We know that children can learn on their own or in small groups. The question is whether children can learn as effectively or as fruitfully when they work by themselves or in frequent interaction with their peers as they can through the well-planned guidance of a skilled and knowledgeable teacher. Learning under the guidance of someone who has familiarity with the material derived from earlier exposure can, under appropriate conditions, be an efficient and rewarding way to learn.

Organizing the classroom into small groups limits the opportunities that each individual has for benefiting from the presence of the teacher, who must move from group to group throughout the class period. This means that any child or group receives only a limited amount of the teacher's time. With effectively managed whole-class instruction, all children receive the same amount of instruction during every lesson.

A basic assumption behind whole-class instruction is that all children should be able to learn the content of the curriculum if they are taught well and study diligently. Japanese elementary school teachers plan their lessons with this in mind. They present each topic thoroughly and systematically so that all students are given adequate opportunity to master the material. If students do not understand the material the first day they know they will have another opportunity the next day, for the pace of instruction is geared to the rate at which the majority of the children give evidence of understanding the content of the lesson.

Neither tracking among classes nor grouping by ability within a class occurs in Japanese elementary schools, despite the fact that the average class size is around forty pupils. Children at each grade level are assigned to classrooms randomly with the restriction that, to the degree possible, there is an equal number of boys and girls in each classroom. Children with profound disabilities are enrolled in special schools, but extra attention is seldom given during the regular class periods to children who may have special needs, such as slow learners or gifted children. These children's needs must be met outside regular classes through individual sessions with the teacher, after-school classes, private tutoring, or attendance at *hosyu juku* (special schools) that provide remedial help for students who are falling behind in their work. (A description of provisions made for the education of gifted and talented children in East Asia may be found in Stevenson, Lee, & Chen, 1994.)

Japanese elementary schools serve the residents of each region of the city. However, in contrast to the differentiation of neighborhoods according to socioeconomic status that occurs in the United States, wide strata of society are represented in a typical Japanese elementary school. Thus teachers must teach in a fashion that will accommodate differences in rate of learning and learning style among students. Teachers must respond to the fact that some children in the class learn rapidly whereas others take much longer to master the material. They must also employ techniques that will help students who learn more effectively by seeing than by doing or who understand more readily by hearing than by reading.

The Lesson

A distinction must be made between a class period and a lesson. The former is often conceived of as a period of time devoted to the study of a particular topic. Class periods may begin where the last class left off and proceed in a loosely organized fashion. In contrast, lessons, as they are typically presented in East Asian classrooms, follow a well-organized, coherent sequence. As in a good book, the lesson consists of an introduction, development of the ideas, and a final period in which all the information is brought to some kind of a conclusion. Lessons presented in this fashion are both informative and enjoyable.

Americans' strong rejection of whole-class instruction is partly due to the manner in which this type of instruction is conducted in many American classrooms. The most common pattern in the United States is for whole-class instruction to consist of lectures by the teacher, followed by seat work where students practice the skills and attempt to apply the information the teacher has presented. The teacher is the prime purveyor of information and judge of the relevance or correctness of the students' responses. This is not the type of whole-class instruction found in most Japanese classrooms.

In Japan, the teacher may begin instruction by presenting a word problem and asking the students to discuss the meaning of the problem. The students are then given time to think about how they would go about solving the problem and are asked to write down their solutions. After this, the teacher asks several students to write their approaches on the board and to explain their answers. The students selected are ones who have proposed a type of response that the teacher wants to address and discuss with the whole class. Before doing this, however, the teacher calls on other students to evaluate the relevance and accuracy of what the first students have reported.

Additional activities may consist of the whole class's reading, responding to problems or questions contained on worksheets, and drawing illustrations of the concepts being discussed, or of the teacher's reading a brief selection to the class. The teacher summarizes, clarifies, or elaborates the students' answers in an effort to provide appropriate feedback and to facilitate the children's understanding of the topic.

Rather than retiring to a desk in the front of the room while the children are solving practice problems at their seats, the Japanese teacher moves about the room, commenting to individual students about their responses, giving hints to others. and helping children to clarify their understanding of what they are doing. The class typically ends with the teacher summarizing what was accomplished and, when relevant, providing the rule or law governing the material or processes covered during the course of the lesson.

Whole-class instruction of this type makes great demands on teachers. To maintain an alert, responsive, interactive mode of teaching requires mastery of the material, excellent preparation, great energy, and patience. Teachers also need time to prepare lessons, to interact with other teachers in order to benefit from their experiences, to meet with individual students, and to conserve their energy.

It seems paradoxical that this type of teaching should characterize educational systems that accept large classes as the norm. However, this form of instruction is possible, in part, because Japan and other East Asian countries have chosen to keep class sizes large so that teachers can spend more time outside the classroom preparing lessons and performing other noninstructional duties.

The ratio of teachers to students in Japan is approximately the same as in countries where classes are limited to fewer than thirty students. This means that Japanese teachers actually are teaching during less than 70 percent of the eight or more hours a day they are at school. Even so, the job is a demanding one and Japanese teachers complain about how hard they must work.

The Pattern of Instruction

The typical lesson in Japanese mathematics classes consisted of several three-part cycles: a period during which information is presented, an opportunity to practice what was learned, and some type of feedback about the relevance or correctness of the students' responses. Advantages of this three-step sequence are obvious. Practice, as we know, makes perfect. And appropriate feedback informs both the student about whether the practice needs to be modified and the teacher about whether the children have understood the material.

Most Japanese lessons consisted of repetitions of this three-step sequence, as is evident in figure 2.1. American teachers also followed this sequence at times, but, as is the case with other types of teaching techniques we will discuss, did so much less often than the Japanese teachers.

Individual Differences

At first glance, whole-class instruction seems to take little account of the fact that every classroom contains slow learners and fast learners, highly motivated and less motivated children, and children who differ in their responsiveness to the teacher's efforts. Discussions of American education make much of this diversity and of the difficulties American teachers face in teaching heterogeneous groups.

Japanese teachers, like American teachers, must respond to individual differences among the children they are teaching. Because of the heterogeneity of Japanese neighborhoods and the absence of tracking, variability in Japanese children's performance on tests we have given is just as great as in American first-grade classrooms; by fifth grade, variability was even greater within the Japanese classrooms. We must emphasize that we are not talking about overall variability in the scores of Japanese students, but about *within-classroom* variability, the type of variability the individual teacher encounters. *Overall* variability in the scores of Japanese elementary-school children at the level of the whole city or region, but not of the individual classroom, tends to be less than is the case in the United States. This occurs for many

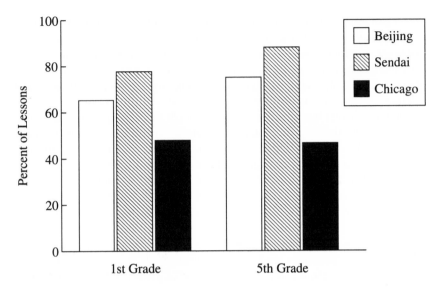

Figure 2.1. Percentage of Lessons in which the Sequence of Instruction, Practice, and Feedback is Used

reasons, including the presence of a national curriculum, textbooks that conform to that curriculum, similarity among teachers in teaching style, and the heterogeneity in socioeconomic status that exists within Japanese neighborhoods.

Japanese teachers put individual differences among children to good use. For example, they rely on individual differences among children to produce the diversity of answers upon which their preferred mode of instruction can build. Inappropriate or inefficient approaches discussed by some students may be just as informative to members of the class as hearing the most cogent and powerful approaches. For such reasons Japanese teachers are less impressed by the need for classes of small size than are most American teachers. They believe that without diversity of answers, students are deprived of opportunities to consider the relative effectiveness of different types of solutions or suggestions.

Japanese teachers respond to individual differences among their students by using a variety of materials and techniques in order to engage and maintain children's involvement during each lesson. They also spend time outside class helping children who may need extra assistance. According to our interviews with teachers. they met with individual children outside of class three times as often as American teachers said they did (an overall average of half an hour compared to ten minutes a day).

Another response to individual differences among students is to organize them in *han* (small groups). Rather than organize these groups so that they are homogeneous according to the students' level of achievement, membership is purposefully made as diverse as possible. All *han* in a classroom work on the same problem. By having slow learners work with fast learners, both types of student can benefit. Slow learners can observe the techniques of fast learners. Fast learners benefit from being forced to clarify their ideas as they try to explain concepts or operations to slow learners. Similarly, the intense interest and high motivation of some members of a small group may have a contagious effect and spread to other, less involved members. It is in this sense that Japanese teachers often practice the cooperative learning techniques espoused by many American educators. However, in contrast to many interpretations of cooperative learning that leave children to discover the basic concepts on their own, activities of the *han* are organized by and remain under the close surveillance and guidance of the teacher.

Members of the *han* work together in many other activities, such as in cleaning the classroom and serving food, and in games and discussions. Participation in the *han* is a central feature of the children's everyday lives in school and leads to a strong identification with the *han*, the class, and the school. Because of this identification with a group, the motivation of slow learners to work hard and perform well may be enhanced and the eagerness of the fast learners to help their slower classmates may be increased.

In addition to presenting information in different manners in an effort to accommodate differences in rate and type of learning, the teacher's use of different approaches has an alerting function for students. Every student in the class knows that he or she may be called upon to present and explain an answer to one of the teacher's questions or may be asked to evaluate the effectiveness of other students' answers. Knowing this, students are likely to remain alert and attentive to the teacher and to their classmates throughout the lesson. Part of the effectiveness of Japanese teaching appears to be due, therefore, to the fact that students are responsive to a much higher proportion of what goes on during the course of their lessons than is the case with their American peers.

Paying Attention

Whole-group instruction clearly depends on the students' paying attention. Our observers who followed the time-sampling procedure devoted part of their observation to tracking the behavior of an individual child. The child was considered to be paying attention when he or she was either attending to the teacher or was engaged in the activity that had been defined by the

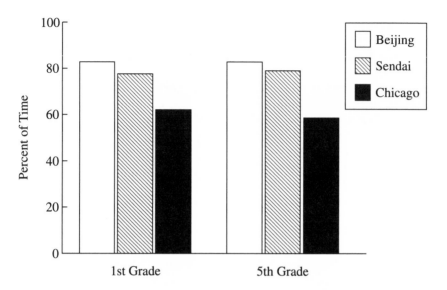

Figure 2.2. Percentage of the Time Children Were Attending to the Teacher or to the Task Defined by the Teacher

teacher. It is evident in figure 2.2 that the children's attention was remarkably high in East Asian classrooms.

There are several explanations of why Japanese children pay such close attention. First, basic subjects such as mathematics are taught in the morning when children are fresh. In American classrooms it is not unusual to observe these subjects being taught after lunch and in the afternoon when children are tired. Second, the frequent recesses appear to contribute to the children's ability to pay attention in class. Students become fatigued if they are required to participate in one class after another without a break. Third, teachers can bring greater vitality and enthusiasm to their teaching if they do not have to be in front of a class all day long. Finally, and perhaps most important, the structure of the Japanese lesson and the varied instructional approaches used by Japanese teachers are likely to engage children's attention and to direct their activities to a greater degree than occurs with the traditional lecture method. Presenting a lesson effectively requires a skilled professional, one who has thought about the ways the concepts or ideas can be demonstrated, the kinds of questions that should be asked, and the times when individual practice or division into small groups can be most productive.

Teachers cannot maintain children's attention if the lesson is repetitious and uninteresting. Japanese teachers know this and, as has been discussed, use various strategies to avoid this pitfall. Even though each topic is taught slowly, instruction is not boring or repetitive. What impresses the observer is how lively and dynamic the lessons turn out to be. Japanese teachers also make strong efforts to present lessons in a meaningful context. Rather than beginning the lesson with definitions and rules, they typically begin the lesson by writing a series of questions on the blackboard or by describing a situation containing an everyday problem that needs to be solved. By engaging the children's interest in the general idea at the beginning of the lesson, teachers seek to increase children's motivation to attend to the details of the lesson. It is evident in figure 2.3 that Japanese teachers are very successful in doing this; an effort was made in nearly all lessons to place them in a meaningful context.

Japanese teachers attempt to create classrooms where the contributions of all children are valued and the teacher seeks to be their knowledgeable, experienced guide. In fact, *teacher* is translated as *sensei* in Japanese, a word composed of two characters, the first meaning "before" and the second meaning "to live" or "to exist." We do not suggest that American teachers fail to act as well-prepared guides. They simply do so less frequently and consistently than Japanese teachers. The view that students must play an important role in producing, explaining, and evaluating solutions to prob-

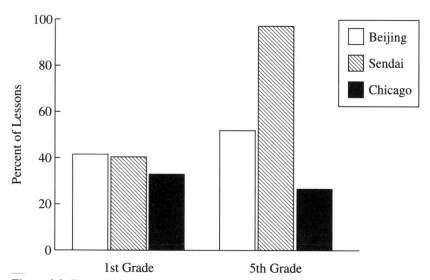

Figure 2.3. Percentage of Lessons in Which the Teacher Placed the Lesson in a Meaningful Context

lems not only helps to maintain children's close attention, it is also a critical element of successful whole-class instruction.

Seatwork as Practice

In classrooms throughout the world, the most common form of practice is seatwork in which the students are given problems or exercises they are expected to complete at their seats. In our observations, seatwork was assigned in over 90% of the Japanese lessons and in 85% of the American lessons. It occupied between 30% and 40% of the time children spent in their lessons in both Sendai and Chicago schools. There was an important difference, however, in the manner in which seat work was handled.

Japanese teachers used seatwork as a time for students to practice each segment of the lesson and for the teacher to evaluate the children's level of understanding. It was an integral part of each lesson. The Japanese seatwork assignment typically consists of a few problems or questions involving the application of what has been learned. Rather than being solvable by mechanically applying routines or formulas that have just been learned, the problems often require novel approaches. "Don't worry about getting the correct answer," the teacher may say, "just come up with your own way of solving the problem." Students, freed of the need to produce a specific solution and faced with nonroutine problems or questions, find seatwork to be helpful rather than boring. The usefulness of seatwork problems is enhanced by the fact that the teacher walks about the class, helping children correct mistakes, answering questions, and probing for more complete answers. In other words, seatwork is not an excuse for abandoning the class, but provides an opportunity for the teacher to scrutinize each child's progress and to interact with individual students.

Observations recently made by one of us in a Japanese classroom indicate how a well-prepared, responsive teacher can give individual attention to children, even when forty or more children must be faced every day. The teacher, following a common practice, had prepared a sheet containing the name of each child and the location of his or her seat. Below each name was a note, indicating the types of difficulties the child was having in mathematics. These notes served to alert the teacher to ways in which different children might need help. During the time children were engaged in seatwork, the teacher glanced at a second sheet. On this sheet was a list of the common errors teachers had observed children to make in previous classes when the concept or information was being taught. The sheet also contained a summary of techniques that had proved to be effective in responding to each type of error. By using memory aides such as these, teachers had a better understanding of how to help individual students and the class as a whole.

The American teachers tended to divide the class period into two parts, the first devoted to lecture and the second to seatwork practice. Our impression is that American teachers, overburdened and fatigued, often use seatwork as an opportunity to have a period of time by themselves. Whereas Japanese seatwork nearly always involved teacher interaction with the children and discussion of the assignment, American teachers were much less likely to use seatwork as an opportunity for feedback or discussion. This is evident in figure 2.4, which contrasts the percentage of seatwork assignments in which East Asian and American teachers provided the students some form of feedback.

The lack of immediate feedback after the seatwork assignment in American classrooms was due, in part, to the fact that seatwork was the last activity in half of the Chicago lessons—a situation that occurred in less than a quarter of the Japanese lessons. On these occasions, American children left the class not knowing whether they had solved their practice problems correctly because there was no opportunity for them to correct each other's papers or to discuss the problems. Teachers, in turn, often faced the task of preparing the next day's lesson without knowing whether the students had

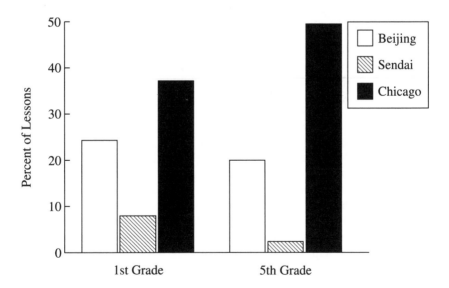

Figure 2.4. Percentage of Lessons in Which Teacher Did Not Provide Feedback to Children Concerning Their Seatwork

mastered the concepts being taught. Because it typically was poorly integrated with the rest of the lesson and failed to provide children with more
than repetitive practice, seatwork often appeared to be an unproductive use
of children's time in American classrooms.

Planning Time for the Teacher

Because Japanese teachers have a lighter teaching load than do American
teachers, they have more time than American teachers to spend with individual students outside of class. Japanese elementary school teachers typically
arrive at school around eight in the morning and remain at school eight or
nine hours a day. American teachers usually arrive by 8:30 and leave six and
a half hours later. According to the teachers' estimates, teachers in Chicago
were at school an average of 36.5 hours a week and in Sendai, 53.5. Part of
this difference was the result of the academic schedule; Japanese schools are
open for half a day on Saturday. Although this practice has recently been
modified so that schools are closed for one Saturday each month, the time
spent in classes still adds up to a longer school week in Japan than in the
United States.

Despite the fact that Japanese teachers spend more time at school, they
actually are teaching in front of the class only a little more than four hours a
day. American teachers, in contrast, are teaching nearly all of the time they
are at school. In Chicago, for example, 72 percent of the elementary school
teachers were responsible for preparing four or more different lessons each
day. Fifty-nine percent taught from five to seven courses.

The skill that Japanese teachers bring to their teaching is due in large
part to the opportunities they have at school for interacting with other
teachers, working together on lesson plans, and sharing ideas about teaching
techniques. It is not uncommon for the mathematics teachers at a particular
grade level to spend several hours planning a single lesson in collaboration
with each other and under the tutelage of the head teacher of mathematics.

Chinese Teaching

Teaching in Chinese classrooms is similar in many ways to teaching in Japan. Chinese and Japanese teachers use similar styles of instruction. The
whole class moves through the lesson together; teaching to the whole class
occurred over 99 percent of the time in our observations of Chinese classrooms. Chinese children engage in rowdy behavior between classes, and
classrooms are crowded. As in Japanese schools, children attend closely dur-

ing the course of each lesson. In our study, conducted in eleven Beijing schools in the same manner as the study in Chicago and Sendai, students were attending to the teacher or to the task they were assigned 84% of the time they were observed—slightly higher than the 80% found in Japan.

The three-step sequence of instruction-practice-feedback found so frequently in Japanese classrooms was also observed in more than three fourths of the Chinese lessons. During these sequences, Chinese teachers, like the Japanese teachers, held the children's attention by varying the tasks. A single lesson might include using manipulatives, representing problems by using abstract equations, practicing calculations, and solving real-life problems. At times this involved listening to the teacher, and at other times the students were asked to engage in group discussions, to answer questions posed by the teacher, to present their solutions in front of the class, to complete seatwork assignments, and to respond in unison as a whole group.

Despite the general similarities of Chinese and Japanese teaching practices, one important difference is immediately evident. Instruction proceeds at a much faster pace in Chinese than in Japanese classrooms. For example, Chinese students were engaged in an average of twenty different activities during each lesson compared to fourteen during the Japanese (and ten during the American) lessons. The fast pace means that many students are called upon to respond during each class period.

Chinese teachers, like Japanese teachers, emphasize conceptual understanding, but they expect students to think about problems and respond in a rapid-fire manner. During a typical Chinese lesson, fourteen students were called on to respond to teachers' questions or to other students' answers. The corresponding number in Japanese classrooms was eight, and in American classrooms, six. Every child in the Chinese classrooms knows that there is a high likelihood that he or she will be called upon during the course of the lesson and is aware of the importance of being alert and paying close attention.

What we have reported about Japanese classrooms, therefore, is relevant to the description of Chinese classrooms. The visitor is aware of being in a Chinese rather than a Japanese classroom primarily by the pace of the lessons, the alacrity with which students answer questions, and the teachers' expectations that rapid answering takes precedence over lengthy thought.

Relevance for the United States

The argument is often advanced by American educators that one of the surest ways of improving American schools is to reduce class size. We believe this argument misses the point, for smaller classes do not necessarily mean that teachers will be able to pay more attention to individual students. After observing East Asian teaching practices and the outstanding levels of academic achievement attained by Japanese and Chinese students, we conclude that the problem in the United States does not lie in the size of the classes in our schools. Rather, we believe that the difficulties are derived from the fact that American teachers teach less effectively than they might, not because of the size of the classes they teach, but because they are required to teach nearly continuously throughout the time schools are in session.

Effective teaching requires time for preparation and energy for imparting this information. Merely reducing class size is less likely to relieve the American problem than would reducing the teaching load. How can we expect teachers to be able to teach productively when we fail to provide them with the time necessary to develop well-planned lessons that deal with the subject matter in an interesting, coherent fashion? Until we realize that good teaching requires teachers who know the subject matter and have the time to organize their lessons effectively, we will continue to search for palliatives and will fail to acknowledge that the most important ingredient of good education is daily guidance of students by well-prepared teachers, rather than the size of the class or the frequency with which the class is broken down into small groups.

Attempts to attribute the poor performance of our students to the large size of elementary school classes is only one of the explanations shattered by careful consideration of what can happen in whole-class instruction. Many criticisms of whole-class teaching prove to be inappropriate. It is inappropriate to equate whole-class teaching with the way it is often exemplified in the United States: a tired teacher lecturing to an inattentive class. Nor is it portrayed properly through the stereotyped image of stern Asian drillmasters. Neither image accurately describes what can be accomplished when interesting lessons are presented in a well-organized fashion by a teacher who concentrates on involving all students in every lesson. Whole-class instruction ensures that each child will have the maximal opportunity to benefit from the teacher, because whether the students are working alone, in a group, or as a whole class, the teacher remains involved throughout the lesson as guide, interpreter, and ultimate source of information about the utility and relevance of students' ideas.

What we have observed in East Asian classrooms involves principles and approaches that would be regarded as sensible, productive teaching practices in any classroom. Indeed, when we describe them to American teachers, they insist that they already use such principles in their teaching.

Our best teachers do work diligently to construct well-organized, meaningful lessons. But this occurs at great personal cost; in order to do this the teacher typically must work alone and at home after school hours.

We realize that practices that are effective in one culture cannot be transported intact to other, different cultures. Nevertheless, the study of teaching practices that apparently produce outstanding students merits our close scrutiny. We may require a mix of whole-class, group, and individualized instruction different from that found in cultures such as those in East Asia, but before criticizing whole-class instruction as an unproductive approach to the education of young children, we can profit from considering the conditions under which this form of instruction can be highly effective.

Looking in the Chinese Mirror: Reflecting on Moral-Political Education in the United States

GAY GARLAND REED

Introduction

Moral/political education is a murky business in the United States and one that policymakers prefer to avoid addressing. This is partly due to our increasingly pluralistic society, which demands that space be made for multiple understandings of what constitutes moral behavior, but it is also due to certain values and beliefs that underpin our system. These values and beliefs are so taken for granted, so embedded, and so much a part of our epistemology that we are unable to fully appreciate their power over the processes of policy formation and implementation. One approach to illuminating these values and beliefs in our own system is to examine them in light of a very different system in which the necessity and efficacy of moral/political education is unquestioned and pedagogies for its implementation have been fine-tuned through the centuries. To do this, I will look into the mirror of Chinese culture.

Investigation into and reflection on Chinese and American policies and practices relating to moral education reveal three areas of contrast that appear to have a particularly significant effect on the way that moral/political education policy is conceived and implemented in these two very different societies.

The first area that I will consider is the strong link in the American mind between religion and morality. This link is so unyielding that any educational policy that addresses issues of morality, ethics, values, or character development is perceived as a threat to the constitutional separation between church and state.

In this respect, there is marked contrast to the Chinese case. Both Confucianism and socialism are human-centered systems that ignore or even reject religious belief and practice. One of the most essential roles of govern-

51

ment, in dynastic China as well as in modern China, is to "educate" the populace and provide moral/political guidance through moral suasion. The secular nature of the Chinese system, coupled with the belief that moral leadership was an essential function of government, facilitated the creation and implementation of moral/political education policy and avoided the tension that is so apparent in the American system.

The second area of contrast that will be discussed in this article is the influence of scientific objectivism in the West, which places "objectivity" at the top of the value structure and encourages us to think of fact and value as separable. Living and working in this paradigm, we accumulate information and knowledge without the constraint of fitting it into some larger philosophical and moral context. This is in marked contrast to the Chinese belief in the inseparability of fact and value and the accompanying assumption that the moral dimension is inherent in the process of knowing.

Finally, in this chapter I will explore the relationship of the individual to the society, which in the West has been strongly influenced by psychology and is marked by a tension between individual autonomy and commitment to the community (Bellah, Madsen, Sullivan, Swidler, & Tipton, 1986). In contrast, in China the tendency has been to define the individual in social terms, thus blurring the individual/society distinction.

By contrasting the values that underlie moral/political education policy in China and the United States, I hope to contribute to a better understanding of why the formation and implementation of moral education policy is so problematic in the United States and, at the same time, to show how economic and social changes in China are beginning to make it more problematic in that country as well.

There is one important caveat that needs to be noted. The material that is presented here on China focuses on form rather than on content. It discusses moral education in China in the past in normative terms. The degree to which the norms and values of Confucian and communist education were actually realized is not clear. It seems that there is always an inescapable gap between what is taught and what is learned. Moral learning is particularly difficult to assess because an individual can demonstrate an understanding of moral principles and even display the desired moral behaviors, but one can only rarely assess the motives that underlie the behaviors.

Through several years of researching moral and political education in China, I have been struck by the fact that the epistemological impediments that make moral education in the United States so problematic have not been historically present in China. It was the impetus to understand the nature of the differences between these two systems that set the present research into motion.

Religion, Morality, and the Constitution

In the United States, the complex and delicate relationship between the church and the state (as it is represented by the public schools) has been the subject of dozens of judicial rulings over many decades. Whereas many of these cases were related to funding matters, others were clearly focused on curriculum and the question of what values should be taught in public schools. More specifically, they dealt with questions about prayer and the infusion of Christian values into the secular public school curriculum. In 1962, in the court case of *Engle v. Vitale*, a nondenominational prayer composed by the New York Board of Regents that was to be said aloud daily was declared unconstitutional. The following year, in 1963, in the court case of *School District of Abington Township v. Schempp*, Bible reading in public schools was declared unconstitutional. In 1980, in *Stone v. Graham*, a state law requiring the posting of the Ten Commandments in public school classrooms was declared unconstitutional despite the fact that the posters were procured with private funds and made note of the fact that the secular application of the Ten Commandments serves as the basis of the legal code of Western civilization. In 1985, the court ruled that the Alabama law authorizing a period of silence in public school for "meditation or voluntary prayer" was unconstitutional (Zirkel & Richardson, 1988). Whereas the intent of these rulings is to maintain a stance that neither advances nor inhibits religion, the effect is quite different. Teachers who are worried that the explicit teaching of values may be perceived as religious indoctrination or the imposition of a personal value system silence themselves.

Even the use of the term *moral education* has inescapable religious overtones. Morality and religion are inextricably linked, at least at the level of common parlance, which is where policy originates. In some respects this is rather curious, given our intellectual tendency toward dichotomization, compartmentalization, and dualism. Nevertheless, the wedding of morality and religion is so embedded in our thinking that in the U.S. Congress, liberals fear that calls for character education are in actuality an effort to mix public education and religion (Sharpe, 1994, p. A20).

In *Culture Wars*, James Davison Hunter (1991) described two key positions in the moral-education debate. According to Hunter, on one side are the Citizens for Excellence in Education, an activist group of Christian educators who want to "take control of all local schools." On the other is the American Civil Liberties Union, which is "seeking to protect nonsectarian education from the meddling of the fundamentalist right." As he describes it, the two camps have made an "all but formal declaration of war over public schools" (p. 197).

The battle is so heated and so politically charged that a very modest proposal made by Congressman George Miller in 1994 to add character education to a massive elementary and secondary education bill was met with snickers and eventually voted down by a 23–6 margin (Sharpe, 1994).

Efforts to promote the teaching of values and character education in public schools are making some headway despite the polemics at the federal level. Communities alarmed by violence and discipline problems are taking matters into their own hands and implementing local policies that promote the teaching of values and character education. The inevitable question is, Given the pluralistic nature of our society and the dramatic technological and social changes that have reshaped our nation and our thinking, can we find a set of core values that we can all agree should be taught to our children? In an effort to discover if there is common ground, a 1993 Phi Delta Kappa/Gallup Poll of 1,306 adults asked what values should be taught in public schools. The values that a significant majority of those polled agreed should be taught were honesty, 93%; democracy, 93%; acceptance of people of different races and ethnic backgrounds, 93%; caring for friends and family members, 91%; moral courage, 91%; the golden rule, 90%; and acceptance of people who hold different religious beliefs, 87% (Sharpe, 1994).

From his contribution to a collection of essays entitled *Values and Public Policy* (Aaron, Mann, & Taylor, 1994), Daniel Yankelovich provides us with another list of what he terms "America's core values." He lists eleven values that he says have remained relatively unchanged and that "make American culture distinctive": freedom, equality before the law, equality of opportunity, fairness, achievement, patriotism, democracy, American exceptionalism, caring beyond the self, religion, and luck (pp. 23–24).

The list from the Phi Delta Kappa/Gallup Poll has a communitarian ring to it, whereas the second list is more civic and nationalistic in tone. Both lists suggest that religion and religious belief are important considerations in the United States even in a "secularized" value system.

Secular morality, except in the more "scientific" sense of Kohlbergian moral development theory, is a concept that many Americans have difficulty with. The notion that an atheistic society could have a well-articulated moral code is difficult for many Americans to accept. This was made clear to me on the eve of my 1990 departure to the People's Republic of China, when a new acquaintance asked what I was going to study. I explained that I was going to study Chinese moral education. He replied, "Isn't that an oxymoron?" This retort set me to pondering why a highly educated American would make the assumption that moral education was impossible in an atheist communist system. This seems to be partly due to our notion of the inseparability of morality and religion. This analysis is supported by the fact that William J. Bennett, former education secretary and author of the best-seller *Book of Virtues*, felt it necessary to point out that one can be a virtuous person without a faith in God (Fineman, 1994, p. 33). Although virtue and morality are not synonymous, many Americans find it difficult to imagine that either can be cultivated in an atheistic society.

As it turned out, through my research in China, I came to the conclusion that the phrase "Chinese moral education" was not an oxymoron, but rather a redundancy. By this I mean that, traditionally, *all* education in China was seen as having a moral/political dimension.

Secular Morality in the Chinese Context

To understand morality and moral education from the traditional Chinese perspective demands that we relinquish our deeply embedded notion that there is a natural and necessary link between morality and religion and that any discussion of values, virtue, morality, and character are preludes to religious indoctrination. The link that we make between religion and morality is not present in Chinese thought. This may be partly due to the fact that there is no notion of a transcendent god who dictates the parameters of human moral behavior. In Confucian China, in Maoist thought, and even now in the post-Mao era, moral actions have been defined as those that contribute to the quality of the "community," whether that is defined as the family, the clan, the collective, or the state. In the past, moral actions were carefully prescribed in texts and based on Confucian principles; there was no transcendent creator to whom an individual must answer. Confucianism is therefore deemed a "humanistic" tradition because it focuses on human relationships (Mote, 1971, p. 62).

To further illustrate this point, it is worth taking a brief look at Confucian thought because it represents the underpinning of much contemporary East Asian thought and, in a reversal of earlier policy, has been officially recognized by the present Chinese leadership as the basis for Chinese social organization and culture. According to Confucius (551–479 B.C.), the cosmos is a moral order, and human beings must be in accord with this order if they are to prosper (Mote, 1971, p. 39). The wisdom to discern what actions are conducive to the maintenance of harmony within the cosmos and the courage to take these actions are virtues that are cultivated through proper education. Indeed, it is this belief in the efficacy of education as an essential element in the maintenance of a human-centered world that unites the disparate strands of thought that came under the rubric of Confucianism.

Whether followers of Mencius (372–289 B.C.), who believed that human nature was essentially good, or students of Hsun Zi (298–238 B.C.), who saw humans as primarily evil, Confucians placed great value on civilization and believed that it could be achieved only through the formal training and personal cultivation of the individual (Mote, p. 57). Even Mencius, the most sanguine of Chinese philosophers of human nature, was concerned that if left to themselves, people were likely to go astray. Despite their natural tendencies toward goodness, in the Mencian view, people need guidance, and education must not be a haphazard business but a carefully planned and directed activity.

Under the Ming and Qing emperors of China (1368–1911), the district magistrate was responsible for the moral education of the people who fell within his jurisdiction. Schooled in the Confucian classics, the district magistrate was encouraged to give regular lectures to the local populace to educate them and to encourage proper adherence to Confucian principles through example. According to Confucian teaching, when moral suasion and education failed to move the constituency onto paths of "proper" behavior, punishment was to be the last resort.

Some Western travelers who took up residence in China were deeply impressed by the moral state that they beheld. The Jesuits, for example, wrote back to their superiors and "described a state where the spiritual effaced itself before the political, where ethics were valued above science and where education played a central role as a way of learning how to act" (Llasera, 1987, p. 30). So impressed were these men by the nobility and morality of the Chinese state that one traveler made the modest suggestion that the Chinese should send missionaries to the West "to instruct us in the purpose and use of natural theology, in the same way as we send missionaries to instruct them in revealed theology" (p. 26).

Whereas the revolutionary educational model of postliberation China (after 1949) has often borne little superficial resemblance to the traditional Confucian model, its secular nature, its melding of the political and the moral, and its belief in the efficacy of education as a means of molding moral character and curing societal ills has never been challenged.

The primacy of moral education was expressed by Chairman Mao Zedong in 1957 when he said, "Our educational policy must enable everyone who receives an education to develop morally, intellectually and physically and become a worker with both socialist consciousness and culture" (Cleverley, 1985, p. 139).

However, what was true in 1957 is not necessarily so now. Although moral education is being revived in other countries with Confucian roots, like Taiwan, Singapore, Hong Kong, Korea, and Japan (Cummings, Gopinathan, & Tomoda, 1988), moral/political educators in the People's Republic of China are facing new challenges. The economic policy of "commodity socialism" in the post-Mao era, disillusionment with the Communist Party leadership, and the "open door" policy have all conspired to bring about what some commentators call "the death of ideology." It is very difficult at this time to predict the outcome of the present social upheaval in China and to imagine the kind of ideological consensus that might emerge. Such speculation is beyond the scope of the present discussion. What *is* important to underscore in this discussion is that however problematic moral education becomes in China, the challenges that Chinese moral educators and policymakers face will probably not be due to legal or constitutional constraints or to linking morality with religion. It is the complex interrelationship among religion, morality, law, and the constitution that poses the most significant challenge in the United States.

Scientific Objectivism and Moral Education Policy

Despite extensive work by neo-Marxists on the hidden curriculum, by scholars like Philip Jackson on the values implicit in classroom settings, and by Joel Spring on ideological management, there is still a belief among many educators that classrooms can and should be value-neutral spaces. Teachers worry that they will impose their own values on their students and, in the context of a multicultural society, such concerns are very appropriate. Nevertheless, it is also important to recognize that all choices that teachers make regarding curriculum, pedagogy, discipline, and even classroom arrangement and decoration are value-laden choices that convey moral and political messages.

The belief in the possibility and desirability of value neutrality can be traced to scientific objectivism. In the movement to adopt scientific practices in education, objectivity became an increasingly positive value for teachers. What this means for educators, administrators, and policymakers is that they can, and should, test and evaluate student skills and behaviors, remediate, develop management strategies for classrooms, and set educational standards and goals systematically and objectively. It also means that in the search for answers to our educational problems, we tend to favor technical solutions over moral solutions, and we often see efficiency as a primary means to better educational outcomes. Objectivism and scientific management continue to inform our educational practice and policy and to encourage us to see fact and value as separate and desirable.

There are some leading American sociologists who worry that we have taken this too far. Bellah, Madsen, Sullivan, Swidler, and Tipton (1992), for example, have pointed out the cultural gap in American society between technical reason and moral practical reason: "As the power of ability to manipulate the world grows, the poverty of our understanding of what to do with that knowledge becomes more apparent" (p. 44). These sociologists worry about our constant reliance on technical solutions, including management science, to solve institutional and social problems. Others, like Parker Palmer (1987), who has described himself as "a recovering sociologist," worry that objectivism as a way of knowing is anticommunal (p. 23). For Palmer, community provides an ethical and moral framework that contextualizes our actions and understandings. He emphasizes that "how we know" is as important as "what we know." In his unwillingness to separate the knower from the known and fact from value, his thinking is more akin to the Chinese view.

The Inseparability of Fact and Values in Chinese Thought

One attribute of traditional Confucian education that was carried over into the modern period is what the scholar of Chinese thought Donald J. Munro (1977) terms the "legitimacy criterion." At the root of this concept is the notion that fact and value are inseparable. Thus any piece of information that is learned must have "value" in terms of the larger ethical system and must be used to further that system (p. 108). This is true even of technical knowledge. The legitimacy criterion that linked fact and value into an indivisible unity became increasingly pronounced under the Communist Party, which brought politics to the fore. The larger ethical system in which a student was operating became the socialist system, and knowledge had value insofar as it benefited the people and the Party and furthered the socialist goals of China. Knowledge for personal gain, or even for its own sake, undermined the socialist system simply by not supporting it. The cultural revolution, disillusionment with the Party, and commodity socialism in the post-Mao era have seriously challenged the larger ethical system, but the notion of the inseparability of fact and value remains a part of the epistemology of China. It is interesting to note, however, that the legitimacy criterion cannot function when the larger ethical system is brought into serious question. This helps to explain why moral/political education in China has become more problematic in the last two decades than it was in former times.

A Question of "Truth"

If this investigation into fact and value is carried a little further, it is possible to illuminate another related cultural difference that has an inevitable impact on the way that moral/political education is conceived and implemented in China and the United States. This has to do with our popular cultural approach to understanding fact as not only separate from value but as essentially synonymous with truth. To many Americans, fact and fiction reside at two ends of a continuum, and truth is a carefully constructed and tested amalgamation of "the facts." The Asian American scholar A. S. Chen (1964) notes what he calls "our Western preoccupation with the distinction between truth and fiction" (p. 236) and suggests that in the Chinese case, truth and facts need not be synonymous. My own experiences doing research in China and presenting that research in the United States serve to illustrate this point.[1]

There was some parallel between my experience presenting research and that of educator Jean Piaget when he presented his stage theory to American audiences. He noted that in America he was inevitably asked, "How can children be accelerated through your stages of cognitive development?" He called this "the American question" (Tobin, Wu, & Davidson, 1989, p. 173). I too have an "American question" that arises almost every time I present my research on the Chinese role model, Lei Feng, the People's Liberation Army (PLA) soldier that Chairman Mao exhorted the entire Chinese nation to learn from: "Was Lei Feng a 'real' person and is the story 'true'?" In this line of questioning, there is the sense that if Lei Feng was not real and the story was not true, then we can dismiss him as a political fabrication of no consequence. My best answer to this question is that he may be largely a political fabrication, but he was certainly real for millions of Chinese people and, therefore, he cannot be easily dismissed. Lei Feng was woven into the belief system, the language, the behavior, and into the lives of Chinese children and adults for three decades through stories, movies, books, plays, and activities. In the context of the American concern for fact and fiction, Lei Feng can easily be dismissed, but in the context of Chinese moral/political education, he cannot. Furthermore, the American question was not a central issue for any of the Chinese people that I interviewed. I once posed the question about the truth of the Lei Feng story to a Chinese intellectual who was deeply influenced by the hero in his youth and who had an obvious continuing admiration for the role model. He recalled with pride an article he had written about Lei Feng when he was a schoolboy. When asked if it would make any difference to him if one day he found out that Lei Feng was a political fabrication of the PLA propaganda team, he said, "No, it wouldn't. But I think the story is true because every culture has people like Lei Feng." For him *true* seemed to mean *authentic* rather than *factual*. Lei Feng was believable to him, and therefore the story seemed true.

Donald Munro (1977), a scholar of Chinese thought, explains the philosophical roots of the differences between East and West concerning this issue of truth:

> In China, truth and falsity in the Greek sense have rarely been important considerations in a philosopher's acceptance of a given belief or proposition; these are Western concerns. The consideration important to the Chinese is the behavioral implications of the belief or proposition in question. What effect does adherence to the belief have on people? (p. 55)

Munro's description of these two very different approaches to belief in China and the West helps to explain why Chinese and Americans view the Lei Feng story differently. For the Chinese, believing in and following Lei Feng was not only politically correct but could also result in more virtuous people and a more harmonious society. For the American, the apparent fabrication is an obstacle to belief.

It should be pointed out that many Chinese are rejecting Lei Feng as a viable model for moral/political education in the 1990s, not necessarily because he is a fabrication but because of their disillusionment with the Party leadership and their sense that the Lei Feng model is not appropriate to the times. A middle-aged intellectual from Beijing discussed this issue and worried about the lack of alternatives for moral educators.

> Now we use Lei Feng to teach children morality. Some people criticize Lei Feng. It's not because *he's* bad but because they don't like the leaders. Now Lei Feng might be a bad idea, but what else do we have to morally educate the children? We have to do something, otherwise the children will grow up only caring about money and business. (Reed, 1991, pp. 229–230)

The importance of institutions that promote moral behavior was evident in an interview that I had in 1990 with Bishop Ding Guang-Xun, a Christian leader who told the story of being expelled from his home by the Red Guards (members of a paramilitary youth organization).

> When the red guards came to this house they drove us out. We were afraid to come back to this neighborhood because we thought the neighbors would have something against us. When we finally returned the neighbors greeted us. Even the non-Christians didn't understand why the church needed to be closed when its main function was to help people to be good. (Reed, 1991, p. 85)

Bishop Ding's story supports the idea that as long as the belief system promotes social harmony and works toward the cultivation of individual virtue and the betterment of the society, the theological particulars and the truth or falsity of the premises on which they are based are of relatively little importance. In short, this is a very pragmatic approach to believing. Once again we must note that changes in China have shifted the focus away from the values promoted by Confucianism and socialism. The loss of a unifying belief system worries some people and makes moral education increasingly problematic in China. An instructor at Nanjing University expressed his deep concerns over the changes that are occurring in Chinese society.

> Chinese people need some religion. They have no beliefs anymore. If we just worry about money, society will deteriorate. We need something to believe in. China is in a period of transition where the old beliefs have disappeared and we have no new beliefs to follow. The new generation is different. They have become westernized. . . . Chinese people have changed. (Reed,1991, p. 230)

His concerns about China's new emphasis on money and the lack of a coherent belief system are not so very different from American concerns about the fraying of our moral fabric. Another informant who had lived in the countryside for most of his youth suggested that the old pedagogical tools for moral/political education that worked so well in the past are not appropriate to the present. He saw propagandizing as an outdated and generally unsuccessful mode of educating: "Propaganda backfires. If you tell them too often, some people get angry. Anyway, it's like a hot pepper. It can make you hot for a moment but in an hour it's gone" (Reed, 1991, p. 199).

This section of the article has focused on differences in Chinese and American beliefs about the relationship between fact and value and what constitutes truth. I have suggested that moral education tends to be problematic in the United States because of our reliance on technical solutions to educational problems, our belief in the separability of fact and value, and our notion of truth as an amalgamation of the facts. The Chinese case presents us with a somewhat different approach to understanding the relationship between fact and value. The legitimacy criterion recognized and promoted a linkage between fact and value and provided a context for behavior that facilitated the teaching of moral education. As was noted earlier, general disillusionment with the Communist Party and the changing economic structure are weakening this traditional linkage and undermining traditional pedagogies that facilitated the system.

The Individual and the Society

The final area on which I will focus in this exploration into the underlying beliefs and values that have made moral education problematic in the United

States is the relationship of the individual to the society. Clearly Chinese and American societies have constructed this relationship very differently over time and have emphasized different values. It is too simplistic and essentially incorrect to say that Americans focus on the individual and Chinese on the society. The interplay between individual and society in the two cultures is more complex and subtle than that. As with the other points that have been made in this paper, I will rely on a certain amount of generalization to discuss this relationship.

Keeping in mind that China has some tradition of inquiry into individualism in non-Confucian texts (de Bary, 1991), one must nevertheless point to Confucianism and socialism as the two dominant social paradigms of the recent, and not so recent, past. In both Confucian and socialist thought, the individual is defined in social terms, and the capacity for relatedness is valued and nurtured. The line between the individual and the society is inevitably blurred in systems that are based upon reciprocity. Confucianism emphasized the reciprocal obligations and responsibilities that members of the family and close associates had for each other; socialism widened this network of reciprocity to include the nation and "the people."

In contrast, Americans in the later years of the twentieth century have increasingly moved away from the early republican notions of the public and focused on individual autonomy and rights. Individualism in the sense that we most often use it implies the inherent dignity and worth of the human being and the notion that the individual has a primary reality, whereas society is a second-order, or derived, reality (Bellah et al., 1986, p. 334). The perception of the individual as the primary reality is promoted through the discipline of psychology, which focuses on the individual as the unit of analysis. Individualism also suggests the right to choose and shape one's own destiny and, as Bellah et al. (1986) pointed out in *Habits of the Heart*, there is a tension that exists in American culture between individualism and commitment to the community.

If we consider these two very different approaches to understanding the relationship between individual and society in the context of moral/political education, we can understand why this type of education might be more problematic in a society that sees the individual as an autonomous decision maker. When the individual is seen as the primary reality and shaper of meaning, then the transmission of societal beliefs and values through codes of morality and rules for social interaction is seen as limiting and even repressive. From this standpoint, moral/political education impinges on the individual's autonomy and right to choose his or her way of being in the world. The American emphasis on autonomy and individual rights has forced us to develop different models of moral education, such as values clarification, which discards the old transmission model in favor of a constructivist approach.

In the Chinese case, the reopening of the door to the West has made moral education more problematic because it offers alternative models and ways of thinking about the relationship of the individual to the society. This experience of opening to new realities, coupled with serious questioning of the system, can be profoundly dislocating.

Conclusion

Looking into the Chinese mirror provides some insight into the ways in which moral education policy formation and implementation are affected by the underlying beliefs and values of a sociopolitical system. At the same time, it helps to illuminate the reasons why moral education policy has been so problematic in the United States.

In the past in China, moral/political education was the central component around which all other education was organized and toward which all education was directed. Over the centuries, sophisticated pedagogies were developed to lead people on the paths to virtue, however virtue was defined at a particular time in history (Reed, 1992). The cultivation of correct political consciousness became a kind of obsession in China in the 1960s and 1970s according to Susan Shirk (1982), who described China at that time as a "virtuocracy." By this she meant that jobs and educational opportunities were more dependent upon demonstrating one's political virtue than on demonstrating one's skills and accomplishments, as in a meritocracy. In the post-Mao era, the emphasis has moved away from demonstrating political virtue toward advancement based on merit. This article indicates that recent economic changes in China have made moral/political education less central to the curriculum and have created challenges for China's moral educators.

In the United States, the search for a common set of values continues, and the three obstacles to the formation of moral education policy that are discussed in this article still influence the process. It should be noted, however, that besides these dominant themes, there are secondary themes and trends that are worth mentioning because they suggest alternative ways of looking at the issues. These secondary themes, or trends, facilitate the teaching of some version of moral education by seeing moral discourse as an integral part of curriculum, by making the issue of values education more visible, and by creating contexts that demand democratic interaction and reflection on process as well as on content.

The first of these trends is the increasing importance of subjects like multicultural education, peace education, antiracism education, environmental education, and global education, which are values-explicit subjects. Unlike some traditional areas of study that might claim value neutrality, subjects like those mentioned above are inherently and explicitly value laden. When subjects like these are included as part of the curriculum, the fact/value dichotomy that was discussed earlier tends to be somewhat ameliorated.

The second trend worth noting is outside the field of education, in the political arena. Because of the integral relationship between school and society, it seems reasonable to expect that this trend might have some impact on schools. It is a new concern for virtue. At the vanguard of this movement are the "virtucrats," political figures from both parties who have put virtue and values on the agenda (Fineman, 1994, p. 31). One of those at the forefront is William Bennett, whose *Book of Virtues* was mentioned earlier. If this trend deepens, public dialogue with regard to what constitutes morality and virtuous behavior will inevitably be facilitated.

A final trend that might offer an alternative approach to thinking about moral education and at the same time might encourage moral discourse is a cluster of policy decisions related to curriculum, assessment, restructuring, and management. These include site-based management, cooperative and collaborative learning strategies, alternative assessment, the movement toward full inclusion of special-needs children into regular classrooms, and the creation of learning communities. By their very nature, these changes encourage attention to democratic processes and promote reflection. At the same time, these policy decisions provide contexts for addressing issues related to morals, values, and character development while avoiding the church/state impasse that has characterized popular debate over the last several decades.

CHAPTER 4

Chinese Teachers as Mirrors of Reform Possibilities

LYNN PAINE

Introduction

U.S. teachers might doubt that they have much in common with teachers in China. They also would likely doubt that they would have much to learn from the experiences of China's teachers in reform. The United States's early introduction of mass schooling, its establishment of teacher certification norms which have meant by the mid-twentieth century all teachers were expected to be graduates of higher education, and the current surplus of teachers (in certain areas and fields), among other things, all make the context of United States teaching very different from China. China only recently introduced compulsory schooling, and mass education for much of the country only goes through elementary school; the norm for elementary school teaching is that teachers have the equivalent of normal school or specialized secondary school preparation, not higher education; and there remain some acute shortages of qualified teachers in much of the country. Yet despite these differences, which are significant, I would argue that there are important ways in which the reform of teaching in China can raise valuable ques-

Author's note: The Committee for Scholarly Communication, the U.S. Department of Education's Office of Educational Research and Improvement, the Spencer Foundation, and Michigan State University supported fieldwork and/or analysis related to this study. I would like to thank them for their support and express my gratitude as well to Brian DeLany, Sharon Feiman-Nemser, Ruth Hayhoe, Liping Ma, Jian Wang, Yi Yu, and Naihua Zhang for thoughtful feedback on my ideas as this analysis has evolved. While very grateful to the financial support of these organizations and the intellectual support of colleagues who have helped me with analysis and critiqued my ideas here, any errors in interpretation are mine. This chapter draws in part on revisions of an earlier chapter I wrote on "Teaching and Modernization in Contemporary China," in Ruth Hayhoe's edited collection *Education and Modernization: The Chinese Experience* (Oxford: Pergamon, 1992).

tions for U.S. educators. In fact, in some regards there are striking similarities to the themes of reform in both contexts.

Both countries have put education reform squarely in the service of larger national reconstruction projects. In both China and the United States public figures and ordinary people alike have invoked educational reform as a crucial means to solve economic, social, and moral crises. There is a long history in both countries of this way of conceptualizing education. Since the 1980s both countries have witnessed a resurgence of this reform discourse. As one Chinese commentator explained, "The 21st century is around the corner. The destiny, fall, or rise of China depends to a large extent on the development of education today" (Feng, 1988, p. 26). And in both contexts, teachers are at the center.

For Chinese teachers, this burden of reform is heavy. "The key to developing education lies in training and expanding the contingent of teachers with both political integrity and professional competence," suggested Premier Li Peng in a speech to teachers at the 1991 Teachers' Day holiday (*FBIS*, 9/11/91, p. 71). It is thus not surprising that China has undertaken an energetic and wide-ranging approach to reforming teachers and teaching. How can that experience speak to the experience of teachers elsewhere?

This chapter explores the practice of teaching and its reform in China as a way of raising questions about the reform of teaching more generally and in particular in the current moment of U.S. educational reform. Teaching in China has been the center of much debate over the past decade and is regularly pointed to as one of the key areas for change if China's education is to be improved. Is teaching technical practice? Is it some cultural enterprise? To what extent does its reform hinge on technical readjustments or social and political changes? Like some Chinese critics, I argue that many Chinese reformers have implicitly suggested that changing teaching is chiefly a technical question; but a technical focus misses some of the more profound and difficult to change aspects of teaching as a practice. More significant change requires considering the culture of teaching and of conceptualizing teaching as a cultural, economic, social, and political practice. China's experience speaks to the challenge for reform to recognize teaching's complexity and the far-reaching potential of genuine reform. In taking this view, U.S. educators may see both possibilities for new conceptualizations of teaching as well as cautionary tales. China's teachers, for example, work in professional communities and with views of teaching that allow for smooth teacher induction, careful reflection, powerful lifelong learning, and real grass-roots experimentation. At the same time, China's experience reminds us that reforms, like many currently espoused in the United States, which come from outside the community of teachers and which impose external control and accountability systems on teachers' practice may do much to inhibit the possibilities for meaningful reform of teaching and learning in schools.

To make this argument, I begin by describing the framing of the problem of teachers and resultant approaches to the reform of teaching that occurred in China in the 1980s and 1990s. I next focus on an alternative framing of the issues and consider the implications of this perspective for understanding teaching as a complex social and political practice. I then explore how Chinese teachers' professional communities encourage alternative conceptions of both teaching and its reform. The discussion that follows draws on interviews and observations I have conducted in China for more than a decade, as well as review of Chinese education literature.[1]

Reforming Teaching: Framing Teachers as the Problem

Beginning in the late 1970s China's political and educational leaders have forcefully and consistently argued for the importance of education to modernization. Central to their argument is the claim that improving education depends on improving teachers and their practice. They have had good reason for this argument. China has millions of teachers (over 8.5 million elementary and secondary teachers at the close of the 1980s) (Department of Planning and Construction, 1992), but over two million are needed simply to fill shortages, and just over half of practicing secondary level teachers are considered qualified. These teaching shortages—in absolute numbers and in terms of qualifications—can be seen as a technical problem, but it is a technical problem of large proportion.

In the late 1970s and early 1980s, this shortage seemed a major obstacle to modernization and educational reform. But as reforms took off and both inservice and preservice teacher education programs expanded, the shortage became less one of absolute numbers and more of teachers who were deemed "qualified" in terms of their degrees. More recently the problem has been of shortages of teachers in particular subject areas, particular levels of schooling, and especially in rural communities.

With the modernizers' emphasis on rational systems and accountability, quality and credentials have been at the center of discussion about teaching. 1990 estimates suggest that only 73 percent of elementary teachers were qualified in terms of years of schooling completed (*ZGJYB* 6/25/91, p. 1) and in 1993 barely half of secondary school teachers (55% of junior high and 49% of senior high) were qualified in these terms ("Guojia jiaowei fuzhuren," 1993, p. 4).[2] Many I have interviewed in central and provincial education offices expressed concern about the proportion of teachers who can cope with a class and comprehend sufficiently the text they are obliged to teach.

China's development patterns makes this general problem of scarcity acute in particular areas. Rural education, junior high schools, and technical schools reflect the problems of the differential distribution of teachers. Rural schools feel more keenly the shortages that do exist. Thus, for example, a central level education official interviewed in 1994 explained that while generally a "quantitative shortage" was no longer an issue, the big challenge facing teacher education was preparing teachers for rural junior high schools. Uneven distribution of the shortage is also clear between academic and vocational schooling. In 1987, 30.7% and 40% of teachers in "general" (academic) junior and senior high schools had the appropriate qualifications, while only 17.2% and 19.9% respectively of agricultural/technical junior and senior secondary school teachers met minimal standards for amount of schooling (Guojia jiaoyu weiyuanhui, 1988, pp. 62–64, 74–75).

The shortage of well-qualified teachers has been exacerbated by two major educational reforms launched in the 1980s that are the linchpins of the education-for-modernization strategy. The introduction of compulsory education, with the goal of extending mass education through ninth grade, has put added strain on the previously underdeveloped junior secondary level of schooling. At the same time, a comprehensive restructuring of secondary education aimed at diversifying and vocationalizing much of secondary education creates an unmet demand for specialists to teach in the many new technical and vocational programs.

These problems are aggravated by the inability of the teaching profession to recruit and retain good practitioners. China's teacher education institutions have historically faced problems in attracting good candidates. In the 1980s and 1990s, despite extensive campaigns and incentive programs, normal universities have been unable to attract top students. The difficulty continues even once young people are officially committed to teaching. Often teacher education graduates manage to "escape" being assigned to "frontline" jobs in teaching; for a period of the 1980s there was in fact a decrease in the percentage of normal college graduates entering teaching (Liu, 1986, p. 6). Finally, the growth of China's "socialist market economy" in the 1990s has encouraged many who actually had entered teaching to leave its security for the possibilities of greater earnings, more status, and fewer political vulnerabilities in other fields. In China the history of periods of political suspicion and persecution of teachers, lack of social respect, verbal and physical abuse, and their comparatively low economic status has been a significant deterrent to attracting and retaining good teachers. These problems certainly were not helped by the well-publicized crisis in 1993 when local governments owed teachers millions of *yuan* (close to US $80 million) in unpaid salaries (*ZGJYB* 1/11/93, p. 1).

As China approaches the twenty-first century, the nation thus faces teaching shortages, an uneven distribution of qualified teachers, and very real difficulties in recruiting and retaining good candidates. This represents a multidimensional problem, one connecting historical practices, recent economic changes, and demographic and political pressures. It certainly stands as a roadblock to national commitments to popularizing education, reducing illiteracy, and preparing a skilled workforce—goals on which the scientific, technological and economic thrusts of the country's modernization strategy rests.

Yet as significant as these challenges may be, I see them as fundamentally a technical problem of supply. As such, there are policy approaches available to the government related to the management of resources that can help address these problems. Many in fact are already in place and have begun to have some positive effect. These solutions range from expanding teacher education opportunities to increasing incentives for teachers. A "television teacher education college" to support elementary teacher preparation; the development of an extensive and articulated teacher education "network" of teacher training schools and colleges, education institutes, and "teacher refresher schools" as sites for preservice and inservice education for both elementary and secondary teachers; and the expansion of correspondence programs for inservice teachers represent significant efforts to strengthen professional development opportunities. Simultaneously the state has pursued high visibility efforts to improve teaching's attractiveness—ranging from creating a national Teacher's Day, to establishing a Teachers' Law to define their rights and responsibilities, to raising teachers' wages. These policy attempts to manage symbolic and material resources can not in themselves solve all the problems related to teacher shortages. But given the sources of the problems—including a prior history that alternately championed, suspected and reviled teaching as a profession—these may be the best policy options available at present, and their potential benefit should not be ignored.

The Need for New Kinds of Teachers and Teaching

Suggesting that these are technical problems of resource management does not minimize their complexity or significance. But to say that they are technical does suggest that these problems are amenable to policy solutions. Framing the problem as a technical one represents only one frame, one interpretation, and leads to only one set of responses. But there are other, equally compelling ways to frame the problem at the heart of China's educational reform. For also central to the success of modernization, as it has been constructed in China's discourse, is the need for new approaches to teaching: in other words, new kinds of teachers. Reformers call for teachers who can teach very differently, who support the thinking skills and independent work that are at the heart of China's technological development. This requires teachers who do not root their practice in teacher-centered, text- and exam-driven views of instruction.

As important as structural and policy changes are for improving teachers, this second set of concerns—centered around reconceptualizing teachers' practice—reflects not only structural conditions but also a teaching culture.[3] This approach focuses less on teachers and more on the practice of teaching. Currently most teaching in China is organized to inculcate conventional ideas and a passive orientation to knowledge, and the educational system produces teachers who continue these practices. I argue that the organization of schooling (particularly the preparation of teachers, their induction to work, and the organization of that work) reinforces the conservative, passive approach to learning that reformers criticize. But teachers' practices are supported by powerful cultural norms as they intersect with the structures of education. Below I consider briefly how the entry to teaching of a beginning teacher can be seen as induction into a professional community, one with a distinct culture.

Teacher Preparation

Today the typical teacher enters the profession by way of teacher education programs. These programs support a conceptualization of teaching that is text-driven and teacher-dominated. We can examine normal university curricula for insight into a dominant conception of teaching, since this higher status institution acts as a model for the less prestigious normal schools and colleges.

Despite some institutional variation and variation among majors, the normal university curriculum clearly defines teaching as the transmission of subject knowledge. While the teacher-education student takes courses in their major field, general education, and professional education, the specialized work in one's major predominates: 60–70% of a four-year B.A. student's program, and up to 75% of an associate (*zhuan ke*) degree student's two- or three-year postsecondary program (Dongbei shifan daxue, 1985; Dangdai Zhongguo, 1986). In sharp contrast, professional education—typically involving three courses (psychology, pedagogy, and subject-specific teaching methods)—receives only about 5 percent of a university student's time.

In my two years of participant observation of a teacher-education university and subsequent visits, I was struck by the dominance of one categorization of knowledge over another (disciplinary subject matter over professional), the relative separation of these two types of knowledge, and the importance given to one orientation to learning over others (classroom instruction over experiential or independent study). With renewed interest in making teachers "scholars" of a certain discipline, my case-study institution and other normal universities around the country established a senior thesis requirement; there was a marked increase in advanced-level electives within a student's major. Even the psychology and education/pedagogy faculty I interviewed, while wistful about the limited time they had to introduce beginning teachers to their areas, shared the view that discipline-based knowledge is the cornerstone of good teaching.

Fundamental to this view is an assumption about the centrality of texts and textual knowledge. Teacher-education courses for the most part rely on texts, and the teaching I observed was uniformly text-centered. Faculty lectured on texts, typically at a pace which allowed the conscientious student to write down verbatim the lecture content. Students reproduced these interpretations on exams. Even the education classes provided reinforcement for this approach. For example, the teaching-methods class is designed to help students "master the teaching materials, apply these teaching materials, and help the student master the basic function of each instructional segment"—in short, to help the students learn how to use the texts (Chen, 1985, p. 51). It is telling that at normal universities the common name for the "methods" classes which each department offers is "teaching materials and methods." This authority of texts is supported by normal university curricula providing primarily required, not elective, coursework organized around a common canon of state-prescribed texts and curricula of precollegiate education. Implicit in this practice is the message that teaching is about the transmission of orthodox subject knowledge.

Associated and reinforcing this message is the view of teaching as performance rather than interaction or joint construction of learning. The preservice teacher first learns this through the "apprenticeship of observation" (Lortie, 1975) and gets repeated exposure to this view in teacher education pedagogy, which puts the instructor in the role of master and the students in the role of disciples as faculty expound on texts. But the theme of teaching as performance is most powerfully enacted in the one experiential learning opportunity all prospective teachers have—student teaching.

Current Chinese pedagogy texts regularly talk about the need for teaching to be active, student-centered, and interactive. Yet the Chinese literature on student teaching and my observations of student teaching over four semesters, including an intensive daily observation of one group during their full experience, suggest that the beginning teacher's first formal encounter with the field (teaching in schools) symbolizes the dominant conceptions of teaching (as subject-oriented, text-driven and teacher-dominated) and learning (as passive). This practicum is a powerful, significant experience for teachers, yet an inherently conservative one.

The distribution of time and activities within the practicum teaches preservice teachers much about how to conceptualize their practice. There is relatively little time in schools (often only four weeks of a six-week practicum in the student's senior year), and even once in schools, only a brief portion of a student teacher's time is spent teaching (or, what the students and teachers call being "at the podium" [*shang jiangtai*]. For the students I accompanied during their practicum, their weeks were organized to emphasize observation and study, rehearsal, and brief performances before students. Student teachers experienced this time as intense and engaging. They uniformly spoke of the importance of their time "at the podium"—often four to ten class periods over a month or more's time. Although this teaching was a high point of their practicum, the time throughout offered consistent messages that supported a view of teachers as experts and performers, that favored passive learning, and which suggested that one learns from masters. The students I accompanied began by listening to experts (teachers who came to lecture during their week-long orientation at the university), then concentrated on observing master teachers and poring over the text they were to teach. The actual amount of text they focused on was small—a single lesson they were preparing—but it was studied in exhausting detail. The student teachers used the same text and accompanying teacher's guide as their main tool for preparation. Their focus was on organizing this material. Accepting the authority and appropriateness of the text, they set as goals precision in interpretation and explanation.

As an observer, it was evident that both the beginning teachers and their more experienced mentors saw concentrated study of textual knowledge and emulation of masters, not extensive time in classrooms or frequent interaction with children, as keys to preparation for teaching. Preparation—based on observing the master teacher teaching, studying the text for the lesson they would teach, drafting a lesson plan, seeking consultation and making revisions to that—culminated in the development, formal rehearsal and finally teaching of a carefully scripted lesson. The polishing process's "trial lesson" (*shijiang*) involved the student teacher performing a dress rehearsal before peers and supervising teachers, followed immediately by a group de-briefing and critique. Only after this sort of full rehearsal could the preser-vice teacher take the podium to teach students.

The level of detail expected in this scripting process encourages instruc-tion that relies primarily on lecture. The students I shadowed showed me that this teaching can be impressive in its precision, artistry, and depth of knowl-edge. But this approach to teaching does not support the active learning reformers claim is important to modernization. Nor does it help a novice conceptualize the teacher's role as a curriculum developer or think about how to develop curriculum materials that go beyond the required canon.

The practicum brings beginners into a community of practice which is explicitly hierarchical. For the ten students I shadowed most closely, the organization of their experience encouraged them to work in groups and to see distinctions within groups as part of teaching. These student teachers were to act as disciples; even the welcoming ceremony at the practicum school the first day reminded the student teachers that they were here to learn from experts. Their learning, arranged for them by the school, was to be chiefly passive and to occur through observation and conversation with "experts," their master teachers. In fact, at this particular school, practicum students as a group were assigned their own preparation room, a symbol of the distinction between experienced teachers and teachers in training. These frequent expressions of role differences among teachers at various stages in their experience reinforce hierarchical arrangements among teachers and the importance of seniority.

In teacher preparation, beginning teachers formally get exposure to re-form ideas of teaching. They are informed of the inadequacy of a tradi-tionally imitative model of teaching. Yet much of teaching preparation tends to perpetuate that model. For example, during the orientation week for stu-dent teachers I shadowed, a distinguished, young local secondary school teacher lectured on "How to be a secondary school teacher of Chinese lan-guage and literature." The teacher talked about the need to teach creatively and in ways that help students think. He reported on observing fourteen classes in which there were 120 questions, and he noted that only twenty of these questions had helped students think. He directly linked the need for teachers to ask tougher and more generative questions to the development of skills needed for modernization. Yet the very medium of his message—a long lecture to a large audience of nervous students anxious about their first days in schools—itself stifled questions, interaction, or developing skills. Furthermore, despite his formal message, his lecture ultimately conveyed traditional ideas about teaching. In criticizing dry teaching that is unresponsive to the dynamics of students, he recommended avoiding staring closely at your lesson plans by writing these plans in very large letters that ease careful, correct reading.

In short, the hidden curriculum of teacher education works to maintain traditional assumptions about teaching and teachers. The content and distribution of the prospective teacher's curriculum and the structuring of time, activities, and roles in the experiential learning of their student teaching convey a consistent, coherent message: teachers' authority is rooted in their deep and correct knowledge of accepted texts, and their authority grows as they devote more time to study and teaching. Teaching involves transmitting—in precise, elegant, but intellectually orthodox ways—knowledge to students, and hence is more a performance than an interaction. It requires careful preparation, is difficult, and can not be very spontaneous or responsive. It is fundamentally conservative.

Induction

These preservice messages are reinforced through the ways in which teachers are subsequently inducted into schools and organized and rewarded for their teaching. For example, new teachers are inducted into a role in a hierarchical institution and an approach to teaching which stresses transmission rather than transformation. The role and approach are mutually supporting in ways that have made a thoroughgoing reform of teaching difficult. New teachers are assigned probationary status in their first year of teaching and often, if schools have the resources to support this, a lighter work load distinguishes them as beginners. The assumption is that they should concentrate on deepening their knowledge and refining their skills through study, working closely with mentors, and rehearsal; that is, they need extended time in which to "prepare classes."

Induction into this work is supported by the system of teaching-research group (*jiaoyanzu*), the basic organizational structure for teachers in both elementary and secondary schools. New and veteran teachers; young, middle-aged and old teachers come together in these groups. Bound by teaching a common subject area, they occupy a shared working space for planning and, among a wide range of activities, meet frequently to plan lessons, prepare and analyze tests, and discuss teaching. They regularly observe and critique each others' practice. While in theory all participants in a group have an equal voice, interviews with young teachers reveal a common pattern of seniority as middle-aged and older teachers' suggestions typically override ideas and objections from newcomers.

In addition to these formal study groups, mentoring arrangements which assign novice teachers to an experienced teacher in their group are common. Findings from a National Center for Research on Teacher Learning (NCRTL) study[4] of weekly mentoring interactions over a year, support what my interviews with other teachers around the country suggest: novices are introduced to teaching in their school through strong encouragement to study textbooks and national syllabi. In our NCRTL study we found that despite wide variation in type and level of school in which they taught, subject background, and orientation to teaching, the most common activity mentors and novices engaged in together was studying and analyzing subject matter, especially the content of their textbooks. Most of these mentors identified studying the text as one of the most important things novices need to do in learning to teach. One mentor's goals for her novice were typical: "I think the most important thing for her to learn is the textbook. As a beginning teacher, one often makes the mistake of wanting to teach all the knowledge she learned in her college period. But the students always find it hard to accept it all. If she masters the textbook, she will know what the important things are that she needs to teach and what can be taught gradually."

The induction phase of teaching highlights the hierarchical structure of schools, the importance of seniority, and the dominance of textual study and repetition. While these practices foster competence, the teaching encouraged comes to accept the wisdom of experience, the power of precedence, and the correctness of the group. It remains subject-oriented, since teachers' primary reference group is subject based, and it remains text-based, since it is the textbook, not the students, that connects teachers in a section and structures their conversations and plans.

Teaching's Work and Rewards

The organization of and rewards for teachers' work further confirms this cultural meaning of teaching. Teachers frequently talk about the way the examination system acts as a "baton" conducting teachers' work. For the many teachers who find themselves "at the podium" yet poorly prepared in their own subject, the pressure to get students to perform well on standardized tests encourages a conformity to common methods that work. The weak teacher inevitably relies on the text and prior practice. And even for the skilled teacher, the press of time imposed by an externally determined syllabus and examination makes staying on target and covering material at a fast pace seem necessary. Teachers I interviewed in 1994 discussed the tremendous pressure they felt to cover everything on the syllabus for the examinations, and, after looking at videos of teaching in the United States and China, many explained the cross-national differences they saw as largely a function of the constraints examinations and the curriculum imposed on Chinese teachers.

The assignment of teachers to classes further supports the maintenance of traditional teaching. Teachers have relatively light class schedules compared to U.S. teachers: secondary teachers typically have between six and fifteen periods of classes to teach each week, and elementary usually under twenty-five. This assignment pattern both reflects and maintains assumptions about the nature and demands of teachers' work: it is assumed that at the heart of teaching is preparation and study of the text. The large class size common to China's schools further encourages traditional orientations to teaching and its teacher-centered focus. With classes that often have 50 to 60 students teachers lack structural supports for individualized instruction, the active participation of large numbers of students, and the encouraging of questions. When faced with the constraint of class size, student diversity, and teachers' own limits of knowledge, time and attention, educators often persist in performance methods of transmitting knowledge to students, rather than reaching out to students to help them develop their own understandings or encouraging open-ended inquiry.

Finally, the system of rewards reinforce the persistence of dominant conceptions of teaching. Student performance on examinations remains the commonly accepted criterion of good teaching. Despite reforms in recent years to reduce the importance accorded memorization skills, the exams give relatively little weight to the creativity and independent thinking so often considered cornerstones of social and technological transformation. Instead, the prevalent practice of using exams as measures of teacher effectiveness supports the persistence of traditional teaching methods, since these have proven highly effective in producing mastery of much factual and procedural knowledge. Even the creation of special categories of teachers deserving reward, such as the "special rank teacher" (*teji jiaoshi*), may inadvertently support conventional views. Most significant is the implied necessity to learn from and emulate models. The special rank teachers are honored for their academic knowledge and effectiveness in teaching, two qualities typically understood in ways congruent with dominant subject- and text-centered conceptions of teaching.

Tensions between Practice and Reform Goals: Speculations about China and the United States

In short, views of teaching undergird practices which are at odds with the explicit reform agendas of China's modernization process. These views are communicated to new teachers and maintained in the culture of teaching through the structures and practices of teacher education, the ways by which novices are inducted in school practice, and teaching environments which organize and reward teaching. Teaching in China today is, in most schools and as practiced by most teachers, an inherently conservative act. It relies on what Jackson (1986) calls a "mimetic" or "epistemic" tradition, which "gives a central place to the transmission of factual and procedural knowledge from one person to another, through an essentially *imitative* process" (p. 117). For China's teaching to meet the reform challenge of modernization, the practice of teaching must be transformed to become not "mimetic" but "transformative" (p. 121). This tension between practice and reform goals is widely discussed in education circles in China. It is a tension not unique to China. While U.S. discussion, for example, does not use the same terms of "modernization" to describe national goals, critics nevertheless point out how contemporary school performance does not match our needs in an information age marked by global competition. As in China, the goals of developing a whole generation of young people which possesses basic literacy and numeracy but also conceptual understanding, problem-solving skills, and critical thinking are as yet unattained in the United States. Whether argued from the ideological right or left, U.S. critics lament the fact that U.S. teaching so often remains imitative rather than transformative.

I have painted a picture of contemporary educational practice that rests on mimetic approaches to teaching. I do not intend to suggest that China's teachers, their professional homes, and their beliefs and assumptions are uniform. China's education, like the rest of its society, comprises much diversity in resources and experience. I am not arguing that all teachers embody the conventional norms outlined here. Rather, my goal is to characterize dominant norms. And these, Chinese critics agree, demonstrate the great resilience of tradition.

China has now undergone more than a decade of vigorous policy efforts to reform education. How is it that its educational system remains in many ways incongruent with its scientific and social goals for modernization? And what are the prospects for change? Can teaching come into closer connection to broader goals? In speculating on the apparent tension between goals and reform efforts in China, and in wondering about the future implications of this tension, we can also consider what lessons U.S. educators can draw from the Chinese experience. For while the specifics of the cases are extremely different, it is clear that the United States, like China, has for over a decade been actively engaged in significant effort to reform teaching; this reform is regularly coupled with larger social and structural reform agendas;

and, as suggested above, critics point to the discrepancy between policy reform and substantial change in practice.

The first question asks us to consider why reform has not produced a practice consistent with reform goals. In China's case, one conclusion is that reform efforts as embodied in policy change have tended to focus on one framing of the issues. This framing has been a technical one that has led to policies external to teaching and aimed at supplementing and upgrading teachers. Policies set outside of the school, typically at provincial and even national levels, have attempted to set standards for teachers, to improve their distribution and to professionalize them through teacher education, examination and certification procedures, and increased material benefits. Much of the attention has been directed at structures—rationalizing them, improving their efficiency, strengthening their articulation. It is certainly the case that the number of teachers overall and the number of those with formal teacher preparation have grown as a result of reform policy. It is also clear that teachers' wages and benefits have improved, again clearly influenced by policy effort. And the impressive network of teacher education institutions which now offer a range of programs for a diverse teaching force at many different stages in a teacher's professional development has been the beneficiary of policy reform.

But little of this broad band of policy work challenged conceptualizations of teaching as a practice. If the framing of the issues is not solely technical, then it is essential to reflect on the nature of teacher's work, that which is at the core of their practice, and to consider how the organization and culture of teaching support a particular version of practice. From the perspective of this other framing—one which centers on teaching as practice—cultural practices become the focus for attention. These practices have proven much more intractable to external policy recommendations than the structural dimensions noted above. The wave of policy reform mandated from above (or outside) the school has had much less influence on what occurs in the classroom. To be sure, many within education have in fact talked about, written in defense of and advocated for change in classroom practice. The 1980's actually witnessed a burgeoning literature of reform articles focusing on various aspects of teaching: inquiry methods, active learning, and so on. But even in these discussions, the unstated assumption was that teaching remained a technical activity; reformers need to introduce a new technique for change to be brought about. Few even within the professional education discourse community talked about teaching as cultural practice. And while teachers, like the ones I interviewed in response to videos, can point quickly to the interconnections of cultural norms, structural constraints, and organizational imperatives, few researchers and reformers have considered reform holistically and in ways that consider these interconnections.

Dominant practices remain so untouched by reform in part because of reformers' failure to acknowledge and address these linkages. For it is the interconnection of teacher learning and school organization, of cultural practices and institutional structures, that make conventional conceptualizations of teaching both so powerful and so pervasive. The Chinese story's message for U.S. educators may be to confirm Elmore and McLaughlin's (1988) claim that "the steady work of educational reform . . . must be grounded in an understanding of how teachers learn to teach, how school organization affects practice, and how these factors affect children's performance" (p. 37).

The message seems a timely one, given certain trends in U.S. teaching reform. Here we have witnessed, as in China, a first wave of reform that has focused largely on creating external structures to improve or buttress teaching. The strengthening of testing and certification procedures to tighten entry into teaching and the use of statewide examination of students as accountability measures of teaching have, as in China, certainly exerted influence. But the limits of these reforms to affect the technical core of teaching, to challenge practice and foster a more ambitious, transformative teaching are also clear. The experience of China's reforms suggests that without considering the ways in which these structural changes leave unaffected knowledge, skills, and beliefs encouraged throughout a teacher's learning, such reforms are likely to remain limited in the range of their impact. Chinese teachers who spoke with me forcefully about the ways in which external measures, even if motivated by reformist agendas, can become constraints that encourage conventional teaching to the test might have much to say about the ability of accountability measures to reshape practice.

Structural change, in China and the United States, that derives from technical framing of the problem can be important. But the story of China's reforms would pose questions to U.S. reformers about the limits of such change. The ability to consider an alternative frame of teaching as a cultural practice would lead U.S. reformers to both conceptualize the problem, consider responses, and see the origin of those solutions in very different places. Examining the problems of teaching in China as practice leads one to explore the range of ways in which teaching culture is produced and reproduced. It would encourage U.S. reformers, for example, to avoid disconnecting the reform of teaching from teacher education. It would argue that teacher education must be reconceptualized as teacher learning, and not seen as limited to a single stage (preservice education) in a teacher's career of development. And it would remind us that organizational factors interact powerfully with teacher learning. The establishment of metropolitan and even statewide mentor programs to support teacher induction in the United States may illustrate the limits of structural reforms that leave unaffected cultural norms; a comparative study of two U.S. programs suggest that as long as mentors see themselves as "local guides" to a novice, rather than as "educational companions" in the process of inquiry about and reform of their own practice, novices and mentors support conventional teaching that the reforms often are created in response to (Feiman-Nemser and Parker, 1993).

Neither China nor the United States offers hope that reconstructing a culture of teaching is something that can be addressed simply by structural changes or affected most directly by external policy. The swift transformations that policy might offer are unlikely to generate the sea changes that transforming practices entail. Rather, in the United States, as in China, reforming teaching is best thought of as "steady work." What the analysis of dominant practices in China suggests is that a careful examination of the factors that influence teaching culture is essential to this work. Finally, China's teachers present evidence of the importance of the "steady work" of educational reform coming *out* of practice, rather than simply being *about* practice.

Possibilities for Reform Coming out of the Community of Teaching

Just as China's experience may mirror the challenges of U.S. reform and the limitations of technical framing of teacher reform, so too does China offer some possibilities for thinking about what conditions support teaching reform that grows out of practice. For practice in China, where it has changed, has clearly been transformed by teachers themselves working in a professional community that has certain features of collaboration and collegiality. As one experienced teacher, reflecting on what has most affected her professional development explained, it is teachers working together which has had the most profound affect on practice: "For my first class here, all my colleagues in the teaching research group came, then assessed the class. Then they had me go teach a class for the normal university to observe. This forces you to raise your level. In the trial lesson you go over every part. I was pressed at each step of the way; they press you to improve. You need to push people. It takes about two years, then the school can relax. So I'm very grateful."

The culture of teaching in China is one organized around a professional community (Paine and Ma, 1993). That is both expressed and nurtured by organizational practices that bring teachers together. In China teachers work together in formal organizations, in the teaching-research groups that exist in every school, elementary or secondary, elite or ordinary. They bring teachers together each week to study teaching, to look at curriculum, to talk about materials they are teaching, to talk about reforms, and to engage in research about particular students' learning, about a subject matter issue, about a pedagogical reform or so on. In addition, they work together in mentor-novice relations that exist in all schools, not just reform schools, not just elite schools, not just schools trying out new ideas. They work together informally in all kinds of ways. On a recent observation I serendipitously witnessed a teacher preparing classes; she was in her classroom teaching the lesson to a colleague seated (alone) in a room full of empty student desks. This was just one example of the frequent informal connections that bring teachers together around the practice of teaching. In addition Chinese teachers work together in a lively literature of teacher research, teacher autobiographies, and teacher biographies.

In short, teachers in China are members of multiple groups—formal, informal, and even across distance. Together these groups construct and maintain a culture of teaching which encourages teachers in particular ways. While not all Chinese mentors and novices would work together in the same way, it is clear from our NCRTL research that mentors are helping novices join a community that is authentic and active, that assumes a collective commitment to teaching and to student learning, and that expects teachers to pursue this commitment through frequent collaboration.

How does China's experience of teacher community serve as a mirror to help us see possibilities for reform of teaching practice, reform that grows *from* practice? Some speculation comes from teachers and researchers examining daily interactions among teachers. In the NCRTL study of beginning teachers working with mentor teachers in England, the United States, and China, we see that in all three cases, the majority of talk about teaching in the interactions between beginning and experienced teachers centers around teaching, planning, and broad philosophical issues about teaching. Much less attention gets given to discussing testing, homework, assessment, or other issues, although those are also important. But, interestingly, in China (and not in the United States or the United Kingdom), the vast majority of time focuses on teaching. This is possible in part because teachers feel they actually can talk about each other's lessons. In most schools, teachers in fact are required to observe other teachers' lessons at least twenty lessons a semester. In the United States, although teaching is a major part of discussion, the majority of discussion is about planning, what you *might* do. Very little is a chance to reflect on what you've actually done, or to critique one another's practice in constructive ways. Chinese mentors participating in our study considered the patterns of teacher-teacher interactions in the three country

samples and were struck by the difference. Their confusion about U.S. patterns implies a question important to considering deep reform of widespread
cultural practices: How can teachers work together towards any real transformation of teaching if the scope for their interaction excludes talking critically about what and how they are actually teaching? Watching teachers in
China, and observing and listening to the stories of teachers engaged in
trying to transform practice, I am left with the deep impression of the importance of reform building on community, and in particular a community that
fosters collaboration around meaningful work, that supports development of
a common professional language, and that allows for teaching to be understood as a shared practice, rather than as a privatized activity (Little, 1990).

Conclusion: Defining Teaching in its Complexity

China's difficulty in defining and addressing the problem of teaching and
teachers suggests some of what is hard about educational reform of teaching
elsewhere. In pondering the possibilities for change in China, three questions
become central. Are the resources available to support change? How can this
change be conceptualized and rationalized? How can it be accepted? These
questions suggest that teaching reform has economic, social, and political
implications.

In China a major impediment to the reform of teaching and learning is
the shortage of resources. For decades, China's teachers have not fared well
economically, socially, and politically in relation to many of their peers. This
situation helped produce the technical shortage of committed and qualified
teachers. If the state is to be able to resolve this problem, changes in the
allocation of resources are needed. Some have already taken place. Yet as
these reforms have been put in place, the expansion of the market economy
has undermined the intended consequences for teachers and generated new
or exacerbated old problems regarding economic security and social and
political valuation. Without a reassessment of the significance of teachers
and their work to broader national goals, patterns of resource management
are unlikely to change, and the technical problem will be relatively slow to
be resolved.

But while resource shortages make the allocation problem burdensome,
there is more hope for change in that regard than in others. For over a
decade state leaders have articulated the importance of teacher recruitment,
retention and standards. In contrast, the argument for a new kind of teacher,
one who teaches in what we might think of as adventurous and unconven-
tional ways, is less widely made. Politicians and lay people have provided

little justification for such a need. Certainly there has been a growing outcry against the overly academic emphasis ("bookishness") of schooling, the heavy homework burden given children, and the pressure and appropriateness of the examinations. But there has been much less direct examination of how these concerns connect to views of teaching and the need for fundamental, transformative change, instead of change in emphasis or amount. Comprehensive and fundamental change would depend on a reinterpretation of learning, a different conception of knowledge, and a new conceptualization of authority relations. These are far more challenging goals than updating the curriculum or introducing specific new methods. One reason for their difficulty is that they extend beyond the classroom or even the school to include the examination system, social structures, and social and political norms.

This leads to the third and most serious obstacle to a transformative reform of teaching; this hurdle is fundamentally political. The technical supply problem is most often understood in economic terms. The difficulty of demanding new teaching in many ways stems from social and cultural practices. But a political basis underlies all of these if we consider the implications of the new teaching espoused by leaders and reformers. If teaching is to encourage questioning, intellectual independence, and creativity, how can one set boundaries for its consequences? Reforming the teaching-learning relationship potentially calls into question notions of orthodoxy, authority, and power. The official response to the 1989 Democracy movement and the criticism of student and teacher participation in that movement reminds us of how threatening revisions of authority relations are.

Considering the future possibilities for the reform of China's teaching profession and their practice forces us to remember the ways that teaching is not only a technical activity, but also one with significant cultural, social, and political dimensions. The limited success of reforms in China, mirroring in interesting ways the challenges of reforms in the United States, may serve as encouragement to consider multiple frames for defining the problem, as well as to be reflective about the complexity of teaching as a social practice. In understanding where success has occurred, we are led to think about how U.S. policy efforts can come out of practice, rather than be aimed at it, and can take as a starting place understanding and working with the versions of community which shape the culture of teaching here.

II

Secondary Education

CHAPTER 5

Restructuring Japanese High Schools:
Reforms for Diversity

NOBUO K. SHIMAHARA

When the National Council on Educational Reform (NCER), the so-called *rinkyoshin*, began its deliberations on educational reforms in 1984, the public displayed an exceptional interest in its agenda, reflecting public concern over critical problems with schools. However, when the final report of NCER was completed in 1987, its recommendations to overhaul Japan's school system seemed to lack the anticipated sharp thrusts and lasting impact. Yet the nationwide reform campaign in the 1980s has led to important initiatives in restructuring both high school and higher education. At both levels, meaningful if not major reforms are currently under way. In the post–World War II period, the nation has witnessed a phenomenal expansion of both upper secondary and higher education. Its concern, however, is now no longer a quantitative extension of education and student enrollment at the secondary and tertiary levels, but the quality of programs and teaching. In this chapter will explore the initiatives to restructure high schools and ask these questions: Why are reformers interested in restructuring high schools? Where is the restructuring campaign headed?

In the United States, restructuring initiatives since the early 1980s have emphasized core curriculum, national standards, and assessment. Recently, America 2000 identified "the new world standards" in all five core subjects and the "new American achievement tests" as a critical school reform target for the 1990s. It is evident that one of the pivotal concerns in American education policy is framed in terms of standards and national goals (Doyle, 1991). In contrast, Japanese policymakers are seeking to diversify high school education.

Author's note: I wish to express my appreciation to the National Institute of Multimedia Education in Chiba City, Japan, for its support of my research on the culture of teaching in Japan. Data used in the article were collected as part of the research.

Educational Accomplishments

To appreciate the foreground of the problem, I will first briefly reflect on its background. After World War II, the Japanese social structure opened to further social mobility as the sweeping, occupation-initiated land and corporate reforms broke up the monopoly of wealth and power. Under this new system, youths' enrollment in secondary and higher education grew at a phenomenal rate, as their rising aspirations for mobility were translated into employment in an expanding national economy. For example, the 1960s witnessed industrial and economic expansion unparalleled in Japanese history. Personal incomes tripled, as did international trade. Industry was desperate for ever greater numbers of better trained people, and it demanded that education be upgraded (Shimahara, 1992). Since then, Japan has enjoyed an enviable position in terms of both unparalleled growth of secondary and higher education and the level of academic achievement (Husen, 1967; LaPointe, Mead, & Phillips, 1989; Stevenson & Stigler, 1992). In 1993, high school and college enrollments were 96.2% and 40.9%, respectively, although high school education is not compulsory and entrance examinations are required for admission (Ministry of Education, 1994). The high school dropout rate declined to 1.9% in 1992 from 2.2% in 1989, reaching the lowest rate in recent years.

Through the 1970s, however, the nation's development was still guided by what is identified in Japan as the catch-up ideology (Economic Council, 1983). To accomplish modernization in a much shorter time than did the West, Japan developed uniform state-controlled schooling throughout the nation, and by this means it attained high literacy. In the post–World War II period, Japan hardly deviated from uniform schooling with respect to the curriculum, other school programs, and control of education.

Now that Japan has caught up with the West, it is seeking a new paradigm of development to replace the catch-up ideology. In the mid-1980s this undertaking was expressed as an emerging national concern (for example, Economic Council, 1983). But, short-term, immediate school reform issues were much more directly related to the effects of uniform schooling and the centrifugal social forces generated by economic affluence, social mobility, changing family structures, and information-dominated social life. These social forces represented a far-reaching transformation that had occurred between the late 1960s and the early 1980s. It became increasingly evident in the early 1980s that Japan's school system, which was effective in meeting the needs of modernization and industrialization for a century, had become dysfunctional in satisfying diversified youth values and needs. The absence of diversity in schooling was declared to be a cause of deviant adolescent behavior—a national obsession in the late 1970s and early 1980s—as society became diversified, creating a lack of fit between the school system and social change.

Problems of High School Education

Prior to discussing high school problems in detail, it is relevant to make a brief remark on Japanese governance of schools. Until recently, the Ministry of Education had concentrated on developing the nation's compulsory schools, although it also oversees upper and higher education (Kitamura, in press). This is clearly reflected in the ministry's substantial share of fiscal responsibility for public elementary and lower secondary schools (50%). Governance of public high schools, which constitute about 75% of the nation's upper secondary schools, is the primary responsibility of the prefectural governments (equivalent to states in the United States). Therefore, the ministry set up an ad hoc task force, identified as the Office to Promote High School Reforms, to coordinate and support high school reforms at the prefectural level. It is sufficient to suggest that given this structure of school governance, prefectural initiatives are critical in promoting high school reforms.

Major issues in today's high school education in Japan stem in significant measure from the fact that high school education has changed relatively little, although it has attained universal attendance. High school enrollment escalated progressively in parallel with the nation's economic growth. In 1955, when Japan was nearly restored to its prewar economic strength, only half of eligible youths attended high school; the enrollment rate was up 6% by 1960, and it reached 82% and 92% in 1970 and 1975, respectively. However, between 1975 and 1994. the enrollment rate increased by only a few points, manifesting that youth enrollment in high school had reached its highest level. Unlike high school youths during the 1960s, for whom high school education was still a privilege, today's students regard schooling at the upper secondary level as mandatory. They represent far greater variance in their academic ability, needs. and values (Kadowaki & Jinnouchi, 1992; Terawaki, 1993). Yet the legacy of uniform schooling at the secondary level still remains potent, countering the divergence in youths' needs and differentiating industrial and employment structures. This has resulted in the alienation of students who cannot follow demanding academic requirements (Amano, 1993).

Since the first postwar high schools were created in 1948, major curriculum reforms have been under taken in 1951, 1956, 1960, 1970, 1978, and

1992 (Jinnouchi, 1992). The 1960 reform established the fundamental structure of the high school curriculum in the postwar period, emphasizing disci-
pline-centered, uniform, and methodical instruction. The 1970 reform further
upgraded the curricular content, reflecting demands for better trained human
resources for industrial development, and it was implemented at a time when
nearly 90 percent of eligible youths began to attend high school. It became
quickly evident that the revised curriculum was too demanding for large
numbers of students. Consequently, initiatives that demanded "humanization" of the curriculum were launched, resulting in the 1978 revision. This
revision called for a less demanding curriculum and what is commonly identified as *yutori*, latitude and relaxation in schooling in response to students'
diverse needs and interests. The latest revision took effect in 1994, emphasizing internationalism, changes in industrial and employment structures, and
a broad latitude in the curriculum.

It is apparent that one of the most critical problems in today's high
school education in Japan is a lack of fit between the uniform curriculum
and changing students with heterogeneous interests and abilities (Central
Council of Education, 1991, pp. 24–25). This is a salient issue even though
high school entrance examinations serve as a sorting device that assigns
students to appropriate schools relative to their academic abilities. In response to the problem, ability grouping has been implemented since the
1978 curriculum revision, but it solves only part of the problem.

Another obvious problem stems from university entrance examinations
(Rohlen, 1983). They have a dominant, perpetual influence on high school
students with respect to their cognitive and motivational orientation toward
schooling and instructional programs. Thirty years ago Vogel (1963), author
of *Japan's Middle Class*, noted:

> No single event, with the possible exception of marriage, determines the course
> of a young man's life as much as an entrance examination, and nothing, includ-
> ing marriage, requires as many years of planning and hard work. . . . These
> arduous preparations constitute a kind of *rite de passage* whereby a young man
> proves that he has the qualities of ability and endurance for becoming a
> salaried man. (p. 40)

Vogel's comment is based on his observation at a time when only 10 percent
of high school graduates went to college. Now the intensity of preparation
for entrance examinations has escalated even more, because the preparation
begins much earlier and requires prolonged institutionalized drilling at *juku*
or *yobiko* (private preparatory schools existing outside the public school system). As part of the early preparation, well-to-do families place their chil-

dren in examination-oriented private schools that have both middle and high school programs. Moreover, as Amano (1986) observed,

> The tendency toward increased stratification is especially evident in the relationship between secondary and higher education [in the 1980s]. The school hierarchies within both of these educational levels are strengthening, as is the tendency for the position attained in lower high schools to determine students' place in the higher level. The opportunity for admission to the top universities is now virtually monopolized by graduates from the top high schools. (p. 24)

Suffice it to suggest that most of the academic high schools, where 75 percent of the nation's high school students are enrolled, find their raison d'être in preparing their students for entrance examinations (Central Council of Education, 1991, p. 92). Given the constraints forced upon them by entrance examinations, these academic high schools are reluctant to diversify their programs. The Central Council of Education (1991) points out in its reform report that these schools' definition of mission as preparation for entrance examinations is a prime source of uniform schooling at the high school level (p. 92).

Diversity as a Reform Issue

In this section I will explore the evolution of policy initiatives to promote diversity in high school education. Although the continued dominance of uniformity in high school education is evident, reformers considered the need for diversity as early as the 1960s. For example, they were instrumental in increasing offerings in vocational high schools from 171 areas of study in 1966 to 252 in 1970, in response to the nation's rapid economic and technological advancement in the 1960s (Kurosawa, 1994). Nevertheless, their campaign to expand offerings failed to meet the changing economic and industrial demands of the times, because the fast-changing demands made these programs obsolete even as they were being developed. As a result, the campaign hardly interested students in the new programs, whereas, in contrast, academic high schools gained greater popularity when high school enrollment was rapidly growing in the 1960s.

The most comprehensive school reform report since the postwar occupation-led reforms emphasized choice and diversity in course offerings in academic high schools. This report was completed in 1971 by the Central Council of Education, an influential advisory body to the minister of education. The reforms proposed by the Central Council were very ambitious and far-reaching, but their firsthand impact on the nation's school system was relatively limited, partly because they did not receive undivided support from the Ministry of Education and national legislators (Schoppa, 1991). Top bureaucrats within the ministry, who guided the development of Japan's postwar school system, stubbornly defended the status quo. Nevertheless, the proposal (Central Council, 1971/1994) offered a fundamental conceptual framework for school reform initiatives in the 1970s and 1980s, including the reform campaign launched by the NCER. In this regard, the 1971 report is highly significant and conceptually more cogent than the NCER's reports.

In brief, the council recommended that the high school curriculum be diversified in response to increasing variance in students' ability, aptitude, and aspirations. In the council's (1971/1994) words:

> It is essential to diversify the educational content of schooling in accordance with divergence in students' ability, aptitude, and aspirations. Sufficient advisement should be given to students so that they may make an appropriate choice in selecting courses from a broad range of offerings. (pp. 125–126)

In the context of postwar Japanese high school education, the council's recommendation was futuristic and consequential, leading to a policy formulation at the prefectural level in the late 1970s. In response to the Central Council's call for diversity in high school education, the National Association of Prefectural Superintendents in 1975 began a campaign to consider innovative high school programs, creating a task force on high school problems (Kurosawa, 1994). In 1977 it issued a report proposing new programs and new types of schools. That report became the basis of the association's (1978/1994) final report, completed the following year, which delineated detailed plans to transform high school education. The report was timely because the Ministry of Education announced a major revision of the course of study for high school education in the same year, which underscored *yutori*, or latitude and relaxation in the construction of school programs, humanization of student life, and the promotion of individuality. The new course of study reduced the required credits for graduation and the number of instructional hours and introduced imaginative strategies to adapt to the diversity of students. The revised course of study provided the Association with additional legitimacy for its campaign.

I will present highlights of the association's (1978/1994) final report, because it involves several important proposals that provided a new direction in the development of innovative high schools. The report proposed broadening course offerings to allow students' choice and increasing academic programs as special fields. The report recommended that students be encouraged to take required courses in the sophomore year, to allow them to explore their areas of interest in the junior and senior years. Further, it proposed what the Association called "new types of high schools," which included the following:

1. "Credit-based" high schools—schools that will enable students to graduate when they complete the required credits. Students would be encouraged to advance in their course work on an individual basis.
2. *Shugogata sentakusei* high schools—the clustering of two or three high schools on the same site to permit students to select courses in a given area of study offered by any cluster school. Each school is encouraged to develop unique programs and to provide students in the cluster schools access to them. Further, facilities of the cluster schools are to be shared. The rationale for the proposed shugogata sentakusei high schools is to offer students a broad latitude of choice and rich facilities.
3. Boarding schools—all residential schools to promote all-around education, providing supervision on both academic and social aspects of students' lives.
4. Six-year high schools—schools that provide effective continuity between middle and high schools to render *yutori*.

This report was timely in another notable respect. Suburbs of Japan's large cities, especially Tokyo, were expanding fast in the 1970s, demanding a considerable expansion of high schools. Also, a significant demographic surge of high-school age population was anticipated throughout the country in the 1980s as a result of the second postwar baby boom. These demographic changes and the increasing political and fiscal support for school reforms enhanced the relevance and the subsequent public acceptance of the report.

The recommendations made by the association (1978/1994) eventually became a blueprint for the development of new types of high schools. The second recommendation resulted in the realization of clustered schools and *sogo sentakusei*, or comprehensive high schools, in various prefectures in the 1980s and 1990s. This development will be explored later. Nationwide promotion of new types of schools, however, required broad public support, financial backing from prefectures across the nation, and above all, political legitimation. That political legitimation was offered by the NCER, whose deliberations on school reforms attracted widespread, intense public attention in the mid-1980s, and by the 1991 reform report of the Central Council of Education.

It should be noted here that during the American occupation, comprehensive high schools were initially introduced but failed in the 1950s owing to several reasons. The first critical reason is that Japanese policymakers, who were unaccustomed to the concept of comprehensive high schools, considered them ineffective, and the second was funding shortfalls (Kaneko, 1986). Consequently, high schools were differentiated into academic and vocational schools. This reorganization of high school education was part of an extensive national campaign to restructure occupation-led reforms in the 1950s (see Komori, 1986).

For the reader who is not acquainted with Japan's school reform movement in the 1980s, a brief review of the movement is in order. In 1982, when the Nakasone cabinet was first formed, the nation's mood for school reform was growing apace. Nakasone successfully marshaled support for the movement from the heads of other political parties. The preparation of the national bill to establish NCER was already under way, and the bill passed in the national legislature in the summer of 1984. NCER took three years to complete its recommendations for reform in four areas: education for the twenty-first century, educational functions of society, elementary and secondary education, and higher education (Shimahara, 1986). In its first report, NCER (1985) pointed out that Japanese education was suffering from a "grave state of desolation" and declared:

> Most important in the educational reform to come is to do away with the uniformity, rigidity, closedness and lack of internationalism, all of which are deep-rooted defects of our educational system, and to establish the principles of dignity of individuals, respect for the individual, freedom and self-discipline, and self-responsibility—in other words, the principle of putting emphasis on individuality. (p. 26)

Aside from its rhetoric, NCER was interested in loosening up the rigid school system. NCER made few new specific recommendations relative to high school education, but it reinforced the earlier recommendations to overhaul high schools by affirming them in general terms, thus providing political legitimacy for the reform initiatives undertaken by the Association of Prefectural Superintendents.

Subsequently, to fill the gap left by NCER, the minister of education charged the Central Council of Education in 1989 to recommend further requisite reforms of high school education. The council's report to the minister, completed in 1991, included a broad range of recommendations, including those formulated by the Association of Prefectural Superintendents and university entrance examinations. Especially, that report urged what was later identified as *sogo gakka*, literally translated as comprehensive programs: in the council's words, "various programs that synthesize both academic and vocational programs" (p. 31).

To implement the council's recommendations, the Ministry of Education set up the Committee for Enhancement of High School Reforms in 1991. The committee (1993) issued four reports in two years to recommend plans to improve high school education. Its central motif was to revamp high school education to empower students to link their personal interests and future aspirations to formal learning in the school. The committee underscored several points, which in part overlap the recommendations made by earlier reformers. At the risk of redundancy, its recommendations will be noted here to highlight consistent emphasis on strategies among reformers in the past twenty years. They include broad latitude in the selection of courses, a comprehensive program, a credit system, interschool collaboration by which students may earn credits at schools other than their own, and improved procedures for selecting applicants for admission to high school by vigorous consideration of interview results, recommendations, and school reports.

The committee's principal recommendation, however, was to implement a comprehensive program in each high school with the central aim of promoting students' career aspirations based on a broad study of both academic and specialized vocational subjects. This comprehensive program would attract students by offering an alternative to the exclusively college-bound program. Students who would choose the comprehensive program would be one of three types: those who are actively interested in linking academic work to career aspirations, those whose primary goal is employment after graduation, and those who have aspirations for college.

The comprehensive program would consist of four parts. The first would include the common requirements for all high school students. The second part would highlight three common areas for students in the comprehensive program, designated as industrial society and human life, basic studies of information technology, and independent study on selected problems. The third part would consist of rich clusters of elective courses, including: information, industrial management, international cooperation, regional development, biotechnology, welfare management, environmental science, and art and culture. Additional optional studies would make up the fourth part.

Implementation of Innovative Schools

The current school reform movement seems to be giving a new complexion to high school education at last. Important innovative changes are now being introduced piecemeal. Let us first turn to new types of schools whose development precedes the latest campaign to establish comprehensive programs.

The 1978 report of the Association of Prefectural Superintendents of Schools, bolstered by the 1978 revision of the course study, led to the emergence of these new types of schools in the early 1980s. These schools include *sogo sentakusei* or comprehensive high schools (not the comprehensive programs proposed in the 1990s), schools for international studies, schools for information science, schools for economics, and the like. These schools varied in terms of their programs, course work latitude given to students, and other characteristics. Stimulated by school reform initiatives in the 1980s, the number of innovative schools has been gradually increasing, reflecting enhanced public support for distinctive high schools designed to meet divergent individual and social needs.

Although comprehensive schools are not defined uniformly, schools characterized as comprehensive seem to display common features (Kurosawa, 1993). They include:

distinctive programs

a broad selection of courses

encouragement of study in specialized fields from the junior level

an inclusion of both academic and vocational studies

recruitment of students from the entire prefecture, rather than the traditional school districts

an emphasis on foreign languages

competence to process information

international studies

arts (including music and calligraphy)

math/science

the humanities

Although the development of these schools is still in an embryonic stage, they are expanding throughout the nation, offering alternative high school education to youths. For example, according to the latest survey conducted by the Ministry of Education (1993), 42 schools distinguished as new types were in operation in 23 prefectures, and 14 such schools were scheduled to be opened within a few years. There were 224 innovative vocational schools in 51 prefectures, with such unique programs as biotechnology, information technology, electronic mechanics, international economics, and the like. Programs are planned soon in 74 schools in 31 prefectures.

By way of illustration, I will cite a few schools identified as new types of schools. To date, the best-known comprehensive school in Japan is Ina Gakuen High School outside Tokyo, established in 1984 (Nishimoto, 1993). It enrolls 3,300 students and offers 164 courses; its seven programs include the humanities, natural science/mathematics, languages, health/physical education, arts, home economics, and business. At this school, students are permitted to choose half the courses that make up their entire program, providing them with latitude to select courses that promote their interests.

One of the most fascinating plans is to open an audacious comprehensive school in 1996, a proposed public school in Makuhari, Chiba City (H. Furuichi, personal communication, May 31, 1994). The construction of school buildings is currently under way, while a task force consisting of six full-time members has been mapping details of programs, staffing, methods of selecting students, and the operation of the school. It will enroll 2,100 students from the entire Chiba Prefecture and offer five programs, which include the humanities, natural science/mathematics, international studies, information science, and arts. According to the plan, students will take all the required courses in their sophomore year, enabling them to choose the remaining courses with few restrictions in the junior and senior years.

The school will adopt a credit system whereby students will graduate when they complete the required graduation credits. The task force is considering granting students the opportunity to enroll in college courses offered by the University of the Air as part of their program. This school will be most liberal in terms of students' course work.

Among other types of innovative schools, Narita International School in Chiba Prefecture and Tokyo Metropolitan International School may be mentioned here. Narita, which had been a prefectural academic high school, was changed to an international school in 1991, incorporating both English and international programs. Tokyo Metropolitan was opened in 1989. Both schools emphasize strong language and international studies programs, in addition to a regular academic program. Students in these schools receive rich language training and an exposure to cross-cultural studies.

In contrast to new types of schools, comprehensive programs, or *sogo gakka*, have just begun to emerge as a result of the policy initiative by the Central Council of Education. The Committee for Enhancement of High School Reforms (1993) suggested conceptual models of these programs. The comprehensive program must be conceptually distinguished from new types of schools, which include comprehensive schools or *sogo sentakusei* high schools. The former is a new program to be developed within an established high school to provide an alternative to students whose interest is not met in distinctly academic or vocational programs. This program would meet needs of a large proportion of students, especially in an academic high school.

Although 75% of all high school students currently attend academic high schools, 30% to 35% of them end up seeking employment, and about 10% of vocational students aspire to college. These students would be a primary target for the comprehensive program. The Ministry of Education's survey (1993) indicates that six prefectures have already decided to open a comprehensive program in six high schools in 1994; eight prefectures in eight schools will being programs in 1995. Another thirty-eight prefectures are considering adding a comprehensive program in public schools. All in all, given the fact that the comprehensive program is in its trial stage, it seems to be off to a good start.

Appraisal of Reform Initiatives

Reformers' interest in enhancing diversity in high school education began in the 1960s when enrollments escalated, and it has been pursued through periodic reform campaigns for more than two decades. The need for diversity in high school education became a more intensified concern as Japan achieved universal high school attendance. Diversity was a central theme of the school reform movement in the 1980s (NCER, 1987). The creation of innovative schools and comprehensive programs is a response to that need. In addition to these innovative drives, initiatives are being advanced in a small number of high schools to adopt a credit plan and an exchange system involving two or three schools whereby students are able to take courses at collaborating schools. These practices are aimed to increase students' choice and latitude in their coursework.

Overall, these initiatives illustrate a departure from the traditional academic and vocational curricula, articulating a promising and bright direction in high school education. At present, however, only a small fraction of the nation's 4,181 public high schools are participating in these initiatives. In assessing this high school reform movement, one needs to ask if it is genuine or faddish. If it is genuine, it will involve more schools, entailing a tangible impact on secondary education. However, I would be remiss if I did not point out that there are potent constraining circumstances that could impede the movement.

First, university entrance examinations are a perpetual force hindering diversification of high school education. As confirmed by principals whom I interviewed in the Tokyo and Chiba areas, innovative schools, especially comprehensive and international schools, may offer highly attractive choices to students, but their viability depends in significant measure on how effectively they can prepare students for university entrance examinations. This constitutes a pivotal constraint, but so far these schools are popular and competitive as well as financially sound. Second, because these schools intend to offer unique programs like international studies, they require far more resources than traditional schools. Third, innovative schools also require the faculty's intrinsic motivation and competence to construct a unique curriculum and provide a stimulating teaching approach, as well as skilled guidance. To maintain a positive public image, these schools are expected to meet these challenges. The trend suggests that they will grow further if public support and financial backing continue.

In contrast, because the comprehensive program has just started, it is unrealistic to assess its merits and adoption in high school education. Notwithstanding reformers' ardent drives to implement the comprehensive program, it appears that the concept of the program has so far not received widespread national acceptance by prefectural boards of education, which have authority over public high schools. Although this does not suggest that prefectural boards are reluctant to finance schools with comprehensive programs, it may suggest that the concept is not as appealing to public schools as reformers expected. In the absence of surveys and publications regarding public schools' reaction to the comprehensive program, one may speculate that public school teachers have a sense of uncertainty. Administrators and teachers whom I interviewed told me that despite its high cost the program does not effectively address pressures stemming from university entrance exams. Although teachers tend to be conservative, they supported the rationale underlying the program. In any event, its success remains unproven.

Conclusion

Finally, I will comment on a few policy concerns relevant to American high school education. Comparatively speaking, Japanese and American school reforms are now evolving in opposite directions. Japan is slowly diversifying its schools while the United States is trying to promote new national academic standards. Both initiatives are significant in terms of the policy orientations that they aim to enhance, in light of the historical development of highly contrasting school governance in the two culturally different nations. The Japanese governance of education is quite centralized, whereas local control of schools at both district and state levels is dominant in the United States.

What Japanese postwar education reveals is that uniform standards for school programs fail to accommodate diverse student needs and values at a time when such needs and values are increasing in postindustrial society.

Realizing this problem, Japanese reformers began to restructure high schools, an important initiative to expand students' alternatives. Meanwhile, the need for reframing American high schools is evident in light of numerous reform reports issued in the past fifteen years. The Japanese history of education, however, suggests that American initiatives to develop national standards in core subjects taught at high school will have to proceed prudently.

One of the emerging common constraints imposed on both Japanese and American high schools is testing. The national assessment of school achievement has become a priority policy issue in the United States. Its need and legitimacy was extensively debated in the 1980s and further articulated in the America 2000 campaign (Howe, 1991), a policy initiative launched under the Bush administration. The primary purpose of national tests is to measure the extent to which American students have achieved national goals—national standards. Although Japan does not employ such tests, its university entrance examinations serve similar purposes by influencing what is taught at high school.

National tests would augment uniformity in the U.S. high school curriculum. As pointed out earlier, university entrance examinations, which measurably determine what is considered to be relevant in the high school curriculum, have contributed to perpetuating uniformity in instruction at the secondary level in Japan. These tests in both countries seem to have a common effect on high school education: promotion of uniformity rather than diversity.

In Japan, academic standards at the high school level are not so much a critical policy issue as the need for diversity. Japanese reformers are seriously considering how to make high schools an attractive place for students with different abilities and interests. In contrast, standards have become a priority issue in the United States. A critical American policy issue, however, is creating an appropriate balance between standards and diversity, instead of promoting one at the expense of the other.

CHAPTER 6

Disruption and Reconnection: Counseling Young Adolescents in Japanese Schools

GERALD K. LeTENDRE

Young adolescents in the United States face a staggering array of problems that strain the resources of school districts and force teachers and administrators to deal with a wide range of behavioral disorders, family problems, and delinquent activities. At many middle schools across the country, discipline and classroom management have become major issues. In several states, reduced budgets have forced a reduction in key support staff. The resources of most school districts, not just those in economically depressed urban areas, are either insufficient or inadequately organized to support school staff in counseling adolescents.

Since the 1960s, Japanese adolescents have also faced an array of problems. Middle schools (also called junior high schools—three-year schools equivalent to our grades seven through nine) have been associated with high rates of juvenile delinquency. In 1989, 15,215 cases of *ijime* (bullying) were reported in middle schools, as compared to 2,523 in high school (Somucho, 1990, p. 278). In the same year, there were four times the number of incidents of *konai-boryoku* (in-school violence) at middle schools as at high schools (Somucho, 1990, p. 273). Age breakdowns for shoplifting (one of the most common juvenile offenses) show that most offenses are committed by minors ages 13 to 16 (Homusho, 1990, p. 211).

Yet Japanese middle schools are able to promote nearly 98 percent of their students to high school (Ministry of Education, 1992). Ethnographic accounts of Japanese middle schools suggest that teachers have created highly effective strategies for counseling students with problem behavior (Fukuzawa, 1994; LeTendre, 1994a; Yang, 1993). How do Japanese teachers and administrators deal with disruptive students or acts of juvenile delinquency? What are the behavioral signs or signals that teachers worry about? How are schools and districts organized to support the counseling of adolescents?

In this chapter I analyze how Japanese middle-school teachers and administrators respond to adolescent problems, and I highlight the various subsystems—committees, clubs, counseling services—that are at their disposal. Through two cases, I present a general overview of how teachers deal with specific problems, the committees they form, and the external resources they have access to. I isolate key Japanese routines and practices and compare them with reforms documented in U.S. schools.

Sample and Methodology

From 1986 to 1989 I worked as an assistant homeroom teacher in the middle schools and high schools of Kotani City, a city of some 80,000 people located about one and a half hours from Kyoto. During 1991 and 1992, I returned to these schools to conduct fieldwork on guidance processes (in Furukawa and Aratamachi Middle Schools) on a Japan Foundation grant. I used an identical fieldwork strategy (in 1992) to study two U.S. middle schools (Wade and Pleasant Meadows) in the Oak Grove School District near San Jose, California. During the fieldwork, I "shadowed" a total of fifteen teachers in the two largest middle schools in each district and recorded hourlong interviews with teachers, administrators, and local officials (45 in Japan and 25 in the United States). I participated in all teacher meetings, guidance meetings, school planning sessions, and extracurricular trips, and I observed counseling sessions with students.

Some readers may object to a comparative study of Japanese and American schools due to the fact that cultural differences account for Japan's low rates of juvenile behavior and crime. This kind of reasoning ignores evidence of Japan's problems and the specific procedures Japanese use. Rates of violence and crime are comparatively lower in Japan than in the United States (see table 6.1).[1] Yet, despite overall low rates of crime, Japanese youth commit a greater percent of the total number of rapes, burglaries, and robberies than American youth. Although Japan may represent a more ordered society in general, the problems of early teenagers are of great significance to Japanese educators (see Kitao & Kajita, 1984; Kondo & Tsukamoto, 1988; Mochidzuki, 1982; Sengoku, Haruhiko, & Gunei, 1987; Wagatsuma & DeVos, 1984).

During my fieldwork in Japan, I documented several cases in which Japanese teachers counseled students with serious emotional or mental disorders (e.g., anorexia nervosa, obsessive-compulsive behaviors) or students who engaged in acts of delinquency (substance abuse, shoplifting, gang involvement). In the next section, I begin with cases that are typical of the

TABLE 6.1
Comparative Rates of Juvenile Crime: Rates of Felonies for Youth (under 18 years of age), U.S. and Japan, 1988 (per 100,000)

	United States	Japan
Murder	6.5	0.3
Robbery	88.9	2.4
Assault	140.8	52.3
Burglary	1,914.0	1,033.8
Rape	15.1	1.7
Arson	22.7	1.6

Comparison of Crimes Committed by Juveniles (under 18 years of age), as a rough Percentage of All Suspects Charged, 1988

	Japan	United States	Germany	England
Murder	3	11	5	2
Arson	25	42	27	37
Assault	23	22	19	17
Robbery	27	13	8	11
Rape	17	15	7	15
Burglary	57	31	23	24

Source: Homusho, 1990, pp. 406, 459.

more severe behaviors that Japanese teachers handle. These two examples demonstrate both the routine workings of the counseling system and the extraordinary situations to which Japanese teachers must occasionally respond.

Case 1: School Refusal

In early October 1992, Mrs. Sachiko Hayakawa, a third-year homeroom teacher, presented the case of Yamamoto Hiroshi to the third-year grade committee. Hiroshi, like a growing number of Japanese students, has what is termed *tokokyohi* (school refusal syndrome). He has not attended school for several weeks. Mrs. Hayakawa visited Hiroshi at his house and reported on the meeting.

> Every time I tried to talk about school he said, "Stop it, cut it out, I don't want to talk about that." His father died of cancer and his mother thinks he is afraid of dying. I asked her "How about going to a private counselor?" She said she didn't know any, so I suggested Dr. Tsukamachi.
> We were in the entry way for about an hour and forty minutes talking

about his dog, a Siberian husky. His mother bought him a book on animals, but he was only interested in the dogs.

Mrs. Kawaguchi, the third-year grade committee chair, said she would try to get the movie *Benji* for Hiroshi. She asked if some kind of rhythm could be established in Hiroshi's life using the dog, for example, watching it every day at a certain hour. Mrs. Kawaguchi mused that by caring for the dog Hiroshi could create a feeling of *aijyo* (compassion) in his life. Mrs. Ritsukawa, the school counselor, noted that even if he didn't come to school, he still needed to take the practice exams. The teachers brainstormed about materials on dogs that might excite his academic interest, rejecting *101 Dalmatians* as too childish.

After the meeting Mrs. Hayakawa continued to visit the boy's home. She tried to introduce him to other boys in the neighborhood with dogs and asked members of her class to visit Hiroshi. She continued to encourage the mother to see a counselor. Mrs. Ritsukawa also visited the home, bringing along various materials that had a canine theme.

Case 2: Foster Homes and Juvenile Detention Facilities

About two weeks after the grade committee meeting on Hiroshi, members of the school governing committee held a tense meeting with the homeroom teacher and the foster home director of Kaneko Yamanaka. Kaneko was a third-year student with a history of absenteeism, truancy, cigarette smoking, gang involvement, and substance abuse. Kaneko's birth mother refused to deal with her, and the school governing committee negotiated her placement in a private foster home. The situation at the meeting was tense because Kaneko had accused a boy in the foster home of raping her.

The foster home director started by stating that the rooms at the home are monitored by microphones and that tapes of the night in question give no indication of an assault. This evidence was corroborated by the results of a physician's examination, which found no evidence of sexual assault. The director was distraught because the incident had disrupted the group life of the home, and he asked that Kaneko be removed. At no point were the police involved with this incident.

The teachers discussed Kaneko's emotional and mental state. They reiterated that she felt rejected by her mother, who refused to even visit her on weekends. The foster home director speculated that Kaneko may have accused the boy in question because he is very popular and has made much more rapid progress than Kaneko. The teachers noted that their only alternative would be to remit Kaneko to a locked juvenile detention facility—an option that is both long-term and highly stigmatizing in Japanese society. The principal suggested that Kaneko and her mother attend sessions at the prefectural counseling center. Mrs. Kawaguchi and the homeroom teacher volunteered to arrange a meeting. The foster home director agreed to let Kaneko stay while the prefectural counselors attempted to resolve the differences between Kaneko and her mother so that Kaneko could return home.

School Committees and Clubs

As shown in these two examples, Japanese homeroom teachers are supported in their work by a variety of organizations (see figure 6.1). All Japanese teachers are required to participate in several of the committees that oversee the management of the school, implementation of the curriculum, and the counseling of students. Chairs of committees are appointed by the principal in consultation with senior teachers: Both experience and demonstrated ability are required to take on positions of responsibility.

The grade committees, student guidance committee, and school governing committee are central to both day-to-day issues of discipline and in dealing with students who have more severe problems. Each committee meets

FAMILY

CLUBS   NURSE'S
                                                         OFFICE

HOMEROOM TEACHER

GRADE COMMITTEE   COUNSELOR

GUIDANCE DEPARTMENT

SCHOOL GOVERNING COMMITTEE

                                             OTHER
POLICE   MUNICIPAL   SCHOOLS
                     YOUTH CENTER

JUVENILE   REGIONAL   MEDICAL/
DETENTION   COUNSELING   PSYCHIATRIC
FACILITY   AGENCIES   FACILITIES

Figure 6.1. The Organization of Discipline and Guidance in Japanese Schools

weekly, starting with the grade committee early in the week, followed by the student guidance committee and the school governance committee. In this way, pressing problems can be referred to the next level and addressed by senior members of the teaching staff in rapid order. Some of the more urgent matters I heard discussed at the Furukawa school included several runaways, three children abandoned by their parents, children drinking off campus, and plans to curtail gang activity.[2]

The student guidance committee regularly communicates with the guidance committees at the other schools and with the Municipal Youth Center. The chair of the guidance committee meets monthly with the municipal police. In any given week, Mr. Shimada, the chair of Furukawa's guidance committee, will spend a considerable amount of time talking on the telephone with his counterparts at other middle schools. Although problems of misconduct are usually referred back to the homeroom teacher, incidents that occur out of class were occasionally referred directly to Mr. Shimada.

When teachers discover that students have a problem, or if they find that students have not performed certain routines, they can discuss the matter with the students themselves (the most common option) or bring it up with the grade committee. The grade committee functions as the workhorse committee of the school, handling classroom management, curriculum implementation, and school activity planning in addition to addressing student problems. If the problem is more than a minor one, the grade committee chair will take up the matter with the school governing committee.

Few problems require the intervention of the governing committee because teachers can call on other groups and individuals for support. Clubs play a major role in the treatment of student problems. Participation in club activities is quite high in Japanese public middle schools. Because most Japanese educators equate problem behavior with a disruption in routine or a disconnection from peers, teachers often try to use club participation as a way to reintegrate children with their peers and establish a daily regimen. Once children have a sense of "belonging" in a club, teachers reason, they can more easily be brought back into the classroom. Consequently, teachers who act as club advisers play a key role in the overall guidance system of the school. Because teachers have multiple roles in the school, any club adviser will supervise a wide range of students, some of whom may be in his or her own homeroom class. This built-in overlap makes it possible for several teachers to address the needs of a specific child.

The school nurse also has a key role in supporting homeroom teachers. She records the name and complaint of each student who comes to her office and transmits this information to the homeroom teacher and the student guidance department. Furukawa's nurse, Mrs. Hokubei, conducted periodic examinations of students, paying particular attention to the condition of hair and fingernails. Bitten nails, brittle nails, and discoloration all were signs to her that students might be experiencing emotional or mental problems—information that should be transmitted to teachers. Mrs. Hokubei also coordinated a nutrition program for parents. sending out material detailing how mothers should make their child's lunch (see Fujita, 1989, on the role of mothers in lunch preparation).

Finally, a small but growing number of Japanese middle schools have formal "counselor" positions. At all of the Kotani middle schools, this position was filled by a teacher. Only one of these teachers, Mr. Deguchi at neighboring Sakuragawa Middle School, had taken a formal course in counseling techniques. Mr. Deguchi and the other counselors are still required to teach a normal load of classes for a senior teacher (about eighteen per week), and they were not exempted from participating in the various teacher committees that run the school.

The Furukawa counselor, Mrs. Ritsukawa, was a physical education teacher who had taken an interest in working with *mondaiji* (problem children). She set up an office in an unused classroom where she met with students who, like Hiroshi, had school refusal syndrome. Coordinating her efforts with the homeroom teacher, Mrs. Ritsukawa allowed students who felt uncomfortable in the classroom to do their schoolwork and take tests in her office. Once students were established in a routine of coming to school and working in her office, she gradually began to have them spend part of the day in classroom activities. In no case did Mrs. Ritsukawa, or any other counselor I worked with, "pull out" students from a class.

The close links between the nurse's office, clubs, the committees, and the homeroom teacher provide teachers with manifold sources of information and support. Teachers are called upon to be the primary counselors and sources of discipline for their class, but they can enlist a wide range of help within the school on short notice. The committees themselves have access to a wide range of external sources of support and are often the primary actors involved in negotiating external counseling or care for students. Although some teachers may advise parents directly on counseling options, as Mrs. Hayakawa did, most of the referrals are reviewed by the school governing committee.

The Importance of Routines

The guidance "system" of Japanese schools is not limited to the system of committees and clubs. Japanese educators have developed elaborate *seito shido* (student guidance procedures). Student guidance can refer to any of the committees, clubs, and school activities that teachers organize, but on a daily basis, guidance means any of the routine activities that Japanese homeroom teachers supervise: morning meetings, cleaning, end-of-the-day meetings, club practice, uniform inspections, and so on. These routines focus on the prevention and early detection of student problems.

Teachers organize multiple opportunities to observe how children perform a variety of specific tasks. These procedures are critical, teachers explained, because minute aberrations in the performance of these tasks may indicate unexpressed problems. What seemed inconsequential to me were points of great interest to the homeroom teachers. Was Yamamoto's jacket unbuttoned? Did Murata remember to wear his name tag? Did Kaneko clean vigorously? The Kotani teachers believed that the first appearance of a problem is likely to be evinced in such a manner. Consequently, middle-school teachers placed considerable emphasis on observing and maintaining the physical health of the adolescent as well as on proper appearance and deportment.

Mondai kodo (problem behavior) or *nayami* (worries), teachers reported, are first exhibited in some disruption of daily routines. The teachers at Furukawa and Aratamachi saw a straightforward progression from lapses in the proper uniform to association with juvenile delinquents and acts of delinquency. Mrs. Chino, the head of the Furukawa second-year teachers, believed that there was a direct progression from cigarette smoking to substance abuse at the middle-school age. In Sato's (1991) study of motorbike gangs, his informants described the same general sequence of events leading to juvenile delinquency that the Kotani teachers discussed.

Juvenile delinquency in middle school has a distinct pattern throughout Japan (see Sato, 1991; Wagatsuma & DeVos, 1984). Beginning with minor offenses such as missing school or wearing modified uniforms, students move on to smoking at home, truancy, and perhaps petty shoplifting. As students become more distant from school routines, they inevitably get more involved with *hiko shonen* or *furyo* (juvenile delinquents). They exhibit more defiant behaviors—sleeping over at a friend's house (forbidden in Japan) or running away. Involvement with other delinquents usually involves substance abuse: inhaling paint thinner or glue. Clothes and other outward forms of appearance are considered by teachers to express the inner emotional state of the child.[3] Even the use of seemingly innocuous clothing or accessories can be taken very seriously.[4]

Recently some girls have been wearing bracelets—the rope/string kind. This kind of behavior should not be allowed. Please guide (remonstrate) your students not to do this and make inquiries about those who are wearing the bracelets. (Shimoda Hidenori, Homeroom Teacher, Furukawa)

Minor lapses can be treated harshly (see Fukuzawa, 1994, for a powerful description of a schoolwide investigation of a chewing-gum incident). At Furukawa and Aratamachi, a missing name badge and a girl wearing her gym sweats (rather than a skirt) or a bright-blue rather than a dull-blue headband were reason enough for a scolding not only by the homeroom teacher but by the head of the student guidance section.

Uniforms and strict rules of deportment are also used as treatment for minor problems. Teachers at both Furukawa and Aratamachi used attention to proper dress as a main way to guide children. Several times teachers expressed to me the concern that sloppy dress indicated a lassitude of spirit. If students were meticulous in their dress and deportment (loudly greeting each other in the morning, bowing with military precision) the atmosphere of the school would be taut or "tense." This tension was seen as a useful force in maintaining positive behavior. The greatest fear teachers had was that during lapses in the overall school spirit, *furyo/warui nakama* (misbehaving students) would *hiparu* (pull) other students into problematic or illegal behavior.[5]

Teachers also used scolding, *hansei sho* (reflection papers), and occasionally physical punishment as ways to correct minor lapses. These procedures are generally used more in discipline cases and not in instances like that of Hiroshi or Kaneko. For example, students who are disruptive or noisy in class may be asked to kneel at the teacher's desk in the teacher's room, after class, while the teacher lectures them about their behavior. In the case of theft during club activities, Mrs. Kawaguchi made extensive use of reflection papers to correct the offending students (LeTendre, 1994a).

Finally, teachers also facilitate communication between students, parents, and teachers by using a *seikatsu dayori/noto* (lifestyle diary) in which students record their daily activities—including study time and time spent watching television. The teachers review these journals on a daily or weekly basis. These journals, teachers explained, allow students a more private means of communication than having to come to the teacher's desk to discuss some problem. In this way, teachers provide students with a private means of discussing problems before the child exhibits aberrant behavior.

Much of a teacher's time is spent on the preventative aspects of *seito shido*, that is, in attempts to diffuse or interrupt what teachers believe to be the inevitable progression of negative behavior. As Mrs. Kawaguchi explained, teachers try to "catch" or "pick up" students who are falling from the precise routines laid down for them in school. The responsibility of the teacher extends far beyond the bounds of the school. Furukawa teachers patrolled the city at intervals during the summer break to observe local "hot" spots. They discussed how to alert parents to an adult talk-line number, and toyed with the idea of taking down the registration number of bicycles parked outside a local *karaoke* establishment where students might consume alcohol.

Theories of Causality

The daily attention to detail or discipline, the monthly inspections of uni-forms, the teacher patrols of hot spots during vacation, point to the fact that in Japanese schools, teachers are responsible for the moral and legal conduct of the child. Japanese theories of discipline, learning, and counseling differ significantly from Western theories—themes of moral inculcation and the prevention of negative habits are common (LeTendre, 1994b; Rohlen, 1983; Rohlen & LeTendre, 1996). Much of a homeroom teacher's responsibility is directed toward prevention of bad habits or negative attitudes. For most Ja-panese teachers, guiding students in attaining self-knowledge is a crucial part of the curriculum as is instilling such qualities as *gambare* (endurance) or *omoiyari* (thoughtfulness) (Fukuzawa, 1994; LeTendre, 1994b; Singleton, 1989). By establishing solid routines and intimate connections with peers in a variety of settings, teachers try to promote student's self-realization: the realization that each person is deeply embedded in networks of family, school, and work.

In Japanese culture, a child's character must be molded from the earliest ages (see Peak, 1991). In the Confucian philosophy adopted in Japan, char-acter is synthetic, that is, it is man-made and self-perfected (Rohlen, un-dated; Tucker, 1989; Wei-ming, 1985). Teachers believe that students experi-ence an upwelling of energy at puberty—a rapid growth in body and spirit that has tremendous potential. The energy released by puberty opens up pos-sibilities for cultivating or strengthening positive characteristics in the young child, but this requires specific guidance and hard work by parents and teachers.

This cultivation of internal characteristics through external routines is common in a wide variety of Japanese organizational settings, from monas-teries to company-sponsored training sessions to therapy programs (Hori, 1994; Kondo, 1990; Okano, 1993; Reynolds, 1980; Rohlen & LeTendre, in press). Character is built up through group organization and groups activities and supported by individual counseling and reflection. Understanding one-self in a Japanese school means having a strong awareness of one's role and responsibility in a group, whether it be a class preparing for the entrance exams, a team readying for a sports festival, or a choir practicing for the choral contest. Awareness of responsibilities and character development are simultaneous. To promote a child's sense of self is to promote a child's sense of duty, responsibility, and awareness of his or her capacities.

The Limits of Guidance

The diffuse nature of the teacher's role, as well as the linkages between schools, hospitals, and formal counseling centers, open up avenues for Japanese teachers. Japanese guidance functions largely as a preventative mechanism, but there is strong dissent among some teachers and a growing national concern (as evidenced in the media) that schools are too strict. Teachers often complained bitterly to me that the counseling and guidance demands of their jobs were simply overwhelming. Long hours spent in tracing down runaways, visiting student homes, or patrolling local trouble spots take up a great deal of teachers' time and energy. Those with formal training in counseling techniques voiced dissatisfaction with the general lack of psychological understanding among most teachers. Even more pervasive was the worry that the all-encompassing guidance system of middle school prevents children from expressing their individuality and creativity.

The severe treatment of students who violate the dress code sometimes works to acerbate rather than reduce a student's problems. Especially in cases of severe emotional distress, Japanese teachers find themselves forced to quickly abandon any pretense of making students follow school rules. In cases of school refusal, anorexia, and certain obsessive-compulsive problems, traditional Japanese techniques appear ineffective, and teachers generally attempt to reach out and access counseling support from the community while simultaneously trying to reestablish a "human connection" with their students. This task, in the case of Kaneko, became frightfully time-consuming.

The guidance system also places teachers in a position of trying to address emotional problems with which they have little or no experience. Given the dearth of counseling in Japan and the limited psychiatric facilities, for most cases, the system functions well. But in severe cases, like Kaneko's, teachers can be led into areas where they exert incredible amounts of energy with questionable results. Kaneko eventually returned to her birth mother's home, but not until she experienced a series of seizures, was hospitalized, and was treated by a spiritual practitioner called in by the foster home director (LeTendre, 1994b). Clearly, Kaneko's access to trained emotional counseling was limited, and the strain placed on the school governing committee during this time was substantial.

Comparisons with the United States

Putting aside the culturally embedded paradigms of causality and folk "psychology" employed by Japanese teachers, does the Japanese system of committees and its concomitant organizational links with outside school agencies hold any lessons for American schools? In my work with schools in the San Francisco Bay area, I noted several recent middle-school reforms that have key features in common with the Japanese committee system. Some of these techniques have already been widely disseminated via popular reform texts (for example, see Glasser, 1990, and Sizer, 1992).

School Management

Pleasant Meadows Middle School in San Jose created a committee similar to the school governing committee I saw at Furukawa and other Japanese schools. This committee met on a weekly basis and consisted of senior teachers representing multidisciplinary teams, the principal and vice-principal, a representative of the special education program, and the school counselor. The committee met weekly to attend to "burning" issues and to plot out overall directions for the school in terms of curriculum, discipline, and extracurriculars. The committee responded quickly to pressing problems, and administrators were kept well abreast of emerging patterns of disruption. The role of senior teachers in these meetings was extensive, and the principal was able to effectively delegate a substantial amount of planning work to the teachers. Conversely, classroom teachers tended to feel that they had a closer link to the principal. Rather than having to address the principal directly, the teachers could take their problems to their team leaders, who would present the issues before the committee much in the way Japanese teachers do.

Compared to the other schools in the district, teachers at Pleasant Meadows appeared to have greater control over what behaviors were to be designated as problems and what policies were to be implemented concerning these behaviors. The school was also able to coordinate with some local agencies. The school counselor was brought in from a local counseling center. The committee members maintained direct contact with the police and the local Drug Abuse Resistance Education (D.A.R.E.) program rather than being forced to "go through the principal." At the time I left, the district was submitting a proposal that would have funded elementary schools to coordinate many of the available social services.

Classroom Management

A second feature that helped to alleviate the tide of discipline referrals flooding the school office was the use of specific teaching strategies such as cooperative group work. The theoretical model for certain cooperative group work programs (see Cohen, 1994) is similar to Japanese models in several key regards:

• There is an emphasis on group roles and norms.
• The teacher consciously works with the student's social hierarchy.
• Peer expectations are used to shape behavior.
• Emphasis is put on connecting each individual to the group process and assuring that each child is able to participate in the group process.
• Classrooms where cooperative group work was successfully implemented tended to have lower levels of disruption.

Peers and Teachers Counseling

Finally, the use of peer counseling measures is growing in the Oak Grove district. Eighth graders at some middle schools received training in peer counseling/conflict resolution techniques. Under the supervision of the school counselor or administration, students were allowed to choose to meet with peers to discuss problems. The peer counselors also functioned to keep the staff abreast of the latest developments—fights, conflicts, depression—in the student body. These measures strongly resemble the emphasis on group participation, student hierarchy, and student committees, which also play a role in Japanese student guidance (see Fukuzawa, 1994; LeTendre, 1994a).

Conclusion

The Japanese system provides clear warnings. Caution must be taken not to burden already overworked teachers with new responsibilities. An emphasis on external order (note that some California schools are now adopting uniforms) can rapidly deteriorate into a repressive atmosphere. For Japanese senior teachers and administrators, the system demands that they intervene early in supporting younger or inexperienced teachers, identify problems that are beyond the scope of the staff's capabilities, and move quickly to engage outside agencies that can provide services students need.

Organizing American schools along a Japanese committee system may not be the answer to our problems, but certain key features of the system may indeed be of benefit, *if they are adopted as part of a system of reforms.*

Any change in the structure of counseling and discipline must provide teachers with a system of adequate support structures that will allow them to take on new roles. Districts or schools must:

- Engage senior teachers in leadership positions
- Organize regular contacts with external agencies
- Provide teachers with instances where they can closely monitor behavior
- Increase communication between students, teachers, parents, and administrators
- Organize and engage students in resolving their own conflicts.

If such systemic reform can be implemented, then U.S. teachers and administrators will have access to strategies that approximate the most effective Japanese organizational techniques.

Human Capital Formation and School Expansion in Asia: Does a Unique Regional Model Exist?

DAVID P. BAKER and
DONALD B. HOLSINGER

The most recent education crisis in the United States was precipitated by a sense of falling behind emerging national economic powers like Japan and Germany. As is often the case, a substantial portion of the blame for our international economic situation was placed at the doorstep of the formal American education system. The concern is that our schools are producing future workers who will not have the skills or knowledge to compete internationally in a global economy. At the same time, a series of international comparisons of school achievement in mathematics and science, dramatically demonstrating the inferior position of American students relative to students in other countries, further defined our feeling of educational inferiority (e.g., Robitaille and Garden, 1989; Postlethwaite & Wiley, 1992; Lapointe, Mead, & Phillips, 1989). Moreover, since in most of these studies Japanese students outperformed all others, the concern over economic competition and educational productivity were joined together and a logic quickly emerged for comparing American and Japanese schooling. Over time this turned to a more general comparison of American schooling with Asian schooling (e.g., Stevenson & Stigler, 1992). Just as the Sputnik crisis and the Cold War of the 1960s pushed comparisons to Soviet education, a new world economic order in the 1980s and 1990s hypothesizes that Asian

The authors would like to thank Thomas Smith, Che Fu Lee, William Cummings, and York Bradshaw for helpful comments and Reed Garfield and John Crist for assistance in data compilation.

During the preparation of this chapter, Baker was the 1992–94 AERA senior fellow at the National Center for Education Statistics, U.S. Dept. of Education, funded by NSF grant #RED-9255347. The opinions here reflect those solely of the authors and do not reflect official policy of any of the sponsoring agencies.

education is exemplary and offers Western countries a model for improving educational productivity.

Thus American education policymakers are deluged with material about the high-performing Asian system, even though usually Japan and, to a lesser degree, South Korea stand in for all of Asia in these cases. Almost all of the comparison has centered on what can be copied from Asian education to improve student achievement, usually in mathematics and science.

This relatively narrow objective—organizational tinkering to increase achievement gains among U.S. students—has overlooked a second major interest in Asian education held by a different set of Western policymakers. Within the economic development literature there has been a preoccupation with the Asian model of human capital development, which of course is closely tied to Asian schooling (e.g., World Bank [WB], 1993; Appelbaum & Henderson, 1992). Again driven by comparisons with some Asian countries' economic development, the idea has arisen that the development of education in Asian countries offers a model for other developing nations.

For U.S. policymakers who may have been chiefly aware of the achievement comparisons with Asian education, this chapter serves as an introduction to a broader view of educational development in Asia and what this may mean for the U.S. international role in fostering economic development through education. We investigate the degree to which Asian educational development, specifically the development of secondary schools in developing Asian countries, represents a cohesive regional model that could be used in other parts of the world. This is a timely subject as the U.S. government and its leading science establishment agencies (i.e., the National Science Foundation, the National Research Council) are increasingly engaged in international education comparisons (OECD, 1994; Griffith, Owen, & Baker, 1994), the use of cross-national studies for American educational policy (National Academy of Science, 1993), and interested in human capital development of its trading partners.

Human Capital and Asian Development

Much credit for the recent and highly acclaimed economic success of some Asian countries is given to their production of human capital through rapid expansion of schooling (e.g., WB, 1993; Johnson, 1982). Supplying high-quality primary and secondary education to large proportions of national populations over the past several decades is one of the key ingredients for a highly competitive labor force in these countries. Japan, the Republic of Korea, Singapore, and Hong Kong—the more economically developed

Asian nations—have seemingly taken an older model of national development through education and applied it more vigorously than ever before. For example, Japan, a country noted for both for its early educational development and economic successes, expanded mass (i.e., nonelite) education shortly after World War II to near universal primary enrollments and also had high secondary enrollments (over 80 percent) by the 1960s. This expansion of schooling did not preclude comparatively high levels of achievement among students and generally standard curricula (Baker, 1993; Tan & Mingat, 1992; Stevenson & Stigler, 1992). Human capital needed for the "East Asian economic miracle" has come from strategic national policies aimed at high quality universal schooling up through the secondary level.

Some have suggested that there is a unique, singularly identifiable and effective Asian human resource approach (Cummings, 1995). Of those who see Asian educational development in this way, a small set consider this approach as one forged out of a common religiocultural Confucian tradition in political action (Berger & Hsia, 1988) while the rest see it as a modern reaction to threatening Western economic and political dominance (Black et al., 1975; Moulder, 1977; Cummings, 1995). Stripped of its refinements, the basic "Asian education as unique" argument states that Asia, as a post–World War II developmental laggard fearful of Western dominance, rejected the traditionally Western approach to human capital and Western school development, and instead constructed its own approach and then eventually beat the West at its own game.[1]

This scenario goes on to point out that developed Asian countries with the strongest market economies followed a *uniquely Asian educational trend* in an accelerated fashion. Rapid economic transformation from agriculture to service and industry has been paired with the rapid accumulation of a competitive labor force, and nowhere has this been celebrated more than in the discussion of successful Asian nations. In fact, so much has been made recently about the role of education in Asian economic and social development that many Western educational professionals may have come to assume that there is a successful and reproducible regionwide "Asian model" of human capital production, and that the school expansion effect behind the East Asian miracle is working its way through the region.

But is this so? Is there really a unique and uniform Asian model of rapid expansion of high-quality primary *and* secondary schooling? Have the so-called "Tiger Cubs" (e.g., Malaysia, Thailand, Indonesia) followed the lead of "Asian Tigers" (e.g., Hong Kong, Singapore, Taiwan, and South Korea), so loudly acclaimed for their aggressive economic growth, into a regionwide trend in the production of human capital through rapid school expansion? Asian regional trends are frequently confounded by regional diversity. A broad view of Asia might include such different countries as Pakistan, Nepal, and India or China, South Korea, and Japan, representing a wide variety of cultures, demographies, economic health, and political structures. Is it possible, then, that a more or less uniform Asian model of economic development resulting in expanded national education systems producing large stocks of human capital (e.g., WB, 1993) really exists?

In contrast to the position of "Asian as unique," we explore the alternative—namely, that highly successful Asian countries have followed a century-long trend in broadening access to schooling starting mostly among Western nations with the establishment of large national systems of primary education, followed soon in time by expanding secondary education. For example, by 1960 most West European and North American countries had close to universal primary education, and secondary education for over one-half of all secondary school-aged youth. The next three decades saw secondary schooling expand for all youth and the beginnings of large tertiary systems. Educating national populations on this scale has had considerable effects on developed nations' economic output (Walters & Rubinson, 1983), as well as social and political benefits (McMahon, 1994).

Since the middle of this century, developing nations also invested heavily in educational expansion, following the similar route already taken by developed countries. Starting in the 1960s education observers identified a worldwide explosion of enrollment rates and the systematic development of state-supported, formal educational systems. Some researchers went so far as to call this a "world revolution" in national educational supply (Meyer et al., 1977). Fueled by the proliferation of new nations emerging from the declining colonial political order, many developing nations began educational expansion just as the more developed countries had done some decades before.

This paper examines this position in two steps. First is a regional comparison between the developing Asian countries and other developing countries in the expansion (or lack of it) of secondary education. We focus on secondary education because primary education has been expanding in most of the region for some time and the human resource challenge created by West European and North American economies has now shifted to job entry skill levels corresponding to secondary and even tertiary level schooling. This regional analysis is followed by a short case study of contrasting national policies towards secondary education in two high growth, developing Asian countries—Thailand and Malaysia—to see if they used national educational development strategies similar to those employed earlier by the more industrially advanced nations in the region.

Regional Comparison of Secondary School Expansion

The regional analyses here have two purposes. First, we see if the expansion of secondary education in developing Asian countries as a group has outpaced expansion in other developing countries. In other words, have the developing Asian nations followed the trends set by more developed and economically successful Asian nations in widening access to the secondary sector? Second, we examine the consistency of any identifiable "Asian regional" patterns of secondary school expansion across the entire spectrum of developing Asian countries.

We analyze educational data for developing countries from standard UNESCO sources and from the World Bank's data archive—Bank Economic and Social Database.[2] Our basic indicator of educational coverage and individual access to schooling is the enrollment rate, which is the number of students in the subsectors of primary or secondary schooling divided by the corresponding total number of school-aged children in the population.[3] A growing enrollment rate over time for a particular school subsector indicates a tendency toward mass education and away from elite education. Enrollment rates are considered a critical proxy for human capital growth and indeed participation in formal schooling is substantively central to human capital development for any modern population (Becker, 1975; Williamson, 1993).

We focus on the period 1960 to 1990, which witnessed a crucial transition from near universal primary coverage to accelerated secondary-school growth among many developing nations. For example, the average enrollment rate at the secondary level for developing countries was about 10 percent in 1960 but by 1990 it had grown to just over 33 percent (Baker, 1994).

Analyses of the history of educational sector growth in developed countries show that access to schooling tends to take on a logistic growth pattern—slow and stable growth from lower enrollment levels until about 20 to 30 percent enrollment ratios at which point growth often accelerates until a slowing at very high rates of over 90 percent enrolled (Trow, 1961; Carroll, 1981).

Over the period from 1960 to 1990, secondary education expansion in fully developed Asian countries increased to enrollment ranges associated with accelerated economic growth (i.e., from about 30 to 80 percent enrollment ratios). Having mostly completed a universal primary system, these countries moved to construct mass secondary systems. As figure 7.1 shows the growth rate among selected developed countries in secondary enrollments was steep—over a one hundred percent increase in thirty years.[4] In part because of lower overall educational development, developing countries

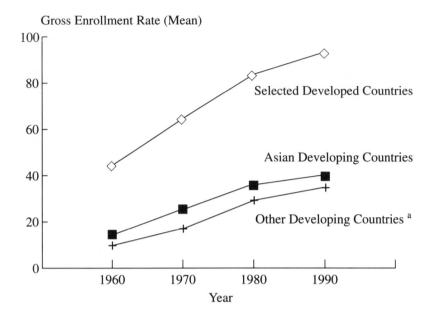

Figure 7.1. Growth in Secondary Enrollment Rates, 1960–1990

'Eastern Europe excluded.

started this period at a much lower rate of secondary education enrollments. Their efforts toward education supply were largely focused on primary education or in some cases on elite tertiary education.

Contrast this to the growth of secondary schooling in developing Asian countries. Compared to other developing nations, Asia began the period with higher secondary school enrollment rates and maintained these throughout. These same developing Asian countries, however, do not show a substantially different education growth rate from other developing countries; both groups, on average, doubled their enrollment rate. Asian countries *did not* produce higher growth rates of expansion than all other developing countries.

When we break down secondary expansion in developing countries, region by region, the Asian picture becomes more complicated. Figure 7.2 displays both primary and secondary 1990 enrollment rates for the five regions of the world containing most of the developing nations. The Asian countries are behind all other regions except for the large Sub-Saharan African region. Note that both in terms of average primary and secondary rates,

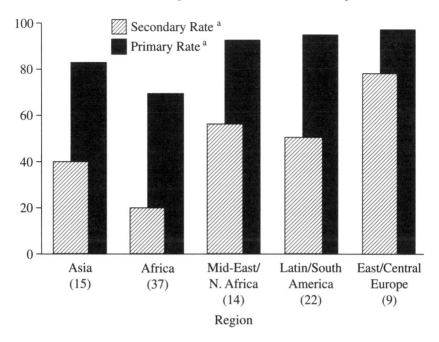

Figure 7.2. Primary and Secondary Education Enrollment Rates, 1990, Developing Countries by Region

developing Asian countries are behind countries in the Mideast and North Africa as well as in Latin America. Stated differently, other than for Sub-Saharan Africa, the developing Asian countries as a group have less secondary education coverage than may often be assumed.

In part this is due to the high degree of variation among developing Asian countries. Compared to the four regions (excluding Sub-Saharan Africa), developing Asia has the largest variation in secondary enrollment rates in 1990.[5] For example, by 1980 countries such as Afghanistan, Bangladesh, Laos, and Pakistan had secondary enrollment rates at or below 20 percent of the age-cohort and in these countries secondary education was still relatively elite. At the same time countries such as China,[6] India, Malaysia, and the Philippines were enrolling 35 percent or more in secondary school. By 1990 the Republic of Korea, China, Malaysia, and the Philippines had secondary school systems enrolling one-half of all age-eligible youth; the same enrollment level from which rates took-off among developed countries in the 1960s.

In large part what is happening in the Asian region is also happening worldwide among all developing nations. Economic development is increasingly associated with high coverage of secondary schooling. The more economically successful developing nations have greatly expanded primary *and* secondary education coverage during this period, while the poorer nations have either expanded only the primary sector or only modestly opened up access to secondary schooling. The secondary enrollment rate difference between wealthier and poorer developing countries across all regions in 1960 was only about ten percentage points, but by 1990 this difference has grown to forty percentage points. The same is true for Asia, where the difference in 1960 secondary enrollment rates between the poorer and wealthier countries was only four percentage points and by the end of the period the difference has grown to about ten percentage points.

Additionally most of the growth in secondary enrollment rates worldwide among developing nations over this period has been in nations within the middle of the economic development spectrum (Baker, 1994).[7] For example, just over one-half of the total developing-world growth in secondary-school enrollment from 1960 to 1990 occurred in middle-level developing nations, while the wealthiest and poorest of developing nations each accounted for only a fourth of the growth. Among developing Asian nations, only a fourth of the countries are in the middle to upper level of economic development. The large number of poorer countries also explains why Asia has lower enrollments relative to most other regions. Thus while some Asian nations have expanded access to secondary school during this critical period, others have done so only modestly.

An informative way to examine the growth of an educational subsector is to determine the degree to which the development of the prior subsector influences its growth. In other words, the actual eligible population for secondary school attendance are those students enrolled in the primary subsector.[8] But this is more than just a better identification of the eligible population. Organizationally a major outcome of an expanding educational system is to link subsector enrollments together. Thus an expanding primary system will eventually create some increase in secondary enrollments and so forth. When large proportions of primary finishers are not attending secondary school, it is either because elite schooling is maintained in the upper subsector (by national policy or otherwise) or there is an inefficiency in the supply of access to the upper sector because of a lack of resources or policy mitigating against secondary expansion.

Among all developing countries there has been a great effort to expand primary enrollments and this has had some success (Lockheed & Verspoor, 1991). For example, the average rate for primary-aged children in 1970 was 77 percent and this has grown to 88 percent by 1990 (Baker 1994). And the difference between primary and secondary enrollment rates (i.e., small differences means a more efficient match between subsectors) has been decreasing slowly among all developing countries over this period.

The same is true for developing Asian countries. Most countries in the region have continued to expand primary education and the difference between primary and secondary enrollments has been declining slowly. For example, in 1970 the average developing Asian primary subsector enrollment rate was 54 percentage points higher than the secondary rate but this difference declined to 47 percentage points by 1990.

Another way to examine the relationship between subsectors is to model the secondary enrollment rate as a function of earlier primary enrollment rate. We add to such a subsector model: (1) the size of the age-eligible population (10 to 19 year-old, five years prior), (2) the economic level of the country, and (3) a variable modeling Asia as a region versus all other developing countries. We examine secondary enrollment rates in the middle of the period (1975) and at the end (1990). Table 7.1 displays the ordinary least squares estimates of these models.

TABLE 7.1

Effects of Primary Schooling Development, Country Income, Age-Eligible Population on Secondary Enrollment Rates, Developing Asian Countries versus Other Developing Countries (Dependent Variable: Secondary Enrollment Rate)

Equation	1975		1990	
	A	B	C	D
Main Effects				
Primary Enrollment Rate, Lagged 5 Years	.41**	.37**	.43**	.49**
Age-Eligible Population, Lagged 5 Years	8.2^{-08}	-2.1^{-06}	1.4^{-07}	1.3^{-06}
Income Level	6.2**	7.5**	16.1**	15.3**
Asia Region	7.6*	-6.9	7.4	1.4
Interaction Effects (Asian Developing Countries)				
Primary Enrollment Rate, Lagged 5 Years	–	.36**	–	-.17
Age-Eligible Population, Lagged 5 Years	–	1.9^{-06}	–	1.7^{-06}
Income Level	–	-8.4	–	11.3
Constant	-14.8**	-13.4**	-27.3**	-26.4**
R^2	.60	.63	.66	.67
N	78	78	73	73

*Coefficient 1.5-times it standard error.
**Coefficient 2-times it standard error.

Equations A and C show just the main effects of the variables described above for 1975 and 1990 respectively. At both the middle and end of this time period the earlier rate of primary enrollment significantly predicts the level of secondary school enrollment rate. For every additional percentage point in the primary rate, the secondary rate increases by four tenths of a point in 1975 with some increase by 1990. This kind of an intensifying connection between subsectors is indicative of an expanding educational system.

As would be expected from the discussion above, the wealthier countries expand secondary enrollments faster than do poorer nations, regardless of the primary enrollment level, and this effect greatly increases by 1990.

One of the main insights about the human capital success of the already developed Asian countries is the notion of closely linking secondary expansion with primary expansion. But how true is this of developing Asian countries and has any such effect persisted over this period?

To examine this we estimated an interaction model which shows the additional effect of being an Asian developing country on each of the variables in the main effects models in 1975 and 1990 (equations B and D, respectively). First note that there is an "Asian effect" in 1975 and not one in 1990 and this is reflected in the lack of interaction effects in 1990 (equation D). In 1975 (equation B) however, there was an important effect, namely that Asian countries capitalized more on prior primary enrollments than did other developing nations. To see this effect more clearly we can rewrite equation B separately for Asian and other developing countries 1975 as follows:[9]

$$Y' \text{ (Asian)} = .73(X_1) - 2.0^{-7}(X_2) - .09(X_3) - 20.3$$
$$Y' \text{ (Other)} = .41(X_1) - 8.2^{-8}(X_2) + 6.2(X_3) - 14.8$$

Where Y' = 1975 secondary enrollment rate; X_1 = 1970 primary enrollment rate; X_2 = 1970 age-eligible population; X_3 = income level.

The effect of primary enrollment rates on developing Asian countries' secondary enrollment rates is almost double that of other developing countries. Further, the economic level of Asian countries has little effect on secondary enrollments, but the economic level has considerable effect on enrollments in other developing nations.

One should be cautious in assuming that the 1975 effects represent a long-term Asian effect. First, as shown in table 7.1, the 1975 Asian "primary-rate effect" vanishes by 1990; Asian countries by this point are not expanding access to secondary school for primary-school finishers more than other developing nations. Further, the effects described above are dominated by the superior Asian expansion of secondary enrollments compared to Sub-Saharan Africa. When other regions are compared directly to Asia, the effects above diminish (analysis not reported here).

To illustrate the variation in the size of the 1975 "Asian effect" across developing Asian countries, we plot actual secondary enrollment rates against those predicted from equation B for the developing Asian countries. In figure 7.3 those countries on or near the diagonal line are expanding enrollments at a rate similar to the average developing nation given various levels of primary enrollments and economic development (the two significant main effects).

Countries above the diagonal have lower secondary enrollments than would be predicted from their inputs. For example, in 1975 countries such as Thailand, Indonesia, India, and China had much lower secondary rates than would be predicted from their prior primary rate, and income level, although the latter two did significantly increase access to secondary schooling over the next fifteen years.

Countries below the line such as Malaysia and South Korea had secondary education coverage beyond what would be predicted from their inputs. The two countries, whose educational development policies we examine be-

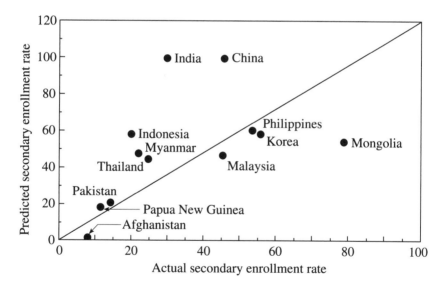

Figure 7.3. Plot of Actual and Predicted Secondary Enrollment Rates for Developing Asian Countries, 1975

Note: Predicted values calculated from table 7.1, equation B. See text for explanation.

low in the short case studies, Malaysia and Thailand, show marked contrasts
in their policies concerning secondary education expansion in 1975 that continues through until the current period.

Two Cases Studies of Contrasting Educational Policy

Thailand: Supremacy of Primary Schooling

Thailand has undergone a major social and economic transformation since
1960. Its economy has moved from reliance on agricultural exports and
placed it in the company of some of the high-growth Asian nations (WB,
1993). It has been grouped with eight "high-performing Asian economies"
with a thirty-year gross domestic product (GDP) growth exceeding the average growth for developing countries, at its overall level of development
(WB, 1993). It has a sizable work force of about 33 million, a large pool of
potential human resources for future economic growth.

Thailand's economic miracle, however, has been less complete than
other Asian countries, accompanied by indications of some underlying problems which may hamper its future economic growth. At the core of these
problems is a serious mismatch between the economy's requirement for
skilled workers in newly developed manufacturing and service jobs and the
government's slowness in providing access to secondary (and tertiary) education for large parts of the future labor force. A failure to address this
human capital problem risks exacerbating short-term inflation and stalling
long-term economic growth.

One cause behind Thailand's labor market problem is its approach to
education development over the past three decades. Thai policy has been to
concentrate state resources on complete coverage at the primary level before
any widespread secondary schooling was supplied. This policy has had measurable effect, as primary enrollment rates reached over 80 percent by 1970.
Although relatively successful, this drive toward universal primary schooling, until recently, deflected interest away from secondary education, particularly in rural areas. Metropolitan Bangkok was favored with ample places at
the lower and upper secondary levels, but the national labor force, with its
exceptionally high levels of agricultural employment, presented a different
picture. Transition rates from primary to lower secondary were low among
rural Thais and there was a shortage of school places beyond the primary
level.

While government policy to include the three lower secondary grades in
an eight-year initial level has already dramatically improved coverage beyond the traditional primary grades, transition to upper secondary is still low

and coverage at the upper secondary level lags well behind its Asian neighbors. For example, the 1990 secondary enrollment rate was only just over 30 percent, which is below the average for the full Asian region, and enrollments grew at a relatively slow rate during this period.

A consequence of this uneven sector development has been the continuation of regional inequality in educational opportunity within the country. As is typical of nonuniversal educational systems in other developing nations, the access to better and more education is unevenly distributed in Thailand. High-quality post-primary education is more readily available in Bangkok, with a number of private and quality public schools serving the elite in the capital city. The effect of this uneven distribution on quality is clear. Although Thai education shows signs of reasonable effectiveness, this is quite likely to be limited to schooling in Bangkok (Chantavanich & Fry, 1985). For example, single-sex schooling for Thai female students is very effective in terms of achievement, but this kind of schooling is almost completely for Bangkok students from the middle-class and above (Baker, Riordan, & Schaub, forthcoming; Jimenez & Lockheed, 1989).[10]

The economic consequences of slower growth in secondary schooling and uneven access to educational opportunity are of concern to the long range development of Thailand. For example, there is a serious shortage of skilled workers such as engineers, specialists in manufacturing, technicians, healthcare workers, and analysts, thus competition for the smaller finite pool of skilled workers is bidding up wages and will add to inflationary pressures. "Poaching" of workers from one Thai firm by another is becoming an acute problem, especially in the services sector. In recent years, the Thai economy has shifted to a "full employment" one without surplus labor, but the unemployment rate is about 3 percent, although several hundred thousand foreign workers (mainly illegal immigrants from Burma and elsewhere) are currently employed in the economy.

The large proportion of the labor force in agricultural employment has contributed to underemphasis on secondary and higher education outside the capital and a few other large urban centers. Sixty percent of the Thai population is still employed in agriculture although this sector produces only about 12 percent of the GDP. Conversely, industry, which contributes around 30 percent of the GDP, employs a disproportional small share of the work force. A limit on industrialization may be the undereducation of the Thai labor force. Thai industries, both domestic and foreign firms, have been reluctant to decentralize operations to outside of Bangkok, in large measure because of a lack of sufficiently well-educated workers.

The current situation has caused some increase in income inequality that parallels the unequal distribution of educational opportunities. As with education, income is sharply skewed in favor of Bangkok with its larger share of manufacturing and service jobs. Even allowing for the fact that many Thais registered in rural areas, in fact, work in urban areas, the lower opportunities in agriculture still dominate the rural economy.

These patterns do not hold well for future economic development and the Thai state has taken steps to remedy some of the situation. Its most recent focus is on expanding secondary education. One of the driving forces behind the Thai government's prior, less expansive, educational policy was a lack of overall financial resources. In a sense, the central state could only afford primary education, and a limited version at that. This is beginning to change with higher tax revenues and declining government debt. Due to a more favorable budgetary position, the fiscal 1994/95 budget presented in July, announces an increase in financial resources devoted to improving secondary education.

In addition to improving quality, there have been several recent attempts to expand the secondary sector, including distance education and night schools. Part of the problem faced here is organizational since the expanded primary system faces sharp declines in the Thai birth rate and thus a reduction in potential entrants. The challenge has been to shift financial resources and teaching personnel from primary to secondary schools. One of the obstacles to the reorganization has been the division of primary and secondary which reside administratively in different parts of the same ministry. In centrally controlled systems, such a division can effectively block needed changes in resource allocation. Relatively short-term problems such as physical infrastructure deficiencies and a lack of adequate numbers of primary teachers with subject-matter competence at higher levels are being addressed with the assistance of the international donor community.

Malaysia: Nation-Building and Managed Sector Development

A multi-ethnic, multicultural country of 18 million, Malaysia and its history of schooling clearly demonstrates a common postcolonial dynamic between modern nation-state building, economic development, and educational expansion. Faced with ethnic diversity and social inequality, the new Malaysian state turned in part to mass schooling to promote national unity and in so doing explicitly developed a large secondary education sector along with a universal primary sector. This central policy of dual primary and secondary educational development has yielded high rates of enrollment; and what was in the earlier period a nation-building necessity has turned into a national human capital advantage. The Malaysia pattern tightly parallels the Western, and now worldwide, pattern of national-state building and education expansion (Meyer et al., 1977).

The end of a British colonial regime left Malaysia a new country made up of three main ethnic-language groups: indigenous Bumiputera (currently at 61% of total population), Chinese (28%), and Indian (8%). From its independence in 1957, the Malaysian state has had to address the uneven distribution of economic and educational opportunity across ethnic groups. Early in its history there were violent ethnic riots and the nation's founding politics were bound up in ethnic conflict. The colonial period had also left an elite system of education with access to secondary education controlled by an examination (given in English) and leading to the civil service or colonial administration. Secondary schooling was in English and for a small minority of students; the so-called vernacular school, taught in the indigenous language of Bahasa Malaysia, was for primary education only. The route to universal education was intertwined with the politics of language of instruction.

The early Malaysian state linked primary and secondary education together first by having automatic promotion through nine years of schooling and then in 1964 eliminating the secondary entrance examination (MSSEE) and lastly by establishing Bahasa Malaysia as the main medium of secondary instruction. This has the effect of pushing expansion of both primary and secondary education. What had been a moderately sized primary sector filtering down to a relatively small secondary sector prior to independence, became in a decade a system with almost universal primary coverage (90% in 1970) and expanding secondary coverage.

The subsequent strategy to expand secondary education even further has been twofold. First, the main part of the secondary sector was divided into two levels: a three year lower secondary, which is now part of basic compulsory schooling, and two years of upper secondary. Second, since two types of primary schools were maintained, again to deal with language diversity, one being taught in Bahasa Malaysia and the other in Chinese or Tamil, an additional transition year (the "Removal Class") of primary schooling was added for students from the latter primary schools to learn Bahasa to participate in secondary schooling and to know the official national language.

These mechanisms have had the effect of expanding lower secondary enrollments rates from about 50 percent in 1970 to over 80 percent by the 1990s. And upper secondary, entrance to which is controlled by performance and curricular selection in lower secondary school, has also expanded from 20 percent in 1970 to about 50 percent in the 1990s (Zainol, 1994). Malaysia's gross enrollment rate for fourteen to nineteen year-olds was about 55 percent in 1990 (Baker, 1994). In addition to these enrollment figures, the explicit policy of dual sector development is evident in the way financial resources are used to develop secondary schooling versus primary schooling.

In the later 1970s the ratio of funds used for educational development of secondary schooling to primary schooling was about one and a half and has grown to over double by 1990, all while the overall pool of educational development funds has been expanding.

An important consequence of these educational policies has been a labor force which has increased its average amount of schooling just as the Malaysia economy has undergone substantial structural changes. For example, in 1980 18 percent of Malaysian workers had no formal schooling and 15 percent had three to four years of secondary schooling. By 1990 only 6 percent had no formal schooling and almost a fourth had the standard secondary school training (Zainol, 1994). This comes precisely at a time when manufacturing and service sectors overtook agriculture in the make-up of the Malaysia economy, with the former now contributing over 60 percent to the country's GDP. There has also been an improvement in the per capita distribution of income with less overall inequality.

Malaysia has been identified as one of the high performance Asian economies that have made up the Asian development miracle. Its policies toward educational expansion over the past thirty years yielded a pattern of education development that is line with the assumed Asian model of human capital production: initial high primary expansion followed by a quickly expanding secondary sector. What is of additional interest here (and with some irony) is that much of this expansive policy was initially more the result of nation-building and ethnic conflict than a rational long-term development plan.

Conclusion

What has this regional analysis of thirty years of secondary school enrollments found? First, contrary to what Western educational professionals may have come to accept as the image of Asian production of human capital, developing Asian countries are not leaders in the developing world in terms of expanding enrollment rates in secondary schooling. But neither is secondary education expansion as low in this region as it might be, given that many countries in this region are less developed. So, for example, Asian countries have done better in educational development compared to Sub-Saharan nations, and some of the countries with the largest populations in the world found in this region have made considerable strides in opening access to secondary education.[11] But compared to the large growth in secondary education in Latin America and the Middle East, the average Asian country is still behind.

Second there is a fair amount of intraregional diversity in educational expansion. Contrary to what others have recently argued (e.g., Cummings, 1995), there does not appear to much that is truly unique here in terms of educational development. Some developing Asian countries have provided large access to secondary school over the past thirty years, while others have had more modest growth. The region as a whole does not appear to have produced significant accelerated growth of a secondary-level educated labor force. In part, this is due to the large and generally successful effort toward primary education in this region, which was the recipe for the now developed Asian countries of the "Asian miracle" image. But the slower growth in secondary enrollments for some Asian developing countries may place them behind in the human capital race of the 1990s.

Finally, there is some evidence that Asian countries have linked the primary and secondary sectors more intensely, so that expansion of the primary sector more efficiently leads to expansion of secondary enrollments. Yet there is some counter-evidence to suggest that this was a short-lived trend among these countries, as an earlier "Asian effect" on secondary enrollments vanishes by 1990.

The brief descriptions of education expansion strategies and policies in two Asian countries which have had some recent economic success, show how contrasting national situations lead to different patterns of secondary education expansion. The extreme emphasis of Thailand on primary schooling, which was the old recipe for economic success, has left it with a labor force that is "educationally behind" its anticipated industrial transformation. The concern over ethnic integration, politics of language and nation-state building has led Malaysia to develop secondary education more fully, along the lines of more developed countries and a very Western logic. The Malaysia national policy may situate this labor force in a better position than the Thai labor force for the next round of economic development.

These kinds of contrasting national policies show how the Asian region has generated a considerable amount of diversity in terms of educational development. It is perhaps best not to consider the existence of one clear and uniform "Asian model" of educational expansion. Although it is true that parts of Asia have used a rapidly expanding educational system to produce a well-trained labor force for industrialization, it is not true that this is a regionwide trend. It may be best to think of Asian education development as representing both the fastest, as well some of the more stagnated, growth in the developing world today.

The Private Sector

CHAPTER 8

Private Education in Eastern Asia

WILLIAM K. CUMMINGS

Central government control looms large in the image of Asian education. For example, accounts of Japanese education often focus on the monolithic Ministry of Education which occupies a pentagon-shaped building in the heart of the all-powerful Kasumgaseki District; the ministry supposedly steers with a strong hand dictating the course of study for all school levels, determining requirements for teacher qualifications and school facilities, inspecting school processes, and otherwise shaping the educational process from one end of the country to the other. *Yet within the framework of this centrally controlled system, there is a vigorous private sector, whose share has, if anything, expanded in recent decades.* Japan's private sector provides over half the places in upper secondary education and nearly 80 percent of the places in tertiary education.

A similar pattern can be found in several of the more dynamic Asian nations, nations that have carved out major niches in the international marketplace and which are striving for more open and participatory institutions. Specifically in Taiwan, Korea, Indonesia, and the Philippines at least 75 percent of the preschool enrollees and at least 50 percent of tertiary-level enrollees are in private institutions. In other Asian countries the private sector tends to be somewhat smaller, but in several cases has experienced rapid growth during the past decade—Malaysia, Thailand, and China are notable.[1]

Private education takes many forms in different parts of the world. In some countries, it serves elites and is of exceptionally high quality, whereas in others it is a low-quality moderate-cost option for those who cannot get into the elite public sector. The public role in private education also varies from completely hands-off to extensive control and subsidy. What is the situation in Asia, and more specifically Eastern Asia? This chapter illustrates the exceptional prevalence in Eastern Asia of private education that complements a strong public sector focusing on manpower and elite education priorities. Why is it the case that Asia is hospitable to private education? What might American educators learn from Eastern Asia's experience with private education? These are the questions addressed in this chapter.

is Education?

Most of the current international discourse on education focuses on formal education, making distinctions between preschool, primary, secondary, and tertiary. To gain a better sense of the prevalence of the private portion of formal education, it is helpful to divide secondary education into the lower and upper levels as most governments guarantee places in the former but many do not for the latter. Also it is helpful to make distinctions at the tertiary level. In most societies, private schools are more common in the nondegree and/or proprietary sectors.

From an Eastern Asian perspective, it is also important to look beyond formal education to what might best be called informal education. In many Eastern Asian educational systems, the curriculum outlines stringent demands which cannot be fully realized in the formal school settings—at least for a significant number of students. It is assumed that these students will seek help outside the formal system through one-on-one tutorials or special schools established for remedial and/or enrichment education.

In Japan such schools are widely prevalent; up to 25 percent of students at the primary level, 40 percent at the lower secondary, and 60 percent at the senior secondary participate in informal education (see also Russell in this volume). Reports indicate that these schools are also common in Korea, Taiwan, and Indonesia. In Eastern Asia, the informal schools are almost always private.

Our presumption is that these informal schools are relatively more prevalent in societies with large and salient private sectors. Regrettably, the lack of comparative statistics precludes a rigorous test of this presumption. However, at several points in our discussion we will refer to the contribution of informal schools.

Defining and Measuring the Private Sector

What is *private*? Readily available international statistical sources accept as private those schools that are legally private and thus classified as such by the statistical bureaus of the respective nations. But as Cummings and Riddell (1994) and others note, there is considerable variation in the fiscal and regulatory arrangements accompanying this legal status.

In some countries, the privateness of private institutions is relatively straightforward. Privately selected trustees have responsibility and the revenues derive strictly from tuition and fees. In some cases, the institutions are allowed to realize a reasonable profit which can be distributed to the owners,

while in other cases they are expected to forego profit with all surplus revenues being returned to the institution for future use. More common are the not-
for-profit institutions that conform with certain government regulations in
order to benefit from a tax-free status. This first group of schools share the
common characteristic of not benefiting from direct government subsidies.

Somewhat less private are those legally private institutions that receive
public subsidies. In some cases the subsidies are for specific purposes such
as school lunches or science laboratories. In other instances the subsidies
may extend to cover part or all of the salaries of staff and even a significant
portion of the operating expenses.

In some nations, government subsidies extend to virtually 100 percent
of the operating expenditures of private institutions; usually, in these cases
the government exercises considerable influence over such matters as admissions, textbooks, and even the selection of personnel. In such cases, the
schools are legally private but defacto public. So, within the rubric of private
there is considerable variation. The Eastern Asian tendency is toward moderate to no subsidies.

While it is useful to note the diverse nature of privateness, there remains
the question of deciding which schools legally constituted as private are
sufficiently private to be classified as private and which are not. In the
Netherlands and Ireland, most primary schools are legally private but fully
funded from public sources; yet in these societies, scholars and officials
think of the schools as private. In contrast, in Hong Kong and some other
Commonwealth nations where the same situation prevails, distinctions are
made between private or independent schools, government-aided schools,
and public schools. Hong Kong once treated the first two groups as private;
currently it only treats the first group as private. Our approach in the table
below is to follow the local convention, listing the enrollment ratios for
Asian nations at different school levels for 1988 (or the nearest year for
which data are available).

Why A Private Sector?

Estelle James (1993) has provided a useful economic explanation for the
relative prevalence of private schools. In this explanation, she argues that the
key factor behind private provision is cultural heterogeneity, particularly religious heterogeneity: the greater the heterogeneity the more prevalent are
private schools. In other writings, James links cultural heterogeneity with the
likely supply of educational entrepreneurs who have the will and skill to
establish private institutions. She also notes that public policies can influence

TABLE 8.1
Percentage of Enrolled Pupils That Are in Private Schools, by School Level, circa 1988

	Level			
	Preschool	*Primary*	*Secondary*	*Tertiary*
Japan	77	1	14	80
Strong Ties with Japan:				
a) Former colonies				
South Korea	60	1	41	79
Taiwan	79	1	10	70
b) Trade partners				
Thailand	25	10	11	30
Indonesia	100	17	51	65
Malaysia	55	0	6	8
Singapore	72	24	27	0
In East & Southeast Asia:				
Philippines	55	7	37	85
Hong Kong	100	10*	22*	
China	–	–	–	0
North Korea	0	0	0	0
South Asia				
Bangladesh	100	13	90	58
India	–	25	52	57
Nepal	4	5	10	23
Sri Lanka	–	2	3	0
Industrial Nations				
Germany	66	2	8	0
Ireland	100	100	70	100
Italy	30	7	6	0
Netherlands	70	69	72	55
Sweden	7	5	9	0
United Kingdom	–	4	10	47
USA	36	11	8	20

Sources: The primary source is UNESCO, 1991; Cummings and Riddell, 1994, is used to supplement as are Kitamura, 1987; Republic of China, 1994; Tan and Mingat, 1992; and Altbach, 1992.

Note: Insofar as possible, figures are computed based on full-time equivalent students. The -dash means credible figures were not available.

*For Hong Kong, the sum of private and government aided at the primary level is 94% and at the secondary level is 96%.

private provision: (1) large public subsidies to private schools enable increases in the private share; (2) in contrast large public expenditures on public secondary education discourage the private sector.

While the James argument is helpful in pointing to key dimensions influencing the provision of private education, it begs the more basic questions of (*a*) whether there will or will not be a private sector in a particular country, (*b*) if so what will be the philosophy affecting its shape, and (*c*) who will establish the schools? To approach these questions, it will be useful to carry out a brief review of the genesis of Asian education.

Premodern Traditions

Prior to the modern era, most education was privately provided on the intiative of transnational or subnational actors, with nations providing little or no legal obstacles (Archer, 1979). These actors included the Church and guilds in Europe, the Islamic *ulama* in the Middle East, and the Buddhist priests in Japan, China, and Thailand. While in Asia many premodern private schools were sponsored by religious or transnational organizations, the leading East Asian nations also fostered a parallel tradition of individual sponsorship of schools. This tradition was most evident in China, Korea, and Japan, where distinguished retirees from public service set up small schools to share their knowledge (Rubinger, 1982). So alongside the tradition of institutional sponsorship, we also find in several Asian countries an accepted pattern of individual sponsorship of schools.

The Modern Revolution

Over the "long modern century" when educational provision expanded in Western Europe and North America (Boli & Ramirez, 1987), reasonable arguments were presented both for public and private education. In the more determined nationalist and/or socialist nations, the public provision arguments tended to dominate. A major thrust of the French Revolution was to eradicate the Catholic Church's role in education, and this same "separation of church and state" logic had a profound influence on education in other nations under Continental influence, including much of Latin America, the United States, and French Indo-China (including Vietnam, Cambodia, and Laos).

Russia, following the communist revolution of 1917, took immediate steps to nationalize all educational institutions, and that approach has tended to prevail in all countries that have adopted the Socialist model. In Asia, this eventually came to include North Korea, China, Cambodia, and Vietnam.

A Counter-Tradition of Diversity

While some European nations adopted a comprehensive public approach to education, others, including England and the Netherlands, opted for a major private role in mass education. These latter nations also came to assume a major role in the colonization of Asia, thus spreading this private tradition to the colonies.

In both the English and Dutch cases, a dualistic colonial educational structure emerged with a small and elite upper tier of public schools featuring instruction in the metropolitan language and an extensive and diverse lower tier of private schools relying on instruction in various vernacular languages; often the schools of the lower tier were supported, at least in part, by missionary groups. In the English case, an explicit policy emerged of fostering diversity so as to "divide and conquer" the colonized population—various Protestant sects as well as Catholicism were encouraged in the various regions of the Indian subcontinent including Ceylon. Indigenous religions were not cultivated and the schools associated with indigenous religions were discouraged. In effect, the colonial policy sought to socially construct an approved cultural heterogeneity so as to enhance the authority of colonial rule (Panikkar, 1959).

Among these nations, Indonesia was among the first to be granted independence (by the departing Japanese in 1945). The Dutch, who had ruled in Indonesia prior to World War II, returned with force after the war to reestablish their colonial authority. In the independence struggle that continued through 1951, youth and teachers from the diverse indigenous educational institutions played a critical role. Upon final liberation from the Dutch in 1951, the Indonesian government rewarded the contributions of these educational interests by allowing each group generous legal space for its educational initiatives. Most Islamic schools were located under an independent Ministry of Religious Affairs while private Christian and independent schools (e.g., Taman Siswa) as well as some Islamic schools (e.g., Muhammidiyah) were coordinated under the private school directorate of the Ministry of Education. Relative to other Asian nations the regulations on the formation of private schools were comparatively lenient.

While the liberation of Indonesia was accompanied by a hospitable orientation to private schools, in the former British colonies of Malaysia and Singapore there was a contrary development. One reason was that certain of the private schools tended to be closely associated with ethnic or political factions that challenged government policies, so the respective governments decided to crack down. Some private schools were closed, whereas others had their private privileges including their authority to collect fees curtailed by extensive government regulations. Only in the past several years have these regulations come under review.

The American Experiment

While the European nations were active in establishing colonies in Asia, the United States as the "first new nation" sought in the first half of the nineteenth century to preserve the independence of non-European nations. Thus in Latin America the United States with its Monroe Doctrine resisted European interference and similarly it promoted an "Open Door" policy in China. Meanwhile American missionaries and foundations sought to strengthen the leadership capabilities of independent nations through establishing schools and offering funds and training to indigenous educational initiatives.

However, in the latter decades of the nineteenth century the United States became involved in imperialistic conflict. Actions taken against Spain in Cuba had their corollary in American intervention in the Philippines; by the turn of the century the United States had acquired an Asian colony, and had become responsible for developing an overseas educational policy. The eventual outcome was a commitment to universal basic public education, while allowing independent groups to establish schools that conformed to public laws. Both the Catholic Church which already had a strong foothold in Philippine education and U.S. Protestant groups became active in founding new institutions. They were particularly active at the secondary and tertiary level where the U.S. colonial authorities evidenced little interest.

Following World War II, the American model achieved wider impact in Asia as the United States occupied and reformed Japanese education along American lines and, through heavy-handed foreign aid, exerted a similar influence on Korean and Taiwanese education. Since then American influence has been exerted on other Asian countries through U.S. foreign aid as well as the prominent role of American experts in the World Bank.

Asia's First Modern States

European colonialism starting in the Mideast and gradually moving eastward alarmed Asian leaders, and those in Thailand and Japan were able to avoid subjugation. In the case of Thailand, an enlightened monarch constructed a response stressing a public monopoly on education. Out of deference to Western pressure, a limited role was allowed for certain Catholic missionary effort and the associated schools. However, the main thrust of official policy was to discourage private education; this policy continued into the sixties thus limiting educational opportunities until it was finally agreed that private schools at the secondary and tertiary level could be established to help in responding to the rapidly expanding demand for advanced education; a particularly interesting feature of the Thai legislation is to allow private tertiary institutions to return a limited proportion of their annual profits to the private owners.

In the case of Japan, the inward-looking Tokugawa shogunate (1600–1868) proved unable to mount a satisfactory response to western pressure. In

1868, the government was deposed by a modernizing coalition determined on the one hand to "expel the foreigners" and on the other to "restore the emperor," who had long been neglected by the former regime. The new government sought to establish policies that would modernize the nation while preserving national autonomy from foreign incursions. In the field of education, universal basic education was proposed as early as 1872 and thereafter the government developed implementing laws. Among the many influences on government thinking was the voice of Fukuzawa Yukichi, an independent intellectual unaffiliated with any religious group or other institutional actor, who had founded his own private school in 1854 and who had strong views on the Encouragement of Learning.

In the early years of the Meiji era (1868–1912) prominent local educators as well as foreign missions established schools at various levels with government permission. By the early nineties, some elements in government became critical of the "de-stabilizing" influence of these private schools and sought to restrict their privileges. The eventual outcome was a policy of minimal to no public support for the private schools and a ban on government jobs being offered to graduates of private schools. Regulations for the establishment of private schools were tightened up, now requiring new private schools to set aside substantial amounts of land and capital in a private school foundation. Despite these restrictions, numerous local educational entrepreneurs established private schools, and these schools were able to recruit students.

The above legal framework continued with little change until 1946 when the U.S. occupation removed the employment restrictions for private school graduates. Over the postwar period, private schools have become eligible for increasing levels of public subsidy providing they conform to official regulations.

Korea and China faced challenges to national autonomy analogous to those experienced by Japan, but were less successful in responding. Following a long series of concessions to western imperialist powers, China lost a war to Japan in 1895, which led to Japan's occupation of Taiwan and the imposition of the above-described Japanese legal framework on Taiwan (Tsurumi, 1977). Subsequently, in 1910 Japan occupied Korea and once again imposed this framework (Hong, 1992). Japan retained control over these colonies until it surrendered to the Allies in 1945. Reforms introduced in the immediate postwar period by the Allied Powers and subsequently by the respective local governments resulted in many modifications of the Japanese colonial imprint; but these reforms did little to reduce the favorable legal provisions affecting private institutions or their prominence.

Current Tendencies

As should be apparent from this institutional review, the private sector tradition in Eastern Asia is quite varied. Of particular note in the more Confucian nations is a tradition of individual sponsorship of schools as a form of self-fulfillment and independent of any religious auspices; thus whereas James sees cultural heterogeneity as an important determinant of privatization, in Asia the culturally more homogeneous nations of Japan, Korea, and Taiwan have large private sectors deriving largely from secular entrepreneurship. In recent years as population growth has leveled off and the educational systems have matured, the private sector's shares have tended to peak.

As indicated in chapter 16 below, Japan has come to occupy a central or core position in Eastern Asian development. Close to Japan are several other nations (see Figure 16.1) which might be said to belong to the semi-periphery. Beyond these are yet another group that are less intensively involved in the mutually reinforcing interchanges of trade, capital and technology that radiate from the Japanese core.

Among the semi-periphery nations, Thailand's effort to preserve autonomy tended to restrict the private sector, whereas Indonesia's independence struggle tended to promote the privileges of private institutions. While the early histories of these two systems have varied, in recent years the private sectors in both countries have enjoyed a growth spurt.

Other semi-periphery Asian nations, colonized by the British, once had a significant private sector which, following independence, was nationalized or transformed to a government-aided status; as these nations have achieved greater political stability, certain of these legally private institutions have experienced a restoration of greater financial and regulatory autonomy.

Distinct from the British influence has been the American model, promoting a common school for basic education while showing considerable openness to private schools at all levels.

Finally, despite the relative cultural complexity of China and Indochina, where there were at one time relatively vibrant private sectors, since the late forties all schools in the systems were nationalized by the ascendant socialist regimes; but over the past several years some of these regimes have begun to relax their regulations thus allowing the reemergence of a fledgling private sector.

In summary, diverse institutional traditions have had a differential impact on particular Asian countries, leading some to be more partial to a private sector than others. Table 8.2 summarizes the differential incidence of these factors in the core and periphery countries of East Asia. *To the extent*

TABLE 8.2
Incidence of Institutional Factors Promoting a Private Sector

	Indigenous Institutional Heritage	Indigenous Entrepreneur	Mission Schools	Foreign Colonial Policy	Foreign Influence
Japan	+	+	+		+
South Korea	+	+	+	−	
Taiwan		+	+	−	
Thailand			+		
Indonesia	+	+	+		
Malaysia			+	+	
Singapore		+	+	+	
Philippines			+	+	
Hong Kong	+	+	+	+	
Cambodia			+		−
China	+		+	+	−
Vietnam					−
North Korea			+	−	−

Key: + means a positive influence; − means negative; blank means a neutral influence, or not applicable

that a country is more exposed to these factors, it can be anticipated that it will be more partial to the private sector.

Private Educational Empires

While various institutional and economic factors have encouraged the emergence of private schools, these schools have also faced institutional and other obstacles. For example, in Japan through World War II graduates of private schools could not obtain government jobs. And public resources were used to support an extensive public sector that could offer quality education for little or no tuition. For private sectors to succeed they have had to offer experiences or opportunities that make them attractive to sufficient numbers of students. The following are several strategies that have proved effective.

One obvious attraction referred to by James as "differentiated demand" is the inclusion of a religious or ideological program in the curriculum which may appeal to the members of groups committed to those beliefs such as the Catholics in the Philippines or the Protestants in Korea and Singapore. While this attraction has proved important in the West, that is not always the case in Eastern Asia. In certain Eastern Asian countries we find the paradox that the numbers committed to these nonmainstream ideologies have been small, yet the number of attendees at ideologically based private schools has been substantial. For example, in Japan the proportion of the population committed to Western religions was (and is) quite small, yet the Protestant mission schools have prospered.

A second attraction is the development of job placement links with nongovernment employers. While government sponsored universities may offer a challenging academic education, private schools may seek to differentiate their image by claiming to develop more well-rounded youth who have energy, initiative, ambition, and creativity—all traits sought by dynamic private firms. Private institutions seek to build links with particular employers, so that large proportions of their graduates obtain jobs. To the extent the private schools can deliver on jobs, they are able to recruit new students.

Yet another attraction is the possibility of a young person pursuing continuous education from kindergarten through university within the educational empire, while never facing the threat of failure and expulsion because of substandard performance on a critical exam of passage. Public sector education typically involves a wide base of basic education followed by a narrower range of opportunities at each successive level in the educational hierarchy, with students having to pass rigorous exams in order to advance; large proportions fail and either have to terminate their education or move to the private sector. While the public sector progressively narrows with each successive level, the private sector tends to have a complementary shape: narrow at the basic education level, progressively wider at the secondary level, and topped off by extensive opportunities at the tertiary level.

While some private schools are content to accept the rejects from public sector exams, others decide to develop comprehensive systems offering those who enter at the ground level the opportunity of continuing without exam through each successive level until university graduation. An example is Japan's Keio Gijuku which began as a secondary-level institution in the mid-nineteenth century. It successively added a collegiate or university-level institution, a primary school, a kindergarten, after World War II a junior college, and most recently an International School outside New York City. Today Keio's highly selective kindergarten takes in approximately 200 new students each year, while its highly regarded university takes in over 10,000 students; among those entering the university without exam are the numerous students who have progressed within the Keio educational empire from its kindergarten, lower and upper secondary schools, and its International School.

Yet another attraction offered by private schools is flair. Teikyo University is the topmost institution of a gigantic private educational empire, built mainly over the past two decades. As Japanese culture has broadened to show new respect for culture and leisure, Teikyo has responded by offering a diversified range of opportunities. Perhaps most noted is its stress on sports and particularly on baseball. To strengthen its university-level baseball team, Teikyo has established feeder high schools and has used these high schools as a recruitment site for top junior ballplayers. The Teikyo high school teams invariably perform well in the national high school competition, and they supply the university with some of the nation's best athletic talent. The high visibility of Teikyo baseball enhances the image of the university and stimulates demand. Today Teikyo has ten high schools across Japan, two junior colleges, a Japan-based university that enrolls nearly 80,000 students, and six overseas colleges (four in the United States, one in Germany, and one in Switzerland).

Similar to the above Japanese examples are the systems of Catholic schools in the Philippines and Indonesia, the Taman Siswa and Muhammidiyah systems in Indonesia, and others.

As these examples indicate, private schools may start out small, but over time certain of them enter into parallel strategies: to complement the public sector they focus on those levels in the vertical school hierarchy where public provision is limited, and to take advantage of economies of scale they engage in massive horizontal expansion at these levels. The outcome is the emergence of large to mammoth private school empires that provide a wide array of educational products crafted to the particularities of evolving local demand. It can be hypothesized that the longer a private sector is in place, the larger will be the proportion of enrollees in these empires. Also, as empires have the liberty to worry about economies of scale, they are likely to press for larger, more efficient schools. Hence the longer a private sector is in place, the larger the average size of private schools.

Private Education Supplements the Public Sector

In the core and semi-periphery Eastern Asian nations, private education tends to be most prevalent around the edges of public education. In these nations the public sector is obligated by law to provide places for all children at the primary and lower secondary levels and beyond that to provide places for those that "have ability." The public sector meets its responsibilities in these areas with free education of reasonable quality, and the private sector cannot compete. Thus the private sector's share of primary education in several core and periphery countries is only one percent. Table 8.3 which differentiates private sector shares for the lower and upper secondary levels, indicates that the private sector share in lower secondary tends to

TABLE 8.3
The Private Sector's Share of Secondary Education in Selected Asian Countries and
the Gross Enrollment Ratio, circa 1988

| Country | Private Share (%) | | Gross Enrollment Ratio for Secondary Level* |
	Lower Secondary	Upper Secondary	
Japan	1	50	100
Taiwan	6	49	100
Korea	1	70	87
Philippines	25	58	71
Singapore	27	27	69
Malaysia	6	6	57
Indonesia	40	50	48
Thailand	1	40	28

Sources: The primary source is UNESCO, 1991; Cummings and Riddell, 1994, and national sources are used to obtain the lower/upper secondary breakdown

*Gross enrollment ratio is the number enrolled in secondary institutions divided by the number in the 13–17 age cohort.

be small in those countries where lower secondary education is compulsory; Indonesia is an exception, as until 1988 lower secondary was not obligatory there. In contrast, at the upper-secondary level, where the number of places in public education are limited and offered at cost, the private sector's share is substantial.

Concerning preschool education, the public sector has a limited responsibility (mainly relating to recent daycare legislation for women in the labor force), and thus the public provision of places tends to be limited; in most core and periphery Asian nations the private sector has moved in to fill the gap.

Similarly, concerning tertiary education, in several countries the public sector has assumed the limited responsibility of focusing its provision on elite formation and training in selected technical and scientific areas deemed essential for national development; as with preschool education, the private sector fills the gap.

Finally, concerning informal education the public sector assumes little or no responsibility. Japan has pioneered in the provision of informal education, and Korea has also been innovative. In Japan, the major informal education organizations tend to differentiate their products: For example, Kawaijuku offers high-quality tutorials, while Fukutake offers correspondence courses. Over time, the scale of the major educational firms in these nations has expanded. Currently, several of Japan's largest firms are exporting their educational products to nearby Asian nations as well as to the United States (see Russell in this book).

Policy Innovations

The countries of East and Southeast Asia have evolved a variety of innovative approaches in the course of developing their respective private sectors. Among these, the following seem to be relatively widely practiced:

1. *Dualism*—in several of the countries, the state establishes a clear demarcation between the public sector which is responsible for critical national purposes and the private sector which is allowed to respond to private demand. The state generously funds its own sector, while leaving private sector funding up to the initiative of constituent schools. Private schools achieve greatest success when they find areas of supply underserved by the state sector, as in upper secondary education, in the humanities and social sciences at the tertiary level, and in kindergartens. The private sector, in effect, acts as a buffer for the state sector. At some points, however, the private sector may have difficulty generating adequate revenues, and thus may engage in unfair practices. When this happens, the public sector may intervene with new regulations, and in some instances may initiate a subsidy program. A particularly interesting case is Japan's Private School Promotion Foundation, which utilizes quality-based incentives to encourage private schools to offer higher quality education.
2. *Private Sector as a Laboratory*—The private sector often serves as a generator of new approaches, or alternately as a testing ground. For example, in Japan the idea of a six-year secondary school was first launched in the private sector and now is being imitated by several public systems (Shimahara, 1995). Similarly, in Singapore the government has turned to the private sector to try out two new initiatives in school-based management (Tan, 1995).
3. *Private Sector as a Back-up*—Public sector education in the Asia teaches to the good student, but it does not assure the student's mastery of the curriculum. In several Asian countries, private schools have founded informal schools to provide remedial and enrichment education.

Policy Implications

Asia's permissiveness to private schools has a significant impact on the overall policy environment:

1. *Privateness can breed more privateness.* Once private sectors get started, they tend to expand rapidly both because private school empires experience economies of scale through expansion and because new entrepreneurs find the entry costs for establishing schools to be reasonable. Private sectors in Western countries have generally had less success in expanding. The difference may lie in the Western commitment to the public sector providing mass secondary and tertiary education, while in Asia the public sector's function is defined more narrowly.

2. *Large private sectors may thwart the achievement of certain public goals.* Whereas public officials can presumably order public schools to comply with various policies, they may encounter greater difficulty in dealing with private schools. Some public policies require control of admissions policies for all schools. For example, public policies that seek to allow children to attend "neighborhood" schools require public control over admissions. But the public officials may not be able to enforce such admissions policies on private schools. In Japan, at the high school level, public policy once sought to make all high schools equal in quality. To compete with the public sector, some private schools decided to stress quality. The success of these schools in placing graduates in elite universities forced the public sector to designate some public schools as elite preparatory schools, that is, more equal than others.

3. *Private schools may recruit critical staff from the public sector.* To gain recognition and to operate their programs, private schools need staff. If established late in the cycle of educational development, private schools will need to draw on staff from available sources which include the graduates of teacher training schools, graduates of overseas programs, and staff already employed at established institutions. In many instances, private schools will choose the last option in order to gain the wisdom of experience and the prestige attached to particular recruits. Different recruitment options include the hiring of recent retirees, the hiring of staff who are in mid-career on a full-time basis, and the hiring of staff on a part-time basis (as a second job). Particularly, the latter two options may weaken the quality of the public sector.

4. *Private schools may be corrupt.* In most educational systems, educational institutions are expected to use objective standards in admission and grading. There are sometimes exceptions, often induced by financial payments. The incidence of such exceptions appears to be most frequent in the private sector.

5. *Private schools may promote controversy.* Private schools are often established by entrepreneurs who hold certain reservations about the policies of government leaders. In such cases, the schools may establish programs

that foster criticism of government policy. At a minimum, private schools tend to foster a contrasting ethos and life style.

Eastern Asian Privateness and Outcomes

Educational systems are often compared in terms of outcomes such as access, equity, quality, and relevance. Privateness is often tainted with negative imagery—it is thought to be more elitist, to allow lower quality, to promote excessive efficiency yet charge high fees. Unfortunately, the quality of comparative statistics does not allow a careful assessment of the Eastern Asia's private sectors in all these dimensions.

In terms of quality, many private institutions stand high in terms of quality while others sink low. For example, in Japan, Korea, and Indonesia, a disproportionate share of the top students competing for university admissions come from a small group of private schools, while other private high schools tend to direct their graduates to junior colleges or the job market.

Student-teacher ratios at private institutions tend to be high relative to public sector institutions, in some instances amazingly high; for example, some faculties of Japanese and Korean private universities have student-teacher ratios in excess of 60 to 1. Private schools also tend to employ a comparatively large number of part-time teachers. Through these and other mechanisms, they are generally more successful than their public competitors in controlling expenditures. Tan and Mingat (1992, p. 118) suggest the prevalence of a moderate-sized private sector tends to stimulate greater efficiency in the public sector; once, however, the private sector exceeds 40 percent of enrollees this demonstration effect weakens.

In one respect it is clear that private sectors make an unequivocally positive contribution. In Asia, to the extent a nation has a large private sector, access to secondary and tertiary education is enhanced. Asian nations that adhere to statist and/or socialist ideologies of exclusively publicly sponsored education such as North Korea, Vietnam, and Cambodia restrict access. Those that are partial to private education excel in access: Asia's four leaders in terms of privateness, Japan, Korea, Taiwan, and the Philippines, are also four nations that stand near the top of the international ranking in terms of access both to secondary and tertiary education (and also are quite respectable in terms of quality).

Conclusion and Lessons

The core and semi-periphery nations of Eastern Asia have encouraged the emergence of a sizable and vigorous private sector. This has benefited these nations in terms of expanding access and promoting diversity in educational approaches and even in political and cultural perspectives. At the same time, it has enabled the respective states to contain their level of expenditure below that characteristic of the typical welfare states of Western Europe and many of the centrally controlled states of the former Eastern bloc. Notable in Eastern Asia has been the stimulation of private solutions both for school education and for out of school or informal education; it is partly because Asian young people participate in this combination of formal and informal education that they perform so exceptionally in international tests of educational achievement. The apparent success of Eastern Asia's public private mix in promoting access, diversity, and quality raises several questions for educators in nations with restricted private sectors, such as the United States:

1. *Is formal education enough?* Asian educational systems expect their schools to convey knowledge in an effective manner, but they hold students and parents responsible for learning. Rather than provide extensive remedial and enrichment opportunities in the schools, they allow a complementary sector of informal schools to offer these services. It may be that this approach is inequitable, favoring children from more affluent homes. But is that any different than the U.S. approach where such services are relatively more available in suburban schools attended by children from more affluent homes?

2. *Need the public sector be responsible for all educational challenges?* Most Asian educational systems limit the public obligation to completion of a particular school level such as junior secondary education, and leave much of the rest of education to the private sector. It turns out that the private sector has been remarkably responsive; indeed, in hot areas such as computer sciences, business management, hotel management, international education, and environmental studies, the private sector has been far more dynamic than the public sector.

3. *Might not the emergence of a strong private sector stimulate greater efficiency and effectiveness in the public sector?* While this issue is still being debated in the United States and in Western Europe, most Asian educational leaders would answer in the affirmative.

4. *Might not the emergence of a strong private sector help in containing public sector educational expenditures?* Asian states which allow large private sectors tend to spend from 4–6 percent of Gross National Product on education, while Western states with restricted private sectors spend much more, circa 5–8 percent.

5. *Might not the availability of a vibrant private sector offer more options for educational workers*, including both more jobs and the prospect of supplementing income through holding second jobs? Private schools are resourceful in identifying undersupplied niches in educational markets, and

thus expanding the scale of educational services. This expansion leads to the creation of new educational jobs that can be filled both by full-time and part-time employees. One of the great contradictions of U.S. personnel policies is to restrict educational workers to one job and then to pay submarket wages for that job. In Asia, the strength of the private sector opens up a wide range of second jobs for educational workers, thus enabling those who need more to supplement their income.

CHAPTER 9

Lessons from Japanese Cram Schools

NANCY UKAI RUSSELL

The traditionally brisk business of supplemental tutoring and cram school operation in Japan has boomed into a vast commercial industry with annual revenues of ¥1.4 trillion ($14 billion).[1] According to a recent government survey, nearly 70 percent of Japanese students will experience going to an extracurricular school, known as *juku* or *yobiko*, by the time they leave middle school. At any given time, 35 percent of all students are actually enrolled in one. While some such tutoring schools can be roughly compared to afterschool learning centers in the United States, the Japanese variety forms an integral part of modern childhood, a perennial topic for national debate and an important, although difficult to quantify, contributor to Japanese academic achievement.

Japanese public education is renowned for its high levels of average achievement, making the phenomenon of private lessons at *juku* and *yobiko* all the more intriguing. Studies indicate that 24 percent of elementary students, 60 percent of middle school students, and 30 percent of high school students attend *juku* lessons (Ministry of Education, 1994a; Tokai Bank, 1995). The government study, moreover, reports that rural enrollments in *juku* are increasing rapidly, narrowing the traditional urban-rural gap and spreading the phenomenon more evenly throughout Japan. Enrollment in afterschool classes supplements Japan's 240-day school year, which is one-third longer than that of the United States.

The pattern of using supplemental lessons continues in high school, but assumes a different character when university exams approach and the educational stakes increase. It is at this stage that a high-pressure category of *juku* called the *yobiko* becomes prominent. Only a tiny percentage of ambitious high school students actually cram at *yobiko*. But this small group fascinates because, like athletes training for their personal Olympics, they symbolize what is believed to be necessary for educational success in Japan: single-minded dedication and hard work.

Yobiko also serve another important group of students. This is the population of recent high school graduates who did not get into the university of their choice on the first try. Hoping to pass the following year's exam, they decline enrollment at less prestigious schools and devote a year to cram fulltime at a *yobiko*. One-third of all Japanese college students have been fulltime crammers at *yobiko* before reaching their goal on their second (or even third) effort. The proportion of repeaters in the entering class of the most competitive and prestigious universities, such as Tokyo University, rises to an astonishing 50 percent and higher (Tsukada, 1991).

Supplemental institutions similar to *juku* can be found elsewhere in Asia. Such schools are known as *hagwon* in South Korea and *buxiban* in Taiwan. China and India have long traditions of private tutoring to prepare students for examinations. But Japanese *juku* are by far the most commercially developed, forming the basis for an "education industry" that goes beyond conventional concepts of private enterprise involvement in education. The largest Japanese company in this business, Kumon Educational Institute, trains housewives to teach its mathematics, English, and Japanese language curriculum to children. It now distributes its mathematics worksheets to over one million children in twenty-seven countries, including 70,000 in the United States (Ukai, 1994). Nine *juku* firms are listed on Japanese stock exchanges. Although the vast majority of *juku* are mid-sized and local, it is the aggressive efforts of the largest dozen firms that are driving technological innovation, changing business methods and providing new models of how instruction can take place outside school.

Despite the institutionalization of *juku* and *yobiko* in modern Japanese life, the subject and its many implications are rarely discussed with objectivity. *Juku* are an embarrassment to the Japanese government and a threat to teacher union ideals that stress "whole person" education. The flourishing *juku* business also contradicts public sentiment, which outwardly favors a lessening of educational pressure on children. Meanwhile, *juku* enrollments have continued to rise, despite the declining pool of school-age users.

The purpose of this chapter is to provide an exploratory description of the current state of Japanese *juku*. We also will ask what Americans might learn from the example of massive, private learning that is increasingly driven by the methods of commercial enterprise. Three main areas will be of special interest.

1. *Complementary aspects of* juku. It can be argued that *juku* continue to thrive because they complement specific aspects of Japanese public education. *Juku* are free to track children by ability, offer smaller classes and focus solely on test preparation, which the public schools cannot or may

not want to do. The way Japanese families use private *juku* to comple-ment public schooling can be taken as evidence of how families use pri-vate schooling to provide educational advantage.

2. *Commercial influence of* juku *on education.* *Juku* companies, selling an educational product, view education in market terms, thus introducing a new vocabulary and paradigm for educational provision. Profit-driven providers introduce aggressive advertising, industry competition and in-vestment in technology to classrooms outside school. How private, com-mercial activity begins to drive educational content and philosophical focus is a deeply interesting, if also disturbing, question. In concrete terms, the most innovative *juku* use state-of-the-art technology, video-conferencing, CD-ROMs, and satellite transmission to relay material and lectures. *Juku* are usually considered a Japanese phenomenon, but the ways in which they respond to market forces, create new demand and influence already existing institutions is not limited to Japan.

3. *Continuing education and the* juku *model.* The evolution of an educa-tional culture in Japan that includes voluntary *juku* attendance by large numbers of people may lead to expanded concepts of lifelong learning, particularly outside schools. As knowledge and knowing how to learn become more important in information-based economies, the ability of a citizenry to continue to learn will be critical. Has the widespread custom of attending *juku* already habituated many Japanese to the idea of disci-plined study outside school? This may help the Japanese move into a future in which education will increasingly take place outside traditional schools.

Defining *Juku*

The term *juku* is derived from the Chinese character that means the "smallest scale of school run by a teacher from his home" (Rubinger, 1982, p. 8). Modern Japanese *juku* present a much more bewildering array of choices, ranging from neighborhood abacus lessons to nationwide companies traded on the Tokyo Stock Exchange. Indeed, the term *juku* lacks clarity because it covers such a wide spectrum of arrangements.

What all *juku* have in common are three characteristics identified by Rubinger that profoundly shape the character of education that is provided:

1. *Administration.* *Juku* are administered in a separate educational sphere outside the constraints of compulsory education and the ideology of the Ministry of Education (Mombusho). Their position vis-à-vis the govern-ment can be muddled. Some *juku* are purely commercial enterprises, and

are regulated as such by the Ministry of International Trade and Industry (MITI). Other *juku* are classified as *gakko hojin*, in a separate legal and tax category for special educational institutions, which puts them under the jurisdiction of the Ministry of Education. In either case, the important point is that *juku* work outside the official requirements for compulsory education, enabling them to operate flexibly.

2. *Curriculum*. *Juku* can teach unorthodox subject matter, such as essay writing for tests or a foreign language not offered in public schools. Working outside the school system enables *juku* to sculpt educational niches, customized to students' needs. They can be nonideological about the moral and philosophical issues swirling around the realities of the examination system and teach only to the test.

3. *Constituency*. Participation is voluntary and fee-based. Customers are free to enroll, quit, or switch to a competing *juku*.

The private nature of *juku* is the critical characteristic because it enables companies to flexibly develop their own educational agendas. This characteristic is amplified by the lack of administrative coherence, as seen in the involvement of both the commerce-oriented MITI and the educational ministry Mombusho. The commerce ministry seeks to encourage the growth of education-related businesses, while the education ministry views *juku* as a threat to the established school system.

A problem that arises from the private nature of *juku* is the difficulty of determining what counts as one. Our focus will be on academic *juku* and the *yobiko* that are its upward extension. These coaching and cramming *juku* are at the heart of educational debate in Japan. But before proceeding to this discussion, other types of supplemental education (*hoshu kyoiku*) that can be considered a part of the multifaceted *juku* world should also be mentioned.

A survey of various sources, including Ministry of Education studies, business reports, news accounts, and popular references, resulted in the following list of activities that can be considered to be a *juku* or *juku*-like in name or spirit.

- Cultural and hobby-type lessons
  (piano, swimming, calligraphy, judo)   *keiko-goto*
- Home tutoring   *katei kyoshi*
- Educational correspondence services   *tsushin kensaku*
- Schools for academic enrichment   *gakushu juku*
  Remedial content   *hoshu juku*
  All-around curriculum   *sogo juku*
- Schools to hone test-taking skills   *shingaku juku*
- High-pressure *juku* for test preparation   *yobiko*

Yobiko serve two constituencies:
(1) high school students who want expert coaching for exams; and
(2) full-time crammers, also known as *ronin*. They have failed to enter their first-choice university and prepare full-time at *yobiko* for the next year's test.

This wide-ranging—and incomplete—list will probably provoke debate. Cultural lessons would not be construed as a *juku* by Japanese parents, but the Ministry of Education counts them as a variety of supplemental education, emphasizing the positive dimension of private lessons. Very few would describe *tsushin kensaku* as a *juku*, since correspondence services have neither classroom nor teacher, but given that families use *tsushin kensaku* in the spirit of an academic *juku*—to build a competitive edge—the Ministry of Education polled usage of this category for the first time in 1993.

Gakushu juku and *Yobiko*: Supplementing Education through High School

Supplemental education in Japan has flourished during the last two decades. A research organization that regularly surveys the field reports that total Japanese spending on all types of extra lessons for children in 1994 was ¥2.3 trillion ($23 billion), triple the corresponding figure for 1985 (Yano, 1994, p. 78). About 25 percent of the pie ($5.5 billion) went to *keiko-goto*, or music, sports, and hobby lessons. The remaining 75 percent of spending went to *juku* (52 percent) with annual revenues of $12 billion and *yobiko* (10 percent), with $2 billion. Ten percent of children use home tutors ($2 billion). Early education and English lessons make up the rest.

The academic *gakushu juku* and *yobiko*, therefore, account for over 60 percent of all supplemental education spending and over 80 percent of what families spend on private tutoring. *Gakushu juku*, literally "study and learn" *juku*, are the less pressured supplement used mainly by elementary and middle school students. *Yobiko* are the more intense, narrowly focused supplement for high school students and full-time crammers. It should be added that these categories occasionally overlap. Some 11-year-olds attend *yobiko* to cram for private school exams. Conversely, most high school users of private tutoring choose *juku*, not *yobiko* to prepare for college entrance tests. But the *gakushu juku* —or *juku*, as most Japanese call them—and *yobiko* are generally used as described above.

Juku can be envisioned as a slow-moving ramp that starts gathering passengers as early as kindergarten, with more children climbing on board until sixth grade, when 40 percent of all elementary school children are riding along. Participation rises sharply during the middle school years. It peaks in the ninth grade, when nearly 70 percent of students are taking extra classes to prepare for the entrance exams to high school. According to the exam results, students are streamed into various academic, technical and vocational high schools and *juku* enrollments drop to the 30 percent range as seen in figure 9.1.[2] An estimated 130,000 high school students, or less than three percent of the total, step on to the equivalent of an express elevator—a *yobiko* (Yano, 1994). *Yobiko* academies feed students into different strata of the national and regional hierarchy of universities.

Juku blanket Japan. Approximately 46,000 *juku* in Japan serve some 6.5 million students, or 35 percent of the school-age population from first to twelfth grades (see Nomura, 1994; Tokai, 1995). This average, however, obscures the high enrollment rates found in certain grades. For example, the government reports that 67 percent of all ninth-graders and well more than 50 percent of all middle school students attend *juku*. Current *juku* enrollment rates are the highest on record. The percentage of elementary students attending *juku* doubled from 1976 to the present and the proportion of middle school students in *juku* rose 50 percent from 1976 to 1993. The ministry reports that users go to *juku* an average of 2.5 times a week, which represents two or three hours of *juku* study per week.

Average monthly expenditure on *juku* increased by a large margin, from ¥9,200 in 1985 to a high of ¥15,300 in 1993 ($92–153) over the eight-year period between ministry surveys. This level of spending is expected to remain flat, judging by slower enrollments and polls that report parents' unwillingness to pay more. Nevertheless, educational spending remains a priority. In the annual Tokai Bank survey, 37 percent of families expressed little concern about *juku* expenses and 49 percent responded that they "feel a slight burden but this cannot be helped, because it is for education."

This is a view of national averages. A more complex picture emerges with an examination of the details that explain why families continue to use *juku*, how children experience them, and how choice is differentiated by age, family income, and region. Recent surveys fill in some of these gaps. *Juku* are frequently depicted as dark dens of cramming and memorization, but probably come closer to being extracurricular homerooms, at least in the elementary years. One report observes that *juku* must offer "interesting classes that hold the interest of primary and middle school students, provide general guidance in all subjects, and create a homeroom-type atmosphere" (Nomura, 1994, p. 6). From the viewpoint of many parents, attending a *juku* at this level should be a low-key activity. A newspaper survey of Tokyo households found that the most popular reason for enrolling children in *juku* was "to raise children's motivation to study" (75 percent), not test prepara-

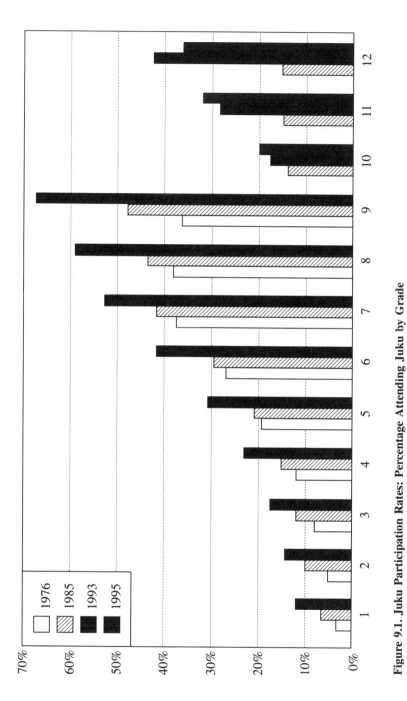

Figure 9.1. Juku Participation Rates: Percentage Attending Juku by Grade

Source: Ministry of Education, Tokai Bank.
Ministry of Education, 1994a.
Tokai Bank, 1995.

tion per se (Tanaka, 1992). Another poll found that the least cited reason for going to *juku* was "to learn test-taking techniques" (Shimomura, 1994). In the ministry's study, parents of elementary school users most often said that the benefit of attending *juku* was that the child "learned how to study by him/herself" (33.8 percent), as seen in table 9.1.

In terms of academic content, *juku* may complement school lessons by filling in the gaps for slow learners, pushing quick students and providing a different classroom atmosphere. While Japanese class sizes often exceed forty, a *juku* industry journal estimates that 70 percent of *juku* classes have a teacher-student ratio of 1:20 or less. Twenty-five percent of *juku* have less than ten students per teacher (Shimomura, 1994). Such extra attention is highly valued by parents. When upper elementary students were asked in the ministry survey what was "good" about attending *juku*, the most frequent response was, "I understood my schoolwork better" (47 percent), followed closely by, "I learned things beyond what we were studying in school," as seen in table 9.2. *Juku* also offer unorthodox teaching methods and material. Approximately one-third of elementary-school *juku* users are enrolled in a Kumon arithmetic franchise, which follows a self-paced worksheet curriculum that emphasizes skill mastery through repetition. This method, criticized by some teachers, complements Japanese classroom teaching, which is

TABLE 9.1
What Were the Benefits of Attending *Juku*? (Parents' View)

	Elementary	Middle School	Average
1. Understood school lessons better	30.3	36.8	34.1
2. Became more interested in studying	31.5	24.4	27.3
3. Learned to study by him/herself	33.8	22.1	27.0
4. Child was taught with enthusiasm	19.9	29.7	25.6
5. Was able to go beyond school lessons	24.9	20.5	22.3
6. Was able to obtain information on tests and future course	7.9	20.9	15.5
7. Nothing in particular	12.9	13.2	13.1
8. Less time for TV, playing too much	11.5	13.3	12.6
9. Made more friends	13.0	10.3	11.4
10. Learned to study without parental guidance	8.6	13.2	11.3
11. Helped child pass test into private or public middle school	—	1.4	0.8
12. Other	7.2	4.3	5.5

Source: Ministry of Education, 1994a

TABLE 9.2
What Were the Benefits of Attending *Juku*? (Children's View)

	Upper Elementary*	Middle School	Average
1. Could do my schoolwork better	46.8	51.8	50.1
2. Could go beyond school lessons	44.4	44.7	44.6
3. Could make friends	41.4	28.2	32.6
4. My grades improved	20.3	27.2	24.9
5. Learned something that helped on tests	9.1	22.1	17.8
6. Could make friends with teacher	22.7	14.4	17.1
7. Studying became more fun	23.2	13.9	17.0
8. Learned something about the school that I planned to attend	3.4	14.6	10.9
9. Nothing in particular	9.4	9.9	9.8
10. Got out of helping at home	4.7	4.4	4.5
11. Made my parents happy	5.8	3.1	4.0
12. Other	3.1	2.2	2.5

*Lower elementary children's views were not solicited for this part of the survey.
Source: Ministry of Education, 1994a

largely devoted to discussing concepts and group problem-solving, as Stevenson and Stigler (1992) describe.

Close friendships may develop in *juku*, especially in the small, neighborhood classes run by retired teachers and housewives. One report describes a *juku* teacher who consciously tries to create a club-like atmosphere, providing students with "club" book bags and organizing weekend hiking excursions (Hendry, 1995). The Japanese author of a book on how to choose *juku* writes, "People might be surprised to hear this, but *juku* have a role as neighborhood hangout spot more than one might expect" (Komiyama, 1991, p. 8). In the ministry survey, 40 percent of elementary-age users said they liked going to *juku* because they made friends, and a Japanese sociologist has observed that many middle school girls and boys find *juku* to be socially exciting, with the trading of notes, flirting, and the opportunity to meet students from other schools.[3]

By middle school, however, *juku* students are working harder to master the academic subjects that will appear on high school entrance exams. Many middle school parents complain that the level of competition to enter elite academic high schools is so intense that it is not possible to succeed without supplemental help. In contrast to the 85 percent of elementary school *juku* students who study arithmetic, the ministry survey shows that middle-school *juku* users are taking English (92.9 percent), mathematics (89.2 percent), and

Japanese language (49.1 percent), the three subjects critical for exam success. *Juku* homework assignments increase, so that the amount of time required to do *juku* homework may be equal to the school workload. A *juku* consultant estimates that middle school students studying English, mathematics, and Japanese should expect about an hour of *juku* homework per night, more perhaps than many American middle school students spend on regular school homework (Komiyama, 1991).

In ninth grade, *juku* enrollments peak. Sixty-seven percent of all ninth-graders nationwide are studying at *juku*, often in evening classes that run until 10 p.m. Until middle school, family income may be a strong factor in determining whether or not children attend *juku*, but by eighth and ninth grades, the correlation between income and *juku* attendance seems to diminish. A Tokyo metropolitan government survey is cited as finding that at the fifth-grade level, two in three families with monthly incomes of ¥500,000 ($5,000) or more were sending their children to academic *juku*, compared to a rate of only one in three for families earning $3,000 or less per month. By the eighth grade, however, the corresponding figures were 63 percent enrollment for the higher income group and 47 percent for the lower income group. The study concluded that higher-income families who used *juku* for their elementary-age children were better able to afford private lessons or were using *juku* before entering private schools. By the eighth grade, however, the looming high school entrance exams and the increasing difficulty of schoolwork made lower-income families feel that they, too, must enroll their children in *juku* (Sengoku & Iinaga, 1990).

The *Yobiko* Express Elevator

The high *juku* enrollments in ninth grade plunge in tenth grade to the 25–30 percent range, where they plateau. This dramatic drop seems puzzling given that the next hurdle looms, university entrance exams. The sharp decline might be attributed partly to the academic sorting that has just been executed by the high school entrance exams. Approximately 96 percent of middle school students continue on to high school. Of this group, about one-fourth enter technical and vocational high schools and the remaining three-fourths of graduates enter academic high schools. The latter group exists in a meticulously ranked hierarchy and feed into different strata of higher education. Students who attend competitive high schools in Japan are already in rigorous preparatory programs (Rohlen, 1983). The low *juku* enrollments seem less mysterious when one further considers that the advancement rate to four-year colleges and universities is 30 percent. The 25 percent of students in technical high schools will not advance to higher institutions of learning and of the remaining 75 percent of students in academic high schools, half are women, who disproportionately attend junior colleges.

A high-intensity option for a tiny fraction of ambitious high school students is the *yobiko*. According to one estimate, 130,000 Japanese high school students, or less than three percent of the total, enroll part-time in approximately 200 *yobiko* nationwide. The "big three" urban *yobiko*, Kawaijuku, Yoyogi Seminar, and Surugadai, reportedly enroll 80 percent of *yobiko* students and account for 60 percent of all *yobiko* revenue (Yano, 1994).

Although they are much less used, *yobiko* are extremely interesting and deserve attention as the pinnacle of supplemental education taken to its logical end in the Japanese context of families competing for educational advantage. If *juku* are analogous to a ramp that gradually grows steeper, the *yobiko* are a vertically launched express elevator hurtling toward the upper echelons of the educational pyramid.[4] Society bemoans the use of *juku* in the lower grades, but once nine years of compulsory education have ended, it is widely accepted that young adults must cram to get into the best university for which they are qualified. *Yobiko* help do this efficiently.

In addition to part-time high school students, *yobiko* also enroll a large full-time population. These are the high school graduates who fail to get into their first-choice university and decide to try again for their goal the following year. Such "repeaters" are called *ronin*, or "masterless samurai," wandering about in educational limbo. Some 200,000 *ronin* enroll in *yobiko* every year (see Kawaijuku, 1985; and August, 1992). Unlike the United States, where college-bound students take the SAT, may apply to as many as ten institutions, and explore a range of options, Japanese high school seniors are much more limited in their choices. This is due to the complexities of test scheduling, different examination content, limitations on the number of applications one can submit to national universities, and so on. Students must therefore carefully evaluate their raft of practice test scores and set their sights on one or two schools which represent their best chance at success. If one's score falls short, for many aspirants it is well worth investing an additional year to cram for the next round.

Ronin routinely make up one-third of the entering classes of Japanese institutions of higher learning. In the case of the prestigious national universities, *ronin* comprise 44 percent of the first-year class, and at Japan's most elite institutions, such as Tokyo University and Kyoto University, more than 50 percent of the freshman class is comprised of *ronin* (Tsukada, 1991). In turn, graduates of the latter category are overrepresented in the leadership of Japan's corporate, bureaucratic, and professional worlds (Ishida, 1993). *Yobiko* are therefore a crucial component of Japanese education, especially in considering university student populations and the composition of Japanese elites.

Yobiko also exhibit the gender gap that exists at higher levels of Japanese education. All along, parents have lower educational expectations for daughters. In the Tokai Bank study, 76 percent of parents said they expected boys to go to university while only 55 percent held the same expectations for girls. In 12th grade, 33 percent of girls are still enrolled in cultural lessons, compared to two percent of boys, and the top three areas of study parents hope their children will pursue further are engineering, science, and economics for males, and education, art, and literature for females. Nationwide, *yobiko* enrollments are 85 percent male and 15 percent female (Tsukada, 1991). Mamoru Tsukada found a slightly more extreme male-female ratio in his study of a Hiroshima *yobiko* and no female teachers. His description of some male *yobiko* students' attitudes toward women were reminiscent of a culture commonly associated with male military academies in the United States.

When Education Becomes a Business

The influence of *yobiko* also extends into the area where education becomes a business that, in turn, heavily influences students' educational decision making. *Yobiko*, along with other companies, administer practice tests by mail to the general public on a fee basis, for ¥5,000 ($50). According to a report by the Yano research group, two million tests are distributed each year by *yobiko* alone. Such tests provide practice opportunities, but also function as widely accepted statistical measures of one's probability for academic success. Computer analysis of the test results by *yobiko* yields precise data on one's standing among the group who took the test, the cohort which plans to apply to the same school, and so on. Based on many years of comparing mock test results and later university acceptances, *yobiko* data are considered authoritative and are widely used by *ronin*, high school students and public school counselors as a means for finding the right "fit" between applicant and institution. *Yobiko* also correlate student test scores to data on acceptance rates at the desired school, and since the higher scores signify the more prestigious departments, the tests effectively rank the prestige of universities and their departments. An expert in this area points out that the *yobiko* tests are only simulations, yet the results carry very real implications for students, families, and the educational institutions themselves (Tsukada, 1991).

It is also in *yobiko* where the private, market-driven model for educational services is most clearly expressed. In the vocabulary of the market, *juku* offer educational services to savvy consumers who comparison shop. *Yobiko* shoppers are the most serious of *juku* consumers because of what is perceived to be at stake. These circumstances are expressed in the commercial behavior of teachers, students, and in the ways schools approach teaching and learning.

In the classroom, for example, *ronin* are demanding customers. They have signed a contract, and in many cases have been screened, to pay an average ¥660,000 ($6,600), the equivalent of a year's college tuition at some public universities, for an educational product they hope will deliver competitive advantage. (Part-time high school *yobiko* students pay about one-third this figure, according to the 1994 Yano report. Tsukada, in his study of a *yobiko* noted:

> *Ronin* students attend their teachers' classes several times, listen to their friends' evaluations, and decide whether or not they will continue to attend. Once the trust between salesmen and their consumers is broken, the consumers never buy goods from the salesmen any longer. (Tsukada, 1991, p. 33)

Unlike their high school days, *ronin* study only test-based curriculum with an instructor of their choosing whom they regularly evaluate. Some classrooms are monitored by video cameras, so that *yobiko* staff can observe *ronin* reaction and judge the instructor's popularity. *Yobiko* teaching must pertain to the examination, but also should be energetic and exciting to *ronin*, who need inspiration and for whom studying the test material is review. The dynamic teaching style characteristic of *yobiko* sometimes leads *ronin* to unfavorably compare their high schools with *yobiko*. One male *ronin* at a mid-sized *yobiko* of 2,000 students observed that his public high school teachers were like "civil servants" while *yobiko* teachers "will be fired if they lose their popularity among students." A young woman *ronin* noted that her former high school teachers were secretly employed at the *yobiko* and "had to save their energy" to teach there (Tsukada, 1991, pp. 50–51).

Depending on the institution, the quality and profile of *yobiko* teachers differs. The most reputable *yobiko* employ a high proportion of full-time instructors. The best teachers will attract the best students who, by passing their examinations, will attract more users. But many *yobiko* hire a mix of full-time teachers, graduate students who work part-time, and moonlighting university professors and secondary school teachers. Full-time *yobiko* teachers trade the traditional high standing and job security of public school teachers for the chance to earn high salaries and celebrity status. A Nomura industry review states that "it is difficult to retain the best (*yobiko*) teachers since many are very independent and hold conflicting views with management over salary and educational goals." A job-search book for college graduates states that "hot" *yobiko* instructors can earn ten times more than their public school counterparts. At Kawaijuku, Japan's largest and oldest *yobiko*, August reports that top instructors who teach 12 to 18 hours a week earn ¥30,000–¥50,000 ($300–$500) per 90 minutes of instruction.

The reality, however, is that while *juku* industry wages are considered to be higher than other service industry wages, they are not appreciably higher on average than public salary scales while representing a higher employment risk. Some figures show that the average starting monthly salary for new college graduates is ¥200,000 ($2,000) monthly at large *juku*, and ¥167,300 ($1,673) at Tokyo public high schools. These figures remain comparable after several years' experience, when the average annual wage is ¥5.2 million ($52,000) for a 30-year-old *juku* teacher and ¥5.4 million ($54,000) for a 32-year-old Tokyo public high school teacher (Shimomura, 1994; and Daiei, 1994).

The Place of Technology in *Juku* and *Yobiko*

Where *juku* and *yobiko* most clearly display the promise and problems of market-driven education is in their use of technology. The use of technology

1. Makes data retrieval, the lifeblood of *yobiko* and *juku*, more accurate and efficient, thus strengthening their credibility.
2. Changes educational processes and concepts from the small, personally crafted and uneven to the distant, automated, and uniform.
3. Accelerates the development of the "manufacturing" aspects of education and widens the divide between small *juku* and large, capital-intensive companies.

These aspects of applied technology are best seen in the activities by the largest firms, including the nine *juku* companies listed on the stock exchange. Nagase Brothers Inc., for example, is closely watched for its "satellite *yobiko*," a new genre that uses satellite technology to relay lectures by Tokyo professors to 30,000 high school students and *ronin* sitting in 680 franchise and company-owned classrooms nationwide. Students listen to the lecturers, whom they already know through test prep books, in screening rooms. They can fax questions to the lecturer and review the lesson by re-watching a video or studying a company-published booklet. The company plans to produce 2,000 new lecture tapes a year, for which it owns the rights. By applying technology and business approaches to traditional methods of instruction, Nagase is creating an educational system reminiscent of Japanese manufacturing processes that can be economically reproduced and distributed to far-flung markets. It has enabled a relative newcomer to leapfrog over the long-established *yobiko* which have traditionally relied on the lengthy, expensive process of building schools near train stations and hiring local teachers.

For nervous test-takers, the use of technology seems to upgrade regional standards of test preparation. Using a computer-generated data base assures more uniform information and higher quality. A few years ago, the Ministry of Education, uncomfortably aware of the extent to which public middle schools relied on privately generated test data to advise their students, banned the use of such data. According to Nobuo Shimahara, this action has had the unintended effect of driving public school students further into the arms of *juku*, which possess the most reliable data.

Fewer Children Means Business Decline

Despite the space that has been devoted above to the large *juku* firms, the industry is still comprised mostly of relatively small schools. Over 90 percent of *juku* are defined as small- and medium-sized enterprises of 2,000 students or less with gross annual revenues of less than ¥100 million ($1 million). Business reports forecast flat growth for the *juku* business, given the recession of the 1990s and the decline in school populations due to lower fertility. After experiencing 10–15 percent growth rates in the boom economy of the 1980s, when some families used two or three *juku* at a time, the *juku* industry is expected to grow slowly, at a few percent annually until 2010, when the next generation of children comes of age. Moreover, the *juku* business is not greatly profitable. It is labor-intensive and smaller firms are vulnerable to economic swings.

Demographic trends present the greatest threat to the vitality of *juku*. The 18-year-old population peaked in 1992, sobering news for *juku* and *yobiko* which rely on this group and younger age-brackets for business. The population of Japanese 18-year-olds reached 2.05 million in 1992, but by 2002, the corresponding figure will drop to 1.5 million, a drop of more than 25 percent in ten years (Ministry of Education, 1994b).

Given the steady erosion of its core constituency, one could justifiably ask if there is any need to be concerned about *juku*. The president of the Kyoiku Soken company heretically foresees a day when there are no more entrance exams and no more *juku*. Japanese parents, after all, criticize *juku* for the same reasons that Americans find them oppressive and cruel. *Juku* rob children of free playtime and pressure them to learn trivial facts. According to the Ministry survey, parents who do not enroll their children in *juku* said: "I would rather have them play" (52.7 percent) and "They have enough to study at school" (50.5 percent). The third most frequent response, "My child doesn't want to go" (29.5 percent) was also the No. 1 reason for families to quit using *juku* (50.4 percent).

As we have seen, however, the *juku* phenomenon cannot be so easily dissociated from what we know about the progression of Japanese public schooling, a system whose accomplishments we continue to study and selectively admire. While young children are forming social bonds in the warm, nurturing public school environment that Catherine Lewis evocatively describes, so too are private *juku* a low key place to make friends and learn study skills. The "we're all in this together" lesson that children are pleasantly learning about cooperative play in elementary school is carried through the years and applied in a cruelly different way when all are cramming together for exams—at school and in *juku*. School achievement, particularly in mathematics, is linked to the extra instruction given privately at *juku* (see Whitman, 1991). *Juku* gladly accept students who fall behind in school, perhaps because of peers who benefited from private tutoring. In other words, *juku* and schools, in a variety of specific ways, coexist in a relationship of symbiosis and complicity. From different spheres, both institutions are guided by the same goal: to ease children into an education system governed by examinations.

A Learning Society, Private and Public

The question again arises, why should this be of concern to Americans? We are not forced to contend with a ruthless examination pyramid like that which exists in Japan. But surely Americans would benefit by having a comparable level of voluntary interest in and commitment to pursuing education that Japanese families display. The single most compelling factor about *juku* is that they flourish without government policy or budgetary support. *Juku* represent a massive private education system that is internally driven. Children go to *juku* without being told to by their teachers. Parents pay what is necessary to keep up with the neighbors. This is not to deny the inequalities that surface when private funds are used to purchase extra education. A Nihon Keizai newspaper survey reportedly found that a surprising 8.5 percent of Japanese families spend ￥50,000 ($500) or more per month on supplemental tutoring (Smith, 1994). At least 25 percent of the population apparently never uses *juku*. As it should be, rising inequality is of serious concern to Japanese policymakers. It also must be noted that the "bottom-up" phenomenon of *juku* study is fueled by an essentially "top-down" system that has everyone competing for the best position in an educational hierarchy. Thomas Rohlen has suggested that "schools pace society" in Japan (Rohlen, 1983). If, as we have seen, *juku* pace schools, then it may not be too far-fetched to suggest that in some important ways, *juku* also set the pace for society.

At the same time, Americans should not allow the potential for unequal access to deter ways of presenting education as something worth striving for. American children seem more apt to compete over the latest sports sneaker and find their role models in popular culture than to perceive education as something of value. Japanese children also have a youth culture, but more likely than not, they're discussing it on the train ride home from *juku*. While they were at *juku*, they might, incidentally, have learned a new way to solve problems. They no doubt are learning to persevere and be disciplined. These are not our ideal conditions for learning. Nevertheless, it is difficult to ignore the cognitive, behavioral and academic achievements that have been developed along the way.

Juku also carry an important lesson for Americans about the range of roles that the private sector already plays in education. It is clear that corporate *juku* help shift educational values toward that which is efficient, commercial and private. What must not go unnoticed is that market-driven education in Japan also enhances educational productivity, while private sector activity and ideology in the United States represents a more open effort to supplant what already exists. *Juku, yobiko,* and other forms of extra tutoring function as invisible supports to Japanese learning and amplify the academic achievements of schools. In the United States, the debate about private participation in education mostly centers around voucher systems and the role of private companies in weak public systems. These are not supplemental to school education but an overt political threat to it. The result is increased conflict and instability in society and the schools. The American analogue of *juku* does exist, in the form of SAT cram courses for college-bound students. Their social and educational impact, though growing, is not yet comparable to that of *juku* and *yobiko*. They are estimated to be a $100 million market, less than one percent of the value of the *juku* and *yobiko* industry, and represent a one-time shot at cramming. Americans are wary of the raw commercial activity that is allowed to penetrate classrooms, with cornflake makers distributing nutritional pamphlets and educational firms leasing video equipment in exchange for the opportunity to broadcast commercials. In Japan, market-driven education tends to shape students into educational consumers. In the United States, the focus is on students as consumers of material goods.

This leads to the question of how a culture of educational consumers, such as exists in Japan, might alter the nature of society, education, and how these evolve in the future. It would seem that continual studying, in and out of school, might accustom people to the attitudes and habits of learning (if not actually inspire them to do so). Peter Drucker, looking not so far ahead, argues that in future knowledge societies, "the school becomes the institution of the adults as well, and especially of highly schooled adults" (Drucker, 1993, p. 208). He asserts that postcapitalist economies will require the continual development of knowledge, the retraining of adult workers, and lifelong learning by all members of society. In such a context, the concept of schooling as an activity that takes place, for example, in a 6–3–4–4 configuration and then stops, is obsolete. Conventional schools will lose "their monopoly as providers of schooling." *Juku* are a clear example of a nonschool institution that provides opportunities for learning. Japanese who have experienced going to *juku*, teaching in one part-time during their university days, or paying for their children to attend one, can be expected to adjust to the concept of attending such future "nonschools" with relative ease.

Meanwhile, *juku* companies are developing new business offerings in the race to survive. The one place in which *juku* business is expected to grow is in urban areas, where the trend is toward more competition to enter private schools[5] due to growing public school violence and the perceived decline in public school education. *Juku* also are targeting preschool learners, foreign language education, and preparatory courses for professional licensing exams. Some are trying to cultivate user loyalty by sponsoring cultural and philanthropic activities. Overseas, they operate schools to serve expatriate Japanese families and domestically, *juku* are opening their own private schools. The annual market for supplemental education is ¥2.3 trillion, but total spending on all school and educational services in Japan is approximately ¥30 trillion ($300 billion).

Juku are an example of how private business has developed a certain role in Japanese education that is different from our common understanding of how private education or market-driven education works in the United States. The critical factor in Japan is that the system is driven by parental demand. But big *juku* companies add commercial momentum. Given current movements in the United States to privatize public programs and large private sector firms already interested in educational markets, knowing about Japanese *juku* may throw light on how American education also could develop in the future.

Linking Education to Society

CHAPTER 10

Education and Work in Japan: Implications for Policy

SAM STERN

In May 1994, President Clinton signed the School-to-Work Opportunities Act of 1994. At the press conference following the signing, President Clinton commented on the remarkable bipartisan support for the law and on how its implementation would benefit individuals, employers, and the national interest. In describing the need for the law, the new School-to-Work Act (1994) stated,

> The United States is one of only a few industrialized nations that does not have an organized, comprehensive system to help young people prepare for and enter the workforce. Because of the increasing demands of a highly competitive global economy, employers have difficulty finding workers with the academic, analytical, and technical skills they need. (p. 1)

In May 1894, exactly 100 years earlier, Kowashi Inoue, the Japanese Minister of Education, appeared before the Diet to describe the need for passage of a national law that would promote technical training. In his speech Inoue said:

> It is clear that competition in the world is essentially industrial, rather than military. Our science has advanced satisfactorily, but not our technical training at the lower levels. This condition is like an army with plenty of good generals, but not enough noncoms. (Passin, 1982, p. 97)

Author's note: The author is grateful to the Japanese workers and managers who graciously participated in interviews and shared their experiences and thoughts, and is especially appreciative of the advice and assistance received from Professor Rupert Evans of the University of Illinois; Professor Takashi Sakamoto and Professor Hiromitsu Muta of the Tokyo Institute of Technology; and the Japan Management Association.

Separated by a hundred years and half the globe, the United States and Japan have both responded to increasing international competition, technological changes, and workforce changes by calling for government support of work-related education and training. However, the nature of the government support and the resulting activity of schools and employers have been and continue to be fundamentally different in the two countries.

A hundred years ago, the United States knew little, if anything, about the emerging Japanese educational policy toward work-related education. Then, as today, we looked to Europe (primarily Germany) for models of how to best connect education and work At the same time that Japan passed its first national legislation in support of technical training, representatives of the newly formed National Association of Manufacturers (NAM) visited Germany and strongly advocated for the adoption of the German system of differentiated vocational training programs aligned with the hierarchical skill needs of German industry (Wirth, 1992). NAM, along with other organizations representing industry, unions, and educators, participated in vigorous debates that eventually led to the passage of the Smith Hughes Act of 1917 and to federal support for vocational education programs in public secondary schools (Gutek, 1991). Returning to its roots, the contemporary version of the Smith Hughes Act, the Carl D. Perkins Vocational and Applied Technology Act of 1990, recommended sending a national commission to Germany to study its vocational training programs (Wirth, 1992). Since passage of the Perkins Act in 1990, a number of educators, politicians, and policymakers have traveled to Germany and northern Europe and recommended that the United States adopt their approach to workforce preparation (Frantz, 1994; Hamilton, 1990; Marshall & Tucker, 1992).

The nature of the relationship between education and work is a basic question that transcends time and national borders. Consideration and analysis of the relationship between education and work in Japan, as well as in Western countries, can contribute to a better understanding of the basis for work-related education programs. Toward that end, the purpose of this article is to describe the basis for the relationship between education and work in Japan and, in particular, policy implications for the role of employers in workforce development.

Workforce development in Japan emphasizes the active role of employers in promoting internal skill development through extensive within-company education and training, as well as the supportive role of schools in preparing students for potential success in a wide variety of work settings. The role of employers in workforce development in the near and medium term is especially important because more than 75% of those who will make up the workforce over the next decade are already working (Office of Technology Assessment, 1990).

To better understand the role of Japanese employers, consider the example of a recent graduate of one of Japan's most prestigious universities. After finishing a master's degree in engineering, he began working for one of Japan's major private railroad companies. His first eight months of employment were devoted almost completely to *shinjin kenshu* (new employee training). Along with about 100 other new university graduates, he spent the first three weeks of training at lectures on a variety of topics, including the recent conversion of the public Japan National Railways to a group of private companies, the management structure, and union relations. Cairncross and Dore (1990) refer to this as the standard form of initial training provided by most Japanese companies to all new employees (college and high school graduates). Lasting from several days to several weeks, this first part of initial training serves to orient the new employees to the company, its philosophy, and its operations. Afterward, the initial training varies based on company size, company type, and type of employee (college or high school graduate, technical or humanities major). In our example, after the first three weeks, new recruits spent several weeks each at a wide variety of jobs, including selling and "punching tickets," railway maintenance, train operation, rail maintenance, and even pushing people onto crowded trains. They then received four months of general on-the-job training.

The new employee training experiences of this new employee are not unique. An investment of several months to a full year in new employee training has become the norm for large Japanese companies and the ideal of smaller ones (Cairncross & Dore, 1990; Levine & Kawada, 1980; Stern, 1988). University graduates who enter a major Japanese trading company spend some of their training time unloading fruit and vegetables onto trucks. Major Japanese electronics companies have their newly hired engineers spend a month or more working on an assembly line. Several of them arrange to have their newly recruited engineers work in a retail electronics store where they sell products, answer customers' questions, and even clean the store at the end of the day. A distinctive feature of initial training in Japanese companies is an emphasis on hands-on work. Rather than hear about or read about work in the company, new Japanese employees do work that is representative of the work of the company, not necessarily representative of their own future work.

Before entering the railway company, the young graduate in our example had no idea what type of job he would do in his new company. Even after completing eight months of initial training, he still had no idea what job, section, area, or where in Japan he would work. Finally, after eight months of education and training, he was assigned to a regular position in the Hotel and Restaurant Division of his company. Although his new assignment had almost nothing to do with what he had learned in school, he was happy because his new assignment would provide him with the opportunity to learn new things in an area that was of interest to him.

During the time this young man spent learning how to punch tickets, as well as other jobs, the intent was something other than the training about the jobs themselves. It is unlikely that he will ever punch a train ticket or push passengers onto trains again. During an impressionable time in this young man's career, important relationships were formed. Relationships were developed between him, other workers, his work, and his company. His extensive initial training helped him form relationships with *dokyusei* (other new recruits of the same age), with *senpai* (those who received similar training in the past), and with *kohai* (those who will receive it in the future), as well as with the experienced workers who taught them. Like the bonds formed between those who experience a common, and sometimes difficult experience, this initial training fosters strong and lasting relationships.

This extensive initial training also helps the new recruits form their perspective on work. The flexibility of Japanese workers is nurtured by exposing them to a wide variety of jobs during their initial training, and then reinforced by rotating them among different jobs throughout their career. Rapid rotation is a sign of success and future promise. Through job rotation, most Japanese workers are expected to continually learn new skills. Such job rotation results in a more flexible workforce and lower resistance to technological change. Conversely, it limits worker affiliation to a specialty or profession.

Through this extensive initial training, mutually dependent relationships between workers and their company are also formed. Workers come to depend on their company to initiate and provide work-related education, and thereby control an important source of information and influence. The companies depend on the workers' willing participation and trust that both they and the company will benefit in the long term. Work-related education, as practiced by the Japanese, is a long-term investment in human resources. In turn, Japanese companies fully expect to receive long-term benefits in the form of increased worker capacity, flexibility, and loyalty. Accordingly, their educational investment is not made equally in each employee, but instead is based on the expected return. Those workers who will remain with one company throughout their career (mostly male college graduates, as in our example) will receive the largest investment. Similarly, varying human resource investments are made in workers based on their age, sex, and educational background, as well as the type and size of company. It is important to recognize that Japanese companies are motivated to provide or sponsor education and training by their belief that it is related to the health and wealth of the company. Similarly, U.S. companies invest in education and training as they recognize its relation to company performance. Motorola, often cited as an example of a U.S. company with progressive educational and training programs, encourages all employees to receive at least five days of training annually (Motorola University, 1993). An important difference between Motorola and a similar Japanese company, such as NEC, is that NEC or other large Japanese companies are much more likely to provide the training inside the company. Although Motorola does provide education and training inside the company, American companies are more likely to purchase training on the open market from private and public providers.

Figure 10.1 provides a general framework for the analysis of the rela-

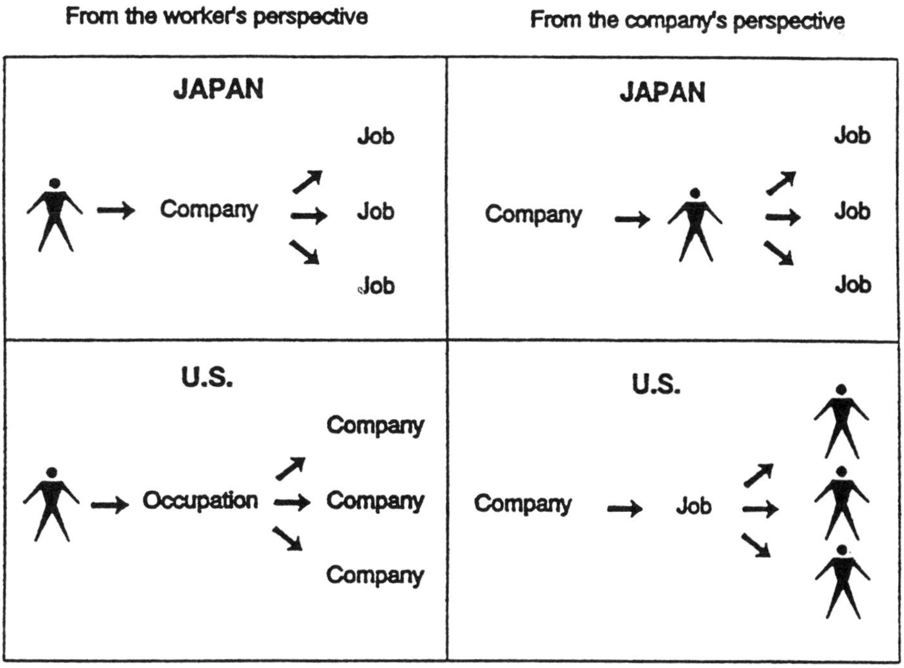

From the worker's perspective   **From the company's perspective**

Figure 10.1. A Framework for the Analysis of Workforce Development in Japan and the United States

Note: A job describes the work assignment in a particular company. An occupation describes similar work performed in any work setting.

tionships between workers, their work, and their companies in Japan and the United States. The figures on the left are drawn from the perspective of workers, and those on the right from the perspective of the companies who employ them. The upper figures represent the perspectives of most Japanese companies and workers, whereas those on the bottom represent most U.S. companies and workers.

As in our example, new Japanese graduates from high school, special training school, or college typically decide which company to enter rather than which job or professional specialty they will perform. Japanese high schools and colleges, compared with their U.S. counterparts, provide relatively general learning and little preparation for professional specialties (Cairncross & Dore, 1990; Hashimoto, 1990; Imada, 1993). In Japan, if you ask college seniors what they will do after graduation, they most likely will tell you the names of the companies they will enter. If you ask what they will do in those companies, they probably won't be able to tell you. They realize that after initial training, they will be rotated through a variety of jobs within the company.

In contrast, new graduates from U.S. high schools, technical schools, or colleges typically associate themselves with occupations and then search for companies that want to hire them in that specialty. If you ask U.S. college seniors what type of job they plan to do after graduation, they will probably be able to give you a detailed description. If you ask them what company they will work for, they probably won't be able to tell you (Stern, 1988).

Japanese companies carefully recruit prospective workers without paying particular attention to specific job skills. Instead, they rely heavily on the colleges, technical schools, or high schools the applicants attended. Using the schools as filters, companies try to select graduates who, on the basis of passing difficult school entrance examinations, have proven their abilities as efficient and motivated learners. The company assumes that as efficient and motivated learners, the new recruits will be able to receive a variety of training and rotate through many different jobs within the company.

As reflected in figure 10.1, most U.S. companies tend to pay much more attention to jobs and specific job-related skills. They prepare detailed job specifications based on job and task analyses. They actively recruit experienced workers from other companies who will need minimal initial training for specific jobs, or they seek workers with several years of successful experience in particular jobs. At its best this approach promotes a good match between prospective workers and predictable work needs. At its worst, it can lead to a "dumbing down" of jobs, limiting both worker and company flexibility.

The countries' different perspectives on education, employment, and work help promote different relationships between workers, their work, and their companies. In Japan, workers develop a primary relationship with their company and a secondary relationship with an occupation. In contrast, U.S. workers develop a primary relationship with an occupation and a secondary relationship with their company. As these relationships are strengthened, so are the bonds of mutual dependence. The Japanese approach to education and work promotes company dependence, whereas the U.S. approach promotes occupational dependence.

Differences in Japanese and U.S. labor unions also reflect this fundamental difference in policy. Traditional U.S. labor unions are organized on the basis of trades, crafts, or professions. Newer industrial U.S. unions cover an entire industry, such as automobile or steel worker unions. Unlike U.S. labor unions, Japanese unions are typically organized on a company or enterprise basis, rather than a trade, skill, or industry basis. As a result, the future of Japanese unions and union members is closely tied to the future of the company. Another important feature of Japanese labor unions is that they represent both blue-collar and white-collar workers. As a result, the unions do not restrict the rotation or reassignment of workers to and from different jobs and skill levels. Japanese labor unions strengthen the relationship between workers and their company, whereas U.S. labor unions strengthen the relationship between workers and an occupational area (Abegglen & Stalk, 1987; Sumiya, 1990).

The predisposition of Japanese companies to provide education and training within the company—*kigyonai kyoiku*—rather than have it provided by an outside source, reinforces these relationships. Even in cases where it appears economically advantageous to use an outside provider, Japanese companies prefer to provide the training themselves or to rely on a company with which they have an existing relationship. Based on extensive studies of small and medium Japanese companies, Koike (1988) reports that even small and medium companies with less resources available for education and training prefer to develop skills internally rather than to rely on external providers.

The foundation of Japanese within-company education has traditionally been an informal but planned use of on-the-job training (Cairncross & Dore, 1990; Hashimoto, 1990; Koike, 1988). On-the-job training takes place on a one-to-one basis during the time of work. It happens at the workplace, while employees are primarily involved in producing a product or delivering a service. Through on-the-job training, workers of all ages and all types are expected to share their knowledge, skill, and way of thinking with others and to learn from others while they work. Experienced workers model the application of knowledge, skills, and attitudes in the work setting and take responsibility for sharing their knowledge with younger, less experienced workers. The division between education, training, and attitude development in on-the-job training in Japan is not at all clear, but the intent is. Workers realize that their on-the-job experiences are intended to enable improved work performance in a specific company setting. While learning a specific skill on the job, a Japanese worker also learns the attitudes and behaviors modeled by the more senior worker, including the value of sharing knowledge and skill with others. Workers who learn together, from each other, and within the company develop common attitudes, understandings, and language.

To better understand the potential power and flexibility of planned on-the-job training, consider the following. In a major Japanese electronics company, a thirty-year-old mechanical engineering graduate works in a television circuit-design group. Although he has never had any formal course work or training in electronics, he designs integrated circuits. Over a period of several years, he learned about integrated circuit design on the job, by reading books on his own, asking questions of workers in his group, and watching more experienced workers. A new worker will soon enter his group, and the now-experienced engineer expects to spend about half of his time teaching and helping the new worker learn. In this manner each worker can be both student and teacher, reinforcing continuous learning through continuous teaching.

On-the-job training, as practiced in Japan, does have disadvantages. The same conditions that make on-the-job training possible, can also prevent it from occurring in different circumstances. Evans and Herr (1978) point out that on-the-job training as typically practiced in the United States has been relatively haphazard, a process where a worker "observes, practices, learns by trial and error, and occasionally receives direct instruction (if the experienced worker does not feel threatened by the potential competition)" (p. 10). For on-the-job training to succeed, the participants must share the same physical space and time; have a common base of perceptions, language, and understandings; and have a true willingness to share and receive knowledge and skill with and from each other. Furthermore, the content of on-the-job training is limited to the knowledge and skill that exists in the company. To overcome this limitation, Japanese companies have long supported *ryugakusei* (study leaves) for a select group of employees. Each year Japanese companies select key personnel between the ages of about 25 and 35 who are sent as visiting scholars or regular students to universities or research institutes for periods of professional development that may last from several months to several years. Their activity is primarily related to an important need of the company, but it is also related to the development of the individual. It may or may not result in a graduate degree and is often closely focused to a topic of interest to the company. Based on a study of creativity in Japanese companies, Stern (1992) identified study leaves as a strategy that contributes to the development and expression of creativity in the workplace. Although the practice of study leaves has been institutionalized in U.S. universities as sabbaticals, it is rarely practiced in U.S. companies.

An example of how study leaves can provide access to knowledge and skill, as well as contribute to the development of a key individual, can be seen in the example of the development of the world's first quartz watch by Seiko. In 1960, a twenty-eight-year-old engineer with a background in precision mechanics was sent to Tokyo University to study electronics for a year. After his return, his combined background in mechanics and electronics, along with his specific knowledge of watch design and manufacturing, enabled him to make a significant contribution to the development of the quartz watch and the emerging area of mechatronics. At the time of our interview in 1988, he was a managing director of Seiko Epson. This example of a successful study leave contributed to the development of the quartz watch, the area of mechatronics that led to the development of the dot matrix printer, and the development of a key person.

In response to changing economic and international conditions, Japanese companies have established many production, service, and research facilities in countries throughout the world. As a result, the composition of their workforce has changed dramatically. More and more Japanese companies employ workers who do not share the same physical space, language, understandings, or attitude toward learning and work. More and more of the work in Japanese companies requires knowledge and skill that did not previously exist. In spite of these significant disadvantages, Japanese companies continue to try to use on-the-job training. Although the cost is high and the investment risky, many Japanese companies bring their non-Japanese workers to Japan, where they can receive on-the-job training from Japanese workers while working in a Japanese setting. During a case study at a medium-size Japanese manufacturing company, I met a group of ten young Malaysians who were participating in a six-month on-the-job training program. Employees of a Malaysian subsidiary of the Japanese company, the Malaysian technicians were learning the operation of automated equipment that would soon be installed in their factory. Although they spoke little Japanese and had never been out of their country, they viewed their experience as positive. They contrasted their training in Japan with the more formal, classroom-style training they had received in Malaysia, where some students succeeded and some did not. They were surprised by the Japanese style of on-the-job training, where each of them worked with an experienced Japanese technician who, using broken English and gestures, carefully explained and reexplained the operation of the equipment. During my time in the company, the six-month training program was extended by several months to assure that the needed skill level was obtained by each of the Malaysian trainees.

For another view of Japanese attempts to extend their approach to on-the-job training to non-Japanese employees, consider the case of a young American graduate, who after receiving his electrical engineering degree in the United States, was hired by an American subsidiary of a Japanese electronics company and then sent to Japan for a full year of training. In describing his experiences in Japan, he told me that he had expected to receive extensive training in an "American-style" classroom, complete with text and technical content. Instead, he moved around the company, from section to section, seemingly without a plan. At first he was frustrated, but he gradually came to realize that he was learning many different things in a wide variety of areas. To the surprise of the Japanese company, less than a year after returning to the U.S. subsidiary, he resigned to pursue other opportunities.

Bringing foreign workers to Japan for on-the-job training is expensive, time-consuming, and risky. Although it is possible for Japanese companies to provide such training to a small number of non-Japanese workers, it is not practical to provide it to all. Those who do receive intensive on-the-job training in Japan or in their home country often find their new skills to be highly sought after in their local job market. For these reasons and others, Japanese companies have been steadily increasing their use of off-the-job training (Taniguchi, 1993; Yahata, 1994).

Off-the-job training may be conducted at or away from the work site. It is distinguished from on-the-job training by its exclusive educational intent. Off-the-job training is more formal than on-the-job training and may be distinguished by several characteristics, including:

Group learning instead of one-to-one instruction

A predetermined time period for training

The use of specialized training staff

More emphasis on general as opposed to context-specific training

A greater use of systematic evaluation

The use of off-the-job training does have several advantages. Through off-the-job training, uncommon skill and knowledge may be shared more effectively with a larger group. That is especially helpful in areas of new and emerging technology, where only a limited number of people have expertise. Standardized training materials, another characteristic of off-the-job training, also can ensure broad reach and consistency among training procedures and content. The principal advantage of standardized approaches is that they make it easier to reach a larger number of learners. The principal disadvantage is that it is difficult to meet individual or context-specific needs.

Even when Japanese companies move training from on the job to off the job, they continue to try to provide the training within the company rather than use outside trainers. It is common for top Japanese managers and engineers to be assigned to develop and teach classes within their company. Consider the example of an experienced engineering manager. After twenty years in a variety of engineering positions, he was rotated to a position as a manager for training and development in his company, a large Japanese electronics company. One of his first assignments was to coordinate a major technical training curriculum revision. He had no training, specialized education, or preparation related to education or the more general area of human resource development. On his own initiative, on his own time, and at his own expense, he enrolled in a four-year course in pedagogy conducted by Japan's University of the Air. He received lectures by television and radio and attended class twice a month at a nearby university. He also began reading studies and publications related to education and training. Through his efforts in self-development he became very knowledgeable and was instrumental in developing a major curricular revision for his company.

When it is necessary to go outside of the company for training, Japanese companies try to use companies or associations with whom they have an existing collaborative relationship. Just as the relationships among people are influenced by the provision of work-related education, so are the relationships formed by companies. Every small, medium, and large Japanese company maintains a complex set of relationships with a select group of other companies. Many of these relationships are maintained and strengthened through collaboration for work-related education. Large Japanese companies provide extensive training to their subsidiaries, subcontractors, and customers. Using work-related education as the medium, both information and influence are exchanged. Large companies are able to share technical knowledge, standards, and other information with related smaller companies. In a similar manner, a company's purchasing patterns can be influenced by the information it receives in the education provided by the companies who sell products or services.

NEC, a large Japanese computer and communications company, operates one of the approximately twenty within-company two-year colleges authorized by the Ministry of Labor. While attending NEC Technical College, the students are full-time paid employees of NEC or NEC subsidiaries. After graduation, they will work as C&C technicians (specialists in computers and communications) in NEC or an NEC subsidiary. The approximately 200 students of NEC Technical College receive education in a wide variety of subjects, ranging from English and mathematics to mechatronics, control, and systems engineering. By way of comparison, Motorola University offers extensive educational and training opportunities for Motorola employees, but it does not offer a full-time degree program (Motorola University, 1993). In addition to the full-time two-year program, NEC, like Motorola, offers many short-term, off-the-job, technical training courses to more than 1,000 experienced technicians per year. Reflecting the increasing diversification of NEC, more than half of the participants in both the NEC Technical College and the short-term training courses are employees of NEC subsidiaries. Through the medium of work-related education, NEC is able to develop and maintain important relationships with its subsidiaries.

The evolution of NEC Technical College is an indication of the importance that Japanese employers place on maintaining and strengthening their relationships with workers through the provision of within-company education and training. Today's Japanese workers enter the workforce with higher levels of formal education than ever before. In 1950, 45% of Japanese lower secondary graduates began working at age fifteen, after completing compulsory education, and 43% entered upper secondary school. In 1993, only 2% of lower secondary graduates began working after completing compulsory education, and 95.3% entered high school (Ministry of Education, Science, and Culture, 1994). As younger Japanese enter the workforce with higher levels of formal education, one might assume that companies will choose to reduce or eliminate their within-company education programs. However, rather than eliminate extensive educational programs for new employees, many Japanese companies have raised the educational level of their programs.

As shown in table 10.1, in 1956 when only half of lower secondary school graduates went on to upper secondary school, NEC started a three-year vocational training school for graduates of lower secondary schools. In 1970, when more than 80 percent of lower secondary school graduates went on to upper secondary school, NEC opened a one-year course for upper secondary school graduates. In 1977 the course was expanded to two years, and in 1986 the course became the first within-company technical college authorized by the Ministry of Labor under the 1985 Human Resource Development Promotion Law (NEC Technical College, 1993). By authorizing companies to operate company colleges and providing subsidies to groups of small employers, such as the cooperative that operates the Nara Cooking

TABLE 10.1
History of NEC Company Schools and the Japanese Educational Context

Year	NEC Company School Event	High School Advancement Rate
1956	Vocational training school for lower secondary graduates is established	51.3% of lower secondary graduates entered upper secondary school; 42.6% entered the workforce
1970	1-year machine course for upper secondary graduates is established	82.1% of lower secondary graduates entered upper secondary school; 16.3% entered the workforce
1977	2-year machine course for upper secondary graduates is established	93.1% of lower secondary graduates entered upper secondary school; 4.8% entered the workforce
1980	3-year machine course for lower secondary graduates is discontinued	94.2% of lower secondary graduates entered upper secondary school; 3.9% entered the workforce
1986	NEC Technical College is established, with 2-year courses in mechantronics and information technology	94.9% of lower secondary graduates entered upper secondary school; 3.6% entered the workforce

School, a two-year postsecondary school serving the employees of small restaurants in the Nara area, the Japanese government continues to promote workforce development for the currently employed through employers.

Through public schools, public training programs, and partial support for private postsecondary schools, the Japanese government attempts to facilitate access to employment. As described earlier, education in Japanese schools is relatively general, with little or no systematic intent to relate educational content to occupational application. This is true even in vocational schools, which represented 24.1 percent of upper secondary enrollment in 1993 (Ministry of Education, Science, and Culture, 1994). In distinguishing between the roles of employers and schools in workforce development, Imada (1993) said,

> Workers acquire skills primarily through on-the-job training rather than at schools and vocational training institutions. They learn and acquire skills by watching their superiors and through rotations from easy to gradually more difficult tasks. Knowledge and skills which are general rather than specialized are more suitable. Thus, the potential for training rather than a wealth of acquired knowledge, is what is desired. (p. 7)

In addition to a more general academic and occupational curriculum, Japanese secondary schools (under the authorization of the Employment Stability Law) accept responsibility for providing extensive vocational guidance and assistance in job placement (Imada, 1993). Similarly, cooperation between Japanese universities and industry typically has more to do with recommendations for employment than recommendations for curricular change. In this manner, cooperation between Japanese schools and industry is not based on collaboration for curriculum or instruction, but instead on facilitation of the school-to-work transition, which, in the ideal, will benefit both employers and individual students.

Japanese schools aim to develop the basis for entry into the largest possible variety of occupational areas; they do not aim to prepare students for specific jobs. In contrast, policy and practice in the United States, in general, continues to promote job-specific preparation to the detriment of both employers and students. It is this fundamental difference that merits our careful consideration, not for the adoption of Japanese approaches to work-related education and training, but for the reconceptualization of policy and practice in the United States.

This reconceptualization can be furthered through the consideration of policy implications of education and work in Japan. One of the most important policy implications is the need for clear recognition and support of public and private purposes in workforce development. The primary participants in workforce development are individuals, companies that employ them, and society as a whole. In general, companies are primarily interested in the development of the currently employed (specifically, their employees) and, depending on labor market conditions, the development of likely future employees. Society as a whole has a major interest in promoting workforce development to assure access to good employment for the largest number of individuals possible. The United States, in marked contrast with Japan, has been reluctant to define good employment in terms of either national or individual interest. Individual interest is primarily related to the enhancement and protection of individual employment opportunities. Although each of these participants has a strong interest in workforce development, their interests are not always the same or even compatible. In an attempt to secure a broad base of support, U.S. policy and practice tends to understate the differences and overstate the sameness. By way of example, one of the purposes of the School-to-Work Opportunities Act of 1994 is "to use workplaces as active learning environments in the educational process by making employers joint partners with educators in providing opportunities for all students to participate in high-quality, work-based learning experiences" (School-to-Work Opportunities Act, 1994). Embracing public-private partnerships as primary means for workforce development without clear communication of purposes, substance, *and differences* is likely to result in a dilution of efforts and confusion of purposes.

A second policy implication that can be gained from an analysis of education and work in Japan is the need for a better understanding of the benefits that can be derived from purposeful on-the-job training. As described in this chapter, Japanese companies receive many benefits from the promotion of on-the-job training. The formation of strong relationships based on the exchange of knowledge and skill; flexible and responsive learning opportunities; and effective integration of learning and working are all benefits of on-the-job training. In particular, on-the-job training is a primary means of providing work-related education and training for the currently employed. As such, it should be carefully considered in the formulation of workforce development policy and practice.

A third policy implication concerns the need for specific and strategic rather than general and unfocused government support of workforce development. As articulated by President Clinton when he signed the School-to-Work Opportunities Act, workforce development is well recognized as being important to our economic development and national interest. In spite of widespread support from politicians, business leaders, and educators, the appropriate role of government in the support of workforce development is the subject of much debate. Our view of models for government support of workforce development has been strongly influenced by the experiences of Western countries, such as the French and Mexican systems that require employers to dedicate a percentage of employee payroll to training, and the German system of requiring industry and schools to cooperate on apprenticeship programs (Bishop, 1993). Japanese government support of workforce development is specific and strategic, and in addition to support of public schools and agencies, includes limited support of private schools and employers. Within-company technical colleges are authorized by the government through the Ministry of Labor, but only those that serve the employees of small companies receive financial assistance. Similarly, the Japanese government authorizes and promotes skill certificates, but it only offers financial assistance on the basis of company size and worker age. Consistent with its approach to supporting the development of key industries, the Japanese government also provides support for education and training in specific areas considered to be important to national interest. Efforts to define a limited and strategic, as opposed to comprehensive and grand, national policy for workforce development may prove especially effective.

As in the United States and other countries, the relationships between education and work in Japan have been and continue to be important to the country's development. In addition to the policy implications identified in this chapter, consideration and analysis of education and work in Japan, as well as other countries, can contribute to a better understanding of important variables that affect workforce development.

CHAPTER 11

Education Policies in Taiwan (China) and Hong Kong

KIN BING WU

In recent years, high academic achievement, particularly in mathematics and science, of students from Japan, South Korea, and Taiwan (China) in international comparative studies has made headlines in the United States, leading to growing public interest in East Asian education. This chapter surveys education policies in Taiwan (China) and Hong Kong, two of the Four Newly Industrialized Economies (NIEs) of East Asia, in order to provide the context for understanding the *diversity* of educational policies and learning outcomes in this region. As will be suggested in the concluding section, there is equal value in examining the diversity of education policies elsewhere, such as among regions and states within the United States.

Taiwan and Hong Kong represent two major Chinese communities outside mainland China. Today, Taiwan has a population of about 21 million, and Hong Kong, 6 million. Both have pursued an export-oriented strategy of development and have enjoyed fast economic growth rates. Between 1965 and 1990, the average annual Gross National Product (GNP) growth rate was about 10 percent in Taiwan, and 6.2 percent in Hong Kong,[1] compared to 4.1 percent in Japan and 1.7 percent in the United States (Government of the Republic of China, 1993a, p. 25; World Bank, 1992, p. 219). In 1992, the per capita GNP was over $10,000 in Taiwan, and $15,400 in Hong Kong, compared to $23,200 in the United States, and $28,200 in Japan (GROC, 1993a, p. 1; World Bank, 1994, p. 163). According to a World Bank study, education was by far the single most important contributor, more so than investment, to the predicted economic growth rates of these two economies between 1960 and 1985 (1993, pp. 52–53). However, these two economies have very different political structures, which have led to marked differences in educational policies and outcomes. This chapter describes and assesses the education policies of Taiwan and Hong Kong.

Taiwan

Background

The island of Taiwan was part of China, except during the period between 1895 and 1945, when it was a Japanese colony, ceded by the Imperial Qing government of China after being defeated in the first Sino-Japanese War (1894–95). Taiwan was returned to Chinese sovereignty at the end of the Second World War. After the establishment of the People's Republic of China in the mainland, the Nationalist government retreated to Taiwan with 1.5 million mainlanders. In the early 1950s, about one in six of the population in Taiwan was an immigrant.

Throughout the 1950s, economic development was pursued as an integral strategy to ensure the political viability of the Nationalist government in Taiwan. The development of agriculture in the 1950s was followed by the promotion of exports in the 1960s, infrastructural improvements and industrial upgrading in the 1970s, and high-technology development in the 1980s. Since 1987, restrictions against overseas investments were removed, thereby opening a new era of Taiwan as a major investor in Southeast Asia, China, and even the United States. Within four decades, the structure of the economy was transformed dramatically. Between 1952 and 1990, agriculture declined from 32 to 4 percent of the Gross Domestic Product (GDP), while industry grew from 20 to 43 percent, and services from 48 to 53 percent (GROC, 1993a, p. 42).

Stages of Educational Development

The aims of educational development have been to develop the human potential, to promote social cohesion, and to support economic development. The educational agenda is enshrined in the Constitution, which not only guarantees educational opportunity for all, but also spells out the level of administrative and fiscal responsibilities for education to be assumed by central, provincial, and municipal governments. Educational policy is made by the Executive Yuan, which is advised by the Manpower Planning Department (MPD) of the Council for Economic Planning and Development (CEPD) in consultation with the Ministry of Education (MOE) (GROC, 1993b).

In the early 1950s, about 42 percent of the working population was illiterate. The priority then was to ensure that the next generation would not suffer from the same incapacity. Primary education was provided free of charge; children from low-income families were supplied with free textbooks. Girls, as well as boys, were enrolled. By 1960, primary education was universalized. As the demand for secondary education grew, nine years of basic education (primary and junior secondary) were made free and compulsory in 1968. The next stage was expansion of senior secondary education, including senior vocational education, as well as junior colleges in the 1970s (GROC, 1991). The 1980s marked a period of expansion of universities and colleges. By 1990, 85 percent of junior secondary graduates enrolled in senior secondary schools; about 30 percent of men and women between the ages of 18 and 22 enrolled in tertiary education, which comprised 75 junior colleges, 25 colleges or technology institutes, and 21 universities (GROC, 1992, p. 286).

The attention of the 1990s is on increasing enrollment in science and engineering (S&E), updating of curriculum, expansion of graduate programs, upgrading of academic qualifications of faculty members and researchers, and recruitment of overseas Chinese experts to guide and direct research and development (R&D). Enrollment in S&E in 1991 was raised to 66 percent of total enrollment in junior college, 43 percent in undergraduate programs in universities and colleges, 63 percent in master's programs, and 73 percent in doctorate programs. Public investments in the R&D infrastructure have been increased; national laboratories and precision instrument centers have been established in universities to strengthen R&D; and national science and technology (S&T) conferences have been convened to identify strategic R&D areas for future development. All of these drives were synchronized with the push towards high technology development in the economy.

Finance of Education

Between 1951 and 1992, total public expenditure on education has risen from 1.2 to 6.6 percent of GNP, placing Taiwan ahead of Japan (4.7 percent), Germany (4.1 percent), and the United States (5.3 percent) (GROC, 1993a, pp. 157, 159; UNESCO, 1993, pp. 153–155). Over this period, the share of education, science, and culture grew from 14 to 20 percent of net expenditures of all levels of government, the share of economic development increased from 10 to 25 percent, and the share of social security rose from 6 to 17 percent. By contrast, the share for defense and general administration fell from 64 to 29 percent (GROC, 1993a, p. 158). Increasingly, education, economic development, and social security have become cornerstones of social stability and national defense.

Public resources have been concentrated on providing and improving primary and junior secondary education, financing teacher training, and supporting a few elite universities to train future leaders, while private resources have been mobilized to finance senior secondary education, vocational education, junior colleges, and colleges. Even today, more than 98 percent of primary and junior secondary schools are publicly funded, compared with only 55 percent of senior secondary schools. Most junior colleges and about half of colleges are private; most universities are public (GROC, 1992).

One of the direct social benefits of investment in basic education in the 1950s and 1960s was the decline in total fertility rates in the 1970s and 1980s (World Bank, 1993). In turn, this demographic transition reduced the share of public expenditure on primary education from the peak of 39 percent in 1961 to 25 percent in 1991, and that on junior secondary education from 37 percent in 1971 to 14 percent in 1991. These savings have enabled the shifting of public resources to finance higher education by increasing its share from 15 percent in 1950 to 24 percent in 1991 (GROC, 1992). In this way, adequate resources have been secured to finance the formation of ever higher levels of skills as the economy has become increasingly diverse and sophisticated. Meanwhile, the decline in the share of the school-aged population has enabled increased public spending per student in real terms between 1976 and 1990—by 332 percent in primary education, 240 percent in junior secondary education, 276 percent in senior secondary education, 189 percent in junior college, and 210 percent in university education.[2] The increased resources have tremendous positive impact on the improvement of quality in education.

The Status, Education, and Remuneration of Teachers

The single most important feature in the education system in Taiwan is, perhaps, the very high status of the teacher, compared to that in mainland China and the United States. A 1980 survey on the prestige levels of forty occupations found that university professors ranked at the top alongside cabinet members and Supreme Court justices, and that school principals and secondary school teachers ranked second, equal to legislators, medical doctors, and engineers (Dahlman & Sananikone, 1990). Those who enter teaching are the dedicated and the academically able. This has been translated ultimately into a culture of learning and achievement. To attribute the high status of the teacher solely to the Chinese Confucian culture is to deny due credit to the policy that has fostered this status. It should be noted that China was also steeped in the Confucian tradition before 1949, but the past policy, particularly during the Cultural Revolution (1966–76), was to destroy the status of the teacher, thereby also undermining his or her contribution to education.

Given that the teacher plays a pivotal role in the formation of values and skills of students, the government has paid great attention to the education, placement, and remuneration of teachers. In the early years, a major constraint to educational expansion was the lack of qualified teachers. This has resulted in relatively large class size. Even in 1991, the average number of students per class was 41 in primary schools, 44 in junior secondary schools, 49 in senior high schools, and 46 in senior secondary vocational schools (GROC, 1992, p. 32).

In the 1950s, primary school teachers were trained in senior secondary normal schools, junior secondary school teachers in normal colleges, and senior secondary school teachers in universities. After the implementation of nine years of compulsory education, training of primary school teachers was upgraded to junior college. The 1970s and 1980s saw continuous upgrading of teachers' qualifications. By 1991, 94 percent of primary school teachers have received teacher education, 98 percent of those in junior high schools have had junior college education, 87 percent of the teachers in senior high schools and 78 percent of senior vocational high school teachers held a bachelor's degree (GROC, 1992, p. 34).

All teacher training institutions are public, and provide tuition waivers, free meals and living accommodations, as well as subsidies for books and clothing. In return, graduates must teach for a minimum of five years in a location determined by the government. Teacher education has high standards. Because education is a process through which individuals can cultivate their character and improve their conditions, to be the initiator of this process, the teacher, is a sacred calling. It is the obligation of the teacher to set an example of moral conduct, to impart knowledge and skills, and to give instruction without discrimination against students' background or ability. The failure of students is attributable to the negligence of the teacher (Smith, 1991).

These values and expectation for teachers are fully reflected in the education of teachers. Teachers are expected to need "a combination of interrelated, co-supportive learning experiences and curricula to be fully prepared in this most important profession" (Smith, 1991, pp. 156–157). Preservice secondary teacher education emphasizes general education (20 percent of coursework), subject specialty (60 percent), pedagogical training (20 percent), and educational foundation (integrated into other areas). In addition, schools are expected to be a model for the ideal world, and teachers are expected to set an example of cooperation and continuous learning for students to emulate. The collegiality and mutual support teachers give each other have been observed in the study of Stevenson and Stigler (1992), and contrasted with the professional isolation of American teachers.

The policy has been to encourage the best persons to enter and remain in teaching by instilling a strong sense of pride and professionalism, and by providing generous remuneration. Teachers' salaries are higher than those of civil servants of similar qualifications. In addition, teachers also enjoy a number of benefits, such as exemption from income tax, a special treatment that no other occupation in Taiwan is accorded. Unmarried teachers are given housing in dormitories, often near the school. Vacation hostels and low interest rate loans are available for personal housing. Rations for rice, edible oil, and fuel (which were important in times of scarcity), a free insurance plan, health package, a disaster relief fund, and benefits for survivors are provided for teachers. Upon retirement after a full career, teachers are entitled to a pension equal to 75 percent of their regular salary or a lump sum payment (Smith, 1991, pp. 158–159). Because of these policies, competition for admission to teacher education institutions has been keen, and the government has been able to place highly qualified and nationally certified teachers even to the remotest areas, thereby minimizing urban and rural disparity in educational quality.

These policies have been in sharp contrast to those in the United States, where salaries are not only low relative to other professions that require a similar duration of training, but also vary from state to state. This has resulted in difficulties recruiting and retaining the academically able into the profession, particularly in teaching mathematics and science, and in disadvantaged school districts. For example, the mathematics and verbal SAT scores of college-bound seniors planning to major in education were significantly lower than the average scores of all students (USNSF, 1993a, p. 19). Furthermore, elementary school teachers in the United States are less likely than teachers in Taiwan to have majored in a subject specialty other than education, and less likely to have taken more courses in substantive areas. The mathematics and science preparation of some middle school and high school teachers is not strong either. Students attending schools with a high percentage of minority students are more likely than students from high socioeconomic backgrounds to be taught by teachers who majored in education only or in a subject different from one they teach.

The attitudinal difference between teachers in Taiwan and the United States is also an important factor because it drives all other teaching practices. The motto of teachers of Taiwan is that all students are capable of improvement. Therefore, student mistakes are treated as an indicator of what still needs to be learned, whereas American teachers tend to believe in differences in innate ability among students, and interpret errors as signs of failure (Stevenson & Stigler, 1992, p. 40).

Achievement

The results of Taiwan's educational policy and investments are well known. In mathematics and science tests administered by the Educational Testing Service to thirteen-year-olds in twenty countries in 1991, Taiwan students' average science score was second only to South Korean students, and their average mathematics scores ranked at the top along with South Korean students (Educational Testing Service, 1992a, 1992b). In cross-cultural comparative studies, Taiwan's students in grades 5 and 11 also did exceptionally well, with very small variability in the learning outcomes (Stevenson et al., 1990, 1992, 1993).

The strength of the education system is also manifested in the strong performance of scientists and engineers from Taiwan. Bibliometric analyses of the databases of the Institute for Scientific Information show that between 1988 and 1990, the number of papers authored by researchers in Taiwan published in international journals increased by 58 percent from 1,086 to 1,720, and the scope of research activities also increased from 12 to 17 percent in all scientific fields within three short years. By comparison, the scope of research activities of the United States covered 98 percent of the scientific fields, and that of Japan, 69 percent. The number of American scientific papers remained unsurpassed by any country in the world, growing by 9 percent from 147,335 in 1988 to 160,384 in 1990, while that of Japan increased by 13 percent from 25,417 to 28,641 (Coward, 1994, pp. 18, 22). Although the scope of research and the volume of output from Taiwan remained very small in comparison with those in the United States and Japan, the rate of increase has shown much promise. Taiwan was rated ahead of South Korea, Hong Kong, and Singapore in three out of four leading indicators of technological competitiveness in socioeconomic infrastructure, technological infrastructure, and productive capacity (USNSF, 1993a, p. 471).

Scientists and engineers from Taiwan have made many contributions to the United States. Of the United States immigrant scientists and engineers in 1992, more than 10 percent were from Taiwan (USNSF, 1993a, pp. 82, 323). Many high-achieving Chinese-American students in the United States are children of these overseas students from Taiwan. The number of U.S. patents granted to inventors from Taiwan grew rapidly, from 80 in 1981 to 898 in 1991, a ten-fold increase, compared to the increase of U.S.-originated patents by 30 percent from 39,221 to 50,895 and that of Japan-originated patents by 149 percent from 8,387 to 20,916 over the same period (USNSF, 1993a, p. 455). While the total number of Taiwan-originated patents was small, the growth rate is impressive.

Lessons of Taiwan

Taiwan's success in economic and educational development is the result of an integrated approach that was pursued consistently over four decades. The government has played a key role in setting priorities, allocating public resources to capture the synergy of a coordinated approach, and mobilizing private resources to achieve the best results under conditions of constraints. A broad-based foundation in basic education was built first, while a few elite schools, higher-education institutions, and research institutes were developed to set the standards for others to emulate.

Four areas in Taiwan's educational policy are worthy of note for American educators. The first one is the emphasis on education as one of the cornerstones of social stability and national defense (McNamara, 1991). Taiwan's reallocation of public resources from defense to education, social security, and economic development undoubtedly has contributed to its economic and educational success.

Second, it is the policy towards the strengthening the status and professionalism of teachers through attention to the education and remuneration of teachers in return for dedicated service to *all* students, rich or poor. This is perhaps one of the most important factors in ensuring high quality education.

Third, great attention has been paid to ensure equity in access and equality of educational outcomes. Entire cohorts of students have been moved through the education system with minimal dropouts.

Fourth, the high achievement in mathematics and science among Taiwan students is attributable to the strong emphasis placed in these subjects throughout the school system. These subjects have become an integral part of education in the way the Confucian classics used to be in traditional education. With this foundation, it is relatively easy to improve undergraduate and postgraduate education, to establish the R&D infrastructure, to generate a workforce that industries can quickly equip with specific technical skills, and to build a national consensus for S&T development.

Hong Kong

Background

Hong Kong provides a case study of contrast with the experience of Taiwan in human resource development. Although both have export-orientations with high growth rates, Hong Kong was a full decade behind Taiwan in universalizing both primary education and junior secondary education. Moreover, university education was highly elitist, restricted to about 2 percent of the relevant age-cohort up to the late 1970s, although higher education was expanded rapidly in the late 1980s and covered 18 percent of the relevant age-cohort by the mid-1990s (Hong Kong Government Secretariat, 1981; Cheng, 1987; Hong Kong Education Commission, 1988).

The major reason education in Hong Kong has lagged behind other NIEs is its colonial status, although this will change when the territory is returned to Chinese sovereignty on July 1, 1997. The territory has been under British rule since 1842, ceded by the Qing government after China's defeat in the First Anglo-Chinese War, better known as the Opium War. The governor of Hong Kong, who is appointed on a renewable five-year term by the British Secretary of State for Foreign and Commonwealth Affairs, is responsible for the overall administration of Hong Kong. He makes policies in consultation with the Executive Council (Exco), and presides over the Legislative Council (Legco). Before 1984, all Exco and Legco members were nominated by the governor and appointed by the British government. Key policymaking positions in the Hong Kong government were held by British nationals. Britain's overriding concern was that the territory should not become a financial or political liability, and that it provide a base to advance British interests (Miners, 1986). For these reasons, public finance was managed prudently, with an annual average surplus of 9 percent of the budget, and a noninterventionist economic policy which facilitates free trade was adopted. However, there was not any long-term plan for social and human resource development.

While Hong Kong is administered by the British, its economy has been built by the Chinese. The massive immigration to Hong Kong from China after the establishment of the People's Republic in 1949 brought to Hong Kong industrialists, engineers, and technicians from Shanghai, which was the most developed East Asian city outside of Japan before the Second World War. They were instrumental in starting the textile and clothing industry which made Hong Kong world-famous as an apparel exporter. The continuous influx of peasant immigrants supplied the labor to make Hong Kong's export highly competitive in the world market. Industry was diversified into the manufacturing of plastic goods in the 1960s, and electronic consumer products, watches and clocks, and toys in the 1970s.

Since China opened its doors to foreign investment in 1978, labor-intensive production has been relocated to China, where wages are low. Hong Kong has become a major international financial center, notable for the syndication of loans and international fund management. The transformation of the economy is evident by the decline of the manufacturing sector's share of the GDP from 31 percent in 1970 to 16 percent in 1991, and the growth of tertiary services' share (including trade and catering, and business and finance services) from 60 percent to 77 percent.

Educational Development

Private provision and financing have played a key role in expansion of education in Hong Kong, in sharp contrast to Taiwan. In the 1950s and the early 1960s, government-subsidized secondary school places enrolled about 15 to

20 percent of the relevant age-cohort. With the large influx of immigrants from China, the growing private demand for education was largely met by schools run by Christian missionaries, educators, entrepreneurs, trade associations, and Chinese clan-based or local organizations.

A major phase of government-initiated educational expansion came in the aftermath of the riots of 1967. To diffuse social discontent, primary education was universalized in 1971 and junior secondary education in 1978. This was accompanied by expansion of teacher training in public institutions. The expansion of education also enabled the teachers' union to push for salary increases on par with other civil servants in the early 1970s. As there were substantial wage differentials between the public and private sectors, this has resulted in high economic status of teachers in Hong Kong. As a result of these higher salaries, it has been relatively easy to recruit academically able persons into teaching in publicly funded schools, particularly at the senior secondary level. However, teachers' salaries in private, proprietary schools remained low, resulting in the inability of such schools to attract highly qualified teachers, which eventually translated into the poor academic performance of students in these private schools.

Education expansion from the 1970s to the 1990s has been achieved through extension of public financing to support nongovernment schools. Over the years, public expenditure on education accounted for about 13 to 20 percent of its total public expenditure, or equivalent to about 3 percent of the GDP, less than half of Taiwan's and comparable to that in low-income economies (UNESCO, 1993). Private contribution to education made up for the rest. Fortunately for Hong Kong, increased income as the economy grew has enabled many to finance the education of their children through private resources.

In higher education, the government maintained control through the funding and accreditation mechanisms. Although private colleges existed, the nonrecognition of their credentials by the government effectively limited the supply of graduates until the late 1980s. Recognition was extended only to publicly funded tertiary institutions in Hong Kong, as well as to those in Organization for Economic Cooperation and Development (OECD) countries. Degrees awarded by Chinese and Taiwan universities were not recognized.

The premier institutions were the University of Hong Kong, which was established in 1911, and the Chinese University of Hong Kong, which was established in 1963 to accommodate the coming of age of the first cohort of the baby-boom generation. In 1971, the government also established the first polytechnic to train intermediate skills, and a system of student grants and loans to enable qualified students from low-income background to attend university. The polytechnic was not authorized to offer degrees. Until the early 1980s, the government had been reluctant to relax the restriction on higher-education enrollment, in spite of the strong demand for professional, technical, administrative, and managerial personnel in a rapidly growing economy (Cheng, 1987). The practice of recruiting British nationals abroad to fill the shortfalls in government continued, and high wages were rewarded to them.

Because of the restriction of opportunity for higher education, Hong Kong students tended to seek overseas education. In the mid-1980s, Hong Kong students were among the ten largest groups of overseas students in the United States (USNSF, 1986). On a per capita basis, Hong Kong led the world in sending students overseas. The 1986 census showed that 64 percent of university-educated workers in the workforce were trained overseas (Chung, 1991). However, because of the high cost associated with overseas studies, this option was available primarily to children from families of means. Thus, the restriction of higher education in Hong Kong had serious equity implications.

Hong Kong's policy towards higher education began to change with the launching of the Sino-British negotiation over the future of Hong Kong in the early 1980s. Public pressure has led to the invitation of a team of experts from OECD countries to review overall education policy in 1982. The OECD team observed, "The lack of qualified labor in all areas of social and economic relevance, and over all levels of qualification, is obvious to everyone." The team found "an overwhelming case for the expansion of opportunity for study at the degree level, with particular emphasis on degrees in technological subjects, and in course for higher technicians" (Hong Kong Government Secretariat, 1982, pp. 65, 68, 103). As a result of the recommendations of the OECD report, an Education Commission with broadened local participation was established in 1984 to coordinate the overall education policy in Hong Kong. Also in 1984, the second polytechnic was established.

In the same year, China and Britain reached an agreement over the return of Hong Kong to Chinese sovereignty in 1997. The impending political change has triggered massive waves of emigrations, particularly of those with internationally portable skills, thus depleting the existing low stock of highly educated people. This gave impetus to an immediate expansion of higher education. The third university was established in 1988. Enrollment in undergraduate and postgraduate programs was expanded, as were part-time, mixed mode, and evening studies in existing institutions. Polytechnics were upgraded to universities. Recognition and public funding were extended to private colleges. An open learning institution was also established to provide continuous education to those who seek it (Hong Kong Education Commission, 1988; Hong Kong Government Information Service, various years).

Achievement

Until the late 1980s, Hong Kong's education system, more so than Taiwan's, was driven by the limited educational opportunities at the postcompulsory levels to select students through examination. Until the middle of the 1980s, territorywide open examinations were held in grades 6, grade 9, grade 11, and grade 12 or grade 13 for the selection of students for subsidized places at the next higher level. The highly competitive examination systems weeded out the average students, allowing only those judged to be the best and the brightest to move up the educational pyramid. For example, in 1979, only 9 percent of any age-cohort in grade 7 reached grade 13, and only 30 percent of grade 11 students entered grade 12 (Brimer & Griffin, 1985, p. 20).

The International Association for the Evaluation of Educational Achievement's (IEA) Second Study on Mathematics and Science Achievement, undertaken in the first half of the 1980s, provided the first evidence of the Hong Kong students' academic achievement set against an international standard. The IEA science study found low average scores at the upper primary and junior secondary levels. The scores of Hong Kong's 9/10-year-olds (grade 4 students) ranked 17th among 19 participant countries/regions. At that level, about 77 percent of Hong Kong schools' average score was lower than the lowest school average in Japan (the country which ranked top). At grade 8, the scores of Hong Kong's 13/14-year-olds ranked 20th among 26 participant countries/regions; about 26 percent of Hong Kong schools scored below the minimum score of Hungary (the country which ranked top) (IEA, 1988).

One of the reasons for the poor performance was that the time allocated to science subjects in primary and junior secondary schools in Hong Kong was low, lower than the averages in Asia, Arab countries, and Africa (Holbrook, 1990, p. 70). Moreover, the between-school variance was great. For example, at primary 4, 34 percent of the variance in achievement was between schools; at secondary 2, it was 29 percent. This between-school variance reflected different modes of financing and variation in quality between publicly funded and better resourced schools, and privately funded and poorly resourced schools, the differences in the quality of teachers in these schools due to high wage differentials, and the tracking of high achievers into publicly funded schools. Furthermore, low achievers in primary and secondary schools were from low-income families, whose fathers had no or little education (Brimer & Griffin, 1985; Holbrook, 1990). These results showed that the education system was unable to bring the entire cohort of students to similar levels of achievement.

Hong Kong's 18/19-year-olds in the university preparatory level, however, performed remarkably well in the IEA Mathematics and Science studies. They ranked first in mathematics among participant countries. Grade 13 students ranked first in physics, first in chemistry, and second in biology, and grade 12 students ranked second in physics, fourth in chemistry, and sixth in biology in the same test. There was no correlation between paternal income and education at matriculation level; presumably high achievers who moved up the educational pyramid had the innate ability to persevere and thrive against all odds (Brimer & Griffin, 1985; Holbrook, 1990; IEA, 1988). These results indicated that the Hong Kong government did not place basic education of acceptable quality as its top priority. Quite the contrary, there was a general tolerance of underachievement of the masses, as long as a small elite was educated to keep the society running.

In the recent IEA international study on reading literacy conducted in 1992, the performance of Hong Kong students was mediocre, in comparison with U.S. students. Among the 9/10-year-olds, American students ranked second in the narrative domain (after Finland), among 27 participating countries, while Hong Kong students ranked 18th; in the expository domain, American students ranked third, while Hong Kong students ranked 15th. In the document domain, however, Hong Kong students overtook the United States, ranking second, above Americans' third (Elley, 1992, pp. 19–22). Among the 14-year-olds, Hong Kong students ranked 21st in the narrative domain, lower than American students' sixth-place rank. Hong Kong students performed better, ranking fourth over Americans' fifth, in the expository domain. They ranked second, higher than the Americans' 14th place in the document domain (Elley, 1992, pp. 28–31). These results demonstrated that Asian students, just like any students, could not perform well if they were not prepared properly. There is no miracle about the East Asian success.

How did Hong Kong researchers perform as measured by bibliometric indicators? Between 1988 and 1990, papers authored by Hong Kong researchers published in international journals increased by 45 percent from 462 to 672 (Cowards, 1994, p. 22). Considering the small stock of highly educated people from Hong Kong, this result was very impressive. This outcome was also consistent with the high performance of the elite in Hong Kong's education system.

However, the training of an elite without bringing the masses along cannot generate large positive impact on the development of the society as a whole. The same study that rated the technological competitiveness of Taiwan vis-à-vis other Asian economies also found Hong Kong lagging behind Taiwan, South Korea, and Singapore in socioeconomic infrastructure, technological infrastructure, and productive capacity by a very wide margin (USNSF, 1993a, p. 471). Hong Kong is unlikely to become another Singapore in the sense of having the same technological capacity and more options for development in the future, although it has twice the population and had a headstart in every aspect three decades ago.

Conclusion

The above brief comparison of the educational policies of Taiwan and Hong Kong shows different consequences of conscious policy decisions. In Taiwan, the government, through four decades of consistent efforts, has deepened the human capital of that society and provided a strong foundation for sustained development. In Hong Kong, the divergent interests of the government and the people it governed resulted in lost opportunities for many, and limited options for development for the future. While Hong Kong is likely to remain an international center of finance and business after its return to Chinese sovereignty, it is unlikely to become a center for high-technology development which can support China in upgrading its competitiveness. Because of the long gestation period required to build up the human resource base, both the positive effects of investment in education and the negative effects of underinvestment will be felt by future generations.

The entire focus of this chapter has been on two East Asian societies that have taken different paths to rapid economic growth in this new era of global competition. Taiwan, by focusing on developing a strong infrastructure of human resources, is destined to have much more positive and enduring prospects than Hong Kong. It is not too far-fetched to think of particular pairs of American states from a similar vantage point. What can one say about the future prospects of North Carolina, which has stressed science education and the Research Triangle Park, as contrasted with neighboring South Carolina or Virginia? Similarly, how does Massachusetts and its Route 128 haven of high technology and basic research compare with Connecticut? Or, in what fundamental ways do Ohio and Michigan differ in their recent policies and their long-term prospects? This study suggests that two economic systems may over the short run achieve similar outcomes by very different strategies. But through looking at the details of their respective strategies, and particularly those relating to human resource development, it is possible to gain a better sense of long-run prospects. Thus, the major implication of this study is to urge more detailed analyses of the path to success, and to urge less attention to external trappings of success.

CHAPTER 12

Improving School-Community Relations in Thailand

CHRISTOPHER W. WHEELER, JAMES GALLAGHER, MAUREEN McDONOUGH, and BENJALUG SOOKPOKAKIT-NAMFA

The Abbot in his saffron-colored robe listened silently as the two elderly villagers described how parts of the forest surrounding Paiwanwittaya village in northern Thailand had been destroyed over the past twenty years, first by loggers, then by some of the villagers. They talked about how important the forest was for food, fuelwood, and building materials. Unless this resource could be cared for better, they felt the future of the village was in jeopardy.[1]

After a long pause, the Abbot spoke in quiet, measured tones. He talked about how he and the village headman had been concerned about the condition of the forest for many years. But until now they had been unable to get the attention of the villagers. Villagers were aware of environmental problems but they were not prepared to act. The school helped to change that.

He described how this past semester sixth-grade students and their teacher had studied the problem of small forest fires set by some villagers. They learned that burning forest groundcover promoted the growth of mushrooms after a rain which could be picked and sold. These fires also made it easier to capture small animals and insects which could be sold to supplement villager income. They also learned that such activities killed trees and the small saplings needed to regenerate the forest.

Their presentation to the village, he argued, stimulated the kind of discussion he and the headman had been hoping for. He felt that now the three pillars of the local community, the temple, the village headman, and the school, could work together with villagers to address this problem. To him, it represented an important first step in preserving their forest and the village.

These reflections, made to Ministry of Education (MOE) officials and a Ford Foundation representative during a site visit in July 1995, capture the essence of the pilot project, Social Forestry, Education and Participation, now in its third and final year before expansion to other schools in Thailand. Six primary and two lower secondary schools in two provinces in northern Thailand are contributing to the capacity of their local villages to address significant problems related to deforestation and subsequent forest degradation through case studies of local environmental problems. In the process, teachers and villagers in participating schools are reassessing their views of school-community relations. In addition, teachers, students, and villagers are reassessing their views on teaching, learning, and the kind of knowledge important for youth to learn. By engaging youth in the study of local environmental problems and by establishing ways for adults and youth to work together in resolving these problems, teachers are helping students learn how to apply academic knowledge and skills in practical endeavors. The response to this approach has been positive as teachers and students find schoolwork more rewarding and as villagers see immediate and long term benefits from interacting with teachers and young people in the community.

In the United States, where schools and communities are experimenting with new forms of collaboration, the Thai experience provides a glimpse into how schools might improve student engagement in learning while promoting social change. The results of this program suggest one way to address the alienation of youth and the more general malaise so common in schools and society today in many parts of the world. By placing students in a position to contribute to positive, small-scale change at the local level, youth are able to find a more meaningful place in the affairs of adults.

In contrast to other chapters in this work, which examine long-standing educational practices in Asian countries relevant to educational issues in the United States, this project represents an innovation in Thailand which seeks to change the teaching and learning process in that country and to promote new forms of school-community relations in rural areas. While still in its pilot phase, the response by teachers, students, and villagers already suggests that under certain conditions it is possible to stimulate local teacher initiative to improve instruction in an otherwise highly centralized system. It suggests that by using case studies of local environmental problems, it is possible to move from a teacher-centered form of instruction to a more constructivist form of education in which concepts are learned through field studies, application, and interaction. The project also provides evidence that the local school can become a more active partner in efforts to manage local resources in responsible ways. The final two semesters of intervention will test the hypothesis that learning occurs not only through the study of local problems, but also during the process of implementing change in local communities. Taken together, these activities raise the issue of the appropriate role of schooling in relation to societal need for change.

The Thai Educational System

Thai education remained virtually unchanged for six centuries, concentrated as it was in monastic schools (Watson, 1984). Open only to males, it focused on character development to fit into the religious ideas of Buddhism. Vocational training for males and females generally occurred at home, under the guidance of a parent or craftsperson.

Beginning in the mid-nineteenth century, however, structural changes began, largely as the result of growing imperialistic pressures from colonial powers in neighboring countries. As King Chulalongkorn reorganized and centralized the government to meet this threat and to improve the general revenue base of the government, he expanded educational opportunities to meet the need for more civil servants. While his successor mandated compulsory primary education for all children in 1921, it took until the mid-1980s for this to become a reality. By then enough schools had been built and enough teachers trained so that approximately 96 percent of every age cohort is currently enrolled in primary school, which encompasses grades 1–6 and a preprimary program of one and increasingly two years. Moreover, within the past five years, dramatic expansion has occurred at the lower secondary level with transition rates increasing rapidly from about 30% (Meyers & Susangkarn, 1991) to over 73% by 1995 (Beach, Schwille, & Wheeler, 1992).

During the period of rapid expansion of facilities (1960s–1980s for primary school; 1980s–1990s for secondary), several issues surfaced and took on enduring characteristics. These included: the adequacy of teacher preparation, highly didactic forms of classroom instruction (called "chalk and talk" by Thais), disappointing levels of student learning, centralized decisionmaking and its stifling effects on local initiative, and the gap between schools and the communities they served (Suwanketnikom, 1987; Chantavanich, Chantavanich, & Fry, 1990; Amornvivat, 1986; Bhumirat et al., 1987; Valenti, 1979). This distance created a status barrier which not only limited parental involvement to more symbolic participation, but also served to devalue indigenous knowledge held by community members (Tsang & Wheeler, 1993).

Ministry of Education Response to Problems

Like all bureaucracies, the Ministry of Education (MOE) is no monolith. Not only do different departments have responsibilities (sometimes overlapping) for different types of education (e.g., formal and nonformal) and different levels of education (e.g., primary, secondary, and university), but also within departments there are factions supporting various approaches to educational improvement. For example, during the mid-to-late 1980s within the Office of the National Primary Education Commission a group of reformers led by an exceptionally able Deputy Secretary General used a variety of capacity-building and accountability initiatives to improve primary school quality (Wheeler, Raudenbush, & Pasigna, 1989).

Within MOE in the late 1980s and early 1990s, groups and individuals within MOE developed several promising initiatives to decentralize authority to schools to make more decisions about what is taught and how. For example MOE's Department of Curriculum and Instruction Development (DCID) undertook a major revision of curriculum guides for primary education in an effort to stimulate more curriculum integration, a greater focus on conceptual learning, and more student participation in the teaching and learning process. A key component of these guides was the effort to get teachers to use local materials to develop lessons in order to make content more relevant to student interest and to stimulate more integration across subject areas by focusing on problems or issues, instead of facts or chronologies of events.

It is within this stream of events that this project emerged in early 1992 and secured the necessary MOE support to begin implementation in May 1993 for two and a half years (until September 1996), encompassing five semesters. The project is currently in its fourth semester. Behind it was a group of MOE reformers, an outside funding agency (the Ford Foundation) which supported grassroots decisionmaking and was willing to think creatively about possible strategies to enhance such a goal, and a group of U.S. researchers from Michigan State University (MSU) with a view of how educational change might occur that could be adapted to another cultural context (see Wheeler et al., in press, for more details about this process).

The common point of agreement among members of this coalition was the need to develop a meaningful form of two-way communication between schools and their communities. On the one hand, project schools needed to develop a relationship with their respective communities whereby information flowed to the school. By changing the style of student participation and improving teachers' abilities to integrate content across disciplines, such information could improve student learning. In so doing, students and teachers could use the community to gather information to understand key concepts in the curriculum. On the other hand, participating communities needed to use the information generated by the school to better understand their environmental problems and possible alternative strategies to address them. The result of this two-way process of communication, it was hoped, would be a dialogue among community members, with the school as a participant, on how each community might address its problems and what role the school might play.

The Relevance of Social Forestry

Social forestry was chosen as the route to school improvement because it represented authentic content for students to learn, owing to the severe effects of deforestation on many rural communities in Thailand (Viriyasakultorn, 1995; Royal Forestry Department, 1993; Montalemburt Clement, 1983). It provided meaningful involvement with the community, fit the case-study approach, and provided clear opportunities for projects that might reasonably be implemented by schools and communities.

Social forestry is one response by the international development community to lack of access to forest resources by local people. Social forestry is an umbrella term for a wide range of small-scale forestry technologies including community woodlots, on-farm agroforestry activities, and community management of remaining native forests. What these technologies have in common is that they are small-scale, meet local needs, and provide for equitable distribution of benefits to local residents. Participation by local people is a critical element in social forestry projects. Trees and forests are a long-term investment. For forestry projects to be sustainable, they must belong to local people. This sense of ownership can only be achieved through participation.

Participation in social forestry projects has been defined in many ways. Most of the debate centers on the appropriate role of the forestry professional in initiating a forestry project. At one end of the spectrum are projects that are totally community-initiated. At the other end are projects in which local people voluntarily contribute labor or other resources but do not take part in project decision-making. The most successful social forestry projects are those in which there is a balance between community decision-making and assistance from forestry professionals. These projects are considered to be community-driven partnerships (McDonough et al., 1994). Community-driven partnerships are successful because while only communities can be responsible for identifying community needs and socially and culturally acceptable ways to meet those needs, sustainable forestry projects require technical assistance. Communities are often unaware of options available to them for solving forestry problems or of the biophysical constraints associated with forest management.

Linking schools and communities in the ways proposed by this project requires fundamental changes in styles of participation. If schools are to help implement new ideas about tree and forest management in rural villages, changes need to occur in classroom instruction, curricula within classrooms and across the school, administrative support at multiple levels of the educational hierarchy, and school-community relations.

Strategies for School and Community Change

To create school change, the project uses six strategies:

1. *"Teacher as learner" training sessions.* Active teacher involvement in training sessions to create greater initial understanding of project goals and participant responsibilities than more traditional forms of staff development. Such involvement also models the constructivist teaching strategies central to this project.

2. *A "handbook/guide."* The "handbook/guide" elaborates project goals, key concepts, strategies for doing a case study, and a model case. While introduced during the initial training session, it is designed to be used by teachers once they return to their schools. Developed initially by the MOE-MSU project team, the "handbook/guide" is a draft document, to be used and modified by project teachers throughout the pilot in an effort to make it "user friendly" before being used by teachers during the expansion phase of the project and teachers in nonproject schools.

3. *Teacher collaboration.* By involving at least two teachers per building, teachers can share experiences and discuss strategies to solve problems. Principals are encouraged to support teacher efforts to implement the project, and project participants across schools meet regularly to share experiences and problems with colleagues and MOE administrative staff.

4. *Supervision.* MOE staff at different levels of the bureaucracy are trained in a supportive form of classroom supervision which includes a debriefing on teacher decisions made during the lesson rather than judgements on what was done "right" or "wrong." These supervisors visit classrooms on a regular basis to provide ongoing support.

5. *Information.* Teachers are encouraged to develop links to information sources outside the traditional educational system, such as officials in the Royal Forestry Department and community members with valuable indigenous knowledge.

6. *Incentives.* A series of incentives are used to reward teacher participation. In the Thai system, teachers who successfully carry out and document classroom "action research" projects can be rewarded with promotions. The project has provided staff development to teachers in the requirements needed to document and submit their work to qualify for such

promotions. In addition, the project is encouraging policymakers from Bangkok to visit project sites to learn directly from participants about the accomplishments of the project. Finally, the project envisions a series of seminars for neighboring districts where project teachers can present what they are doing to colleagues from other schools interested in this approach to learning.

To facilitate community change, the project creates the conditions for the opening of a two-way channel of communication between schools and communities. The case-study approach is one strategy that provides the opportunity for teachers, students, and community members to interact. While student interviews draw upon indigenous knowledge of the origins and consequences of a specific problem, the process of interviewing adults is also expected to increase awareness by community members about the need to address the problem. A second strategy is presentations made by students and teachers to community members on the findings of student case studies in the community. These presentations should generate interaction between schools and communities regarding possible alternative strategies to address forest-related problems identified by students. Schools should assist villagers in identifying resource people, arranging visits to see related initiatives in other communities, and providing technical advice on specific alternatives. The anticipated outcome for schools and communities is the development of school-community partnerships focused on jointly developed projects.

Teacher and Student Response

From the perspective of teacher change, results at the end of the third term (of five) of this project have been encouraging. With the aid of fieldworkers trained under the auspices of this project, we have monitored the progress of twenty-three teachers in the six primary schools and two lower secondary schools engaged in this pilot.[2] When compared to ethnographic data collected before the initiation of the project (baseline), data collected after each term of implementation show:

1. *Improved teacher knowledge and project implementation.* Most teachers improved their understanding of the project and what was expected of them. They also demonstrated the ability to carry out the steps of a field study more easily, reflecting their experience from the first-term pilot. This improvement has been stepwise, not gradual. Each semester, most teachers made noticeable gains with the greatest coming in the third and most recent semester of implementation (March 1995).

2. *Improved field studies.* There were positive changes in the nature of the field studies each semester. Investigations became a more frequent part of the program and they were extended in time, using multi-day cycles of planning, preparing, field study, analysis, interpreting and reporting of results. This allowed students to prepare better, gather better data, and analyze data in greater depth.

3. *Expanded content.* Teachers included a wider range of content in their project-related teaching. In initiating the project, all teachers and students used interview techniques to acquire information from community members about the history of their respective villages, especially their forests. Later on, they moved beyond just doing village histories to inquire about forest conditions and causes of the major floods that occurred in the region during August and September 1994 and water shortages that occurred during the dry season in that followed.

4. *Curriculum enrichment.* Several teachers used what they had learned in the project to enrich the formal curriculum. In teaching regular lessons on plant reproduction, for example, some teachers took students to the school grounds and to local forests to examine the trees, explore their ecology, and collect specimens for later examination back in school. This increased use of application reflected the teaching-learning model guiding the project (Gallagher, 1993) and was virtually absent from earlier baseline data observations.

5. *Curriculum integration.* Many teachers successfully integrated social science with scientific concepts using an approach adopted by the project, called the "kite model" (Campbell & Olsen, 1991). This model focuses attention on the biophysical, economic, policy and sociocultural components of an environmental issue. In so doing teachers succeeded in connecting their village and forestry activities with the curriculum. Teachers also succeeded in using the "kite" to provide a conceptual organization for findings from the field. This substantially improved student understanding of concepts.

6. *Cross-grade coordination.* Articulation occurred across the grades as teachers took account of what had been learned in an earlier grade through project activities. Teachers in grades 6 and 8 created activities around the skills in interviewing, question formulation, and data analysis developed in grades 5 and 7. They also used materials and data developed in the previous year as additional data sources, and they moved more rapidly than before to begin field studies as part of their program.

7. *Creating professional communities.* At the primary level, provincial and district supervisors worked one-on-one with project teachers. Instead of

telling them what to do, they encouraged teachers to come up with possible strategies to address problems. In each province they brought teachers together on a regular basis to share ideas and discuss possible solutions to common problems. They held workshops to build teacher skills in developing instructional plans and connecting content to field studies.

Cross-school collaboration increased among primary teachers. In one province, by the third term nearly all of the project's primary teachers were meeting regularly after school on Wednesdays and all day on Saturdays. Throughout the entire term, district supervisors helped teachers in organizing the meetings and provided part of the intellectual support during these meetings. With this large investment of time, teachers made significant advances in their internalization of the project's goals. Moreover, teachers' implementation skills also improved greatly. Even more importantly, several reluctant teacher participants also made significant advances in their work on the project.

8. *Student progress.* In interviews at the end of each semester showed students nearly unanimous in their belief that the program made school more interesting because of studying local problems and their solution. Moreover, all students felt they had learned important investigative skills including how to design an investigation, gather and interpret data, and report it to adults. Of equal importance was the claim by students that their writing, oral communication skills, and self-confidence had improved because of community-based work.

9. *Areas needing improvement.* First of all, deficiencies in teacher knowledge of basic forestry concepts and social forestry limited their ability to assist communities in addressing actual environmental problems and in facilitating contact with knowledgeable resource persons. MOE has yet to organize appropriate staff development activities. Secondly, as task complexity grew, some teachers reduced their attention to specific process skills students need to carry out effective case studies, such as question formulation, supervision during data collection, and attention to careful data analysis. Some teachers experienced increased instances of poorly organized groupwork and control of student behavior both inside school and in the field. Finally, participation at the secondary level remained problematic with only three of eight teachers actively or moderately involved in the program by the end of the third term. Resistance remained particularly great among the four science teachers who continued to argue that such a field-based program was inconsistent with the curriculum they were mandated to teach and represented an inappropriate learning style for students in lower secondary school.

In general, however, the effects of the project on students and teachers have been very positive. With rather modest investment of external support, teachers have taken on the responsibility to implement a complex project and fine tune the guidelines to fit their local setting. At present, we are not entirely sure what prompted the majority (16) of the 23 teachers to act with such dedication. Research during the final two semesters of the pilot project will help provide answers to this question.

Community Response

At the end of the third term of implementation and the beginning of the fourth term, participating schools and communities had identified a wide range of forest-related problems confronting their varied communities including: forest burning to clear undergrowth, the need to plant short-term tree crops for fuelwood and cash, the need to plant long-term growth trees to replace those harvested by loggers, unauthorized tree-cutting by local villagers, and forest practices that have led to water shortage during the dry season or flooding during the rainy season.

How have communities responded to such activities? Focus group interviews and a household survey provide answers to the following questions:

• What do community members think this project is about?
• What do they see as results?
• How widespread is knowledge about the project and its effects?

In brief, the data show, first, that after only three terms of implementation, villagers across communities have come to understand that this is an environmental project designed to bring the school and community together and that it uses a new form of teaching and learning. Secondly, villagers see a wide range of effects from the project. For example, they perceive a closer relationship between school children and adults and a new potential for addressing serious problems relating to forests, forest protection, development, management, and utilization. Knowledge of both project focus and effects is substantially higher among villagers who have been interviewed by students as part of the project. There are, however, dramatic differences across communities in knowledge of the project. Several communities have over 60 percent of villagers who know about the project and its effects. Other communities have very low knowledge despite having teachers who are very active in the project. These results suggest that a spectrum of community involvement with the project has evolved across project schools raising questions about the events and activities that serve as the interface between the schools and communities in this project.

Relevance of this Project to Thai Education

This project, and others like it, address directly a number of the major enduring problems in Thai education:

- Teachers' need for new and different forms of staff development to compensate for inadequate preparation and the need for re-training and re-skilling over the length of one's career
- The need to change classroom instruction to make it less teacher-centered and more constructivist-oriented
- The need to involve schools and teachers more in the design and implementation of curricula
- The need to create closer bonds to and involvement by local communities
- The need to make schooling more practical so formal knowledge is related more clearly to actions and decision-making in everyday life.

Progress in this pilot project shows that a "teacher as learner" model of staff development coupled with ongoing supervisory support and teacher collaboration can lead to significant changes in teaching practice and teacher views of what schooling is about. Teachers no longer feel they need to be the sole source of knowledge. Instead they are increasingly ready to take on a new role of "resource brokering"—helping students and community members find out where to obtain resources and information to understand and take action on local problems. Teachers also have learned that students and villagers have much to contribute and that they can learn together as they collaborate on understanding and resolving local problems related to their forests.

Regarding curricula, it is instructive to note that none of the twenty-three teachers in this project, before its inception, had experience with developing their own instructional plans, relying instead on materials sent to them from Bangkok or their respective provinces. Most now display considerable confidence in this area and use it as the basis for experimentation with different forms of learning and evaluation. Finally, this project suggests that a systemic approach to change which creates the conditions for local involvement without prescribing specific directions holds promise for significant involvement at the grassroots level.

It also provides an opportunity for teachers and schools to become a part of the local process of change. The importance of this role was discussed in a paper by Paitoon Sinlarat, Dean of the Faculty of Education at Chulalongkorn University presented in July 1995 at the "World Conference on Teacher Education: Innovative Alternatives for the 21st Century." He described the need to create and support a "Thai model" that combined two major trends in education. The mainstream trend aimed at preparing and producing people to work in business and industry. Under this approach, education serves as a tool for the industrial system. Students are taught different skills and technologies which are in demand. The anti-mainstream trend. he contends, looks at old values and traditions which are said to be lacking in the first trend. He argued that in many less developed countries, the issue is how to progress economically and modernize without losing basic societal values along the way. Thai education, he concluded, needed to create a third approach:

> The third trend is one that equips students with the ability for critical thinking so they can become aware and selective regarding the information pushed into them. They should be able to decide what is appropriate and best for themselves while also being knowledgeable in the valuable traditions of the old ways.
>
> Teachers have long functioned as a tool of society by preparing people for jobs. This attitude needs to be replaced—teachers have to become aware that they can also set the direction of society.
>
> Firm knowledge, the ability to think critically and a socially-oriented awareness are the major elements to be integrated into teacher education—and that is the way to achieve the Thai model as I have defined it. ("Pressure on Teachers," p. 3)

Relevance of this Project to U.S. School-Community Initiatives

Many schools throughout the United States are currently re-examining their relationships with communities. This project illuminates three issues that are central to this process.

1. Linking Schools and Communities to Address Local Problems

Traditionally, U.S. schools have relied on mothers donating their time to participate in classroom activities as "room mothers," aides, or chaperones. They were asked to accompany students on field trips, help with special activities and ceremonies, and assist in the library. Parent-teacher conferences provided opportunities to communicate about the progress of students. Teachers called home to discuss problems certain students were experiencing. Parent groups, such as the PTA or Chapter I Parent Groups, assembled to view student programs, to provide reactions to policy proposals, and to raise funds for the school through various booster activities. And, of course, parents and community members had opportunities to run in local school board elections and to vote for local milleages which determined the funding basis for various school programs.

These more traditional forms of participation, however, assume parents feel enfranchised to participate in school-directed activities. In addition, they do not offer an opportunity for schools and communities to work together to solve local problems. Many U.S. neighborhoods have serious problems that could be addressed by developing better school-community relations. Schools can and should contribute to the capacity of their neighborhoods to address significant problems. Detroit, where one co-author works on an urban forestry project, serves as an example. Detroit has more than 65,000 vacant lots many of which are located in low-income neighborhoods. In addition to being eyesores, these lots pose significant environmental hazards as they are used as sites for dumping a wide variety of hazardous materials. Local block clubs and neighborhood associations are concerned with this problem and are looking for solutions within their extremely limited resources. However, schools are conspicuously absent from these activities. While some schools in Detroit participate in tree-planting activities, there is no effort by the schools to link with neighborhood groups. The Thai project described here suggests that schools and neighborhoods working together to solve the vacant lot problem could offer many benefits for both schools and neighborhoods.

A second illustration shows how the logic of this project can be applied to other issue areas. Another co-author is involved in a long-term effort to improve instructional quality in an urban middle school in Flint, Michigan. Social studies teachers and students are examining the issue of violence as it applies to their local setting (school and community). One component includes providing local block clubs with survey and case data on gang activity and its effects. Teachers and students plan to work with these organizations to develop strategies to reduce the effects of such activity.

While some schools encourage teachers to link in-school learning with out-of-school learning through service learning projects (Nathan & Kielsmeier, 1991; Conrad & Hedin, 1991), the model from the Thai project suggests a more active role for the local school as a partner with the community. While the approach used in well-designed service learning projects uses community resources to improve the learning of concepts, the notion of two-way communication at the heart of this project means that the school uses its technical expertise to assist the community in addressing the problem students have examined. Learning comes not only from the study of a problem, but also from the process of developing and evaluating alternative solutions and from the process of selecting and implementing the most appropriate one.

2. Improved Capability to Use Technical Information

Students, teachers, and community members in the United States are faced with the same difficulties as participants in this project regarding how to access, interpret, and use technical information. This project has shown that interpreting and using technical information requires an understanding of relevant concepts and a set of values that guide appropriate application. For example, unless people know about the manner in which tree roots penetrate soil and how leaf litter in forests forms a spongy mass as it decays, they will not comprehend how deforestation is related to problems of flooding and drought in a monsoonal climate. Moreover, they cannot adequately evaluate proposed plans, such as construction of reservoirs and dams, to reduce the effects of flooding and drought. This solution is costly, temporary, and ineffective because reservoirs typically loose capacity due to siltation in a short time, whereas reforestation provides a longer-term, less costly, and more effective solution to flooding and drought in regions of varied rainfall.

Educating the general public, including youth, to be able to use information effectively not only requires education in how and where to access information from sources such as books, reports, databases, technical experts, and individuals with practical knowledge, but it also requires development of a base of relevant conceptual knowledge and values to aid in interpreting the information and in using it wisely. This is a complex task which requires attention to all three components: technical skill in accessing information, appropriate conceptual knowledge for interpreting it, and values that guide appropriate use.

3. Process of Teacher Change

This project has succeeded in helping teachers make very important changes in the content they teach, in how and where they work with students, and how they relate to resources for learning available in communities. Teachers have also made significant advances in increasing their regard for rural villages and indigenous knowledge. Teachers have made great strides in learning how to use resource persons effectively in school and community work.

Key to change has been the creation of a professional community. A growing body of U.S. literature points to the importance of teachers' professional community as a context in which teachers develop their practice and become a part of systemic reform initiatives which can, and do, develop new linkages with surrounding communities. Such communities should not be confused with professional associations or unions which focus on working conditions and teacher welfare. Instead, professional communities are school-based and focus on the teaching and learning process. Within a school they stimulate increased collaboration and interaction, create extended networks linking teachers to colleagues within the immediate work setting and to sources of professional support and knowledge outside the school, and develop new shared standards of practice and conduct based on substantive expertise and standards authorized by the profession (see Sykes, Wheeler, Scott, & Wilcox, 1996, for a review of this literature and a case study of the creation of professional communities in an urban middle school). What is striking about the Thai context is the creation of such communities in a society where collaboration among equals is often seen as extremely difficult to create (Nakata, 1987). If such strong cultural barriers can be overcome in the Thai setting, the possibility for creating such communities in societies like the United States where collaboration is more accepted, may well be greater than currently anticipated.

In addition, support, guidance, and direction were found to be important in implementing a locally based curriculum plan. Such a plan does not need to be overly detailed; teachers can add components from the local setting. New subject matter knowledge was found to be essential to prevent teachers and students from floundering for want of clear new concepts. Most importantly, incremental change spread over time allowed teachers to gradually incorporate new ideas into existing structures of curriculum and school procedures.

The process leading to teacher change is complex. Some, if not all, of the lessons learned from this project may prove to be valuable for those in the United States and elsewhere who are considering ways to link schools and communities in a common effort to address pressing local needs.

Epilogue

The Abbot turned slightly in his chair. The sun poured through the open windows of the small primary school, touching the back of his robe and head so a shadow fell on the wooden table where he sat. He said that what needed to happen was for this project to expand. The forest was also used by two villages with primary schools on either side of Paiwanwittaya and by vil-

lages over the mountain, on the other side. Collectively they needed to develop a system for managing the forest that would take into account the needs of the poorest elements of each village while ensuring the future of the forests. He felt that was the only way rural villages like Paiwanwittaya could survive. To him, that was the real reason the project the students were doing was so important.

The Relevance of Asian Education

CHAPTER 13

Differences that Make a Difference:
Explaining Japan's Success

THOMAS P. ROHLEN

National systems of education are under comparative scrutiny as never before. The major reason, of course, is international economic competition. One might think that the shrinking of global space due to advances in communication and transportation would inherently encourage comparison. However, our public educational system is far more insulated by national and cultural borders than are our corporations, our military, or our scientific establishment. Left to its own devices, there is little reason to think that American education would be inclined to look outside for answers to its problems. The question of learning from or even understanding the East Asian experience is thus a tricky one, involving a reluctant audience.

The Competitiveness Agenda

The rising tide of naive enthusiasm for education's benefits among economists, scientists, business people, elected officials, and proponents of greater competitiveness is primarily the result of their concern with global shifts in power and prosperity. Whole societies today are being compared in terms of competitive strength and their capacity to keep jobs and attract investment. Education and human resources are a very important part of this story.

Yet the new agenda thrown on the already cluttered table of goals for our schools makes educators uncomfortable. Competitiveness is not a perspective legitimated by familiar ideals. It does not begin with notions of social equality or individual growth or political freedom or humanism or cultural tolerance or democracy or even civilization. Rather, it arises largely from the more mundane ambitions of efficiency, social order, and economic well-being. The focus is on job skills, work habits, and industrial knowledge. The language is one of standards, measurement, benchmarking, feedback, incentives, and accountability. The demand is essentially for success in attaining measurable results, not for inspired ideals or interesting pedagogical experiments. Faith in good teaching and the professional judgment of educators is waning. Most educators, guardians of our secular values, naturally find this new environment uncomfortable. Global competition is thus a mixed blessing for education, and any consideration of East Asian "success" or of learning from countries like Japan, Korea, and Taiwan must begin by recognizing our own ambiguity. Asia, furthermore, is alien cultural territory, and its rising strength is threatening. Not only are many jobs on the line, our national values and very way of life seem to be at issue.

Our defensiveness, for whatever reason, has led to distortions in the public image of education in East Asia. Portraits emphasizing "exam hells," authoritarian teachers, student malaise, lack of creativity, and excessive conformity are common. These portraits raise doubts that there is anything to be learned from school systems with such a seemingly alien character. Success at such a price, we say to ourselves, is actually no success at all.

I cannot agree. I think I speak for most of my colleagues who study Asian education in asserting that there is much to learn. We find many faults with Asian systems of education and do not always agree on what is most important to their success. However, these differences make for lively debate, not dismissal of the topic. We seek to understand first and only then to draw practical lessons.

To learn effectively from Asia is first to understand how the many elements of one large system fit together. I will focus on Japan in what follows. The other East Asian nations share many similarities, but their differences, too, are significant.

A Particular Kind of Success

What do we mean by success in Japan's case? Because Japan's very high standing in international achievement tests is what is most often mentioned, the term *success* is defined by the results of comparative international research and opinion, which provide us with a clear sense of what the Japanese do well and what they do poorly in their school system. In math and science, at all levels, Japanese students perform at or near the top of all participating countries. Here is a concrete measure that gets public attention. It is the measure selected by the state governors in their call to educational arms. If the Japanese performed at an average level on these tests, or if other East Asian nations with high economic growth were not also at or near the top, it is unlikely that we would find these tests raised in importance to the level of being a major policy focus. The unfortunate side of this starting place for comparative (and competitive) educational analysis is that it narrows the debate to specific kinds of accomplishments and becomes preoccupied with the test results rather than with the exploration of the process by which children actually learn. It turns our attention away from many of the most critical lessons.

A second aspect of Japanese success is the way educational outcomes are patterned across the population. The same international test results provide clear evidence that the range in student performance is relatively narrow by international standards. Excellence is not achieved, in other words, at the expense of creating looming gaps in the population. This inclusiveness is further documented by the fact that 90 percent of today's nineteen-year-olds in Japan are graduating from high school, not all with exactly the same amount of knowledge and ability, of course, but educationally much more together than the vast range of Americans their age. Dropouts are few, illiteracy is nil, and even the academically weakest students completing high school get jobs, thanks to their teachers (Okano, 1993). Put another way, Japan educates so as to emphasize the middle range of ability and to minimize the degree of deviation from the norm.

Math and science are not the only subjects where we see high achievement. Music, reading, art, and social studies are taught with great skill and to high standards. No international test results are available, of course, but American scholars and teachers who have spent time observing Japanese classes attest to the quality of the work. On the other hand, Japanese accomplishments in language arts, critical thinking, foreign language instruction, and civics are topics much debated and rarely if ever praised. As far as these subjects are concerned, Japan could do much better and could benefit from adopting practices common in other countries.

Japan's success can be defined in other ways, too, ways less consistent with the current focus on output measures. Quite contrary to the stereotype of rigid, competitive Japanese schools, there is broad agreement that Japanese elementary schools are rich in caring, cooperation, and support (see Lewis, this volume; Peak, 1992; Sato, 1991). Considerable exploratory learning occurs. Enthusiasm and spontaneity are abundant. Yet few would say that Japanese elementary schools are disorderly. There is ample evidence also that students learn to cooperate with one another and to participate in the orderly governance of their environment. Lewis writes extensively about elementary schools in this volume and the reader is referred to her chapter.

An important question to ask at this point, however, is where do we draw the line between a successful outcome and a contributing factor to such an outcome? Are we to view very effective elementary schools as successes in and of themselves or as causes of larger and more inclusive achievements, such as those measured by international tests? Obviously, we can and should do both. The point is, however, that by defining national success in a certain manner (such as international achievement test results or percentage of students completing secondary education), we have arbitrarily begun to order an explanation and fix the direction of cause and effect, dismembering the complex fabric of the actual, systemic relationship to suit our current interests.

To continue, the costs of Japanese education are low, implying that administrative priorities are right and that the organization works well. In terms of educational expenditure as a percentage of Gross National Product (GNP), the United States spends close to 7% and Japan averages about 5.5%. Clearly, the size of public spending cannot explain Japan's student achievement. In summary, expert consensus is that Japan educates nearly its entire population to European academic (relatively elite) standards, while coming close to American ideals for full popular participation through secondary school. It teaches more than the basics very well, but its strength in the basics is most notable. It accomplishes these goals while spending considerably less GNP on education per student than the United States.

Yet we also agree with the Japanese critics that their system is seriously flawed and in need of certain reforms. As far as universities, entrance exams, and secondary teaching to those exams is concerned, there is no question that we think there is much room for improvement. Do we agree with the stereotypes of Japanese education as promoting extreme forms of rote learning, competition, conformity, compliance, and student anxiety? As a rule, no. We acknowledge these qualities to be present, especially in the junior and senior high school years, but not to the degree critics of the system claim. The competitive stress levels are notably high (especially for males) during two 6- to 12-month periods prior to the entrance exams for high school and university. Are students unhappy and are schools like dismal factories? Again, no. But there are greater pressures for academic work than in the United States, and there is a progressive narrowing of focus aimed at serious exam preparation, which contrasts quite remarkably with the flourishing youth culture we have encouraged in grades 7 to 12 (see Fukuzawa, 1989; LeTendre, 1994).

We also find Japanese education to be equitably distributed in the population relative to our own. Is it designed to promote equal opportunity and social justice? Definitely not, in an absolute sense. Officialdom is disturbingly silent on most social issues. Japanese education sponsors a more equitable society (see Cummings, 1980), but it does not grapple openly with many kinds of discrimination and prejudice. By social justice measures, it would get mixed reviews.

Let us note what else is not part of Japan's success. The average achievement level is indeed high, but no one would claim that Japan does particularly well with either those students of exceptional talent or with those limited by learning disabilities. Nor is there any claim that schools are outstanding for their capacity to teach democracy or entrepreneurship or creativity or any of a long list of less strictly academic skills and attitudes. The secondary curriculum is especially limited compared to the American one. Nor are such rhetorical skills as self-expression and argument given much time or emphasis. After the exuberant and participative style of elementary instruction, there is a precipitous dropoff in incidental classroom discussion. Topics from current events or questions of human relationships or debates about political philosophy are rare in high school. What must be learned is increasingly standardized as the student passes upward, and what students have to say becomes increasingly less important. Japanese education is an abject failure if measured by the standards of Western individualism or rhetoric, nor is it notably successful when judged by other yardsticks favored by some in the United States (see Rohlen, 1983). The "basics" are what count, but the basics are not just math, reading, and science. They include art and music, social studies, literature, and foreign language (English). Social skills such as cooperation are also very central to the educational effort.

To repeat, success means high average achievement in a range of subjects distributed with relative equity over the student age population at relatively low public cost. This is no mean achievement, and we next ask how it is explained. My focus will be on those explanations that define the context for classroom instructions.

Entrance Exams: The Competitive Factor

Far better known to us than her wonderfully active elementary schools is Japan's competitive system of entrance examinations. These occur at the entry points to secondary schools and universities. Around exams pivots a system of incentives that greatly shape the behavior of students, parents, and, to a degree, teachers (Rohlen, 1983). Complex as they are, these effects can be boiled down to a simple, logical framework of rewards and punishments, a kind of explanation easy to understand and just as easy to exaggerate. Knowing about the basic rewards and punishments connected to education can tell us much about raw individual motivation and its place in a competitive system, but it cannot tell us about the rest of the sociocultural context that is also critically important.

Entrance exams are a national preoccupation. Hated, respected, closely followed, and intensely debated, they have anxious parents in their grip. As the times for exams approach (that is in eighth and twelfth grades), teachers and students too fall heavily under its spell. During these times it is easy to equate education with exam preparation. The classic distortions that accompany test-centered learning occur. So, also, an enormous amount of effort on learning is expended. The time devoted by Japanese students to cramming, some of it in school and more outside, is impressive. The value of the learning taking place is another matter, of course, and worthy of more serious debate than it receives. As it stands, everyone is against rote learning, cramming, and, therefore, the Japanese exam system. It has no public proponents; nevertheless, it survives.

Despite the many horror stories, I would argue that we cannot ignore the likelihood that much real learning occurs in exam preparation. Obviously, math and science mastery in these circumstances cannot be shallow learning, but what about memorizing obscure English vocabulary and trivial facts from one's social studies text? Clearly, there are sharply diminishing returns to test-oriented study in such instances. Nevertheless, some learning is taking place, and some of the information memorized will stick.

Are there better kinds of learning? Of course. But the issue remains: Compared to what? If we make some ideal form of learning the alternative, cramming looks impoverished, but if our comparison is with the reality of little study at all or a superficial kind of achieved glibness, then even the cramming Japanese students do seems quite positive. It is an intense engagement with facts and ideas; it teaches concentration and sets a high standard of meticulousness; and it lifts the student's capacity for self-discipline—not all that learning in adolescence should be, but important nevertheless.

Entrance Exams: Systemic Effects

But the influence of entrance exams does not rest primarily with the cramming issue. Its influence is much deeper and more systemic. Overt cramming is only the tip of the iceberg. Far more significant are the following: parental concern with their children's education, the national emphasis on effort, the high level of private expenditure on children's learning, and the esteem for educational achievement. All of these are enhanced by the entrance-exam system. First, patents begin attending to their children's intellectual development early, because they know that off in the distant future the entrance exams await them. Parents, who were once themselves exam candidates or those with ambitions for their children are reminded regularly by the media of the educational day of reckoning. They begin strategic planning and anxious supervision early compared to American parents. They pay for supplementary tutoring on a massive scale. Nearly half of Tokyo's sixth-graders, for example, are getting after-school extra help with one or more basic subjects (math and English are the most popular).

The willingness to spend private funds to increase one's child's prospects is notable in Japan, as it is in Korea, Taiwan, Hong Kong, and Singapore, where government budgets tend to be less generous than in the West. Government planners can today count on families to contribute significantly to the overall national effort in education. It would be interesting to compare total public and private spending on education in the East and in the West to discover whether the actual costs in East Asia are not higher than official figures imply.

The shaping of attitudes is even more important. From the time of the establishment of the first government university in 1877 to the present, there has been an almost one-to-one identity between academic success (in entering the top universities) and social prestige (that accrues to talent and high office) (Amano, 1990). The initial goal was to create as meritocratic a system as possible, and this equated access to elite positions with examination results. Naturally, the overall importance of education receives a continual boost as a result. Elite status implies intelligence, of course, but that is never enough. To do well in the exams, then and now, requires great devotion to the task. Diligence, self-discipline, concentration, and perseverance are highly valued character traits (predating entrance exams) that lend successful examinees a halo of virtue. Especially for boys, to be a good student is analogous to being a good athlete in this country—everyone is pleased, and a kind of social grace is bequeathed. If universities were less tied to employment prospects, or easier to enter, or if there were no lifetime employment in government and prestigious companies, or if money and inherited privilege played a more significant role, the emotional and moral hold of exams and education on the population would not be as great, but how much less is difficult to estimate.

It is instructive to note in this regard that government policy (except during the American occupation) has always been to limit access to higher education. It is not clear whether this results from fear of creating unemployment among the highly educated, or an interest in allocating public funds more universally by emphasizing elementary education, or a conscious desire to keep competition levels intense. Even when the government has expanded the number of national universities, public demand has grown even faster, with the entrance of at least three-quarters of the population into the middle class due to economic prosperity. Here too we see a pan-East-Asian pattern of government constraints on higher education, extensive private demand, and the mushrooming of private universities after World War II (when American influence caused governments to cease actively constraining private higher education).

In comparative terms, our system of university entrance began in the private sector, always mixed privilege with merit, and sought to identify capabilities as well as recognize studious effort. Access to higher education, furthermore, expanded rapidly as part of our style of democratic society. Only in limited areas of our society do higher education and academic competition have the same intense hold on families and schools as in Japan. We all know these spheres—the wealthy suburbs, the professions, university people, teachers, and others for whom an elite education means a great deal. Japan's advantage is that this attitude covers perhaps three-quarters of the population.

What about teaching to the entrance exams? The picture is mixed. Elementary teachers generally work very hard to ignore this ultimate reality and are against parents spending money and time preparing their children for it. Both the Ministry of Education and the Japan Teachers Union are strongly against teaching to the exam. Secondary teachers are more ambivalent. They generally complain about the necessity, but teach with exams uppermost in mind, explaining that they feel a duty to their students. Exams are the reality in more than half of Japan's high schools. Not to face their looming power over future careers is to penalize the students. Furthermore, the discipline of preparation is valued at the secondary level as part of the perceived student maturation process for which teachers are responsible.

This does not mean that teachers favor competition in the classroom. The competition is national, and teachers urge their students to support one another in meeting the common challenge. It is one of the great ironies of Japanese education that such a competitive system in the larger sense is also home to a consistent use of cooperative, peer-based approaches at the school level. Except for our best public and private schools, university entrance competition is neither as competitive nor as all-consuming. Put bluntly, we have no equivalent nationwide motivational force. In fact, by creating a system which makes the opportunity for higher education so available, we have reduced the competitive and motivational power of our system. The trade-off between opportunities and incentives is not one we address, but in comparative terms it appears important.

Administration: The National Level

Nothing could be more unpopular in educational circles than to suggest that school systems have much in common with corporations. Yet considering the many systemwide issues involved in aggregate national achievement leads one to ask about organizational forms and management practices. Given our definition of Japan's success, we must ask: What makes for the effective execution of the policies aimed at such goals? The answers point to a fixed context, clear direction, adequate latitude, and ample support for teachers and schools.

It is widely understood that coherence, consistency, stability, and coordination are crucial aspects of sustained implementation. The larger the system, the more important are these properties. A national system of education certainly qualifies as a large organization. Japan's school system is far larger than any other organization in the country.

From its inception, public education in Japan has been relatively centralized and dedicated to national goals. The American occupation led to a devolution downward of some of the powers of the Ministry of Education, but from an American viewpoint the national aspects of the system first command our attention.

National standards are definitely in effect, but they are realized through the rather extensive curricular guidelines that govern what is taught at all levels up through grade 12. Nor are these guidelines so detailed as to appear to dictate teacher conduct. Rather, they are general goal statements. They do not focus exclusively on cognitive matters, but, rather, include moral development, cooperation, study habits, and so forth. Textbooks based on these guidelines provide a great deal of material, and these form a concrete basis for the national system of instruction. Textbooks are privately developed but published only with the ministry's approval. Because the textbooks are standardized nationally, they become the basis for the entrance exams. They also play a major role in shaping the day-to-day conduct of classroom teaching, especially from grades 7 to 12, where the lecture format and entrance-examination preparation are increasingly central. At lower grades, teachers combine their use of texts with considerable locally developed pedagogy. Teachers at all levels may use the texts with considerable latitude in terms of what they add or what emphasis they give. Stevenson and Stigler (1992) note insightfully that teaching in Japan is like learning to play already written music skillfully, whereas in our country it is like learning to play while simultaneously writing and rewriting the music.

The very thought of a national curriculum raises many constitutional and other legal problems for us. Japan, by contrast, is not a litigious nation. Conflicts are dealt with differently, and in education this means that the environment even in the classroom is different. One simply does not encounter a sensitivity to the possibility of legal suits among teachers and administrators. Rules are strictly enforced at the discretion of senior officials, and there is a great sensitivity to those matters that are contested between the teachers' union and the government, but lawyers and courts are not setting policy or shaping teacher conduct. No doubt this tells us less about Japan than it does about our own administrative environment. From a Japanese perspective, as the intrusion of our legal culture into American education must be judged as disruptive, cause for great uncertainty, productive of much risk-adverse behavior, and, most telling, symbolic of our low levels of public trust.

Another aspect of the national administrative environment worth noting is the use of foreign examples. For over a century the Japanese have benchmarked themselves against the advanced nations of the world, always with the goal of constructive self-criticism. They still do this, but they now choose their targets carefully to fit the next stage of improvements they plan for the system. Even when we benchmark, we do it with a crisis mentality and without an underlying clear plan.

National curricular guidelines are not written so as to be measured. There is no felt need for an overt system of accountability, as in the United States. The ministry has not put in place national testing by which prefectures, schools, and/or teachers might be annually measured, judged, rewarded, or chastised. Feedback comes to the ministry via the annual sampling work of the quasi-official National Institute for Educational Research, but the results are for planning and policy purposes only. Teachers get feedback from their own tests, from other teachers, and from local board of education supervisors (themselves career teachers). These supervisors, in turn, continually take the pulse of instructional quality for local administrations. As might be expected, parents and students get feedback from grades and teacher conferences, but their primary attention is actually on the degree of preparedness for the entrance examinations. These are measured by practice tests conducted by private firms specializing in helping students target accurately what universities to apply to. From about eighth grade on, these private tests play a major role in predicting a child's future opportunities. The multiplicity of feedback systems is a response to differences of need.

The Japanese national curriculum forms a context for increased professionalism. The intensity of in-service training conducted for teachers by teachers is very impressive, for example, encouraged by the fact of shared guidelines, texts, and expectations about entrance exams. Teachers throughout the country learn readily from one another because they work within a single common framework. As in all respected professions, skill development is expected regardless of monetary incentives. This professionalism is encouraged by a set of personnel policies that reflect its philosophy, namely:

1. Job tenure after the first year
2. Year-round employment

3. Relatively high starting salaries
4. A seniority-based system of salary increases.

The critical point is that Japan's national curricular guidelines create a fundamental ground upon which much else evolves without central intervention. Despite annual political fireworks regarding history textbooks (especially the handling of Japan's wartime crimes and colonial past), textbook approvals are largely routine. Teachers working among themselves at the local level develop pedagogical skills largely on their own. Finally, the entrance examinations that so motivate parents and students in the secondary years are not a ministry responsibility, but the responsibility of each university department and school.

It is a system tightly calibrated by a national curriculum. Japan's is not a system characterized by the centrality of standardized national testing. Nor is it one in which the central government is continually trying to micromanage teacher behavior. The ministry's authority is thus indirect and generally nonintrusive, and this is probably a key to its success. Even the number of ministry personnel is small.

A national curriculum has other obvious advantages. It greatly reduces duplication of effort in all manner of things—textbook production, teacher training, and so forth. Family mobility (which is sizable due to active corporate transfers) does not lead to problems because of extensive geographical variation in education. Teachers can readily transfer within the system, and they learn effectively from one another regardless of school location.

What then are Japan's problems? If we subscribe to the view that variation in any system serves to maintain its capacity for adaptive change, then we would have reason to worry that the standardized aspects of Japanese education limit such possibilities. Indeed, reform is slow and deliberate compared to the constant sense of change and experiment found in our system. Ministry authority clearly stifles many local initiatives that are contrary to standard forms. In Japan, large-scale change waits on ministry initiative. Only very careful, incremental, and long-term approaches to such change appear possible, short of major political upheavals. Highly calibrated systems have this property, and Japan's is such a system.

Administration at the Local Level: Sources of Equity

Teachers' salaries are paid at the prefectural level. The national government provides a subsidy that covers half of all such costs throughout the country. Within each prefecture (roughly equivalent to a small or medium-size state), all public teachers have the same pay arrangement. This standardization allows them to work in any school in the prefecture at the same level of income, and it facilitates the active administrative transfer of teachers from rural to urban and from richer to poorer areas. A similar policy holds for the development, maintenance, staffing, and furnishing of schools in each prefecture. Disadvantaged areas are given special consideration, and the general effect is a leveling of school quality over large areas, quite in contrast with the highly differentiated character of the American school landscape. Here again, uniformity and general high standards are the defining principles. Rather than massive regulation, however, the desired equity of educational resources is achieved through a combination of large administrative areas, willingness to make resource allocations automatic, and the authority to transfer teachers as necessary.

This means that within the public system it is difficult to develop schools where talented or wealthy students receive preferential access to outstanding facilities and teachers. Uniformity is inherently an outgrowth of administrative mechanisms aimed at equity. The partial exception is the high school level, where entrance exams serve to sort the student populations into clearly demarcated tracks. Neither school facilities nor teacher quality reflect this tracking, yet there is no question that the pace of learning differs from public high school to public high school.

Developing systems of administration that "deliver" high-quality instruction to nearly all students every day is a challenge approached differently in Japan. The logic used is instructive and the effectiveness of the system is a major part of any explanation of Japan's success.

At the school level, too, there are organizational differences worth noting. Rural schools can be quite small, but with this exception, the standardization already so apparent in the overall system is found in most aspects of school design and organization. Most notable perhaps is that middle schools and high schools are kept relatively small. The impersonality and sense of disorder of our giant high schools are not to be found. There are other reasons for this difference. Students stay in their homerooms for their classes. They thus bond more as a group, even taking lunch together in the same room.

Secondary teachers themselves are organized into groups focused on a particular grade level. The homeroom teachers of a particular grade do their regular teaching to the same grade level. They also move up a grade with their wards each year. In essence, like the students they supervise, the teachers are organized as cohorts that stay together as a team for the full three years the students are in the school. Teachers and students are thus placed in a continuous, long-term relationship. One can imagine the many consequences that flow from this continuity and greater concentration of attention. Teachers become collectively responsible for the entire range of student activities. Not only instruction, but field trips, class events, discipline, and career guidance become theirs to manage together. In the course of three years they come to know the students well and individually.

There is clear accountability built in to this system too. Only the teachers are to blame if the students have not been well prepared for the next level, for example, and it is they who will have to remedy the situation. By the same logic, failure to deal with discipline problems early only leads to more work later. Not surprisingly the desks of the teachers of each class are grouped together in the teachers' room, face to face. One finds them sharing detailed information constantly about all aspects of grade management, student guidance, and instruction. Monitoring, control, and support activities overlap. Very little falls through the proverbial cracks in this system.

There are drawbacks to such a tight arrangement. Indeed, teachers and students feel enmeshed in a social fabric that by design constrains behavior. Teachers have less autonomy, less privacy, and less choice. Despite the fact that these matters are highly valued in American culture, I believe our teachers would find much satisfaction in the greater community and sense of teamwork that the Japanese approach establishes.

We should also note that class size is larger than in the United States at the junior and senior high school levels, where they average around 35–45 students. Such large classes are not a serious issue. Smaller classes are not seen as the answer to problems of individual needs or classroom order. The point is that all along the Japanese approach has been to see and use the group as the basic unit for instruction and control. Numbers matter much less given this perspective, one that does not focus on the teacher "one-on-one" with students in class.

It is more than a coincidence that teachers spend less time in class than their American counterparts. A trade-off exists, it seems, between class size and preparation time. One sees this clearly only by adopting a comparative perspective. At the middle and high school levels, Japanese teachers have more time to spend in preparation and more time for matters of guidance and coordination because per period they teach larger numbers of students. We are witnessing here a chain of virtuous effects: more early socialization to group-based classroom order, leading to larger class size, leading to more preparation time for teachers.

The lack of tracking until tenth grade is also a notable aspect of school organization. Students are intentionally mixed in terms of ability for virtually all purposes. On the other hand, tracking begins in earnest after ninth grade, due to the competitive entrance examinations and the subsequent ranked differentiation of students into separate schools. Within each high school, however, tracking is studiously avoided. This pattern is quite the reverse of our own, where disguised tracking begins almost immediately in elementary school.

What explains this disparity? Several things come to mind. First, learning to read Japanese is quite different from learning to read English. Initially, Japanese is much easier, being syllabic and having none of the exceptions in spelling, pronunciation, and grammar that plague English. The start in reading is thus smooth for nearly all students and keeping them together without tracking is possible. As each year passes, however, differences in their mastery of the thousands of characters emerge. The late introduction of tracking appears to reflect this difference in the language. Second, historically, the founding Japanese idea that public schools would create a national citizenry set in place an emphasis on equal treatment through the compulsory level (now ninth grade) and set the stage for the other founding principle that differentiation by merit would determine access to higher levels. The ideal was a meritocracy built on a base of uniformity. The founding principles of our system, by contrast, have emphasized localism and the importance of expanding the opportunity for higher education.

We have never had an overall integrative framework linking compulsory and higher education. One would think that the homogeneity of the Japanese population would also be an important factor, but this is doubtful. We track just as actively in our sociologically most homogeneous schools. Furthermore, in this country, parents, pedagogical theories, and teacher convenience all point us in the direction of early individuation, and this amplifies both our inclination to track and our thinking that class size is important.

Japan's late-tracking approach results in a relatively egalitarian foundation of learning and yet accommodates a very competitive, merit-oriented final race for a highly differentiated set of status rewards at the university level. The fact that the Japanese educational budget greatly favors compulsory over higher education helps us to grasp the policy intent here. We spend about 30% of all public educational monies on higher education, whereas the figure for Japan is 11%. Taken together, all of the above appears to give the Japanese system a decided advantage in the delivery of a relatively high level of educational equity.

Costs, too, are efficiently managed. Centralized though the system is, bureaucratic overhead is relatively small. Japanese education, too, is hedged in by rules and reporting requirements, by slow decision-making, and the rest, but the evidence from ratios of students and classroom teachers to administrators and staff at all levels strongly suggests a very lean system. The number of students per district administrator in 1989, for example, was 960 in Japan and 176 in the United States (Cummings, 1992).

This highly integrated regime obviously stands in stark contrast to our highly diversified, decentralized, and small-district arrangement, which is so unsystematic as to be almost inconceivable as a single organization. There is virtually nothing in our classic vocabulary of social preferences favoring uniformity or centralization. Typically, we see these as smacking of coercion and dependence. It is difficult, therefore, for us to see the obvious advantages in the Japanese system without becoming entangled in our distrust of authority and beliefs about the advantages of diversity. Undoubtedly, many of the personal freedoms we seek to emphasize in American education are much less in evidence in Japan. But in the contrast there is a lesson. It is that we cannot see and give an honest accounting of the price we pay for our many, very particular, forms of choice and autonomy in our schools. We cannot, in other words, make clear choices, despite our preoccupation with choice.

Time on Task

When we look at the behavior of Japanese students, we are confronted with the overwhelming evidence that they spend significantly more time in mastering knowledge of the kind that international tests measure. Another explanation for Japanese success is simply that they succeed because they spend more "time on task." By implication, it is not the national curriculum or the skills of teachers or the school environment or any of the other recognized virtues of the system that really count. The answer lies in the focused investment of time. To some, this kind of accounting will raise the specter of a Dickensian nightmare, but the evidence is quite compelling all the same.

In addition to the often cited longer school year (sixty attendance days or three months more than this country), there is much more to consider. In the case of weekly homework, the evidence points to from 30 percent more time (fifth grade) to better than twice as much in the later secondary years (Stevenson & Stigler, 1992). A longer school year, of course, also means more days of homework.

Then there is the popularity of after-school tutoring and cram activities. About 40% of upper elementary, and 65% of middle school students currently attend privately run supplementary programs. These add, at the minimum, about three extra hours of learning per week for the students enrolled. Stevenson and Stigler's (1992) careful comparative studies show, furthermore, that actual instruction and learning in elementary schools during formal class periods is significantly greater than in the United States. A conservative approximation for the purposes of estimation might be 20 percent more instruction time per hour of class. Then there is the recently published

Prisoners of Time (National Education Commission on Time and Learning, 1994), which has estimated that American high school students spend 1,460 class hours on required core subjects, whereas their Japanese counterparts spend 3,170 hours, or twice as much.

Finally, absenteeism and related problems of attendance appear to be much greater here than there. For example, we know that large city high schools experience absentee rates on the order of 15% to 30%, whereas rural areas of our midwestern states have rates in the neighborhood of 2% to 3%. The Japanese do not publish statistics on this, but personal experience in many schools and conversations with scholars and administrators indicate that the average for Japanese schools at all grade levels would be near or below those for the rural Midwest.

A precise calculation of the differences of time on task is not possible, but a rough and intentionally conservative estimate is worth attempting. A few comments on the limits of such an estimate first. Annual days of school is problematic to a degree, because as everyone knows, not every official day is filled with instruction. Japanese schools have a calendar of non-academic events that absorb time from instruction. Also, the use of substitute teachers at the secondary level is uncommon, and teacher absences can mean no instruction. Of course, American schools have official "half-days," early closings on account of weather, and other similar practices that mean less time for instruction. Clearly, in both countries, official figures overestimate instructional days. To cover the possibility that the overestimate is greater in Japan, I have adjusted the number of school days in Japan downward by twenty days. I have also ignored the evidence that American teachers, following our long summer vacations, spend considerable time (up to one-third of the subsequent year) reviewing the previous year's work. Japanese teachers do not have to review extensively because of both shorter vacations and more tutoring and parental help. Estimating, again very roughly, a half-hour of homework difference between the two student populations per day is also conservative. The difference is almost certainly more on the order of five hours a week, when we acknowledge the greater weekend homework reported by Japanese students. In the same vein, crediting Japanese students with only an additional hour a week of outside tutoring seems reasonable given the complexity of the pattern there and the fact that some American students also receive such help. Finally, because absenteeism is the least uniform of patterns across a population (being chronic for some areas and of little consequence for others, yet important comparatively), I have quite arbitrarily subtracted for every American student one day of school every two months.

What do these assumptions produce as an estimate of the annual time on task differences for the two student populations? Annual days of school: Japan 240 − 20 = 220; United States 180 − 5 = 175; the difference is 45. Hours of outside school study a year: in Japan 2.5 more weekly hours of homework and 1 more hour of tutoring = 3.5 more hours per week. This difference (3.5 hours) × 36 weeks (U.S. school year) + 5 hours of homework and 1 hour of tutoring × 8 additional weeks (the longer Japanese year minus 20 days or 4 weeks) = 174 hours.

By this formula, our typical Japanese student is studying in school 45 days more a year and studying outside (homework and tutoring) 174 hours more than his or her counterpart in the United States. Assuming, again arbitrarily, that 5 hours of outside study equals a day of school instruction, we find the Japanese student studying 74 more school-day equivalents per year. Using the 180-day American school year as our basis and calculating this bundle of differences only from fifth through twelfth grades (when tutoring is common and homework differences are more pronounced) leads to the conclusion that Japanese students spend in that seven-year period what amounts to a phenomenal 3.2 years of extra time on task. Keep in mind that we have made no adjustment for the greater efficiency of classroom instruction revealed by Stevenson and Stigler's work or the amount of review time spent by American teachers following our long summer vacations.

It would be very instructive also if we could capture the pattern of variation within each country using these resources. Almost certainly, the range of variation in absenteeism, homework, tutoring, and classroom efficiency is much greater in the United States. This would help explain our much greater problems achieving outcomes that do not deviate greatly from the mean.

Japanese success, as we have defined it above, is most certainly connected to the startling differences in time on task. What produces them, however, is another question. Would simply lengthening the American school year produce much higher results? The answer is not an unqualified yes. Much more is involved, as we have just noted, including the fact that the two societies are fundamentally different as far as children are concerned.

Societal Differences

We have become used to the notion that education plays a key role in the replication of social differences generation after generation. The same might be argued regarding sociological differences between societies. There was a period in the history of education when public schooling was a major factor moving the structure of industrial societies in new directions, in constructing convergent patterns labeled "modern," but that era is largely past. Today, more characteristically, education can be said to reflect and perpetuate the fundamental problems of each society. It is now a conservative force for continuity in social structure. If we are going to compare Japanese and American education, we must attempt to understand each in its own distinct context. Societal differences, if quite large, constitute an explanation in and of themselves for Japan's success.

To begin with, Japan is not a nation of immigrants. Only a small fraction of its population (less than 1%) are not ethnically Japanese, and many of the Koreans, Chinese, and Europeans living in Japan attend their own schools. There are no established figures on the minority group known as Burakumin, but even the highest estimates place them at no more than 2 percent of the total population. Obviously, the characterization of Japan as homogeneous is correct in a comparative sense (despite a myriad of forms of social differentiation that occupy Japanese attention).

Second, the family situation is different. Children being raised in single-parent households do not amount to even 5 percent. The number of out-of-wedlock births is infinitesimal. Unemployment is roughly in the 3 percent range and, because it is structurally different, it affects children much less than in this country. Women, although very active today in the employment sector, tend to stay at home during their children's infancy and early school years. Family size is quite small, less than two children per married couple. By our standards, Japan has very few at-risk children, few families in poverty, and virtually no illiteracy. It is much less common, furthermore, for families to move from place to place in ways disruptive of their children's schooling as happens frequently in this country.

As is widely known, Japanese communities are virtually free of drugs. Urban crime is generally about a tenth of its level in the United States. The Japanese do have school problems (such as children being teased and bullied) that they worry about incessantly, but the scale of any and all such problems is comparatively small. Nothing better illustrates this than the fact that student smoking in public is a major focus of teacher concern.

Japan, in other words, is a quintessentially stable, middle-class society by American standards, and educational outcomes reflect this profound fact. Education is important to a very high proportion of families. Children on average experience relatively little stress from the destabilizing effects of unemployment, poverty, divorce, and crime. Nearly all parents have the time and energy to focus on supporting their children's education. From generation to generation, this environment helps the schools reproduce the same social conditions and the same distribution of outcomes.

In trying to factor in what such societal differences mean to our interest in explaining educational outcomes, I find it useful to ask what U.S. education would be like, all else unchanged, if 90 percent of American families were like those in our middle- and upper-class suburbs. The change would certainly be dramatic. But it would be felt primarily in our city schools. The few comparative studies that have been designed to screen out the effects of poverty, inner-city environments, and first-generation families conclude that much more than just differences in family and neighborhood is necessary to explain Japan's achievements. Generally, even when income and other such factors are held more or less constant, Japan apparently does much better in teaching its children. The reader is again referred to the chapter by Lewis (this volume), as well as to the work of Stevenson and Stigler (1992). The lesson is not to ignore the social differences, and not to attribute to them an explanatory sufficiency that denies the many other considerations involved.

The Role of Cultural Differences

Modern science, social studies, and much else taught in Japanese schools is of Western origin, of course, as is the idea and institutions of universal public education itself. But if the content of instruction and the conceptual framework of the system have been borrowed by Japan, they have been blended with many native assumptions and values about learning and teaching. Remaining very influential in the face of change have been Japanese (often East Asian) understandings of child development, of adulthood, of learning, of character development, and of the meaning of civilization itself. These are very basic notions, largely taken for granted in any country. They greatly influence how education actually works in Japan and are important, if we are to translate the Japanese system into useful insights for ourselves (see also Hess & Azuma, 1991; Shimahara, 1986; White, 1987).

Culture is a tricky issue for comparative work, because general ideas alone do not directly cause events. Rather, we can say that cultural differences shape perceptions and influence the way institutions are formed and work. Nor is culture a simple, uniform, or unchanging matter. The current system, by embodying cultural predispositions, keeps them alive and evolving. The labels also change. Few Japanese would admit to being Confucian or to thinking they are part of a Confucian society, yet many patterns in education are clearly in that tradition. Our discussion so far has made it apparent that we cannot ignore American individualism or our legalistic traditions when comparing our education with others, and so, too, it is important to highlight how Japan's ideals are related to her educational success.

Civilization is a key concept with which to begin. Going back to seminal East Asian philosophies like Confucianism, the written word, book knowledge, the virtue of study, and ideas of human moral perfection have been bundled together and made central to ideas of order and prosperity. Civilization is thus a pivotal concept that states almost categorically that it is necessary and good for everyone to perfect themselves through learning and that this opportunity and social obligation is lifelong. Before the development of the modern state, Japan did not need public education to support a myriad of systems of intense learning. The social prestige that accompanied study, the assumption that diligence was critical to achievement, and the submission of the student to the teacher were firmly in place. So was the legacy of the Chinese entrance-exam system as a meritocratic means of promoting the most deserving to high office.

A related legacy is the Japanese emphasis on effort rather than ability. Although the culture recognizes the advantage of greater intelligence, it is played down by teachers and parents. Success is interpreted as due primarily to effort. The dominant success story is one of getting ahead through study, not brains. This notion fits neatly with an instructional process designed to keep everyone together through compulsory education. Because the capacity for hard work is universal, the pressure to do well falls on all students. This effort-oriented ideal thus encourages a high average level of homework, school attendance, and extra study—the very pattern of effects we have labeled a major aspect of Japanese success.

A rather different and more distinctly Japanese set of assumptions about how young children learn, however, appears to have conditioned the way elementary instruction has developed. These ideas hold that the child is naturally inclined to learning and that spontaneity should be encouraged as part of nurturing the inherent inclination to curiosity. Culturally, the child is held to be good by nature and inclined to social cooperation and compassionate involvement with others. Teachers should bring these feelings forth through patient encouragement of cooperative practices. To follow this ideal is to build a social order from the foundation of shared relationship. The classroom is a natural place for this socialization and, in the early elementary years, this kind of social learning is given more importance than are cognitive achievements. This socialization lays the groundwork for patterns of classroom conduct that distinguish Japanese schools.

As adulthood approaches, however, we find a very different ideal defining student virtue—one that emphasizes hard work, dedication, and suffering as contributing to character building. This perspective serves to define the drudgery of entrance-exam preparation as a useful challenge. The transition the student experiences from elementary school to high school is a radical one indeed—from a patient nurturing of wonderment and friendliness to a regimen of hard study. An eternal question before Japan is whether this kind of stressful contradiction is necessary and useful. The majority see wasted time, too much stress, rote learning, and lack of creative exploration in the present high school situation. And they are not wrong. On the other hand, learning to settle down and work hard when the work is not pleasant is a necessary part of becoming an adult. Most Japanese are cognizant of this reality. There are many closet pragmatists who agree with the traditional ideals of hard study as virtue. Motivating an entire population of teenagers to learn via "the joy of learning" route is not suggested by anyone.

Our American ideas about the development process from child to adult are quite different. We can understand the Japanese perspectives—our own past had many of the same ideas—yet we are inclined to view the child as requiring early training in independence and self-control. We see the adolescent as needing to learn about his or her own self and individuality. The American approach is to teach responsibility by providing greater choice and thus allowing individual diversity to flourish. Put oversimplistically, whereas we are focused on structure, rules, and cognitive foundations in the early years and then proceed to remove restraints, the Japanese begin by encouraging an atmosphere of shared discovery and familial bonding and proceed to gradually tighten the discipline and structure. Their path to adulthood is not one of increasing freedom but of increasing hard work and duty; the result is greater conformity and compliance, and also more intensely socialized students.

It appears that the kind of elementary socialization and learning that children are given in Japan prepares them for the severities of secondary schooling. There are complementarities, that is, as well as contradictions in their approach. Despite so much exam-oriented instruction, for example, Japanese students are well prepared in their understanding of conceptual and analytic processes. Clearly, their kindergarten through ninth-grade training laid excellent foundations. The point to keep in mind is not only that the culture of Japanese education is different, but also that we oversimplify it at some risk.

Most important, the cultural differences we have discussed contribute significantly to the outcomes in which we are most interested. A brief list would include:

1. The higher status for the entire educational enterprise, for teaching as a profession, for academic achievement, and for scholarship
2. The centrality of learning and study to personal growth
3. The conviction that education is critical to national well-being and security

4. The location of greater responsibility and authority to higher levels of government
5. The emphasis on effort rather than individual ability
6. The conviction that rigidly objective entrance exams are the key to a meritocratic process
7. The pervasiveness of education's high priority in the population as a whole.

These cultural predispositions support the institutional, familial, instructional, and other systems already discussed. Lacking such ideas and convictions, the very same organizations and practices would certainly work differently in our society.

Discussion: Systemic Change as a Cultural Problem

Let us assume that we want the kind of educational success exemplified by Japan. This is a big assumption, obviously, because it is far from clear that this is the definition of success operative in our present system. Nevertheless, it appears to have the bipartisan support of the majority of our political leaders at the national level. It is this circumstance that makes Japan so pertinent.

We begin by noting how plausible the preceding explanations appear. Is it helpful to ask which is most important?

It would be comforting to discover that one or another explanation is the correct one. This would make for parsimonious and elegant insights and clear policy direction. It would also be a relief to find answers in the Japanese example that did not appear unsuitable to an American context. We cannot become Japanese, and although we may admire the relatively egalitarian structure of their society, we know that the United States is too different to expect families and communities to resemble Japan in the foreseeable future. So, too, is it difficult to imagine limiting access to higher education in a manner that stimulates the kind of competitive levels we have noted for Japan's entrance exams. The political unpopularity of such an idea is obvious.

Continuing along a line of increasing pragmatism, we begin to look for systemwide approaches that might work here—the national standards/curriculum approach is one. We are already moving cautiously along this path, and the success Japan has with a national curriculum is worth underscoring. State by state, we are also exploring the reallocation of resources (to lower levels and poorer schools). This, too, is a change that has strong support in the Japanese case.

It is not as clear that we are ready to rethink the fundamental organization of our secondary schools to build greater community among teachers and students and at all levels to establish collective responsibility and more peer-based ordering mechanisms. That Japan has essentially the same socialization and governance practices across the entire country and spectrum of schools seems especially impressive in light of our largely ad hoc and even (in places) unexamined approach to this crucial issue. Perhaps realizing that a different approach produces impressive results can help us in building a widening consensus that school-level reform should move in this direction.

Turning to time-on-task issues, we have seen that the U.S.-Japan gap is very large. But we must also note that simply lengthening the school year will not be enough to remove the difference. A shorter summer vacation is certainly warranted, but of almost equal importance are such things as reducing absenteeism, raising parental involvement with homework, and increasing the time of actual instruction in classrooms. We must also address the very problematic differences of time on task within our population of students.

There are many active proponents of all of these changes already at work, of course, and there is nothing hidden in the Japanese experience that would persuade us not to consider all seriously. Yet the enormous problems in implementing any one of them are also by now apparent. The political will to effect major long-term change in our present political environment is difficult to imagine, especially when we view U.S. problems from the perspective of a well-integrated and advantaged system like Japan's. One feels like a Pollyanna even discussing the Japanese case.

We also must note that we find little confirmation for many of our own perennial panaceas for educational reform. Smaller classes, parental choice, community involvement, more money, monetary incentive systems for teachers and/or students, more computers, the end of tenure, greater focus on the individual child, and so forth receive almost no support from the Japanese case. Even national testing is not a Japanese practice. It is interesting to note how few of our most talked about solutions are found to be important in Japan's success.

Instead of further disassembling the Japanese example in search of things that we might borrow, it is wise to conclude with some lessons that derive from viewing the Japanese case as a whole.

Given the country's advantages, one cannot help but feel that Japan's success in education actually should be even greater. With this in mind, consider the Goals 2000 statement that the United States will be first in the world in math and science in what is a mere five years from now. Our reaction must be one of incredulity—amazement that our political leaders could even imagine catching up to nations like Japan with our present system. It is equally shocking to realize that we have such an unrealistic sense of the time required. Finally, one must be appalled that our state governors and national leaders are so poorly informed as to buy into such a fantasy timetable. Had they looked closely at Japan's advantages, for example, they would have avoided such bravado. Naive international benchmarking as hype is an approach that will wear thin soon enough and is, I am afraid, symptomatic of our deeper national problems with educational reform.

Obviously, many factors converge to produce what we have defined as Japan's success. In practice, the explanations we have considered above generally reinforce one another. They constitute a better, more powerful explanation when combined. In effect, we have been considering cultural, administrative, social, and behavioral dimensions of one complex reality. This reality was not created sui generis, but constructed methodically over a long time. Initially, of course, traditional values were joined to modern institutions, but in time the educational institutions themselves recast the national culture of learning and created its present character.

Our long-term task, too, is to slowly remake our own culture of learning through the creation of better institutions. The same can be said of society. Acknowledging our comparative problems only sets the stage for committing to the long-term task of using education to overcome them. It would be instructive to ask what prevents us from assuming a more realistic long-term perspective, say fifty years, in the effort to improve, to catch up to Japan. This, at least, would be what I would expect of Japanese planners.

Let us say that to understand Japan's success is to understand the complex structure of factors shaping the routine interactions of teachers, students, and parents. Such an approach would focus our attention on the quality of daily behavior in and out of school at the level where learning occurs. If there is broad commitment to the goals and responsibilities involved, adequate resources, and sufficient motivation, the routines work. It helps immensely to have a high degree of regularity in this kind of arrangement. The goals need to be few and the responsibilities clearly understood. Too much variety, change, imprecision, or confusion contribute to uncertainty and a decline of coordination. Under such conditions, the implementation of responsibilities declines in quality and consistency. The "keep it simple" maxim is all the more important when one recognizes how vulnerable children, parents, and classroom teachers are to outside forces that run counter to the necessary conditions for learning. The Japanese have developed a system that is consistent, stable, and simply focused. It is not exciting seen from a distance, and its final stages, namely, university entrance-exam preparation, seem uninspired, but teachers, students, and parents work well together day after day after day. This is what counts.

We Americans take pride in breaking routines, however ubiquitous and necessary. We do this typically in the name of personal independence or in the name of innovation and creativity. Standards and standardization sound inherently threatening, again despite our admission that at some level and to some degree they are absolutely necessary. Our preference is for independence, and we can never agree where critical matters should be decided— the classroom, the school, the district, the state, or Washington. And even when we decide, we reserve the right to reopen the issue the next year.

These cultural assumptions and preferences make for an American style: a systematic amount of lively uncertainty, a dramatic level of crisis and reform, great numbers of experiments and searching questions, and a marked degree of mutually reinforcing hopefulness and frustration. Rarely are reforms committed to for sufficiently long periods of time. Institutional memory problems are rife. Personnel changes, budget crises, competing ideas, or simply too many ideas dilute and wash away so many well-intended efforts. A sense of imminent burnout is typically what we are left with. This pattern, this style, cannot be found in Japan, and it cannot be sustained in this country if the goal is eventually to succeed to Japan's level of achievement.

Viewed from a Japanese perspective, we Americans are continually "reinventing the wheel," although they admire the fact that we are never afraid to try new ideas. Yet viewed in the light of the Japanese case, our approach is obviously flawed. First, we chronically underestimate the extent of our problems and the time we need to solve them. Our optimism needs to be tempered with a wisdom that is built into a deliberate, long-term strategy for the country as a whole. Second, we should value overall coherence and stability as necessary to sustained reform. Third, we should, in setting up other nations as exemplars or rivals, have an adequate understanding of the many contributing factors to their achievements. Fourth, we need to create a true teaching profession by treating teachers and the instructional context as such. Fifth, deep down we must become convinced that a stable national framework is a source of strength.

Changing individual schools alone will never guarantee that such changes survive over time. When such changes are uncoordinated and the initiatives arise from charismatic leadership, as is very often true, they are vulnerable to the erosive effects of time. All of the work that goes into gaining the allegiance of teachers at the school level to a program of change (however appropriate) is perpetually at risk without broad systemic support and reinforcement. Our look at the advantages Japan possesses, in other words, leads to the sobering conclusion that we have no choice but to very carefully draw the many necessary elements of change into a coherent national program that slowly redefines American education far into the next half century.

CHAPTER 14

Education and State Development:
Lessons for the United States?

S. GOPINATHAN

A sense of crisis gripped U.S. education in the 1980s and reports like *A Nation at Risk* (1983) detailed the growing conviction among U.S. policymakers that quality had been seriously eroded in U.S. education and was in large measure responsible for U.S. economic decline, and to a lesser extent, social disruptions. One consequence of these perceptions was a willingness to study other systems to see how other nations organized their education systems and to see if their policies, such as a common curriculum or length of the school year, could be adopted in the United States. By and large, the focus of comparison has been Japan, a logical enough focus since Japanese students seemed to top most academic competitions and because Japan was the most serious economic rival of the United States. Except for the work of scholars like Stevenson and Stigler (1992) and Stevenson, Lee, & Chen (1994) Asian education for U.S. policymakers has meant Japanese education.

This chapter explores the way Singapore, one of the four "dragons" and a major economic and social success story, has organized its education system, and the lessons this may have for the United States. How can the education system of a nation of less than 3 million people be relevant to the United States? One quick answer that will be pointed to here (and discussed later in fuller detail) is that Singapore has full employment, a highly efficient economy and has structured its education system to contribute to economic growth. By all accounts that is what the United States wishes to do. Besides, both Singapore and the United States are nations which welcomed immigrant populations, have a tremendous range of ethnic diversity, and are democratic and market-oriented. It is also clear from the most recent reform efforts and the legislation initiated since 1990, namely, those dealing with school to work linkages, reform of vocational education, and *Education 2000*, that the U.S. policy elite has warmly embraced human-capital approaches to educational planning; *Education 2000* also sets as a goal the

249

development of a competitive education system in which U.S. students do better than their international counterparts. Finally, in a reversal of tradition the United States is contemplating common and rigorous achievement standards for its high school students. This implies that an effort will be made to link school outcomes to requirements of the economy. These features are central in the Singapore system.

The capture of the U.S. Congress by the Republican party and the prospect of a Republican victory in the next presidential election have given focus to long-standing concerns about desirable values and norms to guide U.S. education and society. Debates over abortion, the role of the entertainment industry, and the respect that should be accorded to the U.S. flag, may be today's newspaper headlines but they reflect major debates about values and the roles that the schools could and should play in inculcating values. In Singapore's case the school always had a central role in value inculcation. As in the United States today, there was contestation over what these values should be and how they should be taught. However, these were resolved and values education is a major part of the Singapore school curriculum (Gopinathan, 1988a).

Even as politicians argue about the need for a common national vision, there is fear of overcentralization and the growth of federal power. Singapore's experience may be instructive in this regard. As the discussion below will make clear, the Singapore state at the beginning was without central power and influence; the central state apparatus remained weak because of disputes over education, language, and culture issues. It was only through a resolution of these issues that the state was able to grow strong and through such strength to direct education in ways that contributed to the state's agenda of social cohesion and economic growth. The use of central power was productive in Singapore's case and demonstrates that central power need not always be feared.

U.S. researchers and policymakers also need to move away from an overconcentration on Japan. There is need to draw upon a wider range of countries, for interesting variations can be seen in the ways other successful economies have resolved educational dilemmas. It would be foolhardy to assume simple and uncomplicated borrowing from one system for adoption into another system; what is needed is a commitment to learning from a wide variety of examples.

Singapore shares with Japan both similarities and differences. Size, historical factors and ethnic make-up come easily to mind as differences. It is particularly important to note that unlike Japan and more like the United States, Singapore is ethnically diverse, celebrates ethnic and cultural differences, and is more tolerant of minorities in its midst. Cultural diversity has meant linguistic diversity and policymakers have had to make difficult decisions about which languages to use as the media of instruction and if, and how, the state should provide for such instruction. Similarities lie in the fact that both Japan and Singapore share a secure state, an orderly society and economic growth, which is attributed to getting education policy and practice right. In education, both countries have a centralised curriculum and system of governance, large class sizes, formal pedagogy, and frequent evaluation. In both countries a high premium is placed on student effort and parental involvement.

The role of culture in Singapore's development and education system is more problematic. In the case of Japan it is clear that modernization has occurred without excessive westernization and the Japanese have been able to modernize without having to use English. In part their success may be due to their homogenous society and the fact they began their modernization process before the era of mass and modern communications. In Singapore's case its legacy of colonialism is seen in positive terms, especially in the usefulness of English in the modernization process. As we shall see later, the use of English was welcomed by the state but opposed in the early stages of state formation by significant numbers of Chinese who were non-English educated. The government has also been ambivalent, decrying the undesirable effects of English-mediated culture while insisting that all learn English.

The Singapore government sees value not just in defining a vision for the future but also in constructing a common cultural-historical lineage for Singapore's ethnic groups. It characterizes as Asian values, an emphasis on the group rather than the individual, duties of the individual to his family, social group, or clan and to the wider community/nation, emphasis on education, thrift, preference for consensus, a tradition of self-help, respect for elders and authority, among others. This official view of Singapore culture is strongly promoted and sees expression in language, values education and other policies in education. It could be argued that in Singapore the consequences of pluralism and the stresses created by a rapidly modernizing city state have been held in check with the aid of such constructions.

Education and the Emergence of the Fragile and Strong State: Singapore

A Fragile State, 1950–1965

As education systems are dependent institutions it is necessary to understand history and societal structure before considering educational practice. The model adopted for this discussion is one which sees state-society relationships, especially in developing countries, as contested in the beginning, that is, there is little power in the central authority and the state's influence is weak. In this section we detail the ways in which a fragile state, Singapore, developed into a strong state which maintains its strength through a measure of strong state power, control over civic institutions, especially education, and a growing measure of congruence on values, norms, and assumptions between politicians and bureaucrats on one hand and citizens on the other.

Singapore, at the onset of limited self-government in the mid-fifties, and later independence in 1965, exhibited all the features of a state where the center was weak and where there were multiple centers of power, that is, a fragile state. It was a colonial plural society which, during World War II, had suddenly fallen from a secure, paternalistic colonial order to an oppressive Japanese occupation during which the majority Chinese population was frequently brutalized. Made up of three major ethnic groups, Chinese, Malays, and Indians, fragmented by a variety of languages, religions, and cultures, a fragmentation made visible by housing, educational, and occupational segmentation, Singapore at the beginning of the fifties showed little potential for the successful strong state it presently is.

Singapore had several other features germane to a characterization of it as a fragile state. Singapore's economy in the mid-fifties, made up of entrepôt activities, was incapable of providing employment to a population growing at 4 percent. The trade union movement was largely in the hands of leftists and unions were being used as proxies in the political contest. The schools, the media, and business organizations were all politicized and factionalized. Some Chinese-language newspapers, for instance, were used to whip up sentiment over language and culture issues while Chinese-medium schools were encouraged to oppose the government's language and curricular policies. The defining characteristic of the civil service was that it was colonial-dependent since civil servants had been recruited to serve colonial interests and almost all senior civil servants were English-educated (Chan Heng Chee, 1989).

If the state was weak, community-based civic institutions were strong. In such realms as education and business, community organizations like dialect-based associations and welfare organizations were active and functional. The Chinese community, for instance, was largely responsible for providing its own language schools and by the late fifties had established primary and secondary schools, a university, and a technical college. The Chinese Chamber of Commerce was an active collection of indigenous entrepreneurs; however, many of these organizations fell outside the realm of colonial influence and were oppositional in nature (Gopinathan, 1974, 1985).

Emergence of a Strong State in Singapore, 1965–1995

No one who has recently studied global economic developments can be un-aware of Singapore's emergence since the early 1970s as an orderly, cohe-sive, well-managed, and economically successful nation; its politicians and civil servants have won a deserved reputation as efficient and incorruptible, with an exceptional capacity both to plan and to implement. Singapore today exhibits all the characteristics of a strong state. The state enjoys legitimacy in that at the regional and global level it is accepted as an independent and viable state and the People's Action Party has won every election since 1959.

Though the Singapore state was helped to build up an industrial econ-omy by wooing multinationals, it has never been perceived to be a client state. The Singapore state now has the capacity to support its own macro-economic initiatives, and investment in regional economies is being actively promoted; it is estimated that some US$30 billion has been invested by Singapore companies in South and East Asia. The state continues to be visi-bly and continually active in both the political and civic spheres. In the former it seeks to develop (and its efforts have wide support and credibility) a democratic system relevant to its needs by such innovations as the Nomi-nated Member of Parliament scheme (NMP) and group representative con-stituencies (GRC). In the civic sphere it has been able to dominate profes-sional organizations like the law and medical societies, and religious, cultural, and welfare organizations to ensure that they do not become spe-cial-interest pressure groups. Over the past three decades, state-initiated or-ganizations like the Peoples' Association and Citizens Consultative Commit-tees have become major instruments for control and influence in the civic sphere. Indeed, it might be argued that the Singapore state is not just strong, it is hegemonic.

Singapore has achieved spectacular economic growth in the last twenty years. In 1991, Singapore had a total trade of US$155 billion and was the world's seventeenth largest exporter and the fifteenth largest importer. The GDP in 1991 stood at US$49,965 million; per capita GDP at current market prices reached US$18,473 in 1991 compared to US$2,012 in 1970. Official foreign reserves stood at US$50 billion in 1993; Singapore has the highest foreign reserves per capita in the world. Singapore's savings rate at 47 per-cent of GDP is also the highest in the world. Singapore has negligible for-eign debt and its currency has appreciated considerably in the last two de-cades against such major currencies as the U.S. dollar, sterling, and the mark. The government has implemented policies to achieve better wealth distribution and invested heavily in infrastructure and so the growth of the economy has been reflected in a rise in the standard of living.

Many labels may be applied to the strong state that emerged in Singapore—developmental (Castells, 1988), hegemonic (Clammer, 1985), paternalistic-authoritarian (Pye, 1986). Pye's comment, noted in McCord (1991) sums up the Singapore state: "Authority is expected to combine, with grace and benevolence, both elitism and sympathy. . . . [T]he cultures revere hierarchy . . . but they also expect rulers to be concerned about the livelihood of the masses." The current fashion in some academic circles for a culture-based explanation for the economic success of the East Asian states has won the approval of the Senior Minister, Lee Kuan Yew (1982), who has noted that "the Confucianist belief that good self-cultivation, regulation of the family, and governing of the state will bring peace under the heavens" led to "the people's respect in [Singapore] for their elders which made them accept tough government policies." In a paradoxical way, it helped that the state had such inauspicious beginnings for it forged a steady determination not to fail and gave birth to the "politics of survival." The fear that it may all still go horribly wrong, that present achievements need to be protected for the future, and a measure of self-serving rationalizations continue to lead to policies that entrench the strong state.

Education-State Relations

The key point to note is that in the pre-independence period contestation in education contributed significantly to the state remaining weak. The postcolonial inheritance in education was a divided and fragmented school system, with English-, Chinese-, Malay-, and Tamil-medium schools. Given their demographic majority the Chinese dominated both English and Chinese medium schools, thus dividing an ethnic group already riven by class, dialect, and clan factors by an additional language division. Many of the non-English schools were underfunded, and had poor facilities and indifferent teaching. Standards and years of schooling varied, as did teacher qualifications and conditions of service. Obviously, under these circumstances no common curriculum existed. Such was the hostility that these circumstances engendered that Chinese-stream students in the fifties and sixties agitated openly and defied government efforts to rid schools of communist sympathisers and to standardize curriculum and standards. In the mid-fifties, the Singapore Chinese Middle School Teachers Union was as much a political force as mainstream political parties.

There were other ways in which an anti-state school system influenced state-society relations. Tied up with, and indeed underpinning, agitation in education, were primordial concerns over ethnic identity, culture, and language. Chinese schoolteachers and writers represented the Chinese intelligentsia and were thus active in teachers' unions, the Chinese-language newspapers, and clan associations, among other civic institutions. The Chinese-medium teachers resented their unfavorable status in terms of training and remuneration vis-à-vis English-medium teachers and obstructed moves to standardize and upgrade the system. Writers and journalists in their turn took up the issue, playing it up as an attack on Chinese education and culture. Given a state in which key political actors were uncertain of future political directions, such oppositional culture and language-based politics diminished state legitimacy.

The principal reason why Chinese-medium nongovernment schools, teachers, and pupils were hostile is that they felt discriminated against under British colonial rule. Lack of funding, lack of support, and limited vocational prospects in an English-dominated civil service alienated them. Further, it left them open to communist subversion and to political parties who wished to use them as proxies in first, the anti-colonial struggle, and later against the successor administration. The state was weak vis-à-vis civil society because of the particular nature of the educational problem. The use of English as a medium of instruction and the higher economic returns to English language competence affected and influenced teachers, writers, and businessmen who saw themselves discriminated against because of poor English competence. Exploitation of these grievances turned them against the state.

Policy Responses

Multilingualism

In 1956, members of all political parties accepted in the *All Party Report on Chinese Education* the concept of "equality of treatment." Henceforth, the government would support, equally, instruction in four official languages, build both primary and secondary schools in which the use of Chinese, Malay, and Tamil as media of instruction would be allowed, invest in teacher training for non-English-medium teachers and apply comparable terms and conditions of service to teachers with equivalent qualifications. Isolation of pupils in different language streams would be overcome by integrating different language streams under one administration, thus providing tangible evidence of equality. Such integration was achieved without much difficulty or hostility. Equality of treatment for languages was not, in the Singapore instance, schooling in isolated ethnic enclaves; it was not a separate but equal strategy but a means to stronger social cohesion via bilingualism for all pupils. This again helped to placate the non-English-educated, for the previous practice had been to insist that the English language be compulsory for all in non-English-medium schools (Gopinathan, 1974).

Educational Expansion

A second major policy response was the expansion of access, both by making available more school places and by diversifying the curriculum.

As table 14.1 indicates, the government was able to increase the number of school places from 323,000 in 1959 to 486,811 in 1965, an increase of 163,811 in six years. This increase must be considered significant in that it took place during a period of severe political turmoil, and attests to the fact that the capacity of the government was not seriously undermined during this period; the number of school places continued to expand, to 532,956 in 1975. The number has stabilised since as the government has been able to moderate population growth with an active and effective family-planning policy. Equally impressive has been the steady shift away from a purely liberal arts education to a greater emphasis on science and mathematics in the curriculum, expansion of access to technical and vocational institutes, and the development of vocational and technical streams in secondary schools.

In many countries, educational expansion has often been accompanied by a lowering both of standards and of satisfactory levels of resource allocation, as ministries often expanded education under political pressures but without the necessary resources; this has often resulted in declining legitimacy. In Singapore's case great care and attention has been paid to ensuring

TABLE 14.1
Growth and Change in Educational Enrollments, 1959–1994

	1959	1965	1975	1985	1994
Primary		357,075	328,401	278,060	251,097
Secondary & Junior Colleges		114,736	176,224	190,328	197,981
Academic		102,861	153,029	154,435	
Technical/Vocational	—	11,875	23,195	35,893	
Technical & Vocational Institutes		1,193	9,830	21,161	29,954*
Universities & Polytechnics		13,807	18,501	39,913	73,126*
Total	323,000	486,811	532,956	529,462	552,158

Sources: Chng Meng Kng, et al, *Technology and Skills in Singapore*. Singapore: Institute of Southeast Asian Studies, 1985, Table 11, pp. 47. Ministry of Education, *Education Statistics Digest, 1994*.
    *Figures for 1993.

that standards were maintained in the face of expansion. The percentage of pupils passing the Primary School Leaving Examination rose from 58.7% in 1975 to 88.4% in 1989; at the GCE "O" (General Certificate of Education Ordinary) level examination, the percentage of pupils obtaining a minimum of three "O" level passes rose from 65% in 1979 to 89% in 1990; those obtaining five "O" level passes rose from 38% in 1979 to 69% in 1990. By keeping the quality of pupil outcomes at higher and specified levels, the government was able to signal employers that expansion of educational opportunity did not mean less productive workers. Too much decentralization in the United States means that markets cannot "read" well what the education system is doing and thus schooling and school efforts are not given their due.

As with Japan, Singapore has been able to achieve educational expansion without allowing for a reduction in quality. Even after thirty years of self-government, Singapore has not set up its own high school leaving examinations—though it is well able to do so—preferring to use the British "O" and "A" level examinations to ensure that Singapore students face the discipline of international competition. As with Japan, many have criticized the system as examination-driven and excessively competitive. The Singapore authorities prefer to see the examination regime as necessary for ensuring discipline and effort on the part of pupils and teachers. Unlike Japan, which like Singapore insists on a common curriculum for all, there is direct government pressure for achievement standards in schools, as the government allows the publication of a league table of secondary schools and junior colleges, *The Straits Times 100*, based primarily on examination results. The contrast with the United States is obvious, for there the commitment to equity issues and a desire not to penalize students for the accidents of race, gender, or social class has resulted in an unfortunate retreat from standards, especially in state schools.

Government expenditure on education has been maintained at a high level. According to the Ministry of Education, its budget for the financial year 1992 was 15% of total government expenditure or 3.6% of the Gross Domestic Product; Japan spends about 5.5% and the United States 7%. Total expenditure on education increased from approximately US$156.5 million in 1969/70 to US$1.22 thousand million in 1989/90. Impressive increases in secondary education, polytechnics, as well as universities, indicate rising costs due to both expansion of students enrolled as well as infrastructural development. Nevertheless, such is the surplus that the government has accumulated that it is able to establish an endowment fund with a capital sum of one billion dollars to be topped up yearly to five billion Singapore dollars. The government is also committed to increasing spending on education to 5 percent of GDP in an Edusave Scheme for grants to schools, pupils and special scholarships.

Educational Qualifications and Occupational Mobility

Another major way in which the Singapore state gained legitimacy was in its ability to foster economic growth. Growth is significant for education, not only because it provides a resource base with which to fund educational modernization but because the modernization project patently fails when schooled youths have no jobs to go to (Fuller, 1990; Fuller & Robinson, 1992). The promise that is implicit in government calls for extended involvement in schooling is, especially for hitherto marginalized groups, that it offers incorporation into the mainstream and social mobility. Where a state is able to closely couple education to economic needs, investment in education becomes more productive and the state more legitimate (Hage, Garnier, & Fuller, 1988).

One way of demonstrating the education-economy link is to show that additional years of school pay off in better job opportunities and increased wages. Tables 14.2, and 14.3 show the educational qualifications and the type of jobs for employed men and women who earned more than US$2,158. Going to school and staying in school pays off in Singapore because the economy has grown and diversified and has demanded new skills which schools were able to successfully teach. The strong state built and maintained an orderly school environment, stressing meritocracy and high academic achievement. A strong manpower orientation in policymaking

TABLE 14.2
Highest Educational Qualifications for Men and Women Earning more than US$2158 per month

Highest Qualification	Men	Women
Never attended school	1.1%	0.6%
No qualification (below PSLE)	1.9%	1.9%
Primary school leaving (PSLE) or equivalent	5.1%	2.2%
O or N level or equivalent	17.6%	13.8%
A level or equivalent	22.7%	20.3%
University degree	49.6%	59.1%
Other qualifications	2.0%	2.2%

Source: Report on the Labour Force Survey of Singapore, 1987
A — Advanced Level
N — Normal Level
O — Ordinary Level

TABLE 14.3
Type of Job held by Men and Women Earning More than US$2,158 per Month

Type of Job Held	Men	Women
Administrative, managerial/executive	44.9%	37.5%
Professional/technical	38.3%	50.6%
Sales	9.3%	9.4%
Other jobs	7.5%	2.5%

Source: Report on the Labour Force Survey of Singapore, 1987

ensured that the links between the school system and the needs of the workplace were tight.

The Singapore experience of effectively linking education to the economy should be encouraging for the United States, provided that policymakers move away from a position of seeing schooling solely as a humanistic enterprise devoted to personal growth and development in which a curriculum of choice and lax assessment rules. If the ideology of the nineties is economic competitiveness, then the closer the fit of the school system to the economy, the greater the possibility that schooling will have economic credibility and be productive. It is clear that at least in this area the United States, in the various initiatives to improve vocational training and school to work linkages, is moving in the right direction. Obviously this need not mean that only economic conditions should matter; the challenge is to find the balance and there are many different models from the Japanese to the Swedish and the German, to name a few that U.S. policymakers should seriously examine.

Active Socialisation

We turn next to the state's policies to win "allegiance and identification." Newly developing states faced with a variety of cultural-ethical traditions, with different modes of child socialization, including some seen as oppositional to the press for modernity, have first to reach a political consensus on preferred values and norms. When developing syllabi and materials and implementing them in the school system, both political and pedagogic aspects are important. Two approaches can be identified in the Singapore school system. One had a largely political content, to signal that a new political order had emerged and to describe its ideology, namely, acceptance of diversity via multiculturalism, institutions like the cabinet and parliamentary system, state symbols like the flag, the anthem, the pledge of allegiance, and so on. History textbooks, for instance, quickly changed to include more balanced accounts of colonial rule but also with more emphasis given to the personalities and political struggle involved with winning independence. The teaching of civics, raised in status as a subject, intensified between 1956 and 1965 with the aim of developing a greater understanding in pupils about the workings of the new society. Since the seventies, there has been a daily flag raising and lowering ceremony in the schools, singing of the national anthem, and recitation of a pledge of loyalty. School-uniformed groups like the Police Cadet Corps and National Cadet Corps are encouraged and allowed to participate in National Day parades (Gopinathan, 1988a).

The new state also made an ambitious effort to develop a curriculum for moral education. While multiculturalism had the advantage of making all communities feel equal, it also had the potential to lead to divisiveness and feelings of marginalization on the part of smaller ethnic communities; the Chinese after all made up 75 percent of the population. The government chose to respond to this issue by extending the rationale for bilingualism. English had clear economic value, while the acceptance of languages other than English was a political necessity. The educational argument for the mother tongues (Chinese, Malay, Tamil) was that as language was a carrier of values, the teaching of the mother tongue in itself and the use of it as a medium of instruction for moral education would be beneficial. It was argued that indigenous or "Asian" cultural values were strengths and that to know and prefer only English was to risk becoming "deculturalized." Thus, with English serving as a link language, the ethnic communities were encouraged to rediscover their Asian roots and to develop and strengthen them (Gopinathan, 1988b). Moral education textbooks stressed such values as respect for elders and elected leaders, the importance of the family unit, selfless service to community, and consensual decision-making, among others. Textbooks with titles like *Education for Living* and *Being and Becoming* were used to teach these values.

The government's arguments that the schools should, in a newly independent plural society, teach a common core of values was accepted without much opposition. Memories of interethnic riots in the sixties were fresh. The government, however, decided to take matters further with the introduction of a Religious Knowledge curriculum. The government, in searching for a sociopolitical identity in Singapore, had begun to argue in the seventies that Singapore was an Asian society, that the cultural and ethical traditions of Chinese, Indian, and Malay civilizations were important sources of values. It then argued that in addition to common values, the religions underpinning these traditions ought to be studied in schools. Several religions like Christianity, Islam, Hinduism, and Buddhism were to be taught; later, a proposal to introduce Confucian Ethics as an additional option was made. The proposal to introduce Confucian Ethics created controversy, with some arguing that this was an effort to strengthen the existing conservative political ideology in Singapore; also, while the Chinese were quite amenable to learning Mandarin rather than their dialects as a school language, making choices between Bible Knowledge, Buddhist Studies, and Confucian Ethics was more problematic. Though the course options were duly introduced into the curriculum, the Religious Knowledge curriculum was withdrawn in 1989 when it became clear that in the wider society religious polarization and active evangelism were creating problems for social order (Gopinathan, 1993).

There are some interesting lessons for the United States in Singapore's experiences. The school has a socialization function and it can win both public support and teach a curriculum of core values effectively. By teaching a set of core values neither the state nor schools need to seek to erase ethnic or cultural differences; indeed, in Singapore the state actively sponsors efforts to strengthen each ethnic group's cultural traditions and the state's involvement in these activities is not viewed suspiciously. This may be why it is possible in a state with a large Chinese majority to teach a common set of core values in the schools. It is also interesting to note that the efforts to introduce a Religious Knowledge curriculum failed. It should be noted that the objections to Confucian Ethics came primarily from English-educated Chinese indicating that factors other than ethnicity may be significant. In curricular terms at least, the U.S. tradition of church-state separation in schools seems a more feasible position.

Singapore's policies on bilingualism, the linking of education to economic needs, and the emphasis on a core set of values are all made possible by a commitment to the standardization of educational experience, one that can only be achieved by a high degree of centralization. Unlike Japan the Ministry of Education in Singapore is interventionist and influential, directly so. This may be explained by the earlier experience of a lack of central authority threatening state legitimacy, the smallness of Singapore making centralization both feasible and cost effective but most importantly by the belief that an ethnically divided society cannot allow education to mirror division. Educational centralization in Singapore was sensitive to difference as in the case of bilingualism and values education without being held hostage to it. It enabled the fledgling state to be cost-effective in such areas as syllabus design and teacher training and made feasible the entrenchment of the concept of meritocracy as a central educational principle, even though there were major differences in the beginning between different types of schools.

A major concern in the United States is the differences in achievement between different ethnic groups. In a nonhomogenous society like Singapore with different traditions in educational provision, it is understandable that differences in achievement have not been significantly erased, even under the centralized system that Singapore has. A centralized system, especially in curricula and assessment, can reduce differentials, not eliminate them. In Singapore the Malays have historically lagged behind in educational performance. The government in 1982 forced the issue into the open, providing statistics to show the scope of the problem and listed the consequences that the community and nation would suffer if the problem were ignored or palliatives sought (Lee, 1982). It argued that the community had to be involved in devising and delivering solutions and promised considerable financial and logistical support. The government has since extended similar help to the Indian and Chinese communities.

Though some have argued that the government's strategy has resulted in the re-ethnicization of an educational problem, one that a national system was supposed to eliminate, the government has argued in turn that the national system cannot cope with educational issues all on its own. While the system has relatively little by way of parental involvement in individual schools, the self-help group strategy has enabled a large measure of community involvement in education; through its influence on the appointment of key officials to lead these self-help groups, the government is able to exercise a measure of control without diluting the commitment of the community.

Lessons for the United States?

While no state or polity can claim, nor be expected to, that all legitimation issues have been overcome, it is nevertheless true that in large measure the state in Singapore is secure; key social sectors like the economy and the armed forces are credible and there is a large measure of social cohesion. Education, which, as we noted earlier, has the potential to deepen attachments while providing increased opportunities for occupational and social mobility, is highly valued.

What is the relevance of the Singapore experience to the United States? All comparisons need to be qualified, and especially between such divergent states as the United States, and Singapore. Nevertheless, some points of comparison can be noted. Both Singapore and the United States are nations which welcomed immigrant populations, have a tremendous range of ethnic diversity, saw schools as socializing institutions, are democratic and free-market oriented, and are conscious of the need to be economically strong and socially cohesive. If current rhetoric is to be believed, where they differ is that in the United States the key emphasis is on the individual and his/her rights, the concern to keep education free from central directives and control and the state democratic by leaving education to community and parent groups.

Singapore's efforts in using education for state-building purposes can be seen as a model in the sense that the key assumptions and strategies are those used by the Singapore government in other spheres and with other institutions. The fundamentals of state survival—Singapore's small size, small population, lack of natural resources, volatile ethnic mix, threatening geopolitical environment—had to be addressed first. Education was a key institution in that new political identities, economic development, social cohesion, all depended upon the school—to an extent unthinkable in the United States, where other social institutions were expected to play a pivotal role.

Singapore's model of strong central direction of education may not appeal in the present climate of hostility to a strong and intrusive federal polity. It is, however, worth remembering that democratic nations like France, Germany, and Japan, and now the United Kingdom, tend toward a greater degree of educational uniformity and coordination than the United States is prepared to consider. It should be possible for the states, governors, and state legislatures to be more powerfully involved in educational matters while at the same time retaining the country's long tradition of community involvement.

Neo-conservative thinking in education in the United States seems to ignore the early role of education in state formation. Katz (1976) notes, for example, in his account of the origins of public schooling that by the mid-nineteenth century schools were expected to play a critical role in the socialization of the young and in the maintenance of social order. This was the case even though the United States adopted a federal structure with educational responsibility resting with the states. According to Katz, early educational reformers saw in education a potent way to address the problems of crime and social dislocations, a means to tame wayward youth. The involvement of the state and of political power in education was seen as legitimate, as necessary since the institutions of civil society, such as the church and the family, could not meet the requirements of new societal conditions arising out of urbanization, demographic change, and industrialization. In any event, it has never been the case that local control was absolute; it is more accurate to say that there was an interplay of local state and national influences

(Fuhrman, 1993). Though educational history is contested terrain, it does seem possible to argue for a view of education that is congenial to U.S. traditions.

U.S. policymakers and opinion leaders may also need to consider returning the school to its primary role as an agency of instruction. The school has been used in the United States both to advance the individual student's rights, and as an instrument of social programs. In the Singapore case, the school's role is clear: the school is an agency of the state and students are in school to learn. It is to their, and society's benefit, that they do learn. There is strong emphasis on instruction, on individual motivation and effort, on rewarding academic achievement, and on support for the teacher and the school in matters of discipline. While nonschool factors like socio-economic status, ethnicity and gender are regarded as important, they are not allowed to be used as excuses for failure. Singapore has been able, without positive discrimination, to raise educational standards among minority ethnic groups, though it has not erased differentials. What has not been allowed to happen is a repeat of the politicization of these issues—the endless disputation of evidence and effects with little commitment to action.

There is also concern in the United States about the government's becoming the agent of a set of "national values" as is the case in Singapore. The current debate about school prayer underscores the commitment to the earlier tradition of the separation of church and state. The emphasis on individual choice and responsibility as well as a commitment to diversity might militate against the articulation of a set of national values for use by schools. Though Singapore, like the United States, is an immigrant society, the emphasis in Singapore has been on finding unifying elements rather than the unrestricted expression of diversity. There is far too much evidence of social pathology in U.S. society for the nation to deny the need for a strong reaffirmation of its fundamental beliefs, and for the schools to teach it. Big nations as well as small fragile ones need a common core of beliefs, an ethical basis, not an excessively legalistic one, to hold them together. For what it is worth, this is the educational experience in Singapore.

CHAPTER 15

The Role of the State in Educational Reform in the People's Republic of China

NINA Y. BOREVSKAYA

> Chinese education is not in all aspects backward, as the
> American one is not fully progressive.
>
> He Dongchang, former minister of education (1992)

The World Bank gives high marks to the People's Republic of China (PRC) record in educational reform:

> China's achievements in education since 1949 have been unmatched among developing countries of the same income level. . . . The Government has been able to keep the cost of major education programs under control, and China has—unlike the rest of the developing world—been able to introduce improvements in the educational system without any serious strain on public expenditures. (World Bank, 1985, p. ix)

It can be observed that the United States and the PRC are shifting away from the extremes of decentralization and centralization, correspondingly, to find new equilibria. The promising results China has recently achieved through its comprehensive nationwide educational reform suggest the possibility that some elements of Chinese experience may be useful for educators in other nations including the United States as they search for "centralizing macro-policy (setting a national curriculum and standards) and decentralizing micro-policy (the organization and management of schools and placement of pupils therein)" (Swanson, 1994, p. 785). There is a second rationale for such relevance: large countries, like big numerals, have their own laws of existence. When we consider the implications of China's recent experience, four strategic issues stand out:

1. What is the state's potential for defining goals and principles?
2. What is the best strategy for coordinating reform, a bottom-up or top-down approach?

3. What sanctions and incentives can be mobilized to promote reform and by whom?
4. What is the optimum balance between national standards and regional interpretation?

The State as a Designer of Educational Goals and Principles: The Imperative of Continuity

The PRC state, personified by the government and the Central Committee of the Chinese Communist Party (CCCCP), claims the prerogative to devise educational objectives and policy. Looking forward to the twenty-first century, the PRC leadership seeks "to establish the framework of a socialist educational system with Chinese characteristics." In congruity with the Confucian tradition they articulated "the purpose of education in terms of utilitarianism" (Zhu Weizhang, 1992, p. 4) In 1949, education was expected to contribute to "the revolutionary struggle and construction," in 1958 to "the proletarian policy," and most recently to "building socialist modernization." The 1995 Law on Education states: "Education is to serve the building of socialist modernization, education is to be combined with the productive labor and education is to cultivate the builders of socialism and its successors, who achieve the comprehensive development in moral, intellectual and physical aspects." It should be noted that the views of the democratic-oriented educators, who on the crest of the wave of enthusiasm among intellectuals in 1988–1989 for educational humanization suggested redefining the educational goals, were not incorporated in this latest formulation (Ding, 1989; Gu, 1988).

This review of official discourse illustrates the following: First of all, the Chinese leadership is concerned about the continuity of the political guidelines: the appeal for "successors" reiterates this concern and reveals their fear of possible future political cataclysms. Further, this discourse illustrates the premise from which the Chinese government works: that continuity should be manifested in formulas to facilitate the perception of the political course held by the vast majority of the population. Over the past four decades the key slogans have even preserved the same grammatical construction. Drastic shifts in terms, as the Chinese government evidently is aware of, can hamper the implementation of the policy since the bureaucrats in the educational units and local governments, as well as teachers, students, and parents, expect stereotypes and may overreact to suggestions for change.

However, the rigid structure of official language can disguise drastic changes in tactics. For example, the substitution of "builders" for "laborers" presupposes a move from those engaged in the "physical labor" to intellectuals, while at the same time illustrating the state's view that the schools create a social product essential for development. Indeed, striking in recent rhetoric is the frequency with which the state describes education as a "productive force." The state now seeks to encourage bureaucrats to relinquish their long-standing attitude that education is a form of social welfare. At the CCP 14th Congress, "science and technology" was called "a productive force of the first priority." A new policy guideline envisages a shift to the human capital investments approach, where education will "improve the quality of the nation" (*renmin suzhi*).

Thus the 14th Congress of the CCP declared that education had "a strategic position in basic development." In the 1995 education law the government confirmed its commitment "to guarantee the development of education" and elaborated various measures to ensure that policy. To highlight the strategic position of education the government promised "to reward units and private citizens for special contribution in educational development." The Act on Compulsory Education (1986) included the following provision: "The percentage increment of State allocations for mandatory education must surpass the percentage growth of regular State revenues" by 5% at the provincial level and 2% at the regional, city, and district levels.

Coordinating Plans: The Pitfalls of Decentralization

In conjunction with these ideological shifts, the Chinese leadership has shifted certain responsibilities for the finance and management of education to more local levels. China has in the past attempted decentralization—at the end of the 1950s, during "the Great Leap Forward," and then during the "Cultural Revolution"—but those attempts were not accompanied by the introduction of a market economy. The claim for democratization in terms of mass participation predetermined the transfer of responsibility and decision-making to the lowest level—"people's communes"—bypassing the intermediate levels of provinces and counties. Robinson's study (1986) of "people-run" (*minban*) schools is a fine illustration of the outcome. The absence of an economic basis for alternative funding, the incompetence of local administrators, and the substitution of ideological control for administrative management doomed that decentralization to failure.

Nowadays most Chinese educators and policymakers concur about the need for decentralization but they also recognize the hazards of that process: "The improvement of the school system demands the reduction of the concentration of power. . . . We should not overemphasize the local authorities and self-government . . . otherwise it will lead to chaos" (Liu, 1988). In the educational reforms in China, whether they were driven by Confucianism or Marxism, the idea that education was predominantly a State function was articulated very explicitly. At the same time the PRC leaders were always attracted by the option of local responsibility with the hope of giving impetus to local initiatives and competitiveness. Yet they gradually became aware that decentralization was a double-edged sword: it was a challenge to the central bureaucracy, but at the same time it could add to the power and ambitions of local authorities and exacerbate disintegration tendencies, thus risking the loss of control (as the Great Leap Forward and the Cultural Revolution proved). These centrifugal tendencies already emerged in the Chinese economic domain by the end of the 1980s. As for the educational domain, Robinson (1986) argued that there was "growing dissatisfaction in society with decentralization as a panacea for educational development problems" (p. 87). He concluded: "Central authorities from both the Party and the State are concerned with broad issues of modernization and see specialization and standardization as the ultimate objective for public education. . . . Local officials, in contrast, are concerned with maintaining their authority" while being forced to promote the unpopular measures (pp. 86–87).

The process of decentralization has been fraught with various tensions. The first one derives from the central government's policy of privileging key schools and developed districts. In the scramble for privileges, competition between schools, local authorities, and districts was heightened. For instance, local governments falsified accounts and accelerated the expansion of grades or the types of schools they were most interested in.

The second problem generated from decentralization as the lack of coordination within local administrations. One example can be seen in the area of basic education. The government focused on two complementary targets: universalization of primary education and, since the mid-80s, promotion of compulsory nine-year junior secondary education. While the law gave the state the core responsibility for establishing and operating schools, community and enterprises were encouraged to participate in the process. From the beginning of the 1980s the central government delegated some financial responsibilities to local authorities but soon it realized the inevitability of also delegating them authority to operate and manage schools. Legislative provisions for that shift were included in the 1986 act and the 1995 law. The latter stated that schools up to the secondary level should be managed by the local governments, while those at the tertiary level by central or provincial governments. Key (magnet) schools were under the direct supervision of the provincial government. Compared to earlier decades, administration was being transferred to lower levels. The state declared its commitment to support and stimulate the community educational associations which were organized by schools in conjunction with neighboring enterprises and street or village committees. However, these associations posed a challenge to the local bureaucracy, and since the schools were not essentially autonomous and no legislation existed to guarantee the rights of the public, the associations' activities met with resistance from local educational bodies.

One more pitfall in educational decentralization stemmed from the government policy of region-oriented manpower training. The policy itself does not constitute a radically new approach when compared to the Great Leap or the Cultural Revolution, but it led to chaotic planning and distorted ratios in various specializations. A lack of coordination and the ambitions and incompetence of local leaders were some of the reasons for the poor results of the grandiose plans.

One interesting point of contrast with the United States is that the PRC government rarely sought to influence education through the court system; similarly the legislative foundation for education was always weak. Rather the changes were based on administrative orders. In the last decade more than 250 administrative provisions and statutes as well as some legislative acts of paramount importance designed by the State Council in collaboration with the CCCCP were promulgated.

Designing the System of Sanctions and Incentives

The reform of the financial management structure was of paramount importance in the process of redefining relations between the central and local governments, and the schools. The 1995 law confirmed the major principles of PRC educational funding under market-economy conditions—that is, the bulk of educational expenditures came from central government grants, albeit alternative channels were introduced and the ratio between the state budget allotment and other sources of funding for education had changed. By 1991 the ratio was correspondingly 63.8% to 37% compared with 76% to 24% in 1986 (Wang & Hu, 1993, p. 24).

Government allocations flow to the schools that are under direct jurisdiction of the State Education Council (SEC) and mostly reach those schools that train personnel for the public sector of the national economy and specialists for handling economic priorities and promoting the development of science and technology. Thus funds are largely spent on the key and vocational schools.

Administrative responsibility was transferred to the low levels together with fiscal rights. Such alternative funding as educational taxes, endowments, donations had to be locally levied and locally used. According to the 1995 law, provincial and administrative districts' governments were empowered to determine the amount of the added educational tax (in the previous decade it was fixed by the central government).

The state has set a policy of financial and other preferences to stimulate educational development. One example is the schools' construction. According to the 1995 law, plans for construction had to receive priority in the city or village general construction plans. The same policy pertains to all the publishing houses and enterprises that publish textbooks or manufacture school equipment. Another example is the policy toward school-run enterprises from which partial revenues are returned to schools as a substantial addition to teachers' salaries. These enterprises received tax-exempt status including exemption even for the fees they collect for educational materials, transportation, and construction. The same status went to that part of their production and services financed by schools. The act claimed that the state would pursue preferential policy to stimulate financial bodies and banks to provide schools with loans and assistance.

The government was concerned about diminishing the negative impact of market relations on equal access to education. In 1986 and 1988 the SEC together with the Ministry of Finance worked out a policy to sustain compulsory education in the border areas and poor districts as well as in those inhabited by the national minorities through the introduction of "earmarked grants." Concurrently with the introduction of tuition on the tertiary level, the central government provided fellowships and grants to aid the gifted: they were exempted from any fees and, as teachers were in great demand over the country, the outstanding students at the teachers' colleges were exempted from dormitory fees. In addition, the students who chose a teaching career after graduation were released from loan obligations. To defend the rights of the disadvantaged while promoting compulsory education, the state provided aid to all poor students enrolled in comprehensive or special junior secondary level. At the primary school level, this aid was awarded only to those from national minorities districts or to students living in dormitories.

The lack of a developed system of administrative sanctions and stimuli, as well as a lack of legislative provisions, made most of the former educational decisions in the PRC ineffective. The documents of the last decade manifested the central government determination to establish a system of sanctions and to empower local authorities to implement them. These measures were of extreme importance in China where the "personal relationships network" (*quanxi wang*) could distort the official guidelines drastically as local authorities were constantly under pressure from friends and relatives. The abuses occur at many levels, from school principals and educational administrators to the governmental officials themselves. Common abuses include increase of the school sundry fees (*zafei*), promotion of students with low marks in competitive examinations to upper grades, and the misuse of educational donations for private or different purposes.

The state organized an all-round attack on the problem of educational dropouts with the help of several new tools—legislative provisions and administrative and economic sanctions—and a few old ones—propaganda and inspections. In 1988 the SEC issued a circular on the strict control of primary and secondary school dropouts and initiated inspections on the implementation of the Law, which helped to bring the dropout rates under control.

The 1986 act and the 1995 law claimed that all attempts to impede the implementation of the compulsory education were to be prevented by the court. Local authorities were empowered with these sanctions: to fine or to undertake administrative punishment toward persons or units that hindered the promotion of compulsory education and those who refused to enroll students. The local governments were empowered to prohibit the employment of school-aged children and to fine, suspend the operations of, or annul the licenses of offending enterprises. Measures were also to be taken with respect to parents or guardians who did not send their children to schools (Law on Education, 1995).

These central government efforts led to a decrease in the dropout rate from 3.3% in 1988 to 1.8% in 1994 for primary schools and from 6.7% to 5.1% in junior secondary schools.

National Standards versus Regional Strategy

The main concern of the transitional period for China was to preserve national standards while allowing distinctive regional strategies. At the moment there are three major zones of economic, social, and cultural development in the country: coastal, highly developed provinces; central, medium-developed provinces; and western, less-developed regions (with further divisions and more disparities internally). By the 1990s the vast investments, and the economic, scientific, and technological advantages of the Chinese east resulted in increasing disparities between the latter and the inner hinterland.

The new approach in the central government's strategy was based on differentiation: regions were delegated rights to develop their own specialization and train personnel for local needs, while the central government exercised the functions of organizing interregional cooperation and exchange. The regional strategy and the schools diversification challenged the central control of curriculum and textbooks that the PRC government enjoyed for three decades (excluding the absurd deviations of mass creativity during the Leap and the Cultural Revolution).

The central government was much concerned about preserving the basic level of education and elaborating the national standards. The SEC was entrusted to set up standards for basic education, *guiding* curriculum and syllabus, levels of personnel and teachers staff, criteria for teachers qualification, and norms for their *basic* salaries. Government bodies of the provinces, autonomous regions, and cities under central jurisdiction were entitled to adjust these standards to local needs. They were delegated rights that in the previous decades had belonged to the central government: to define the school age, the school staff commitments and duties, and teachers' salaries; to determine the current duration of basic education (temporally it could be eight years) and the structure of primary and junior secondary grades (6 + 3, 5 + 4, or 5 + 3); to choose curricula and textbooks. For some basic disciplines only 60–70% of the curriculum was to be approved at the SEC level, the rest was supplemented by provincial educational bodies. They compiled teaching materials on local geography and history and included them as optional or required courses; some materials were also compiled at the county level, but needed to be approved by the provincial authorities.

Strict measures were provided to ensure the basic level of curriculum and text books (beyond it any level of difficulty was allowed). In 1986 an independent commission was organized to approve school textbooks for inclusion in a SEC list of recommended literature. The textbooks were diversified and oriented to different types and levels of schools, but the criteria and demands were unified: a Shanghai set for the developed urban districts, a Zhejiang set for economically developed rural districts, a Guangdong set for the special economic zones, and sets for mountain districts with small-sized scattered schools (Borevskaya, 1993). Schools were given options, but those who used the textbooks that were not approved could be strictly punished.

Conclusion

Realignments of the levels and balance of power for educational administration and policymaking are influenced by the economic, political, cultural issues and orientations of particular nations, but in periods of seismic change governments usually endeavor to homogenize schools and strengthen their own control. In the United States, there were movements toward centralization and standardization during the Great Depression, the Cold War, and, most recently, under the pressure of globalization. The increase in role of state and federal government control, aid, and responsibility has been gradually realized, despite the traditional preference for local control. U.S. polls in the mid-1980s indicated that "most people with any opinion on the matter also favor heightened state involvement" (Finn, 1987, p. 315). Following the consolidation of the state's role, the U.S. federal government has become more involved in educational policy. Just as American educators learned their lesson from excessive decentralization and democratization, China and the former USSR learned theirs from the lack of those components.

China's story is interesting, as in a short period this country experimented with two extremes; a highly centralized and a highly localized educational system. In what ways are the Chinese lessons of specific value to other countries, including the United States? The first lesson is that education is never "above politics," if the latter presumes the national goals and policy. This is confirmed by what the United States learned from its own history when it entrusted the task of ruling schools to experts: 'What happened, in essence, is that education politics came to be dominated by interest groups within the field itself' (Finn, 1987, p. 309). The state should shield education from being involved in political or other group interests, but the educational goals and strategy cannot be separated from the state orientation. China provides correspondingly a positive and a negative example.

The current Chinese educational goals were well articulated and entrenched in the state social and economic reforms, became an inseparable part of them (which is not to say that they were not exposed to criticism), so they were easily absorbed and implemented. In contrast, the Russian Federal Program of Educational Development gave the definition of educational goal in terms of revolutionary innovations: "The individual-oriented model in the paradigm of the developing education." Was that one of the reasons that the program suggested for Parliament; approval in early 1994 was not passed until May 1995. It also corresponds with Kelly and Seller's (1985) conclusion: "Our evidence indicates that reforms that are clearly articulated, consistent and within the realm of existing knowledge gave a greater likelihood of being implemented than reforms which are not. . . . Well-intentioned, but vaguely stated goals rarely succeeded" (p. 99).

The PRC government did not just articulate its intention to give priorities to education; it took steps to guarantee them by legislative provisions, financial preferences, and well-organized propaganda. It developed a system of privileges that pertained to the whole educational system and units whose activity faced educational demands. That could be a second lesson.

China is a developing country, at the same time it claimed to be a socialist state. Its experience in keeping a balance between the search for higher efficiency in education and governmental commitments to diminish the negative impact of a market economy by introducing the multifarious policy of priorities and aid is quite unique. This policy pertains to key and ordinary schools, gifted and disadvantaged students, open economic zones, and less-developed regions. It is worth study by other countries.

The PRC, Russia, and the United States are countries with great regional disparities. Therefore, the creation of multiple educational models is a crucial problem for all of them. China experienced both the positive and negative effects of that process while adjusting schools to local economic needs. The practice of Chinese reforms affirmed that the decision-making rights in education should preferably be concentrated on the intermediate level, that is, that of provinces (or states and regions in other countries) that could play the role of moderators and design the standards. Among the crucial negative impacts there are contradictions between the local tactics and the national strategy, and increasing disintegrative tendencies. From its own past China knew the potential of comprehensive planning and macro-control and the necessity to preserve these tools while elaborating original methods to cope with the latent and manifested consequences of educational decentralization. This lesson could be useful for all countries that are anxious "to preserve the united educational domain."

The success of China's recent educational reforms on the threshold of the next century demonstrates that its experience could be instructive for societies in transition from a paternalistic educational model to a democratic one (Russia, Eastern Europe, and the newly independent countries) as well as to the countries that are concerned about national educational strategy.

CHAPTER 16

Human Resource Development:
The J-Model

WILLIAM K. CUMMINGS

Several recent studies maintain that the educational and research institutions of all modern nations are becoming increasingly similar in response to common global economic and political forces (Meyer & Hannah, 1979; Meyer, Kamens, & Benavot, 1992; Sklair, 1991; Ilon, 1993), and, moreover, that these institutions are taking on an increasingly Western form (Ramirez & Boli, 1987). This chapter challenges the prevailing Westernization proposition by asserting that several Eastern Asian nations,[1] radiating from Japan through East Asia and Southeast Asia, have and are developing a distinctive approach to human resource development and utilization that contrasts in important respects with the Western model.

This chapter outlines the sources and nature of the Eastern Asian approach; Japan, which virtually alone among Asian nations avoided the shackles of Western imperialism, is portrayed as the chief initiator and diffuser of the Eastern Asian approach. To minimize ambiguity, the Eastern Asian approach here will be labeled the J-model, in recognition of the fact that *Japan was the first architect of the approach, and most of the components were fully realized in Japan circa the 1960s*. Other Eastern Asian states have rankled at the Japanese influence or, as in the recent cases of Singapore and Malaysia, announced official policies of "Learning from Japan." Nevertheless, all of the nations considered here have made a number of changes in the direction of the J-model. Why they have made these changes is somewhat of a mystery. In the concluding section, we will speculate on the regional processes leading to the apparent convergence on the J-model.

The core components of the J-Model are as follows:

1. The state coordinates education and research with a firm emphasis both on indigenous value transmission and the mastery of foreign technology.

2. High priority is placed on universal primary education, while state investment at the secondary and tertiary level is limited primarily to critical
   areas such as engineering and the sciences.
3. Individual students, their families, and the private sector are expected to
   provide critical backup for the education provided by the state.
4. The Asian state in seeking to coordinate not only the development but
   also the utilization of human resources involves itself in manpower planning and job placement and increasingly in the coordination of science
   and technology.

This chapter also reflects on several global implications of the Eastern
Asian approach. Among these, it is suggested that perceptions of the Asian
model as a challenge or threat to the Western model may account for highly
normatively laden critiques by certain Western observers. A more judicious
perspective could lead to a broadened understanding of human resource development. The goal is to outline a counter-proposition to the prevailing
Westernization proposition that may stimulate future investigations.

Origins of the J-Model

Development was once viewed as nationally initiated; educational reform
was seen as a component of national mobilization. But in recent years, there
is increasing recognition that global forces are creating a nascent world system (Wallerstein, 1980). It is assumed that the influences of states are weakening relative to that of the global market composed of multinational corporations and a fluid international labor market (Fuller & Rubinger, 1992;
Frobel et al., 1980). Meyer, Kamens, and Benavot (1992) observe that global
forces are leading to increasing homogeneity in the structure of modern educational systems. Others argue that the homogenous attributes follow a Western model (Ramirez & Boli, 1987; Ben-David, 1977). The recent stress on
global forces has been accompanied by a relative de-emphasis on national
and regional forces.

While analytical work may now neglect national and regional forces,
this does not mean they are necessarily diminishing in import. Kennedy
(1987) outlines the historical rise and fall of world centers; in the interlude,
where no center dominates, it has often been assumed that global forces
were triumphant. Is it possible that we are currently in such a transitional
period, and perhaps Eastern Asia may be the next rising center, displacing
Western dominance in politics, the economy, and education?

Eastern Asia was the source of great civilizations that, through the six-
teenth century, developed largely independent of Western influence (Lach,

1965). After that time Eastern Asia has been the focus of the West's persistent colonial ambitions (Moulder, 1977). Having survived the Western threat, the region is now moving from a subordinate to an independent position vis-à-vis the West's push for dominance.

Binding several of the Eastern Asian nations is a common Confucian tradition which has endured as a guide for social and political action for over 2,000 years (Berger & Hsiao, 1988). Though some see the Asian model as a reflection of this Confucian tradition (Tai, 1989), many features of the Asian model are at least superficially inconsistent with these Confucian origins, including militancy and the provision of public education. The Confucian origin attribution fails to account for the sharp discontinuities between premodern and modern Eastern Asian states. And it falters in explaining why states lacking in a Confucian tradition have adopted many of the components of the Asian approach.

Rather than think of the Eastern Asian state and the related human-resource approach as emerging from a Confucian past, it is also possible to think of the main components as being rapidly innovated by lead states during a period of intense external threat. Confucianism shaped but need not have determined the nature of these component innovations. These components, developed first in the more prescient and innovative Eastern Asian nations of Japan and Thailand, were subsequently diffused to neighboring Eastern Asian states through processes of regional political and economic colonialism.

The modern Eastern Asian states emerged in opposition to the Western threat (Black et al., 1975; Moulder, 1977). These states drew on the Asian heritage of strong centralized government (Bailey & Llobera, 1981), but whereas the Confucian tradition stressed moral leadership the most successful of the Eastern Asian states came to rely on the forces of order to strengthen their position. Facing external threat, the Eastern Asian states were obstinate, sometimes engaging in conflict with Western imperial forces. Several Eastern Asian states were defeated in the mid-nineteenth century. Japan and Thailand avoided defeat at that time, but continually faced aggression. Japan, in particular, responded with aggression leading to the defeat of Russia in 1905 and ultimately to the struggle with and defeat by the Allied powers in World War II.

Nevertheless, the Allied powers supported Japan's recovery as a means to contain the threat of communism in Asia. And by the mid-sixties Japan's development state was forging a miraculous economic recovery (Johnson, 1982). And since then Eastern Asia's newly industrializing states have demonstrated impressive economic strength (Appelbaum & Henderson, 1992).

Diffusion of the Eastern Asian Approach

The modern form of the Eastern Asian approach was first developed by Japan, though in Japan as in other Asian countries many features of this approach were shaped by past educational traditions, most notably the Confucian heritage. Parallel to Japan's early modern efforts, Korean, Chinese, and Thai political leaders were also initiating more or less independent efforts of educational modernization. However, the imperialistic policies of both Japan and various Western nations terminated most of these autonomous efforts, leaving Japan and Thailand as the only independent Asian innovators.

Whereas Thailand did not pursue a policy of regional influence, Japan aggressively occupied various Asian nations, and through its colonial policies stamped the imprint of its human resource model in those settings (Tsurumi, 1977; Hong, 1992). Japan was most thorough in its influence on the Korean and Taiwanese systems, but it also had influence on other nations through the visitations of students (as in the case of China) and through more limited periods of occupation (as in the case of Indonesia, Vietnam, the Philippines, and China).

And since World War II, the J-model has been fostered through cultural diplomacy and foreign assistance, particularly under the auspices of the Japan-controlled Asian Development Bank. While it would be a gross overstatement to argue that the major objective of these postwar transactions has been to encourage the development of a common J-model, it can be argued that a by-product of many of these transactions has been to export primarily Japanese ideas about education and development (Yamashita, 1991; Stewart & Nihei, 1992).

Recent interest in Asia has been accompanied by a voluminous literature, which can be confusing as, depending on the account, the nations included in Asia differ. This study focuses on those Eastern Asian nations that have been most directly influenced by Japan in their economic and social transformation. Two Asian nations, Taiwan and Korea, were former colonies of Japan; and both by virtue of reparations and economic interest, Japan has invested heavily in the industrial infrastructure of these two nations for several decades. Other Eastern Asian nations, because of special strengths in natural and human resources as well as political stability, have also been the focus of Japanese investment both through Japan's massive OAD funds and through private initiative: Thailand was an initial favorite, followed by Malaysia, Singapore, and currently Indonesia. Figure 16.1 characterizes these two groups of Eastern Asian nations, that have been the primary focus of Japanese attention, as two wings of an Eastern Asian development flock led by Japan.[2]

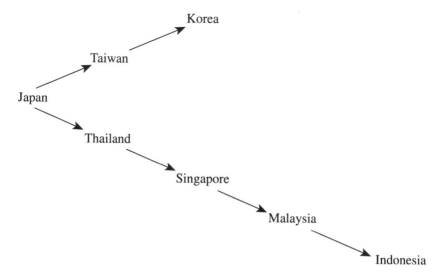

Figure 16.1. The Eastern Asian Flock

In the analysis below, several indicators will be cited to illustrate how the nations in the Japanese flock differ in important respects from other Asian nations (e.g., the socialist and communist republics of East and Southeast Asia as well as the South Asian nations, all of which have relatively weak ties to Japan) as well as other developing countries and the major industrial nations of the West (the relevant data are included in table 16.1.) It is not intended, by grouping Eastern Asian nations in this way, to suggest that these groupings reflect any formal agreement; rather the grouping is analytical, based on differences in levels of mutual trade, investment, and political affinity.

The success of the Eastern Asian development state has led to reviews of its distinctive approach in the economic sphere (World Bank, 1993). But thus far, analyses have provided relatively sparse detail on the human resource dimension of the Eastern Asian state (Fukui, 1992; Deyo, 1992). We suggest below that the Eastern Asian state has devised a distinctive approach to human resource development and utilization, and that this approach which initially served the interests of the Eastern Asian state is now beginning to have a global impact.

Just as Japan has (consciously or unconsciously) exported its educational ideals to other parts of Eastern Asia, Japan has also been the recipient of various Eastern Asian cultural exports. Perhaps of greatest consequence has been the Eastern Asian demand that Japanese textbooks be amended to

TABLE 16.1

Comparison of Japan and Japan-related Eastern Asian Nations with Other Asian
Nations, Europe, and the Developing World circa 1988 (unless otherwise indicated)

Indicator	1	2	3	4	5	6	7
Lean Govt.:							
Govt. expense as % GNP	10	20	22	11	19	44	30
Ed. as % Govt.	34	19	25	17	9	10	13
Science							
Science/Eng. students as % all in higher education	22	37	23	29	24	29	29
Human Resources							
Primary GER 1970	99	107	89	86	54	103	76
Secondary GER 1970	86	48	28	28	20	70	27
Tertiary GER 1990	31	13	7	8	3	21	9
Society Fills Gap							
Private % 2nd	13	33	30	54	49	23	25
Private % H. Ed.	80	75	26	22	35	25	15
Efficiency							
2nd student/teacher	19	30	20	17	22	14	22
% Finished 4th Grade	100	96	82	83	58	95	83
% Primary Repeaters	0	0	6	6	10	4	14

Key: 1: Japan; 2: Korea, Taiwan; 3: Other NICs; 4: Other Asian; 5: South Asia; 6: Western Europe; 7: Developing nations.

Source: Primary source is UNESCO (1991). Additional indicators are from World Bank and SPIE data bank at the University at Buffalo.

GER = Gross Enrollment Ratio

show greater and more accurate recognition of Japan's ongoing relationship with Asian countries (the textbook controversy of wartime activities being a particularly pointed example). Eastern Asian student flows to Japan accompanied by demands that Japanese universities and communities internationalize their services are another channel for Eastern Asian influence on Japan (Hook & Weiner, 1992).

The expanding postwar interaction between the various Eastern Asian nations, with Japan as a particularly active promoter of these exchanges, has resulted in a growing Eastern Asian consensus on the efficacy of many of the features noted above.

This is not to deny the persistence of major intraregional variation in the practice of human resource development. China's socialist approach (Carnoy & Samoff, 1990) and Malaysia's multiracial approach (Mukherjee, 1988) are two distinctive deviants from the main pattern. Also between those countries that are closer to the Eastern Asian mainstream, there are important points of variation: For example, Korea and Taiwan place greater stress on the public sector than Japan; and the Korean state places more emphasis on national unity than do most of the other Asian countries. These differences form the basis for important human resource competition within the region.

The Core Features of the Eastern Asian Approach

The first outlines of the Eastern Asian approach emerged in the late nineteenth century as Japan and other Asian nations responded to the Western challenge. But only Japan and Thailand were able to escape the shackles of Western imperialism and develop distinctive indigenous approaches (Altbach & Selvaratnam, 1989). Since Japan has enjoyed greater developmental success over time, the Japanese approach has been the most influential. Thus it helps to focus first on Japan when seeking to identify the core features of the Eastern Asian prototype; but, as will be indicated below, other Eastern Asian nations have developed important variations on the Japanese model that deserve note. The core features of the Japanese/Eastern Asian approach, insofar as they relate to human resources, are as follows:

The State is Strong but Lean

In view of potential external threats, Eastern Asian states have usually mobilized substantial resources for national defense, somewhat above the average level of other nations. For example, Taiwan and Korea devote circa 10 percent of GDP for defense. But in most other areas the government's expenses are modest compared both to Western industrial societies and the average for developing societies; for example, the Eastern Asian states' expenditures in the field of welfare are negligible and in public health the expenditures are comparatively low. Indeed, Eastern Asian leaders are often explicit in their disdain for the Western welfare state, arguing that the safety net is too generous and discourages hard work. While expenditures in these areas are low, the state nevertheless takes a directive role through its mobilization of community organizations and its emphasis on family and community responsibility. Apart from defense, the two policy areas where the Eastern Asian state allocates relatively large sums are industrial policy and human resources. The limited commitments of the Eastern Asian state result in government budgets that absorb smaller proportions of GNP than are typical of Western industrial societies as well as many developing societies. As noted in table 16.1, government expenses absorb 10 percent of Japan's JDP, an average of 20 percent of Taiwan and Korea's, and 22 percent of the other

Asian NICs, compared to an average of 44 percent for the countries of Western Europe, and 30 percent for other developing countries.

Human Resources are Critical for National Development

Key national leaders who perceived the need to respond to the Western challenge quickly concluded that a major cultural and human transformation would be necessary (Smith, 1955; Hall, 1973). Surveying the factors behind Western political and economic preeminence, Eastern Asian leaders recognized the scarcity of their resources. Whereas the leading Western nations were blessed with generous natural resources, Eastern Asian leaders concluded that people were their major resource. Thus, as indicated in table 16.1, Japan and the countries closest to it, spend relatively large proportions of the lean national budget on education, and this leads to relatively high enrollment rates in primary and secondary education.

In Eastern Asia, stress has been placed not only on the *development* of human resources but also on their *utilization*. To bring this about, they placed educational and cultural policy at the center of plans for national development. In the public sector, educational streams were tightly linked to projected manpower requirements. Governments assumed a coordinating role in the transition from education to work, and in several instances routinely carried out annual surveys to evaluate the success of schools in placing their graduates in workplaces. This legacy of planned utilization of scarce human resources endures.

The State is Responsible for the Framework

Given the concern for maximizing the impact of scarce human resources, the state assumed a central role in their development (Black et al., 1975). Central authorities sought to lay out educational goals and a curriculum as well as to provide textbooks and staff (Ministry of Education, 1980). With these contributions, the Asian state was satisfied it could shape the educational process: given a slim budget, the state minimized its involvement in the everyday management of schools. The trusted principals and staff were expected to do their job. Hence within the centrally prescribed framework, there remained much school-level autonomy in implementation.

Seeking Knowledge throughout the World

Entering late and reluctantly into the modern era, Eastern Asia recognized a need to catch up to the leading Western nations (Levy, 1972). Seeking knowledge throughout the world and particularly from the West became a core element in the Eastern Asian catch-up strategy (Braisted, 1976; Teng &

Fairbank, 1954). Western knowledge, particularly in the areas of science, medicine, and technology was seen as the essential means for developing national strength and competitiveness. The schools were expected to provide a solid foundation in these areas by featuring mathematics and science as required subjects from the first grades of the primary school. Colleges and universities were also expected to stress these fields. The earliest human resource institutions were established to import and transmit scientific and technical knowledge rather than to create it (Bartholomew, 1989); applied faculties such as agriculture, engineering, and medicine were far more prominent than faculties in the basic sciences. This legacy endures.

Western Science/Eastern Values

While Western knowledge was considered valuable, Asian leaders had reservations about the broader societal framework of the West. They believed that Eastern Asia's familistic and political values provided a better foundation for the good society (Hall, 1973). Thus, they sought through schooling and other means to foster continuity in the values realm. Schools included moral education as a core component of their curriculum, and educators were expected to set proper examples so as to lead young people to respect Eastern Asia's enduring traditions.

In contrast with the off-and-on Western interest in multiculturalism, Eastern Asian states identified a common core of values which they sought to convey to all young people in the national language; bilingualism was typically eschewed. The common normative core mainly focused on behavior stressing honesty, hard work, respect for parents and authority, cleanliness (Befu, 1993; NIER, 1981). Religious commitments were left up to the individual, so long as they did not conflict with state priorities: thus the Japanese state made no distinction between Christians and Confucianists and the Indonesian Pancasila emphasized respect for God, without placing priority on any particular religion.

Public Primary Schooling Provides the Foundation

Reflecting the Eastern Asian conviction that excellence derives from a command of the basics, Eastern Asian educators placed special emphasis on the development of effective primary schools (Passin, 1965). Much care was devoted to the curriculum and teaching methods at this level. And adequate funding was provided to insure a solid basic education for all. Eastern Asian nations have tended to realize universal enrollment faster than nations in most other parts of the world (Williamson, 1993); as indicated in table 16.1, the average gross enrollment ratio of 1970 for those nations associated with

Japan was close to 100 percent, well ahead of the average for South Asia (54 percent) or for other developing nations. The stress on primary education meant that advanced educational levels were sometimes given lower priority, at least in the public sector (James & Benjamin, 1988). But through a combination of public and private effort, Asian gross enrollment ratios at the secondary level were also comparatively high as early as 1970.

The Public School Teaches; the Pupil Has to Learn

Always conscious of scarce resources, Eastern Asian educators placed limits on the school's responsibilities: The school's job was to present the curriculum in as effective a manner as possible for the average pupil (Cummings, 1980). It was up to the pupil (and his/her parents) to take advantage of the school's presentation. The school was not required to make special efforts to accommodate slow students or to stimulate the gifted. The responsibility for learning rested on the pupil. To insure this common understanding, the school worked closely with local leaders and parents so as to gain their cooperation. Thus considerable pressure was exerted on young people to exert their best efforts for learning. And when young people encountered difficulties, parents sought through extra tutoring to help them master the required material (Stevenson & Stigler, 1992).

Public Secondary and Tertiary Education Focus on National Priorities

The Eastern Asian state's concern was to catch up and then move ahead. Public resources were allocated in accordance with that objective. Thus in education beyond the foundation level, the public sector had the limited objective of developing critical manpower and training elites (Cummings, 1980; Pang, 1982). The public sector set up a limited number of educational opportunities in critical areas and heavily subsidized these so tuition was low and good students were attracted; in some fields such as engineering, the state actually funded a surplus of opportunities in anticipation of future expansion in the related labor markets. Despite an overall policy of restraint, public institutions oversupplied in certain specialties.

"Society" Welcome to Fill the Gaps

The Eastern Asian state sought to limit its provision in schooling (and other social services), but it recognized that the public might demand more. Rather than contain this popular demand, the state assumed a permissive policy, only intervening when the private response began to conflict with public objectives. Thus a vigorous private sector often emerged to complement the public sector (Geiger, 1987).

One area of private response was at the preschool level. A second was in supplementary courses to help pupils keep up with the curriculum provided in basic education. Private schools also emerged to help young people prepare for postcompulsory level entrance exams. And, because of the limited public provision of public sector opportunities relative to the number of qualified students, private educational entrepreneurs established competing secondary and tertiary institutions. In several Asian societies (Japan, Taiwan, Korea, Indonesia, the Philippines) the private sector provides over 75 percent of all places at the tertiary level. Thus private schools emerged to accommodate the "excess demand," which was sometimes very sizeable (James & Benjamin, 1988.

Yet another area of private initiative was in the utilization of human resources for research and development. While the public sector trained human resources to a high level and supported research in certain critical areas such as health and munitions, it left commercially relevant research and development to the private sector. As the Eastern Asian corporate sector expanded, it became increasingly involved in the self-sponsorship of major research efforts. Thus, in contrast with Western nations where national R&D budgets tend to be heavily subsidized by the state, in Eastern Asia typically three-quarters or more of all R&D activities are supported by the private sector (Johnson, 1993; Ushiogi, 1993).

But All Education and Research Should be "Coordinated"

While the public sector limited its provision, it retained comprehensive responsibility. Thus private schools were required to observe public regulations. And periodically public officials intervened in the private sector to curb excesses, such as unreasonable prices or abysmal quality. A particular challenge for the public sector was the education provided by nonschool media such as journals, the cinema, and lately the television industry. In these areas as well, the state was likely to intervene so as to achieve overall consistency in the educational experience.

Similarly, while state funding of research and development was comparatively modest, the state made important contributions to the coordination of research. Most notable was state sponsorship of overseas research trips and of national facilities for the import and translation of foreign research journals. In more recent years, the Eastern Asian state has come to play a more prominent role in targeting technologies for development by the private sector (Vogel, 1991).

Some Implications of the Eastern Asian Approach

The Eastern Asian approach provides several sharp contrasts with the approaches to education that have evolved in leading Western industrial nations (Cummings, 1992). For example, the Asian educational ideal places greater stress on cooperation and cohesion relative to the Western stress on individualism. Asian pedagogy assumes that the key to learning is individual effort rather than inherent genetic endowment or talent. And Asian systems place more emphasis on insuring that every child receives a standard education than on enabling each child to obtain an education suited to his or her needs; similarly teachers are expected to teach the common curriculum rather than to introduce curricular innovations that express their unique strengths. Eastern Asian educational systems tend to place their greatest stress on basic education, rather than on elite public schools or great universities; though in the schools that provide basic education, some educational conditions such as the numbers of students in a classroom do not conform with the standards characteristic of western systems.

In these various ways, the Eastern Asian approach constitutes an alternative to western approaches, and an exception to the proposition that education around the world is becoming more homogeneous. The distinctiveness of the Eastern Asian approach has provoked a variety of assessments. Many are critical, focusing on lack of quality and on "human costs," and we will turn to these shortly. In contrast are assessments which take the Eastern Asian approach on its own terms, evaluate its effectiveness in promoting cultural and political autonomy in the face of the Western challenge, and then consider its comparative success in promoting national development. Since the Eastern Asian approach has proved to have impressive development effects, this line of assessment inevitably leads to a consideration of the global implications of the Eastern Asian approach.

Social Stability

A major concern of the Eastern Asian approach is to instill accepted social values. Whereas Western educators lean toward a cognitive reasoning approach to values education (Kohlberg, 1981), Eastern Asian educators favor a directive approach involving explicit teaching and consistent reinforcement (Cummings et al., 1988). The school is viewed as the primary vehicle for conveying the values curriculum, and it is partly for this reason that the school calendar is long and the atmosphere is constrained. But constrained is not the same as joyless or inhuman. Observation studies indicate that Eastern Asian schoolchildren enjoy their schooling (Tobin, 1989), and comparative statistics suggest that their schooldays are at least as humane as those experienced by children in other industrial societies: Eastern Asian schools have low absenteeism; high completion rates (see table 16.1); abundant evidence of healthy youth; a comparatively low incidence of neurosis-suicide; as well as a low incidence of other forms of deviance (drugs, delinquency, juvenile pregnancy). The social savings from these healthy and stable child and adolescent years are substantial (UNICEF, 1992; UNESCO, 1992).

Human Resource Edge

A second set of implications is what might be called the Eastern Asian Human Resource Edge. A relatively uncontroversial theme is that Eastern Asian educational systems are slanted towards the provision of math and science education and that they produce relatively large numbers of upper secondary and university graduates in the fields of technology, engineering, and science. For example, Japan with only half the U.S. population trains as many engineers as the United States (Johnson, 1993; U.S. Department of Education, 1987). Despite the comparatively large number of Eastern Asian students specializing in these fields, nearly all obtain employment on graduation. Many of the best end up as researchers in Eastern Asia's corporate laboratories and universities. Some of the less qualified of these graduates take up positions in the lower levels of the modern manufacturing sector, providing Eastern Asia with the best "second half" of the labor force (Dore & Sako, 1989).

But what about the rest? All find employment, but many are by standard human resource measurements "underemployed"; that is, they work in positions that do not require their professional skills such as in sales jobs or as stock brokers and analysts (Kodama & Chiaki, 1991; Muta, 1990). But perhaps the underemployed provide unique perspectives to their co-workers that enhance the productivity of these nontechnological units (Cole, 1989; Lynn et al., 1993).

Not an insignificant number of Eastern Asia's underemployed graduates decide to leave the Asian labor market and seek opportunities in Western labor markets, especially the United States. Indeed, one of the least heralded outcomes of Eastern Asian education's excess production is the extraordinary extent to which it has supplied scientific and technical workers to Western corporations and universities (Cummings, 1984, 1985; Lee, 1993).

While Eastern Asia supplies both indigenous and overseas markets with large quantities of scientific and technical workers, it is sometimes asserted that these workers are not particularly gifted, that they are unable to make creative contributions (Miyanaga, 1991). But the evidence supporting these assertions comes from earlier years when Eastern Asian researchers and research laboratories were underfunded. That constraint is rapidly disappearing, and it remains to be seen how impressive the productivity of the Asian researcher will be under more favorable conditions. Recent indications (based on gains in scientific articles, patent submissions, high-tech product sales) are that Eastern Asian scientists may be highly competitive (Bloom, 1990; Science and Technology Agency, 1991). Their hard-work ethic combined with their willingness to cooperate in joint projects may even give them an edge in some creative endeavors.

Pacific Rim Connection

A third set of implications could be described as the Pacific Rim connection. Over the course of the past three decades, Eastern Asian human resources have become extensively developed and diffused throughout the Pacific Rim.

One facet of the rapid expansion of Eastern Asian human resources has been a fostering of a new level of competitiveness as Eastern Asian corporations seek to outdo each other in the international marketplace. This competitiveness, often fueled by feelings of chauvinism, as between Korean and Japanese construction firms competing for the same contract, pushes Eastern Asian human resources to ever higher levels of productivity.

But an equally interesting and virtually unexplored theme is the extent of cooperation that emerges between Eastern Asian scientists, particularly when they are located in foreign settings. For example, a recent study documents that many Eastern Asian-born scientists working in American research universities retain relatively fluid scientific ties with colleagues in their countries of origin (Choi, 1993). This cooperation across national boundaries may provide an important impetus to the quality of Eastern Asian scientific and technical work.

Yet another feature of the Asian connection is the rapidly expanding level of communication between scholars and scientists within the Eastern Asian region, particularly stimulated by Japan's new commitment to Overseas Development Assistance. Over the past five years, Japan has trebled its intake of students from other Eastern Asian countries. Even more impressive has been the fivefold increase in the number of Eastern Asian scholars spending short study visits in Japan (STA, 1991).

There still remains the question of the Eastern Asian Limit, particularly in the area of research. Will there be an Eastern Asian research edge? Can the Eastern Asian approach move beyond knowledge seeking to indigenous knowledge creation (Cummings, 1994)? This may be a false question—for if

Eastern Asian corporations can buy the other brains and labs of overseas competitors, why do they have to do the work on their own? Thus an extension of the Pacific Rim Connection analysis would be to look into Eastern Asian (and non-Asian) strategies for securing control of off-shore knowledge/value production. In the new era of weaker states, the nationality of knowledge workers has reduced meaning—but there still is interest in who benefits.

Human Rights

Yet another area where the Eastern Asian approach challenges Western perspectives is with respect to human rights (Awanohara, 1993). The Eastern Asian approach places considerable emphasis on the family group and the community, often urging the individual to subordinate personal interests so as to advance the welfare of these broader collectivities. Even more, the individual identifies his/her well-being with the well-being of the broader collective. The welfare of the broader group, it is proposed, results in a better situation for each of the members. Harmony and the consensual negotiation of differences are emphasized as means to reconcile individual and social rights.

In contrast to the Eastern Asian approach, in recent years Western ideologues have urged Eastern Asian states to make greater efforts to conform to universal (or are they Western?) concepts of human rights. The Western critics insist that Eastern Asian nations should foster greater personal freedom and institute more representative forms of democratic government. Issues such as Timor and Tianamen Square have sharply polarized Western critics and Eastern Asian leaders. The Eastern Asian statesmen argue that the Eastern Asian approach places its first priority on social welfare or development, and only as these conditions are realized does it become meaningful to encourage democracy and Western concepts of human rights. Sometimes the Eastern Asian leaders go so far as to point out how much more stable and crime-free are their societies than are the societies of those Western nations that place such high priority on human rights. It may be that these differences in the notion of what constitutes the good society will lead to sharp conflicts between the Asian and Western approaches to human rights over the next decades ("Human Rights," 1993).

Critical Assessments of the Eastern Asian Approach

In contrast to the above relatively sanguine evaluation of the Eastern Asian approach to human resource development is a more critical view, found in many recent publications, that tends to present a "yes, but" argument (Tobin, 1989). The typical critical assessment acknowledges certain accomplishments of the Asian approach such as its success in promoting quantitative growth but then goes on to assert that these accomplishments are realized at considerable cost. Often these critical views are articulated by insiders (Horio, 1988; Lee, 1991), but some of the sharpest comments come from Western observers (Cogan, 1984; Fallows, 1987; Miller, 1982; Shields, 1993).

Big Numbers

International comparisons increasingly rely on national statistics as a starting point for analysis. The quantitative accomplishments are undeniable. Enrollment levels in Asia are high through the tertiary level, and Eastern Asia produces relatively large numbers of science and engineering graduates. Also in various international achievement tests, Eastern Asian school children do exceptionally well—some analysts go so far as to suggest that the typical Eastern Asian high school graduate knows more math than the American university graduate (Rohlen, 1983). But, of course, the international tests do not focus on the full range of cognitive and social skills, and thus may not reflect areas of Western strength and Asian weakness.

Quality is Lacking

The Asian approach may lead to impressive quantitative results at the school level, but what about at the tertiary level and in the critical area of research and development? In particular, critics point to the weakness of Eastern Asia in basic science; few Eastern Asian scientists have achieved distinction in international circles, and those that are well known have generally carried out their best work in Western laboratories (Nagai, 1970; Miyanaga, 1991). Does this not reflect a fundamental weakness of Eastern Asian education? Other critics point to the lack of diligence of Eastern Asian university students and their reputed inability to engage in critical dialogue (Reischauer, 1973). Eastern Asian education is portrayed as creating good vessels for pouring in knowledge, but poor vehicles for the critical processing of ideas.[3]

The Human Costs are Excessive

While Eastern Asian education produces many graduates with an impressive command of core cognitive subject matter, this appears to be accomplished with modest public expenditures (Tan & Mingat, 1992). Eastern Asian governments typically devote 4–5 percent of GNP to education compared with 6–8 percent in leading Western nations. The more centralized nature of Eastern Asian systems and also the higher student-teacher ratios help to account for the savings; in many Eastern Asian systems, primary level classes have forty pupils per teacher.

But critics ask, Might not these savings have their corollary in high human costs (Lee, 1991)? According to some accounts, Eastern Asian children from a young age have to devote long hours to dreary schoolwork, and, moreover, travel long distances with heavy bookbags before enduring this torture (Miller, 1982). Many are said to break from this pressure, engaging in fistfights and bullying. And yet others are said to turn their frustration inward, committing suicide. Western accounts suggest that the incidence in Eastern Asia of these human tragedies is comparatively high, and that these do not justify whatever the Eastern Asian approach may realize in the achievement game (Woronoff, 1984; Fallows, 1987).[4]

Conclusion

Human resource issues are moving to the center of the policy agenda of advanced industrial nations. (Reich, 1991; Malecki, 1991; Thurow, 1992; Marshall & Tucker, 1992). It has been proposed a distinctive approach to Human Resource Development has emerged in Eastern Asia. This approach was developed to insure Eastern Asian survival in the face of potential Western dominance. Only Japan and Thailand were initially successful. But now all of Eastern Asia is politically independent, and through a process of regional diffusion the basic components have become more widely shared. The prestige of the Eastern Asian approach rises, in conjunction with the strength of the Eastern Asian economies. Of course, there is much criticism of the Eastern Asian approach; while much of this criticism comes from within Eastern Asia, the vehemence of external critics is also notable. It could be that this critical view derives from a defensive position of the leaders of Western institutions who feel their assumptions are being challenged and even threatened by the often contrasting Eastern Asian approach. Our goal here has been to identify some of those contrasts and to suggest a range of issues for further exploration.

Notes

Chapter 3

1. Formal in-depth interviews (47) were conducted in China and the United States between 1987 and 1990 (Reed, 1991). Most of these took place in China during the last six months of 1990 in the cities of Beijing, Shanghai, Nanjing, Fushun, Changsha, and Yanji. The data from these formal interviews was augmented by numerous informal conversations in China and the United States that continue up to the present and by data collected from a class of fifty-three senior middle school students in Nanjing. Most of the interviewees are intellectuals, and approximately 25 percent are Chinese Communist Party members. This number is approximate because it was not always comfortable to inquire about party affiliation.

Chapter 4

1. In 1982–84 I spent two years conducting an intensive participant observation study of teacher-education reform and made five subsequent data-collection trips to interview and observe at twenty-two teacher education institutions in very different regions of the country. I have observed and interviewed at education offices (local, provincial, and central government level) and over sixty-five schools, including rural and urban schools, elite and ordinary, public and private in coastal, central and remote parts of China. Systematic analysis of education journals and newspapers, as well as teacher literature, has helped broaden my sense of national developments and tensions.

2. These figures are distressingly low when one asserts, as the Chinese government does, that years of schooling are only weak approximations of qualification.

3. Feiman-Nemser and Floden (1986) make a case for the importance of thinking about cultures of teaching. In this chapter I focus on China's teaching culture but, given limitations of space, will both generalize about a dominant culture (although I acknowledge at the outset that alternative cultural norms exist in particular communities of teachers) and will limit my discussion only to professional culture. Clearly, China's dominant teaching culture rests on and is supported by a broader set of cultural values and givens. For more discussion of the intersection between broader cultural values and teaching culture in China, see Paine and Ma, 1993, and Paine, 1992.

4. As a part of a National Center for Research on Teacher Learning (NCRTL) study, we have examined the forms and content of mentoring that seven pairs of mentors and mentees in three Shanghai schools engaged in on a weekly basis over a year's work together.

Chapter 6

1. Several caveats to binational comparisons of criminal behavior must be recorded. The Japanese tend to report crimes committed by juveniles as part of overall crimes—the status of the offender is changed dependent on age. In the United States, both age of offender and the crime itself are the basis for separate categories (Office of Juvenile Justice, 1992, p. 149). The Japanese system of reporting is centralized; in the United States, it is not. Most of the statistics compiled by the Office of Juvenile Justice are national projections based on ten states.

A second problem with cross-national comparisons is that the Japanese also report "warnings." Middle school or high school students who are detained by police on suspicion of a crime can be admonished and released. Moreover, reporting of violence or disruptive behavior within schools falls outside the scope of the Ministry of Justice and is handled by the Ministry of Education.

2. Involvement in *yakuza/boryokudan/bosozoku* (gangs) in Kotani was considered to be mostly a problem with high school boys or boys who had failed to enter high school. In simple terms, Japanese society hosts a range of gang-type affiliations ranging from *kaminarizoku* (groups of teens on souped-up scooters) to *yakuza* (large crime syndicates). Kotani teachers use the term *yakuza* to refer to the organized family operations in the area, which appear to control the local bars, pachinko parlors, and prostitution. *Boryokudan* referred to "violent" gangs, sometimes youths affiliated with *yakuza* families. *Bosozoku* was used to denote groups of young people, often from outside the area, who staged drag rallies and occasionally engaged in street fights. For in-depth studies of Japanese gangs and gang formation, see Wagatsuma & DeVos, 1984, and Sato, 1991.

3. Boys dress in a modified Prussian uniforms: black pants and white shirts, black jackets in winter. For girl's uniforms, the color of the kerchief or cut of the blouse can vary slightly from school to school. Some middle schools even allow drab brown or green outfits instead of the traditional black and navy blue. Knapsacks and briefcases are regulated and nearly identical from school to school. Students carry little that is not directly connected with school—comic books, makeup kits, and a variety of other items are forbidden. Each student carries a pencil case and a plastic square to be used to prevent ink from penetrating pages in the notebook, and these articles are covered with amusing slogans in Japanese and English. Items that convey personal tastes are allowed but confined to a limited set of possessions.

4. Japanese attitudes about personal appearance diverge sharply from American. Tadahiko Abiko (1987), a Japanese researcher who conducted an ethnography of a

Florida middle school, thought that the freedom in dress, makeup, and expression given to American middle schoolers was the way that schools made American adults out of children (p. 20). Clothes were, in American culture, *watakushigoto* (personal affairs) (p. 21). Dressing in a certain way was not obligatory for participation in school, rather it was the "responsibility of the will of the parent or child" (p. 21).

5. *Hiparu/Ishi ga yowaii* (being bullied into crime or having a weak will) is often given as an excuse by parents for their child's behavior (see Wagatsuma & DeVos, 1984). In her confessional novel, Hozumi (1991) links her initial abuse of paint thinner to the influence of bad companions.

Chapter 7

1. There is also a similar, parallel image in the more narrow school achievement comparative literature on Asia.

2. For purposes of analysis, we have included in the category "developing nations" any country eligible for World Bank support with a population over one million in 1990. The micro-nations are excluded because of both data problems and their radically different scale in terms of educational development. Included in the analysis of developing Asian countries (data availability permitting) are: Afghanistan, Bangladesh, Bhutan, Myanmar, China, India, Indonesia, Kampuchea, Republic of Korea, People's Democratic Republic of Laos, Malaysia, Mongolia, Nepal, Pakistan, Papua New Guinea, Thailand, Sri Lanka, and Vietnam.

3. Unless otherwise stated, all enrollments rates discussed here are gross rates (i.e., enrollment divided by all age-eligible eligible children), without any out-of-age repeaters removed from the ratio (i.e., net rates). In some cases, additional estimation of enrollment rate data was done by the authors.

4. The developed nations selected for this figure are France, West Germany, Hong Kong, Japan, the United Kingdom, and the United States. Other developed nations show a similar trend over this period.

5. A coefficient of variation (standard deviation divided by the mean) for the Asian region is .60 compared with an average of .40 for the other four regions.

6. Unless otherwise listed China refers to mainland not Taiwan.

7. Standard World Bank 1991 categories of national income were used to divide developing countries into *low income*—GNP per capita of $635; *middle income*—GNP per capita between $635 and $7,911; and *high income*—GNP per capita above $7,911.

8. Actually the best indicator of eligible population is primary school finishers, but the data used here do not contain this information.

9. Equation B is:

$$Y' = C + b1X1 + b2X2 \ldots + d1CX1 + d2CX2 \ldots + a$$

where C is a dummy variable coded 1 for developing Asian countries and 0 for all other developing countries. It is written for Asian secondary enrollment rates as

$$Y' = (a + C) + (b1 + d1)X1 + (b2 + d2)X2 \ldots$$

and for other developing countries secondary enrollment rates as

$$Y' = a + b1X1 + b2X2 + b3X3.$$

10. Another example of this is the very favorable mathematics achievement in Bangkok schools versus schools in the countryside evident in early 1980s from the Second International Study of Mathematics (analysis available from the authors upon request).

11. Given the large population in this region, any regional growth in secondary enrollment represents significant numbers, for example the relatively high rate in India and China translate into large additions to the world's population of secondary students (Baker, 1994).

Chapter 8

1. The Social and Political Impacts on Education Data-Bank (SPIE) of the University at Buffalo is the primary source of information for this analysis (Cummings, Vargas, & Williams, 1995). The SPIE data bank combines files from the World Bank Social Indicators, the World Bank's World Development Indicators, the Consortium of Political Science at the University of Michigan's Political Indicators, UNESCO's Educational Indicators, Humana's Human Rights Indicators, OECD's Financial and ODA Flows, and from various national sources. Taiwan entries are drawn directly from official reports. Available data are relatively complete through the late eighties, and from 1970, so most of the comparisons will use the years of 1988 and 1970 (or 1975).

Chapter 9

1. Because of the variety of operations involved and difficulties in obtaining a precise definition of what constitutes supplemental tutoring, revenue figures for the industry are inexact. The estimate used in this chapter is taken from the Yan Research Institute's Annual Report on the education industry in Japan. Calculations are based on the September 1995 exchange rate of ¥100 = $1.

2. The Ministry of Education survey used for the 1976 numbers only covered youth in primary and lower secondary schools (grades 1 to 9).

3. Rika Sato, personal communication, October 1994.

4. Thomas Rohlen discusses in his 1980 article the concept of an "express" *juku* that is part of an "elite" course for students who wish to move ahead of the public school curriculum. I am grateful to him for discussing with me the contrasting nature of *juku* and *yobiko*.

5. Tanaka cites a 1991 Tokyo Teachers Union study which found that 22 percent of Tokyo elementary school students sat for private middle school exams and 14.2 percent enrolled (p. 32). He says that 43 percent of parents did not consult their child's public school teacher about applying to private school, inferring that they made their decisions privately, perhaps with the aid of a *juku* instructor.

Chapter 10

Descriptions of education and training in Japanese companies contained in this article are based on interviews conducted by the author at more than 100 Japanese companies between 1987 and 1994.

Chapter 11

1. The percentage for Hong Kong refers to the annual average growth rate of the Gross Domestic Product (GDP), not GNP. The same applies to the per capital GDP in the following sentence.

2. Estimates are calculated from the Consumer Price Index and per-student total education expenditure (GROC, 1992, p. 54; GROC, 1993a, p. 167).

Chapter 12

1. Pseudonyms are used in place of actual villages and schools.

2. Originally twenty-four teachers began the project. One resigned for philosophical reasons.

Chapter 16

1. An earlier version of this paper appeared as "The Asian Human Resource Approach in Global Perspective." *Oxford Review of Education, 21*(1), pp. 67–81. In speaking of Eastern Asia, we mainly refer to Japan, Korea, Taiwan, Thailand, Malaysia, Singapore, and Indonesia as illustrated in figure 16.1.

2. Hong Kong, often considered an Asian tiger, is not included in this grouping, as at the policy level the leadership has expressed little interest in the Japanese model. China also is not included as it, until recently, has relied on a controlled economy; also China has consciously restrained the development of human resources.

3. Or perhaps the vehicles are prepared but the conditions in Eastern Asian universities are not conducive to creativity, notably the lack of facilities.

4. It should, however, be pointed out that many of these Western accounts are factually wrong.

References

Introduction

Fallows, J. (1987). Gradgrind's heirs: Despite what the U.S. Department of Education says, you would not want your kids to go to a Japanese secondary school. *Atlantic Monthly*, 259:3 March, 16–24.

National Commission on Excellence in Education. (1983). *A nation at risk: The imperative for educational reform*. Washington, DC: Government Printing Office.

Schoppa, L. (1991). *Education reform in Japan: A case of immobilist policies*. New York: Routledge.

Chapter 1

Barrett, M. J. (1990). The case for more school days. *Atlantic Monthly*, November, pp. 78–106.

Boocock, S. S. (1987, March). *The privileged world of little children: Preschool education in Japan*. Paper presented at the annual meeting of the Comparative and International Education Society, Washington, DC.

Connell, J. P., & Wellborn, J. G. (1991). Competence, autonomy, and relatedneess: A motivational analysis of self-system processes. In M. R. Gunnar & L. A. Sroufe (Eds.), *The Minnesota Symposia on Child Development* (vol. 23, pp. 43–77). Hillsdale, NJ: Lawrence Erlbaum.

Cummings. W. (1980). *Education and equality in Japan*. Princeton, NJ: Princeton University Press.

Deci, E. L., & Ryan, R. R. (1985). *Intrinsic motivation and self-determination in human behavior*. New York: Plenum.

Duke, B. (1986). *The Japanese school: Lessons for industrial America*. New York: Praeger.

Easley, J., & Easley, E. (1983). Kitamaeno School as an environment in which children study mathematics themselves. *Journal of Science Education in Japan, 7*, 39–48.

Guilford, J. (1968). *Intelligence, creativity, and their educational implications.* San Diego: Knapp.

Hara, H., & Wagatsuma, H. (1974). *Shitsuke* [Childrearing]. Tokyo: Kobundo.

Hess, R. D., & Azuma, H. (1991). Cultural support for schooling: Contrasts between Japan and the United States. *Educational Researcher, 20,* 2–8, 12.

Kajita, M., Shiota, S., Ishida, H., & Sugie, S. (1980). Sho-chugakko ni okeru shido no chosateki kenkyu [Survey of teaching methods in elementary and junior high schools]. *Bulletin of the Faculty of Education, Nagoya University, 27,* 147–182.

Kashiwagi, K. (1986). Personality development of adolescents. In H. Stevenson, H. Azuma, & K. Hakuta (Eds.), *Child development and education in Japan* (pp. 167–185). New York: Freeman.

Kojima, H. (1986). Childrearing concepts as a belief-value system of the society and the individual. In H. Stevenson (Ed.), *Child development and education in Japan* (pp. 39–54). New York: Freeman.

Kurita, Y. (1991). The culture of the meeting: The tradition of "yoriai" or village meeting. *Senri Ethnological Studies, 28,* 127–140.

Lepper, M. (1981). Social control processes, attributions of motivation, and the internalization of social values. In E. T. Higgins, D. Ruble, & W. Hartup (Eds.), *Social cognition and social behavior: Developmental perspectives.* San Francisco: Jossey-Bass.

Lewis, C. C. (1984). Cooperation and control in Japanese nursery schools. *Comparative Education Review, 32,* 69–84.

Lewis, C. C. (1989). From indulgence to internalization: Social control in the early school years. *Journal of Japanese Studies, 15,* 139–157.

Lewis, C. C. (1992). Creativity in Japanese education. In R. Leestma & H. J. Walberg (Eds.), *Japanese educational productivity* (Michigan Papers in Japanese Studies, no. 22, pp. 225–266). Ann Arbor: University of Michigan Center for Japanese Studies.

Lewis, C. C. (1995). *Educating hearts and minds: Reflections on Japanese preschool and elementary education.* New York: Cambridge University Press.

Lynn, R. (1988). *Educational achievement in Japan.* Armonk, NY: Sharp.

Mackerras, C. Ed. (1995). *East and Southeast Asia.* Boulder: Reiner.

Monbusho. (1989). *Shogakko gakushu shido yoryo* [Course of study for elementary schools]. Tokyo.

Nagano, S. (1983, April). *Docility and lack of assertiveness: Possible causes of academic achievement in Japanese children.* Paper presented at the Conference on Japanese Education and Child Development, Center for Advanced Study in the Behavioral Sciences, Stanford CA.

Peak, L. (1991). *Learning to go to school in Japan.* Berkeley and Los Angeles: University of California Press.

Sato, N. (1991). *Ethnography of Japanese elementary schools: Quest for equality.* Unpublished doctoral dissertation, Stanford University School of Education, Stanford, CA.

Sergiovanni, T. (1992). *Moral leadership: Getting to the heart of school improvement.* San Francisco: Jossey-Bass.

Shimahara, N., & Sakai, A. (1992). Teacher internship and the culture of teaching in Japan. *British Journal of Sociology of Education, 13,* 147–162.

Solomon, D., Watson, M., Battistich, V., Schaps, E., & Delucchi, K. (1992). Creating a caring community: Educational practices that promote children's prosocial development. In F. K. Oser, A. Dick, & J. L. Patry (Eds.). *Effective and responsible teaching: The new synthesis.* San Francisco: Jossey-Bass.

Stevenson, H. W., & Stigler, J. W. (1992). *The learning gap: Why our schools are failing and what we can learn from Japanese and Chinese education.* New York: Summit.

Stigler, J. W., & Stevenson, H. W. (1991, Spring). How Asian teachers polish each lesson to perfection. *American Educator,* 12–46.

Tobin, J., Wu, D. Y., & Davidson, D. H. (1989). *Preschool in three cultures.* New Haven, CT: Yale University Press.

Tsuchida, I. (1993). *Teachers' motivational and instructional strategies: A study of fourth grade U.S. and Japanese classrooms.* Unpublished doctoral dissertation, University of California, Berkeley School of Education.

Uchihashi, K. (1983). Making the most of masterly expertise. In T. Ishii et al. (Eds.), *A look at Japanese technological development* (pp. 13–20). Tokyo: Foreign Press Center.

U.S. Study of Education in Japan. (1987). *Japanese education today.* Washington, DC: Government Printing Office.

Watson, M., Solomon, D., Battistich, V., Schaps, E., & Solomon, J. (1989). The Child Development Project: Combining traditional and developmental approaches to values education. In L. Nucci (Ed.), *Moral development and character education: A dialogue* (pp. 51–92). Berkeley, CA: McCutchan.

White, M. (1987). *The Japanese educational challenge.* New York: Free Press.

Chapter 2

Garden, R. (1987). The second IEA mathematics study. *Comparative Education Review, 31,* 47–68.

Lee, S. Y., Graham, T., & Stevenson, H. W. (1996). Teachers and teaching: Elementary schools in Japan and the United States. In T. Rohlen and G. LeTendre (Eds.), *Teaching and learning in Japan*. New York: Cambridge University Press.

Lewis, C. (1984). Cooperation and control in Japanese nursery schools. *Comparative Education Review, 28*, 69–84.

Lewis, C. (1989). From indulgence to internalization: Social control in the early school years. *Journal of Japanese Studies, 15*, 139–157.

Peak, L. (1991). *Learning to go to school in Japan*. Berkeley: University of California Press.

Rohlen, T. (1983). *Japanese high schools*. Berkeley: University of California Press.

Sato, N., & McGlaughlin, M. W. (1992). Context matters: Teaching in Japan and in the United States. *Phi Delta Kappan, 74*, 359–366.

Stevenson, H. W., Chen, C., & Lee, S. Y. (1993). Mathematics achievement of Chinese, Japanese, and American children: Ten years later. *Science, 259*, 53–58.

Stevenson, H. W., Lee, S. Y., & Graham, T. (1993). Chinese and Japanese kindergartens: Case study in comparative research. In B. Spodek (Ed.), *Handbook of research on the education of young children* (pp. 519–535). New York: Macmillan.

Stevenson, H. W., Lee, S. Y., Chen, C., Lummis, M., Stigler, J. W., Liu, F., & Fang, G. (1990). Mathematics achievement of children in China and the United States. *Child Development, 61*, 1053–1066.

Stevenson, H. W., Lee, S. Y., & Chen, C. (1994). Education of gifted and talented students in Mainland China, Taiwan, and Japan. *Journal for the Education of the Gifted, 16*, 223–250.

Stevenson, H. W., & Stigler, J. W. (1992). *The learning gap*. New York: Summit Books.

Stevenson, H. W., Stigler, J. W., Lucker, G. W., Lee, S. Y., Hsu, C. C., & Kitamura, S. (1987). Classroom behavior and achievement of Japanese, Chinese, and American children. In R. Glaser (Ed.), *Advances in instructional psychology* (pp. 153–204). Hillsdale NJ: Lawrence Erlbaum.

Stigler, J. W., & Perry, M. (1988). Mathematics learning in Japanese, Chinese, and American classrooms. In G. G. Saxe & M. Gearhart (Eds.), *Children's mathematics* (pp. 27–54). San Francisco: Jossey-Bass.

Stigler, J. W., & Stevenson, H. W. (1991). How Asian teachers polish each lesson to perfection. *American Educator* (Spring), 12–20, 43–47.

White, M. (1988). *The Japanese educational challenge: A commitment to children*. Glencoe, IL: Free Press.

Chapter 3

Aaron, H. J., Mann, T. E., & Taylor T. (Eds.). (1994). *Values and public policy.* Washington, DC: Brookings Institution.

Bellah, R., Madsen, R., Sullivan, W. M., Swidler, A., & Tipton, S. M. (1986). *Habits of the Heart: Individualism and commitment in American life.* New York: HarperCollins.

Bellah, R., Madsen, R., Sullivan, W. M., Swidler, A., & Tipton, S. M. (1992). *The good society.* New York: Vintage.

Bennett, W. (Ed.). (1993). *Book of virtues: A treasury of great moral stories.* New York: Simon & Schuster.

Chen, A S. (1964, January–March). The ideal party secretary and the "model man." *China Quarterly, 16,* 229–240.

Cleverley, J. (1985). *The schooling of China: Tradition and modernity in Chinese education.* Sydney, Australia: Allen & Unwin.

Cummings, W. K., Gopinathan, S., & Tomoda, Y. (Eds.). (1988). *The revival of values education in Asia and the West.* Oxford: Pergamon.

de Bary, W. T. (1991). *Learning for one's self: Essays on the individual in non-Confucian thought.* New York: Columbia University Press.

Engle v. Vitale, 370 U.S. 421 (1962).

Fineman, H. (1994, June 13). The virtuecrats. *Newsweek,* pp. 30–36.

Llasera, I. (1987). Confucian education through European eyes. In R. Hayhoe & M. Bastid (Eds.), *China's education and the industrialized world: Studies in cultural transfer* (pp. 21–32). Armonk, NY: M. E. Sharpe.

Mote, F. (1971). *Intellectual foundations of China.* New York: Knopf.

Munro, D. J. (1977). *The concept of man in contemporary China.* Ann Arbor: University of Michigan Press.

Palmer, P. (1987). Community, conflict and ways of knowing: Ways to deepen our educational agenda. *Change, 19*(5), 20–25.

Reed, G. G. (1991). *The Lei Feng phenomenon in the People's Republic of China.* Unpublished doctoral dissertation, University of Virginia.

Reed, G. G. (1992). Modeling as a pedagogical technique in the art and life of China. *Journal of Aesthetic Education, 26*(3), 75–83.

School District of Abington Township v. Schempp, 374 U.S. 203 (diverged from on other grounds by Wallace v. Jaffee 472 U.S. 38) (1963).

Sharpe, R. (1994, May 10). Efforts to promote teaching of values in schools are sparking heated debate among lawmakers. *The Wall Street Journal*, p. A20.

Shirk, S. (1982). *Competitive comrades: Career incentives and student strategies in China.* Berkeley: University of California Press.

Stone v. Graham, 449 U.S. 39 (1980).

Tobin, J. J., Wu, D. Y. H., & Davidson, D. (1989). *Preschool in three cultures: Japan, China and the United States.* New Haven, CT: Yale University Press.

Yankelovich, D. (1994). How changes in the economy are reshaping American values. In H. J. Aaron, T. E. Mann, & T. Taylor (Eds.), *Values and public policy* (pp. 16–53). Washington, DC: Brookings Institution.

Zirkel, P. A., & Richardson, S. N. (1988). *A digest of Supreme Court decisions affecting education.* Bloomington, IL: Phi Delta Kappa.

Chapter 4

Chen, Z. (1985). Tigao shifan yuanxiao xuesheng de jiaoxue nengli ying cong yanjiang nengli zhuaqi [Raising teaching skills of normal college students should start from lecturing skills]. *Jilin Gaodeng Jiaoyu Yanjiu*, (2), p. 51.

Dangdai Zhongguo zongshu jiaoyujuan bianjishi (Ed.). (1986). *Dangdai Zhongguo gaodeng shifan jiaoyu ziliao (shang)* [Selected materials from contemporary higher normal education in China (vol. 1)]. Shanghai: Huadong shifan daxue chubanshe.

Department of Planning and Construction, State Educational Commission. (1992). Zhongguo jiaoyu tongji nianjian 1991/1992 (Educational statistics yearbook of China 1991/1992). Beijing: People's Education Press.

Dongbei shifan daxue jiaowuchu. (1985). Dongbei shifan daxue zhidaoshu (benke) [Northeast Normal University teaching guide (undergraduate program)]. Changchun: Dongbei shifan daxue.

Elmore, R. E., & McLaughlin, M. W. (1988). *Steady work: Policy, practice, and the reform of American education.* Santa Monica: Rand.

FBIS (Foreign Broadcast Information Services: China Daily Reports)

Feiman-Nemser, S.,& Floden, R. E. (1986). The cultures of teaching. In M. C. Wittrock (Ed.), *Handbook of research on teaching* (3rd ed.) (pp. 506–526). New York: Macmillan.

Feiman-Nemser, S. and Parker, M. (1993). Mentoring in context: A comparison of two U.S. programs for beginning teachers. *International Journal of Educational Research, 19,* 699–718.

Feng, Z. J. (1988, December 3). *Guangming ribao*, p. 1, in *Foreign Broadcast Information Service: China Daily Reports (FBIS)* (1988, December 22), p. 26.

Guojia jiaowei fuzhuren Liu Bin jiu 1993 nian zhongxiaoxue jiaoyu gongzuo da benkan jizhe wen [Liu Bin, Vice-Commissioner of the State Education Commission, responds to reporters' questions about elementary and secondary education in 1993]. (1993). *Renmin Jiaoyu* (2), pp. 3–5.

Guojia weiyuanhui jihua caiwuju. (1988). *Zhongguo jiaoyu tongji nianjian 1987* [Educational statistics yearbook of China 1987]. Beijing: Beijing gongye daxue chubanshe.

Jackson, P. W. (1986). *The practice of teaching*. New York: Teachers College Press.

Little, J. W. (1990). The persistence of privacy: Autonomy and initiative in teachers' professional relations. *Teachers College Record, 91*, 509–536.

Liu, B. (1986). Jiaqiang hongguan guanli tigao jiaoyu zhiliang [Strengthen macro management, raise education quality]. *Renmin Jiaoyu* (1), pp. 5–8.

Lortie, D. (1975). *Schoolteacher*. Chicago: University of Chicago Press.

Paine, L. (1990). The teacher as virtuoso: A Chinese model for teaching. *Teachers College Record, 92*: 49–81.

Paine, L. (1992). Teaching and modernization in contemporary China. In R. Hayhoe (Ed.), *Education and modernization: The Chinese experience* (pp. 183–209). Oxford: Pergamon Press.

Paine, L. and Ma, L. P. (1993). Teachers working together: A dialogue on organizational and cultural perspectives of Chinese teachers. *International Journal of Educational Research, 19*, 675–697.

Zhongguo jiaoyubao (ZGJYB) (China Education Daily).

Chapter 5

Amano, I. (1986). Educational crisis in Japan. In W. K. Cummings, E. R. Beauchamp, S. Ichikawa, V. N. Kobayashi, & M. Ushiogi (Eds.), *Educational policies in crisis* (pp. 23–43). New York: Praeger.

Amano, I. (1993). In search of a new direction in high school education reforms: A dialogue. *Monthly Journal of High School Education, 26*(February), 14–23.

Association of Prefectural Superintendents of Schools. (1994). Study report on the development of high schools. In K. K. Henshubu (Ed.), *Primary documents on high school education: Reform reports* (pp. 183–196). Tokyo: Gakuji Shuppan. (Original work published 1978)

Central Council of Education. (1991). *Educational reforms for a new age*. Tokyo: Gyosei.

Central Council of Education. (1994). Basic policy regarding the reform and expansion of school education. In K K. Henshubu (Ed.), *Primary documents on high school education: Reform reports* (pp. 116–151). Tokyo: Gakuji Shuppan. (Original work published 1971)

Committee for the Enhancement of High School Reforms. (1993). Enhancement of high school education reforms. *Monthly Journal of High School Education, 26*(8), 116–154.

Doyle, D. (1991, November). America 2000. *Phi Delta Kappan*, pp. 185–191.

Economic Council. (1983). *Japan in the year 2000*. Tokyo: Japan Times.

Howe, H., II. (1991, November). America 2000: A bumpy ride on four trains. *Phi Delta Kappan*, pp. 192–203.

Husen, T. (1967). *International study of achievement in mathematics*. New York: Wiley.

Jinnouchi, Y. (1992). Present status and problems of high school education. In A. Kadowaki & H. Jinnouchi (Eds.), *Sociology of high school education* (pp. 1–16). Tokyo: Toshindo.

Kadowaki, A., & Jinnouchi, Y. (Eds.). (1992). *Sociology of high school education*. Tokyo: Toshindo.

Kaneko, T. (1986). Postwar education reforms and the establishment of the high school system. In K. Komori (Ed.), *A comprehensive study of reforms of the high school system*. Tokyo: Taga Shuppan.

Kitamura, K. (in press). Policy issues in Japanese higher education. *Research in Higher Education* [Bulletin of the Research Institute for Higher Education, Hiroshima University].

Komori, K. (Ed.). (1986). *A comprehensive study of reforms of the school system*. Tokyo: Taga Shuppan.

Kurosawa, Y. (1993). Present status and problems of comprehensive high schools. *Educational Law, 95*, 12–19.

Kurosawa, Y. (1994). What is the aim of high school reforms? *Monthly Journal of High School Education, 27*(April), 108–113.

LaPointe, A. E., Mead, N. A., & Phillips, G. W. (1989). *A world of differences: An international assessment of mathematics and science*. Princeton, NJ: Educational Testing Service.

Ministry of Education. (1993). *Progress report on reforms of high school education*. Tokyo: Taga Ministry of Education.

Ministry of Education. (1994). *Educational statistical abstract*. Tokyo: Okurasho Insatsukyoku.

National Council on Educational Reform. (1985). *First report on educational reform*. Tokyo: Government of Japan.

National Council on Educational Reform. (1987). *Report on educational reforms*. Tokyo: Okurasho Insatsukyoku.

Nishimoto, K. (1993). How to create a comprehensive program. *Monthly Journal of High School Education, 26*, 23–29.

Rohlen, T. (1983). *Japan's high schools*. Berkeley: University of California Press.

Schoppa, L. (1991). *Education reform in Japan: A case of immobilist politics*. New York: Routledge.

Shimahara, N. (1986). Japanese education reforms in the 1980s. *Issues in Education, 4*, 85–100.

Shimahara, N. (1992). Overview of Japanese education: Policy, structure, and current issues. In R. Leestma & H. J. Walberg (Eds.), *Japanese educational productivity* (pp. 7–33). Ann Arbor: Center for Japanese Studies, University of Michigan.

Stevenson, H. W., & Stigler, J. W. (1992). *The learning gap*. New York: Summit Books.

Terawaki, K. (1993). Toward the realization of comprehensive programs. *Monthly Journal of High School Education, 26*(April), 21–25.

Vogel E. (1963). *Japan's middle class*. Berkeley: University of California Press.

Chapter 6

Abiko, T. (1987). *Yomigaeru Amerika no Chugakku* [The reviving American middle school]. Tokyo: Yuhikaku-sensho.

Cohen, E. (1994). *Designing groupwork: Strategies for heterogenous classrooms*. New York: Teacher's College Press.

Fujita, M. (1989). It's all mother's fault: Childcare and the socialization of working mothers in Japan. *Journal of Japanese Studies, 15*(1), 67–92.

Fukuzawa, R. (1994). The path to adulthood according to Japanese middle schools. *Journal of Japanese Studies, 20*(1), 61–86.

Glasser, W. (1990). *The quality school*. New York: Perennial Library.

Homusho. (1990). *Hanzai-hakusho* [White paper on crime]. Tokyo: Okurasho.

Hori, G. (1994). Teaching and learning in a Rinzai Zenmonastery. *Journal of Japanese Studies, 20*(1), 5–35.

Hozumi, Y. (1991). *Musume no Tsumiki Kuzushi.* Tokyo: (The Decline of Young Women's Guilt Consciousness) Data House.

Kitao, N., & Kajita, E. (1984). *Ochikobore*Ochikoboshi* (Falling Behind in School and Excessively Complaining). Tokyo: Yuhikaku-sensho.

Kondo, D. (1990). *Crafting selves.* Chicago: University of Chicago Press.

Kondo, M., & Tsukamoto, M. (1988). *Chugakko: Hikotaisaku jireishu* [A compendium of delinquency prevention examples for the middle school]. Tokyo: Kyoiku Shuppansha.

LeTendre, G. (1994a). Guiding them on: Teaching, hierarchy, and social organization in Japanese schools. *Journal of Japanese Studies, 20*(1), 37–59.

LeTendre, G. (1994b). *Willpower and willfulness: Adolescence in the U.S. and Japan.* Unpublished doctoral dissertation, School of Education, Stanford University, Stanford, CA.

Ministry of Education. (1992). *Statistical abstract of education, science, and culture.* Tokyo: Author.

Mochidzuki, K. (1982). *Hankoki: Chugakusei no shinri* [Rebellion—The psychology of middle schoolers]. Tokyo: Asunaro-shobo.

Office of Juvenile Justice and Delinquency Prevention. (1992). *Juvenile court statistics.* Pittsburgh, PA: National Center for Juvenile Justice.

Okano, K. (1993). *School to work transition in Japan.* Philadelphia: Multi Matters Ltd.

Peak, L. (1991). *Learning to go to school in Japan.* Berkeley: University of California Press.

Reynolds, D. K. (1980). *The quiet therapies.* Honolulu: University of Hawaii Press.

Rohlen, T. (1983). *Japan's high schools.* Berkeley: University of California Press.

Rohlen, T. (undated). *Notes on concepts of personhood and self in Japanese and English.* Unpublished manuscript, Stanford University. Stanford, CA.

Rohlen, T., & LeTendre, G. (1996). *Teaching and learning in Japan.* Berkeley: University of California Press.

Sato, I. (1991). *Kamikaze biker.* Chicago: University of Chicago Press.

Sengoku, T., Haruhiko, K., & Gunei, S. (1987). *Nihon no chugakusei* [Japanese middle schoolers]. Tokyo: NHK Books.

Singleton, J. (1989). *Gambaru*: A Japanese cultural theory of learning. In J. Shields (Ed.), schooling: Patterns of socialization, equality, and political control (pp. 8–15). University Park, PA: Penn State University Press.

Sizer, T. (1992). *Horace's compromise: The dilemma of the American high school.* Boston: Houghton Mifflin.

Somucho (Seishonen Taisaku Honbu). (1990). *Seishonen hakusho* [White paper on youth]. Tokyo: Government Printing Office.

Tucker, M. E. (1989). *Moral and spiritual cultivation in Japanese neo-Confucianism.* New York: SUNY Press.

Wagatsuma, H., & DeVos, G. (1984). *Heritage of endurance*. Berkeley: University of California Press.

Wei-ming, T. (1985). *Confucian thought: Self as creative transformation.* New York: SUNY Press.

Yang, H. (1993). *The teacher's job: A comparison of U.S. and Japanese middle school teachers.* Unpublished doctoral dissertation, Stanford University, School of Education, Stanford, CA.

Chapter 7

Appelbaum, R. & Henderson, J. (1992). *States and development in the Asian Pacific Rim.* Newbury Park: Sage Publications.

Baker, D. (1993). Compared to Japan, the U.S. is a low achiever . . . really: New evidence and comment on Westbury. *Educational Researcher, 22,* 18–20.

Baker, D. (1994). *The size and structure of secondary education in developing countries.* (Research Report). Washington, DC: World Bank, Education and Social Policy Department.

Baker, D., Riordan, C. & Schaub, M. (1995). The effects of sex-grouped schooling on achievement: The role of national context. *Comparative Education Review, 39,* 468–482.

Becker, G. (1975). *Human capital.* Chicago: University of Chicago Press.

Berger, P. L. & Hsia, H. M. (1988). *In search of an Asian development model,* New Brunswick, New Jersey: Transaction Books.

Black, C., Black, C. E., Jansen, M. B., Levine, H. S., Levy, M. J., Jr., Rosovsky, H., Rozman, G., Smith, H. D., II, & Starr, S. F. (1975). *The modernization of Japan and Russia.* New York: Free Press.

Carroll, G. R. (1981). Dynamics of organizational expansion in national systems of education. *American Sociological Review, 46,* 585–599.

Chantavanich, S. & Fry, G. (1985). Thailand: System of education. In T. Husen & T. Postlethwaite (Eds.), *The international encyclopedia of education.* New York: Pergamon Press.

Cummings, W. (1995). The Asian resource approach in global perspective. *Oxford Review of Education 21,* 67–81.

Griffith, J., Owen, E. & Baker, D. (1994). *Strategic plan for international activities at the National Center for Education Statistics.* (NCES White Paper). Washington, DC: U.S. Department of Education.

Jimenez, E. & Lockheed, M. (1989). Enhancing girls' learning through single-sex education. *Education Evaluation and Policy Analysis 11*(2), 117–142.

Johnson, C. (1982). *MITI and the Japanese miracle.* Stanford: Stanford University Press.

Lapointe, A., Mead, N., & Phillips, G. (1989). *A world of differences: An international assessment of mathematics and science.* Princeton, NJ: Educational Testing Service.

Lockheed, M. & Verspoor, A. (1991). *Improving primary education in developing countries.* New York: Oxford University Press.

Meyer, J., Ramirez, F., Rubinson, R. & Boli-Bennett, J. (1977). The world educational revolution, 1950–1970. *Sociology of Education 50,* 242–258.

McMahon, W. (1994). Education and endogenous growth models in East Asia. (Research Report). Washington, DC: World Bank, Education and Social Policy Department.

Moulder, F. (1977). *Japan, China and the modern world economy: Toward a reinterpretation of East Asian development 1600 to 1918.* Cambridge: Cambridge University Press.

National Academy of Science. (1993). *A collaborative agenda for mproving international comparative studies in education.* Washington DC: National Academy Press.

Organization for Economic Co-operation and Development (OECD). (1994). *Education at a glance.* Paris: OECD.

Postlethwaite, T. & Wiley, D. (1992). *The IEA study of science II: Science achievement in twenty-three countries.* Oxford: Pergamon Press.

Robitaille, D. & Garden, R. (1989). *The IEA study of Mathematics II: Contexts and outcomes of school mathematics.* Oxford: Pergamon Press.

Stevenson, H. & Stigler, W. (1992). *The learning gap: Why our schools are failing and what we can learn from Japanese and Chinese education*. New York: Summit Books.

Tan, J. & Mingat, A. (1992). *Education in Asia: A comparative study of cost and financing*. Washington DC: The World Bank.

Trow, M. (1961). The second transformation of American secondary education. *International Journal of Comparative Sociology 2*, 144–166.

Walters, P. & Rubinson, R. (1983). Educational expansion and economic output in the United States, 1890–1969. *American Sociological Review 48*, 480–493.

Williamson, J. (1993). "Human capital deepening, inequality and demographic events along the Asia-Pacific Rim." In N. Ogawa, G. W. Jones, & J. G. Williamson (Eds.), *Human resources in development along the Asia-Pacific Rim*. Singapore: Oxford University Press.

The World Bank. (1993). *The East Asian miracle: Economic growth and public policy*. New York: Oxford University Press.

Zainol, A. A. R. (1994). *A case study of secondary education in Malaysia*. (Research report). Washington, DC: The World Bank, Education and Social Policy Department.

Chapter 8

Altbach, P. G. (Ed.). (1992). *International higher education: An encyclopedia*. New York: Garland.

Archer, M. (1979) *Social origins of educational systems*. Beverly Hills: Sage.

Cummings, W. K. & Riddell, A. (1994). Alternative policies for the finance, control, and delivery of basic education. *International Journal of Educational Research, 21*(8), 751–776.

Cummings, W. K., Vargas, M. I., & William, J. (1995). *Socioeconomic and political impacts on education database*. Buffalo: Center for Comparative and Global Studies in Education.

Hong, M.-J. (1992). *Japanese colonial education policy in Korea*. Ed.D. dissertation. Harvard University.

James, E. (1993). Why do different countries choose a different public-private mix of educational services? *Human Resources, 28*(3), 571–592.

Ministry of Education, Republic of China. (1994). *Education statistical indicators, Republic of China*. Taipei: Veterans Printing Works.

Panikkar, K. M. (1959). *Asia and Western dominance.* London: George Allen & Unwin.

Ramirez, F. O. & Boli, J. (1987). The political construction of mass schooling: European origins and worldwide institutionalization. *Sociology of Education, 60,* 2–17.

Rubinger, R. (1982). *Private academies of Tokugawa Japan.* Princeton: Princeton University Press.

Shimahara, N. K. (1995). Restructuring Japanese high schools: Reforms for diversity. *Educational Policy 9*(2), 185–200.

Tan, E. T. J. (1995). *Independent schools and autonomous schools in Singapore.* Unpublished Ph.D. research proposal, State University of New York at Buffalo, Department of Educational Organization, Administration and Policy.

Tan, J.-P. & Mingat, A. (1992). *Education in Asia: A Comparative study of cost and financing.* Washington, DC: World Bank.

Tsurumi, E. P. (1977). *Japanese colonial education in Taiwan 1895–1945.* Cambridge, MA: Harvard University Press.

UNESCO. (1991). *World education report 1991.* Paris: UNESCO.

Chapter 9

August, R. L. (1992). Yobiko: Prep schools for college entrance in Japan. In R. Leestma & H. J. Walberg (Eds.), *Japanese educational productivity.* Ann Arbor: The University of Michigan, Center for Japanese Studies.

Daiei Shuppan henshubu. (1994). *Naritai! Kyoiin* [I want to become a teacher]. Tokyo: Daiei shuppan.

Drucker, P. (1993). *Post-capitalist society.* New York: HarperBusiness.

Hendry, J. (1995). *Understanding Japanese society* (2nd ed.). London: Routledge.

Ishida, H. (1993). *Social mobility in contemporary Japan.* Stanford, CA: Stanford University Press.

Kawaijuku Gojunenshi Henshuiinkai. (1985). *Kawaijuku gojunenshi* [Fifty-year history of Kawaijuku]. Nagoya: Kawaijuku.

Komiyama, H. (1991). *Ikasete yoi juku, warui juku* [Sending your children to good juku, bad juku]. Tokyo: Sanseido.

Lewis, C. (1995). *Educating hearts and minds.* New York: Cambridge University Press.

Mainen 7–8 kyoshitsu o kaiko suru kyoiku sangyo no paionia [The educational industry pioneer that is opening seven or eight schools a year]. (1995, March 18). *Shukan Diamond* (Tokyo).

Ministry of Education. (1994a). *Gakushujuku nado ni kansuru jittai chosa* [Survey of *gakushu juku*]. Tokyo: Author.

Ministry of Education. (1994b). *Wagakuni no bunkyoshisaku* [The cultural and educational policies of our country]. Tokyo: Okurasho iinsatsukyoku.

Nomura Research Institute. (1994). *Gunyu kakkyo no gakushujuku gyokai* [Rivals hold their ground in *gakushu juku* industry]. Tokyo: Author.

Rohlen, T. (1980). The *Juku* phenomenon: An exploratory essay. *Journal of Japanese Studies, 6*(2), 207–242.

Rohlen, T. (1983). *Japan's high schools*. Berkeley: University of California Press.

Rubinger, R. (1982). *Private academies of Tokugawa Japan*. Princeton: Princeton University Press.

Sengoku, T. & Iinaga, K. (1990). *Nihon no shogakusei, kokusaihikaku de miru* [Japanese elementary school students in international perspective]. Tokyo: NHK Books.

Shimomura, K. (1994). *Shinkyoiku sangyo* [New education industry]. Tokyo: Nikishuppan.

Smith, P. (1994). Japanese cram school industry. *James Capel Japanese Smaller Companies Monthly*, March, pp. 12–22, London.

Stevenson, H. W. & Stigler, J. W. (1992). *The learning gap*. New York: Summit Books.

Tokai Bank. (1995). *Kodomo no kyoikuhi* [Expenditures on children's education]. Tokyo: Tokai Bank.

Tanaka, H. (1992). *Machigaedarake no juku erabi* [Common mistakes in selecting a *juku*]. Tokyo: Keyaki Shuppan.

Tsukada, M. (1991). *Yobiko Life: A study of the legitimation process of social stratification in Japan*. Berkeley: Institute of East Asian Studies.

Ukai, N. (1994). The Kumon approach to teaching and learning. *Journal of Japanese Studies, 20*(1), 87–113.

Whitman, N. (1991). Teaching of mathematics in Japanese schools. In E. R. Beauchamp (Ed.), *Windows on Japanese education*. New York: Greenwood Press.

Yano Research Institute. (1994). *Kyoiku sangyo hakusho* [White paper on the education Industry]. Tokyo.

Chapter 10

Abegglen, J. C., & Stalk, G. (1987). *Kaisha: The Japanese corporation.* Tokyo: Charles E. Tuttle.

Bishop, J. H. (1993). Underinvestment in employer training: A mandate to spend? *Human Resource Development Quarterly, 4*(3), 223–241.

Cairncross, D., & Dore, R. (1990). *Employee training in Japan.* Washington DC: Office of Technology Assessment.

Evans, R. N., & Herr, E. L. (1978). *Foundations of vocational education.* Columbus, OH: Charles E. Merrill.

Frantz, N. R. (1994). Youth apprenticeships in the United States: Transmission or transformation of the German apprenticeship system. *Journal of Industrial Technical Education, 31*(3), 28–39.

Gutek, G. L. (1991). *Education in the United States: An historical perspective.* Needham Heights, MA: Allyn & Bacon.

Hashimoto, M. (1990). *The Japanese labor market in a comparative perspective with the United States.* Kalamazoo, MI: W. E. Upjohn Institute for Employment Research.

Hamilton, S. F. (1990). *Apprenticeship for adulthood: Preparing youth for the future.* New York: Free Press.

Imada, S. (1993). Transition from school to work. *Japan Labor Bulletin, 32*(10), 5–8.

Koike, K. (1988). *Understanding industrial relations in modern Japan.* New York: St. Martin's.

Levine, S. B., & Kawada, H. (1980). *Human resources in Japanese development.* Princeton, NJ: Princeton University Press.

Marshall, R., & Tucker, M. (1992). *Thinking for a living: Education and the wealth of nations.* New York: Basic Books.

Ministry of Education, Science, and Culture. (1994). *Statistical abstract of education, science, and culture.* Tokyo: Author.

Motorola University. (1993). 1993 Motorola University year-end report. Shaumberg, IL: Author.

NEC Technical College. (1993). *Guide to NEC Technical College.* Tokyo: Author.

Office of Technology Assessment. (1990). *Worker training: Competing in the new international economy.* Washington, DC: Government Printing Office.

Passin, H. (1982). *Society and education in Japan.* Tokyo: Kodansha.

School-to-Work Opportunities Act Section 3. (1994, August 3). *Creating a school-to-work opportunities system.* Washington DC: Author.

Stern, S. (1988, May). *Human resource development and training in Japan.* Tokyo: The Japan Management Association.

Stern, S. (1992). The relationship between human resource development and corporate creativity in Japan. *Human Resource Development Quarterly, 3*(3), 215–234.

Sumiya, M. (1990). *The Japanese industrial relations reconsidered.* Tokyo: Japan Institute of Labor.

Taniguchi, Y. (1993). Role of public vocational training in society characterized by lifelong education. *Japan Labor Bulletin, 32*(1), 5–8.

Wirth, A. G. (1992). *Education and work for the Year 2000: Choices we face.* San Francisco: Jossey-Bass.

Yahata. S. (1994). In-house training and OJT. *Japan Labor Bulletin, 33*(5), 5–8.

Chapter 11

Brimer, A. & Griffin, P. (1985). *Mathematics achievement in Hong Kong secondary schools.* University of Hong Kong, Centre of Asian Studies.

Cheng, K. M. (1987). *The concept of legitimacy in educational policy making: Alternative explanations of two policy episodes in Hong Kong.* Doctorate thesis, University of London Institute of Education.

Chung, Y. (1991). An economic evaluation of overseas university education from the perspective of the sending country. Mimeo.

Coward, H. R. (1994). Bibliometric indicators of research activity and infrastructure. Prepared for the World Bank. Mimeo.

Dahlman, C. & Sananikone, O. (1990). Technology strategy in the economy of Taiwan: Exploiting foreign linkages and investing in local capability. Washington, DC: World Bank.

Educational Testing Service. (1992a). *Learning mathematics.* The International Assessment of Educational Progress, Report No. 22-CAEP-01.

Educational Testing Service. (1992b). *Learning science.* The International Assessment of Educational Progress. Report No. 22-CAEP-02.

Elley, W. B. (1992). *How in the world do students read?* Hamburg: The International Association for the Evaluation of Educational Achievement.

Government of the Republic of China (GROC). (1991). *Educational statistics of the Republic of China*. Taipei: Ministry of Education.

Government of the Republic of China (GROC). (1992). *Education statistical indicators*. Taipei: Ministry of Education.

Government of the Republic of China (GROC). (1993a). *Taiwan statistical data book*. Taipei: Council for Economic Planning and Development, Executive Yuan.

Government of the Republic of China (GROC). (1993b). *The Republic of China year book 1991–92*. Taipei: Kwang Hwa Publishing Company.

Holbrook, J. B. (1990). *Science education in Hong Kong: The national report of the Hong Kong science group*. 2 Vols. Hong Kong National IEA Center, University of Hong Kong, Department of Education.

Hong Kong Education Commission. (1988). *Education commission report no. 3: The structure of tertiary education and the future of private schools*.

Hong Kong Government Information Service. (1992). *Hong Kong 1992*.

Hong Kong Government Secretariat. (1981). *The Hong Kong Education System*.

Hong Kong Government Secretariat. (1982). *A perspective on education in Hong Kong: Report by a visiting panel*.

International Association for the Evaluation of Educational Achievement (IEA). (1988). *Science achievement in seventeen countries: A preliminary report*. Oxford: Pergamon Press.

McNamara, R. S. (1991). The post-Cold War world: Implications for military expenditure in the developing countries. *Proceedings of the World Bank Annual Conference on Development Economics*. Washington, DC: World Bank, 95–125.

Miners, N. (1986). *The government and politics of Hong Kong*. Hong Kong: Oxford University Press.

Smith, D. C. (1991). *The Confucian continuum: Educational modernization in Taiwan*. New York: Praeger.

Stevenson, H. W., Lummis, M., Lee, S., & Stigler, J. W. (1990). *Making the grades in mathematics: Elementary school mathematics in the United States, Taiwan, and Japan*. Reston, VA: The National Council of Teachers of Mathematics.

Stevenson, H. W., Lummis, M., Lee, S., & Stigler, J. W. (1992). Learning from Asian schools. *Scientific American, 267*(6), 70–75.

Stevenson, H. W., Chen, C., & Lee., S. (1993). Mathematics achievement of Chinese, Japanese, and American children: Ten years later. *Science, 259*, 53–59.

Stevenson, H. W., Chen, C., Lee, S., & Stigler, J. W. (1992). *The learning gap.* New York: Summit Books.

UNESCO. (1993). *World education report.* Paris: author.

United States National Science Foundation (USNSF). (1986). *Foreign citizens in US science and engineering: History, status, and outlook.* Special Report NSF 86-305 revised. Washington DC: U.S. Government Printing Office.

United States National Science Foundation (USNSF). (1993a). *Science and engineering indicators* (11th ed.). Washington, DC: author.

United States National Science Foundation (USNSF). (1993b). *Human resources for science and technology: The asian region.* Survey of Science Resources Series, NSF 93-303.

World Bank. (1992). *World development report 1992.* New York: Oxford University Press.

World Bank. (1993). *The East Asian miracle: Economic growth and public policy.* New York: Oxford University Press.

World Bank. (1994). *World development report 1994.* New York: Oxford University Press.

Chapter 12

Amornvivat, S. (1986). *Final report of project: The improvement of teaching efficiency of the primary school teachers* [in Thai]. Bangkok: Ministry of Education.

Beach, K., Schwille, J., & Wheeler, C. (1992). *Transition to school, transition to work: A review of studies and data on primary school leavers and the workplace in Thailand.* Bangkok: United Nations Development Programme.

Bhumirat, C., Kidchanapanish, S., Arunrungreung, P., & Shinatrakool, R. (with assistance of Sirijirakal, V.) (1987). *Research and evaluation on the quality of primary education in Thailand.* Bangkok; Office of the National Education Commission.

Campbell, D. & Olson, J., (1991, February). *Framework for environment and development: The kite.* CASID Occasional Papers Series No. 10. East Lansing, MI: Center for Advanced Study of International Development.

Chantavanich, A., Chantavanich, S., & Fry, G. (1990). *Evaluating primary education: Qualitative and quantitative policy studies in Thailand.* Ottawa, Ont.: International Development Research.

Conrad, D., & Hedin, D. (1991). School-based community service: What we know from research and theory. *Phi Delta Kappan*, June, 743–749.

Gallagher, J. (1993). Secondary science teaching and constructivist practice. In K. Tobin (Ed.), *The practice of constructivism in science education*. Hillsdale, NJ: Erlbaum.

McDonough, M., Vachta, K., Funkhouser, S. & Gieche, A. (1994). *Creating community-forestry partnerships: A participatory approach*. Chicago: Urban Forestry Center for the Midwestern States, USDA Forest Service.

Meyers, C. & Sussangkarn, C. (1991). Education and development of the Thai economy: Issues and options for policy and reform. In Thailand Development Research Institute, *Educational options for the future of Thailand*, vol. I. Bangkok: The Thailand Development Research Institute.

Montalembert, M. R. de & Clement, J. (1983). *Fuelwood supplies in the developing countries*. FAO Forestry Paper No. 2. Rome: Food and Agriculture Organization of the United Nations.

Nakata, T. (1987). Political culture: Problems of development of democracy. In S. Xuto (Ed.), *Government and politics of Thailand*. New York: Oxford University Press.

Nathan, J., & Kielsmeier, J. (1991). The sleeping giant of school reform. *Phi Delta Kappan*, June, 739–742.

Pressure on teachers seen to be growing. (1995, July 13). *Bangkok Post*, p. 13.

Royal Forestry Department. (1993). *Forestry statistics in Thailand: 1986*. Bangkok: Planning Division, Royal Forestry Department.

Suwanketnikom, S. (1987). *Inservice initiatives in Thailand*. Bangkok: Office of the National Education Commission.

Sykes, G., Wheeler, C. W., Scott, J., and Wilcox, S. (1996). Professional community among teachers: How does it form? An inquiry and a case study. Unpublished manuscript. East Lansing, MI: College of Education, Michigan State University.

Tsang, M., & Wheeler, C. (1993). Local initiatives and their implications for a multi-level approach to school improvement in Thailand. In H. M. Levin & M. E. Lockheed (Eds.), *Effective schools in developing countries*. Washington, DC: The Falmer Press.

Valenti, J. J. (1979). Current problems and developments in Thai education. *International Review of Education, 20*, 71–81.

Viriyasakultorn, V. (1995). *Community woodlots and their impacts on rural household fuelwood supply and rural development*. Ph.D. dissertation. East Lansing, MI: Department of Forestry, Michigan State University.

Watson, K. (1984). *Educational development in Thailand*. Hong Kong: Heinemann Asia.

Wheeler, C. W., McDonough, M., Gallagher, J., Sookpokakit, B., and Duongsa, D. (in press). In D. Chapman & L. Mahlik (Eds.), *Improving school quality*. Oxford: Pergamon Press Ltd.

Wheeler, C. W., Raudenbush, S., & Pasigna, A. (1989). *Policy initiatives to improve primary school quality in Thailand: An essay on implementation, constraints, and opportunities for educational improvement*. BRIDGES Research Report Series No. 5. Cambridge, MA: Harvard Institute for International Development.

Chapter 13

Amano, I. (1990). *Education and examinations in modern Japan*. Tokyo: University of Tokyo Press.

Cummings, W. (1980). *Education and equality in Japan*. Princeton, NJ: Princeton University Press.

Cummings, W. (1992). Examining the educational production function: British, American, and Japanese models. *Advances in Educational Productivity, 2*, 21–39.

Fukuzawa, R. E. (1989). *Stratification, social control, and student culture: An ethnography of three Japanese junior high schools*. Unpublished doctoral dissertation, Northwestern University, Evanston, IL.

Hess, R. D., & Azuma, H. (1991). Cultural support for schooling: Contrasts between Japan and the United States. *Educational Researcher, 20*, 2–8, 12.

LeTendre, Gerald K. (1994). *Willpower and willfulness: Adolescence in the U.S. and Japan*. Unpublished doctoral dissertation, Stanford University, Stanford, CA.

National Education Commission on Time and Learning. (1994). *Prisoners of time*. Washington, DC: U.S. Government Printing Office.

Okano, K. (1993). *School to work transition in Japan: An ethnographic study*. The Language and Education Library.

Peak, L. (1992). *Learning to go to school in Japan*. Berkeley: University of California Press.

Rohlen. T. (1983). *Japan's high schools*. Berkeley: University of California Press.

Sato, N. (1991). *Ethnography of Japanese elementary schools: Quest for equality.* Unpublished doctoral dissertation, School of Education, Stanford University, Stanford, CA.

Shimahara, N. (1986). The cultural basis of student achievement in Japan. *Comparative Education, 22,* 19–26.

Stevenson, H., & Stigler, J. (1992). *The learning gap: Why our schools are failing and what we can learn from Japanese and Chinese education.* New York: Summit.

White, M. (1987). *The Japanese educational challenge.* New York: Free Press.

Chapter 14

Castells, M. (1988). *The developmental city state in an open world economy: The Singapore Experience.* Berkeley: University of California.

Chan H. C. (1989). The PAP and the structuring of the political system. In K. S. Sandhu & P. Wheatley (Eds.), *Management of success: The moulding of modern Singapore.* Singapore: Institute of Southeast Asian Studies.

Clammer, J. (1985). *Singapore: Ideology, society and culture.* Singapore: Chopmen Publishers.

Furhman, S. (1993). *Designing coherent education policy: Improving the system.* San Francisco: Jossey-Bass.

Fuller, B. (1990). *Growing up modern: The Western state builds Third World schools.* New York: Routledge, Chapman and Hall

Fuller, B. & Robinson, R. (1992). *The political construction of education: The state, school expansion and economic change.* New York: Praeger.

Gopinathan, S. (1974). *Towards a national system of education in Singapore 1945–1973.* Singapore: Oxford University Press

Gopinathan, S. (1985). "Education." In J. S. T. Quah, Chan H. C., & Seah C. M. (Eds.), *Government and politics of Singapore.* Singapore: Oxford University Press

Gopinathan, S. (1988a). Being and becoming: Education for values in Singapore. In W. K. Cummings, S. Gopinathan, & Y. Tomoda (Eds.), *The revival of values education in Asia and the West.* Oxford: Pergamon Press.

Gopinathan, S. (1988b). Bilingualism and bilingual education in Singapore. In C. B. Paulston (Ed.), *International handbook of bilingualism and bilingual education.* New York: Greenwood Press.

Gopinathan, S (1993). *Religious education in a secular society: The Singapore experience.* Paper presented at the International Conference on Moral and Civic Education, Hong Kong.

Hage, J., Garnier, M. A. & Fuller, B. (1988). The active state, investment in human capital and economic growth: France 1825–1975. *American Sociological Review, 53*, 824–837.

Katz, M. B. (1976). The origins of public education: A reassessment. *History of Education Quarterly, 16*(4), 381–407.

Lee K. Y. (1982, May 29). Education is the road to success. *Straits Times.*

Lee K. Y. (1994, October 6). Confucian values helped Singapore prosper. *Straits Times.*

McCord, W. (1991). *The dawn of the Pacific century: Implications for three worlds of development.* New Brunswick, NJ: Transactions Publishers.

National Commission on Excellence in Education. (1983). *A nation at risk: the imperative for educational reform.* Washington DC: Government Printing Office.

Pye, L. (1986). The new Asian capitalism: A political portrait. In P. Berger & H.-H. Hsiao (Eds.), *In search of an East Asian development model.* New Brunswick, NJ: Transaction Books.

Rohlen, T. P. (1995). Differences that make a difference: Explaining Japan's success. *Educational Policy* (Special Issue), *9*(2), 103–128.

Shee P. K. (1985). The evolution of the political system. In J. S. T. Quah, Chan H. C., & Seah C. M. (Eds.), *Government and Politics of Singapore.* Singapore: Oxford University Press.

Stevenson, H. W., Lee, S. Y., & Chen, C. (1994). Education of gifted and talented students in mainland China, Taiwan and Japan. *Journal for the Education of the Gifted, 16*, 223–250.

Stevenson, H. W., & Stigler, J. (1992). *The learning gap: Why our schools are failing and what we can learn from Japanese and Chinese education.* New York: Summit.

Yeo K. W. (1973). *Political development in Singapore 1945–1955.* Singapore: Singapore University Press.

Chapter 15

Act on Compulsory Education. (1986, April 8). *Renmin ribao.*

Borevskaya, N. Y. (1993). New curriculum in the PRC. *Pedagogica, 3*, 101–108 (in Russian).

Ding S. (1989, March 11). *Renmin ribao.*

Finn, C. E., Jr. (1987). Governing education. *Educational Policy, 3,* 785–790.

Gu M. (1988, December 14). The lessons for us from the global education development. *Guangming ribao,* 3 (in Chinese).

He D. (1992). Speech at the Pedagogic Society Conference. *Jiaoyu yanjiu, 1,* 3–5.

Kelly G. & Seller M. (1985). A history of school reform in New York State: Implications for today's policymakers. in Francis Kemmerer, ed. *National Education Reform and New York State: A Report Card,* Proceedings of the New York Education Policy Seminar. Albany, N.Y.: School of Education, SUNY-Albany. 77–109.

Law on Education. (1995, March 23). *Renmin ribao,* 3.

Liu F. (1988). The changes in our approach to education in the last decade. *Jiaoyu yanjiu, 11,* 3–8.

Robinson, J. (1986). Decentralization, money, and power: The case of people-run schools in China. *Comparative Education Review, 31,* 73–88.

Swanson, A. (1994). American and Anglo perspectives. *International Journal of Educational Research, 21*(8), 751–771.

Wang X, Hu Y. (1993). Our investments in education: Policy, attainment and new steps. *Jiaoyu yanjiu, 2,* 20–24 (in Chinese).

World Bank. (1985). *China: Issues and prospects in education.* Washington, DC: World Bank.

Zhu W. (1992). Confucius and traditional Chinese education: An assessment. In R. Hayhoe (Ed.), *Education and Modernization: The Chinese Experience.* Oxford: Pergamon.

Chapter 16

Altbach, P. & Selvaratnam, V. (1989). *From dependence to autonomy: The development of Asian universities.* Dodrecht: Kluwer Academic Publishers.

Appelbaum, R. P. & Henderson, J. (1992). *States and development in the Asian Pacific Rim.* Newbury Park: Sage Publications.

Awanohara, S. (1993, June 17). Human rights: Vienna showdown. *Far Eastern Economic Review,* 16ff.

Bailey A. M. & Llobera, J. R. (Eds.). (1981). *The Asiatic mode of production: Science and politics.* London: Routledge and Kegan Paul.

Bartholomew, J. (1989). *The formation of science in Japan.* New Haven: Yale University Press.

Befu, H. (1993). *Cultural nationalism in East Asia.* London: Curzon Press.

Ben-David, J. (1977). *Centers of learning.* New York: McGraw-Hill.

Berger, P. L. & Hsiao, H.-H. M. (Eds.). (1988). *In search of an Asian development model.* New Brunswick, NJ: Transaction Publishers.

Black, C. E. Marius B. Jansen, Herbert S. Levine, Marion J. Levy, Jr., Henry Rosovsky, Gilbert Rozman, Henry D. Smith II, S. Frederick Starr. (1975). *The modernization of Japan and Russia.* New York: Free Press.

Bloom, J. (1990). *Japan as a scientific and technological superpower.* Washington, DC: U.S. Department of Commerce.

Braisted, W. R. (Trans.). (1976). *Meiroku Zasshi: Journal of the Japanese enlightenment.* Cambridge, MA: Harvard University Press.

Carnoy, M. & Samoff, J. (1990). *Education and social transition in the Third World.* Princeton: Princeton University Press.

Choi, H. (1993). *Asian scholars in the United States: Roles, careers and contributions to the international knowledge system.* Ph.D. dissertation, Graduate School of Education, University at Buffalo.

Cogan, J. J. (1984, March). Should the U.S. mimic Japanese education? Let's look before we leap. *Phi Delta Kappan,* 463–468.

Cole, R. (1989). *Strategies for learning.* Berkeley: University of California Press.

Cummings, W. K. (1980). *Education and equality in Japan.* Princeton: Princeton University Press.

Cummings, W. K. (1984, May). Going overseas for higher education: The Asian experience. *Comparative Education Review, 28,* 241–257.

Cummings, W. K. (1985). The preference of Asian overseas students for the United States: An examination of the context. *Higher Education, 14,* 403–423 (with Wing-Cheung So).

Cummings, W. K. (1992). Examining the educational production function: U.K., U.S. and Japanese models. In H. Walberg and D. W. Chapman, (Eds.). *International perspectives in educational productivity.* Greenwich, CT: JAI Press.

Cummings, W. K. (1994). From knowledge seeking to knowledge creation: The Japanese university's challenge. *Higher Education, 27,* 399–415.

Cummings, W. K. Gopinathan, S. and Tomoda, Y. (Eds.). (1988). *The revival of values: Education in East and West.* London: Pergamon, 1988.

Deyo, F. C. (1992). The political economy of social policy formation: East Asia's newly industrialized countries. In Appelbaum & Henderson, pp. 227–252.

Dore, R. & Sako, M. (1989). *How the Japanese learn to work*. London: Routledge.

Fallows, J. (1987, March). Gradgrind's heirs: Despite what the U.S. Department of Education says, you would not want your kids to go to a Japanese secondary school. *Atlantic Monthly*, 16–24.

Frobel, F., Henrichs, J., and Kreye, O. Burgess, P. tr. (1980). *The new international division of labor*. Cambridge: Cambridge University Press.

Fukui, H. (1992). The Japanese state and economic development: A profile of a nationalist-paternalist capitalist state. In Appelbaum & Henderson, pp. 199–226.

Fuller, B. & Rubinger, R. (1992). *The political construction of education*. New York: Praeger.

Geiger, R. L. (1987). *Private sectors in higher education*. Ann Arbor: University of Michigan Press.

Hall, I. P. (1973). *Mori Arinori*. Cambridge, MA: Harvard University Press.

Hong M.-J. (1992). *Japanese colonial education policy in Korea*. Ed.D. dissertation, Harvard University.

Hook, G. D. & Weiner, M. A. (1992). *The internationalization of Japan*. London: Routledge.

Horio, T. (1988). *Educational thought and ideology in modern Japan*, tr. Steven Platzer. Tokyo: University of Tokyo Press.

The Human Rights Debate. (1993, September). *Japan Echo*. Special Issue.

Ilon, L. (1993). Structural adjustment and education: Adapting to a growing global market. Mimeo.

James, E., & Benjamin, G. (1988). *Public policy and private education in Japan*. New York: St. Martin's Press.

Johnson, C. (1982). *MITI and the Japanese miracle*. Stanford: Stanford University Press.

Johnson, J. M. (1993). *Human resources for science and technology: The Asian region*. Washington, DC: National Science Foundation.

Kennedy, P. (1987). *The rise and fall of the great powers*. New York: Random House.

Kodama, F. & Nishigata, C. (1991). Structural changes in the Japanese supply/employment system of engineers: Are we losing or gaining? In D. S. Zinberg (Ed.), *The changing university*. Amsterdam: Kluwer Publishers.

Kohlberg, L. (1981). *The meaning and measurement of moral development.* Worcester: Clark University Press.

Lach, D. (1965). *Asia in the making of Europe.* Chicago: University of Chicago Press.

Lee, M.-J. (1993, July). Asian-born scientists and engineers: Their immigration flow and labor market adjustment. *Korea Journal of Population and Development, 22.*

Lee, W. O. (1991). *Social change and educational problems in Japan, Singapore and Hong Kong.* New York: St. Martin's Press.

Levy, M. J. Jr. (1972). *Modernization: Latecomers and survivors.* New York: Basic Books.

Lynn, L. H., Piehler, H. R. & Kieler, M. (1993). Engineering careers, job rotation, and gatekeepers in Japan and the United States. *Journal of Engineering and Technology Management, 10,* 53–72.

Malecki, E. J. (1991). *Technology and economic development.* New York: Longman.

Marshall, R. & Tucker, M. (1992). *Thinking for a living: Education and the wealth of nations.* New York: Basic Books.

Meyer, J. W. & Hannah, M. T. (1979). *National development and the world system.* Chicago: University of Chicago Press.

Meyer, J. W., Kamens, D. H. & Benavot, A. (1992). *School knowledge for the masses: World models and national primary curricular categories in the twentieth century.* Washington, DC: The Falmer Press.

Miller, R. A. (1982). *Japan's modern myth: The language and beyond.* New York: Weatherhill.

Ministry of Education, Science and Culture. (1980). *Japan's modern educational system.* Tokyo.

Miyanaga, K. (1991). *The creative edge: Emerging individualism in Japan.* New Brunswick, NJ: Transaction Publishers.

Moulder, F. V. (1977). *Japan, China and the modern world economy: Toward a reinterpretation of East Asian development ca. 1600 to ca 1918.* Cambridge: Cambridge University Press.

Mukherjee, H. (1988). Moral education in a developing society: The Malaysian case. In W. K. Cummings et al. (Eds.), *The revival of values education in Asia and the West.* New York: Pergamon Press.

Muta, H. (Ed.). (1990). *Educated unemployment in Asia.* Tokyo: Asian Productivity Organization.

Nagai, M. (1970). *Higher education in Japan: The take-off and the crash*. Tokyo: University of Tokyo Press.

National Institute for Educational Research (NIER). (1981). *Moral education in Asia*. (Research Bulletin No. 20). Tokyo.

Passin, H. (1965). *Society and education in Japan*. New York: Teachers College.

Fong, P. E. (1982). *Education, manpower and development in Singapore*. Singapore: Singapore University Press.

Ramirez, F. O. & Boli, J. (1987). The political construction of mass schooling: European origins and worldwide institutionalization. *Sociology of Education, 60*, 2–17.

Reich, R. *The work of nations*. New York: Knopf.

Reischauer, E. O. (1973). *Toward the 21st century: Education for a changing world*. New York: Knopf.

Rohlen, T. P. (1983). *Japan's high schools*. Los Angeles: University of California Press.

Science and Technology Agency, Japan. (1991). *White paper on science and technology 1991: Globalization of scientific and technological activities and issues Japan is encountering*. Tokyo.

Shields, J. J. Jr. (1993). *Japanese schooling: Patterns of socialization, equality and political control*. University Park, PA: Pennsylvania State University Press.

Sklar, L. (1991). *Sociology of the global system*. Baltimore: John Hopkins University Press.

Smith, T. C. (1955). *Political change and industrial development in Japan: Government enterprise, 1868–1880*. Stanford: Stanford University Press.

Stevenson, H. W. & Stigler, J. W. (1992). *The learning gap*. New York: Summit Books.

Stewart, C. T. & Nihei, Y. (1992). *Technology transfer and human factors*. Lexington, MA: D.C. Heath and Co.

Tai, H. (Ed.). (1989). *Confucianism and economic development: An oriental alternative*. Washington, DC: The Washington Institute Press.

Tan, J. & Mingat, A. (1992). *Education in Asia: A comparative study of cost and financing*. Washington, DC: The World Bank.

Teng, S. & Fairbank, J. K. (1954). *China's response to the West*. Cambridge, MA: Harvard University Press.

Thurow, L. (1992). *Head to head: The coming economic battle among Japan, Europe and America*. New York: William Morrow.

Tobin, J. (1989). *Preschool in three cultures: Japan, China and the United States*. New Haven: Yale University Press.

Tsurumi, P. E. (1977). *Japanese colonial education in Taiwan, 1895–1945*. Cambridge, MA: Harvard University Press.

UNESCO. (1992). *World education report 1991*. Paris: UNESCO.

UNICEF. (1992). *The state of the world's children*. New York: Oxford University Press.

U.S. Department of Education. (1987). *Japanese education today*. Washington, DC: U.S. Government Printing Office.

Ushiogi, M. (1993). Graduate education and research organization in Japan. In B. R. Clark (Ed.), *The research foundations of graduate education*. Berkeley: University of California Press.

Vogel, E. (1991). *The four little dragons: The spread of industrialization in East Asia*. Cambridge, MA: Harvard University Press.

Wallerstein, I. (1980). *The modern world system II: Mercantilism and the consolidation of the European world-economy 1600–1750*. New York: Academic Press.

Williamson, J. G. (1993). "Human Capital Deepening, Inequality, and Demographic Events along the Asia-Pacific Rim," in Naohiro Ogawa, Gavin W. Jones, & Jeffrey G. Williamson, eds. *Human Resources in Development Along the Asia-Pacific Rim*. Singapore: Oxford University Press, 1993.

World Bank. (1993). *The East Asian miracle: Economic growth and public policy*. New York: Oxford University Press.

Woronoff, J. (1982). *Japan: The coming social crisis*. Tokyo: Lotus Press.

Yamashita, S. (1991). *Transfer of Japanese technology and management to the ASEAN countries*. Tokyo: University of Tokyo Press.

Contributors

PHILIP G. ALTBACH is professor of higher education and director of the Center for International Higher Education at Boston College. He is author of *Higher Education in the Third World, The Knowledge Context*, and other books, and currently serves as editor of the *Review of Higher Education*.

DAVID P. BAKER is associate professor of sociology in the Department of Sociology, Catholic University of America. His research focuses on cross-national comparisons of school organization, academic outcomes, and national development.

NINA BOREVSKAYA is Senior Researcher in the Institute of Far Eastern Studies, Russian Academy of Science, Moscow. Her research interests center on contemporary Chinese educational policy, educational strategy, and educational reform. Her main publications look at the influence of foreign educational models on modern Chinese educational reform movements. Dr. Borevskaya is currently engaged in research on "individually oriented pedagogy on the threshold of the 21st century." This research explores the possibility of cross-cultural dialogue among China, the United States, and Russia.

WILLIAM K. CUMMINGS is professor and director of the Center for Comparative and Global Studies in Education at the State University of New York at Buffalo. He is the author of numerous articles and books on Asian education, including *Education and Equality in Japan*. In spring 1995, Professor Cummings was appointed the first foreign Visiting Scholar at Japan's National Institute of Educational Research.

JAMES J. GALLAGHER is professor of science education at Michigan State University. He has been active in international pursuits in educational research and environmental education in Africa, Asia, Australia, Latin America, and the United States. He is noted for his international work in the application of ethnographic techniques in science education and for his studies of science teachers' thinking and secondary science thinking. In addition to the Environmental Education Project on Social Forestry, Dr. Gallagher co-directs a project on classroom-based assessment in middle school science and mathematics.

S. GOPINATHAN is dean of the School of Education at the National Institute of Education, Nanyang Technological University, Singapore. He has written widely on education in Singapore, on publishing and book development, and on moral education.

DONALD B. HOLSINGER is a senior education specialist focusing on the development of secondary education in countries in Asia, Latin America, and Eastern Europe. He is currently working with David Baker on a series of analyses about the expansion, organization, and effectiveness of secondary education in developing countries.

SHINYING LEE is assistant research scientist at the Center for Human Growth and Development at the University of Michigan. Along with other colleagues, he has spent the past fifteen years conducting comparative studies of children's academic achievement in Japan, mainland China, Taiwan, Hungary, Canada, and the United States.

GERALD K. LETENDRE received a B.A. in sociology from Harvard University and an M.A. in sociology from Stanford University. He completed his Ph.D. in education at Stanford, writing a comparative study of the social construction of adolescence in the United States and Japan. He is currently on the faculty of the University of Georgia, where he is working with the Third International Math/Science Study investigating the role of schooling (especially math and science) in adolescents' lives in Japan.

CATHERINE LEWIS is director of Formative Research at the Developmental Studies Center, Oakland, and an adjunct associate professor and research psychologist in the Departments of Pediatrics and Psychiatry, University of California, San Francisco. A developmental psychologist who graduated from Radcliffe College and Stanford University, she speaks Japanese fluently and has experienced Japanese education as a high school student, researcher, and mother of two children in Japanese schools.

MAUREEN H. MCDONOUGH is professor of forestry in the Department of Forestry at Michigan State University. Her work focuses on the interactions of people and natural resources and includes community forestry projects in Thailand and Detroit. She has studied public participation in natural resource decision-making in the United States, Thailand, Taiwan, Jamaica, and the Dominican Republic. She is currently involved in projects to expand participation by underrepresented groups in ecosystem planning in both the U.S.

Forest Service and the Michigan Department of Natural Resources. She also has extensive experience in environmental education.

LYNN PAINE is on the faculty of the School of Education, Michigan State University. Her research has focused on understanding intersections of policy and practice regarding teachers, teacher education, and teaching. Much of her research is international. Her publications include research based on fieldwork in schools, teacher-education programs, and universities in China, the United States, and England.

GAY GARLAND REED is assistant professor of educational foundations at the University of Hawaii. She completed her doctoral work at the University of Virginia in 1991. Her research interests include Chinese education, learning communities, Asian-Americans, North Korean education, and moral/political education.

THOMAS P. ROHLEN is professor in the School of Education and a senior fellow of the Institute for International Studies at Stanford University. He is also a fellow of the Canadian Institute for Advanced Research. Professor Rohlen is the author of *Japan's High Schools* and *Teaching and Learning in Japan* (with Gerald LeTendre) and many articles on the subject of Japanese education. He is presently focusing his research on Japan's research and development system, its universities, and the interplay between corporate and school-based learning.

NANCY UKAI RUSSELL is a graduate student in education at Rutgers University. She lived in Japan for fourteen years, where she worked as a reporter for the Tokyo bureau of Newsweek and studied different aspects of Japanese education. Her most recent publication is "The Kumon Approach to Teaching and Learning" in the *Journal of Japanese Studies*. She became interested in *juku* when her two children began studying in the Dallas, Texas, branch of the Kumon Educational Institute.

NOBUO K. SHIMAHARA is professor of education and anthropology in the Graduate School of Education and the Department of Anthropology, Rutgers University. He is currently conducting research on changes in the culture of teaching in Japan as part of an international project involving eight countries. He is an author of *Learning to Teach in Two Cultures: United States and Japan* (with A. Sakai) and an editor of *Teacher Education in Industrialized Nations*.

BENJALUG SOOKPOKAKIT-NAMFA serves as assistant director of the Office of Project Development and Special Activities in the Thai Ministry of Education's Office of the National Primary Education Commission. She is responsible for projects in environmental education, life-skills development, and education for sustainable development. Her main interest is in factors that support teacher change. To this end, she has successfully introduced new forms of staff development and supervision to the Thai educational system. As a member of the Thailand/BRIDGES project, she co-authored a number of articles in research journals about Thai primary education.

SAM STERN is professor of education at Oregon State University. His research and teaching are concerned with education, work, and creativity. From 1990 to 1992, he served as the Japan Management Association Professor of Creativity Development at Tokyo Institute of Technology and led a research team in a study of creativity in the workplace.

HAROLD STEVENSON is professor of psychology and fellow at the Center for Human Growth and Development at the University of Michigan. Along with other colleagues, he has spent the last fifteen years conducting comparative studies of children's academic achievement in Japan, mainland China, Taiwan, Hungary, Canada, and the United States.

CHRIS WHEELER is professor in the College of Education at Michigan State University. Since 1987 he has been involved in collaborative research projects on education in Thailand. In 1991 the National Education Commission in Thailand selected the Thailand/BRIDGES project, on which he served as country coordinator, as the outstanding policy for that year. In addition to numerous articles about changes in Thai education, he co-edited with Jack Schwille an issue of the *International Journal of Educational Research* on primary schools in Thailand. His focus is on schools as organizations.

KIN BING WU was formerly a lecturer at the Chinese University of Hong Kong and the Hong Kong Polytechnic. She recently completed her Ed.D. at the Harvard Graduate School of Education.

Index

SUNY SERIES
FRONTIERS IN EDUCATION
Philip G. Altbach, editor

List of Titles

Black Resistance in High School: Forging a Separatist Culture—R. Patrick Solomon

Emergent Issues in Education: Comparative Perspectives—Robert F. Arnove, Philip G. Altbach, and Gail P. Kelly (eds.)

Creating Community on College Campuses—Irving J. Spitzberg and Virginia V. Thorndike

Teacher Education Policy: Narratives, Stories, and Cases—Hendrick D. Gideonse (ed.)

Beyond Silenced Voices: Class, Race, and Gender in United States Schools—Lois Weis and Michelle Fine (eds.)

Troubled Times for American Higher Education: The 1990s and Beyond—Clark Kerr (ed.)

Higher Education Cannot Escape History: Issues for the Twenty-First Century—Clark Kerr (ed.)

The Cold War and Academic Governance: The Lattimore Case at Johns Hopkins—Lionel S. Lewis (ed.)

Multiculturalism and Education: Diversity and Its Impact on Schools and Society—Thomas J. LaBelle and Christopher R. Ward (eds.)

The Contradictory College: The Conflicting Origins, Impacts, and Futures of the Community College—Kevin J. Dougherty (ed.)

Race and Educational Reform in the American Metropolis: A Study of School Decentralization—Dan A. Lewis (ed.)

Professionalization, Partnership, and Power: Building Professional Development Schools—Hugh Petrie (ed.)

Ethnic Studies and Multiculturalism—Thomas J. La Belle

Promotion and Tenure: Community and Socialization in Academe—William G. Tierney and Estela Mara Bensimon (eds).

Sailing Against the Wind: African Americans and Women in U.S. Education—Kofi Lomotey (ed.)